HERMENEUTICS AND EDUCATION

Shaun Gallagher

State University
of New York
Press

Published by
State University of New York Press, Albany

© 1992 State University of New York

All rights reserved

Printed in the United States of America

For information, address State University of New York
Press, State University Plaza, Albany, N.Y., 12246

Production by Susan Geraghty
Marketing by Terry Swierzowski

Library of Congress Cataloging in Publication Data

Gallagher, Shaun, 1948–
    Hermeneutics and education / Shaun Gallagher.
        p.   cm. (SUNY series in contemporary continental
    philosophy)
    Includes bibliographical references (p.) and index.
    ISBN 0-7914-1175-3 (alk. paper) : $59.50. — ISBN 0-7914-1176-1
    (pbk. : alk. paper) : $19.95
    1. Education—Philosophy. 2. Hermeneutics. I. Title.
    II. Series.
    LB14.6.G36   1992
    370'.1—dc20   91-37120
                                                                      CIP

10 9 8 7 6 5 4 3 2

To Elaine
from whom I continue to learn the most

CONTENTS

PREFACE

This study is concerned with two seemingly unconnected disciplines: hermeneutics, understood as the theory of interpretation, and education. These fields display a *real* disconnection only to the extent that theorists in these respective areas have, for the most part, developed their disciplines independently and generally in ignorance of each other. I believe, however, that these two fields are marked by essential relations once thought obvious by the ancients but since forgotten or obscured. Rather than try to retrieve the ancient view of these connections, I set out in this book to explicate their essential nature within the contemporary context of hermeneutical and educational theories. Within the framework of such a project it is important to note that these fields have never been unified within themselves. Indeed, in bringing them together and in reestablishing their relations it is possible to gain new perspectives on the multiple conflicts found within each. This is one aim of the present study.

The approach taken in this book is not a technical one and is only indirectly practical. It is not technical in the sense that I do not apply predetermined or uncontested principles of interpretation to educational experience. Such a technical procedure would oversimplify both hermeneutics and education. The hermeneutical principles employed in this book are themselves contested in their application to the educational context. As a result, hermeneutics learns from educational experience, just as much as educational theory learns from hermeneutics. By implication, it is hoped that the reader will learn just as much about interpretational processes as about educational processes.

The book is not directly practical in the sense of offering prescriptives about educational practices, or in the sense of developing correct approaches to problems of interpretation. I do not, for instance, say what is wrong or right about educational practices. On this score I do not enter directly into the current frays or contemporary debates about the fundamental aims of education, curriculum design, language education, or what has come to be known as "political correctness." Still, the following studies are not irrelevant to these discussions. I would contend, in fact, that some of the issues raised in this book need to be decided before one can adequately address the prescriptive and policy issues at stake in the previously mentioned discussions. In this book I develop a position which is clearly underrepresented in the current debates. As a matter of convenience I refer to this position as a "moderate" theory of education. The reader will discover, however, that in principle such a theory lacks a general prescriptive dimension. On this point, and in other ways, it is different from conservative, critical, and radical approaches taken in both hermeneutics and educational theory.

The lack of a general prescriptive dimension will not appear as a weakness if properly understood. I am not opposed to designing prescriptives in either the hermeneutical or educational contexts. I believe there are ways to determine whether one interpretation is better than another, or whether a particular educational practice is more or less productive. But I argue that one cannot legitimately do this on the level of general theory. Prescriptives have relevance only to particular and local contexts and so must be designed on that level. Still, even local prescriptives are constrained by the possibilities defined by universal principles. The latter are what is at stake in this book. Because this study is limited to the interface between philosophical hermeneutics and the philosophical theory of education it can only promise practical implications. This limitation, however, opens up a number of issues that cut across most aspects of educational experience. The promise of practical implications is made with respect to all grades of educational institutions, from primary school to the university, and addresses a variety of aspects, from teaching method within the classroom, to the formation and transformation of cultural traditions, to the political determination of educational contexts.

Although it is difficult to avoid assuming too much in writing a book concerned with hermeneutics as much as with education, I have tried to make it accessible even to those who work outside of these fields. I have attempted to clarify the nature of hermeneutics and a number of contemporary debates which define the current problems encountered in this field. Those already familiar with hermeneutics should find this a lucid account, and my hope is that they will be all the more able to see the implications of this work for hermeneutics itself. On the other side, although I do not offer prescriptives concerning educational practice, I do not avoid developing critiques of current educational theories. A hermeneutical approach to education, among other things, helps to define the proper place for the prescriptive reform of educational practice. It calls into question the current models of educational experience and critically exposes their hermeneutical underpinnings. In the end, this approach suggests a new understanding of the nature of educational experience, an understanding as full of implications for hermeneutics as it is for education itself.

ACKNOWLEDGMENTS

Earlier versions of the section on Plato's concept of *paideía* (in Chapter 5) found patient and helpful audiences at an international symposium on *Philosophische Hermeneutik und Griechische Philosophie* held at Heidelberg University in July 1991, and at a meeting of the Heidegger Circle at the University of Notre Dame in May 1989. An earlier version of the section entitled "Paidiá and Paideía" was read at a meeting of the International Society for Philosophy and Psychotherapy at the University of Hawaii in January 1988. A number of people at these conferences and in conversations or correspondence have helped me to clarify my thinking on various points considered in this book. They include John Caputo, John Cleary, Elaine DeBenedictis, Robert Dostal, Hans-Georg Gadamer, George L. Kline, Diane Michelfelder, Richard Palmer, James Risser, and Stephen Watson.

I am profoundly indebted to Canisius College and my colleagues there for their moral and financial support, including a 1988 sabbatical, a Faculty Research Summer Fellowship in 1989, and a Special Assistance Grant in 1992.

Finally, I owe the greatest amount of appreciation to my wife, Elaine DeBenedictis. Without her constant and loving support, time, and sacrifice I would have been unable to start or finish.

ABBREVIATIONS

AG   Gregory Ulmer, *Applied Grammatology: Post(e) Pedagogy from Jacques Derrida to Joseph Beuys* (Baltimore: Johns Hopkins University Press, 1985).

AK   Michel Foucault, *The Archaeology of Knowledge*, trans. A. M. Sheridan Smith (New York: Pantheon Books, 1972).

Betti   Emilio Betti, "Hermeneutics as the General Methodology of the *Geisteswissenschaften*," trans. in Josef Bleicher *Contemporary Hermeneutics: Hermeneutics as Method, Philosophy, and Critique* (London: Routledge and Kegan Paul, 1980).

BN   Jean-Paul Sartre, *Being and Nothingness: An Essay on Phenomenological Ontology*, trans. H. E. Barnes (New York: Philosophical Library, 1956).

Bruffee Kenneth Bruffee, "Collaborative Learning and the 'Conversation of Mankind'," *College English* 46 (1984), 635–652.

BT   Martin Heidegger, *Being and Time*, trans. John Macquarrie and Edward Robinson (New York: Harper and Row, 1962), with English/German pagination.

CL   E. D. Hirsch, Jr., *Cultural Literacy: What Every American Needs to Know* (Boston: Houghton Mifflin, 1987).

D   Jacques Derrida, *Dissemination*, trans. Barbara Johnson (Chicago: University of Chicago Press, 1981).

DD   Diane P. Michelfelder and Richard E. Palmer (eds.), *Dialogue and Deconstruction: The Gadamer-Derrida Encounter* (Albany: SUNY Press, 1989).

DP   Michel Foucault, *Discipline and Punish: The Birth of the Prison*, trans. Alan Sheridan (New York: Pantheon Books, 1977).

G   Jacques Derrida, *Of Grammatology*, trans. Gayatri
            Chakravorty Spivak (Baltimore: Johns Hopkins Uni-
            versity Press, 1976).

HHS   Paul Ricoeur, *Hermeneutics and the Human Sciences*,
            trans. John B. Thompson (Cambridge: Cambridge
            University Press, 1981).

HR   Kurt Mueller-Vollmer (ed. and trans.), *The Hermeneu-
            tics Reader* (New York: Continuum, 1988).

HS   Michel Foucault, *The History of Sexuality*, vol. 1,
            trans. Robert Hurley (New York: Vintage, 1980).

HT   Gayle L. Ormiston and Alan D. Schrift (eds.), *The Her-
            meneutic Tradition: From Ast to Ricoeur* (Albany:
            SUNY Press, 1990).

JG   Jean-Francois Lyotard and Jean Loup Thebaud, *Just
            Gaming*, trans. Wlad Godzich (Minneapolis: Univer-
            sity of Minnesota Press, 1985).

KHI   Jürgen Habermas, *Knowledge and Human Interests*,
            trans. Jeremy J. Shapiro (Boston: Beacon Press, 1971).

LK   Clifford Geertz, *Local Knowledge: Further Essays in
            Interpretive Anthropology* (New York: Basic Books,
            1983).

PH   Hans-Georg Gadamer, *Philosophical Hermeneutics*,
            trans. David Linge (Berkeley: University of California
            Press, 1976).

PMC   Jean-Francois Lyotard, *The Postmodern Condition: A
            Report on Knowledge*, trans. Geoff Bennington and
            Brian Massumi (Minneapolis: University of Minnesota
            Press, 1984).

PMN   Richard Rorty, *Philosophy and the Mirror of Nature*
            (Princeton: Princeton University Press, 1979).

PO   Paulo Freire, *Pedagogy of the Oppressed*, trans. Myra
            Bergman Ramos (New York: Herder and Herder,
            1970).

PR   Jacques Derrida, "The Principle of Reason: The Univer-
            sity in the Eyes of Its Pupils," *Diacritics* 13 (1983), 3–
            20.

RE   Pierre Bourdieu and Jean Claude Passeron, *Reproduc-
            tion in Education, Society, and Culture*, trans. Richard
            Nice (London and Beverly Hills: Sage, 1977).

RH   John D. Caputo, *Radical Hermeneutics: Repetition, Deconstruction, and the Hermeneutic Project* (Bloomington: Indiana University Press, 1987).

SP   Jacques Derrida, *Speech and Phenomena*, trans. David B. Allison (Evanston, IL.: Northwestern University Press, 1973).

Textshop   Gregory Ulmer, "Textshop for Post(e) Pedagogy," in *Writing and Reading Differently: Deconstruction and the Teaching of Composition and Literature*, ed. G. Douglas Atkins and Michael L. Johnson (Lawrence: University Press of Kansas, 1985).

TM   Hans-Georg Gadamer, *Truth and Method*, 2nd rev. ed., revised translation by Joel Weinsheimer and Donald G. Marshall (New York: Crossroad Press, 1989).

WD   Jacques Derrida, *Writing and Difference*, trans. Alan Bass (Chicago: University of Chicago Press, 1978).

CHAPTER 1

The Nature of Hermeneutics and Its Relevance to Educational Theory

The connection between education and interpretation is an ancient one. In the educational practice of the ancient Greeks, for example, the central place of the interpretation of poetry attests to an essential relation summarized in Wilhelm Dilthey's observation that "systematic exegesis (*hermēneía*) of the poets developed out of the demands of the educational system."[1] The relationship between the interpretation of poetry and the acquisition of knowledge in ancient Greek sources shows that the educational value of poetry did not hinge on learning to author it, but on learning to take wisdom from it, that is, on the process of interpretation. According to Plato, for example, not only did poetry require interpretation, but poets themselves provided educational value only by being the "interpreters (*hermēnes*) of the gods" (*Ion* 534a).[2]

At the beginning of the development of the modern discipline of textual hermeneutics the connections between education and interpretation, if blurred, were not entirely lost. Johann Martin Chladenius (1710–1759), in his systematic treatise on interpretation theory, followed Johannes von Felde's pedagogical definition of interpretation: "An interpretation is, then, nothing other than teaching someone the concepts which are necessary to learn to understand or to fully understand a speech or a written work."[3]

Since the development of nineteenth-century Romantic hermeneutics, however, the connections between education and interpretation have been obscured. One might trace this obscurity back to Friedrich Schleiermacher, who excluded *subtilitas explicandi* (exactness of explication) from the realm of hermeneutics. Only *subtilitas intelligendi* (exactness of understanding) belonged to the concept of interpretation. Thus, in contrast to Chladenius's identification of interpretation and teaching, and in contrast to Friedrich Ast's inclusion of explication within the rule of hermeneutics, Schleiermacher proclaimed that "hermeneutics deals only with the art of understanding, not with the presentation of what has been understood."[4] Even when, at the turning point of contemporary hermeneutical theory, Martin Heidegger defined interpretation as a development or education (*Ausbildung*) of the possibilities of understanding, the educational dimension of interpretation was never further explicated.[5] What Hans-Georg Gadamer refers to as interpretation's "merely occasional and pedagogical significance" is overshadowed by every other aspect of hermeneutical theory, from textual exegesis to fundamental ontology. Gadamer refuses to abandon "the insights of the Romantics, who purified the problem of hermeneutics from all its occasional elements. Interpretation is not something pedagogical."[6]

My intention in this introduction, however, is not to trace the connections between education and hermeneutics in historical terms. Indeed, a historical analysis would not suffice to show their essential relations. Even when these connections are not ignored, the understanding of them has been one-sided, for the most part emphasizing only the relation between interpretation and pedagogy. The connections, however, are more comprehensive and are relevant, not only to teaching, but even more essentially to learning. I postpone until the final chapter a discussion of the causes of the obscuring of these relations, which for all practical purposes amounts to a disconnection between hermeneutical theory and educational theory. My more immediate aim is to reassert the essential connections between interpretation and education within the contemporary framework of hermeneutics.

As a first requirement for clearly seeing these connections we need to provide a working conception of hermeneutics. This is not only helpful for those unfamiliar with hermeneutics, but, as those already familiar with the unsettled nature of contemporary interpretation theory will attest, it is a necessary task if some degree of clarity is to be achieved. Furthermore, a consideration of the various aporias or impasses that define the contemporary framework of hermeneutical theory will, in a general manner, help us to define the relevance of hermeneutics to education.

A WORKING CONCEPTION OF HERMENEUTICS

If it has not yet entered into the standard vocabulary of educational theory, *hermeneutics* is a familiar word in many philosophical, theological, legal, literary, and social scientific contexts. Still, any attempt to provide an orderly definition of hermeneutics reveals that this concept has a long and complex history.[7] Moreover, the term *hermeneutics* is used in many senses, and various commentators have pointed to its "definitional vagueness." Thus in various contexts, hermeneutics is said to be a "theory, a philosophy, a view of reality, a methodology, an approach, a hope, a promise, an ideology," or "a slogan, a battlecry . . . a field of study, a discipline."[8] Our first task, then, is to sort out some of these senses and to arrive at a working conception, although not a final or adequate definition, of hermeneutics. The following collection of definitions gathered from various historical and scholarly sources may serve to indicate some of the different conceptions, as well as some of the common features of hermeneutics.

(1) Schleiermacher, writing in the early nineteenth century, defined hermeneutics as "the art of understanding," an art or practice that related discourse and understanding (*Verstehen*) to each other.[9] For Schleiermacher, as for his predecessors and most of his followers, the art of hermeneutics was practiced in the reading of biblical, classical, and legal texts.

(2) More recently, Richard Palmer defined hermeneutics as "the study of understanding, especially the task of understanding texts." The discipline of hermeneutics tries to answer the question concerning "what understanding and interpretation, as such, are."[10]

(3) Another definition might read: Hermeneutics is the study of the explicit and implicit rules and methods that govern textual philology and commentary. For example, according to Paul Ricoeur, hermeneutics is "the theory of the rules that preside over an exegesis—that is, over the interpretation of a particular text, or of a group of signs that may be viewed as a text."[11]

(4) Dilthey, in the late nineteenth century, was concerned about defining the proper method for the social and human sciences (*Geisteswissenschaften*). For him, hermeneutics was a "critique of historical reason" that formed the basis for the methodology of the

human sciences. As a method it improved the "art of understanding permanently fixed expressions of life."[12]

(5) In the twentieth century, Heidegger radicalized the concept of hermeneutics and understood it to be the existential, phenomenological analysis of human existence insofar as "understanding" is an existential-ontological characteristic of human beings (see BT 62/37–38).

(6) Gadamer, following Heidegger's ontological concerns, developed hermeneutics as a theory which illuminates the conditions of possibility of understanding. According to Gadamer, "the best definition for hermeneutics is: to let what is alienated by the character of the written word or by the character of being distantiated by cultural or historical distances speak again. This is hermeneutics: to let what seems to be far and alienated speak again."[13]

(7) Josef Bleicher offered the following, more general definition: "Hermeneutics can loosely be defined as the theory or philosophy of the interpretation of meaning."[14]

(8) Jürgen Habermas, on the other hand, proposed a more specialized meaning: "Hermeneutics refers to an 'ability' we acquire to the extent to which we learn to 'master' a natural language: the art of understanding linguistically communicable meaning and to render it comprehensible in cases of distorted communication."[15]

The variety of these definitions—and this is not an exhaustive list—should be enough to indicate that not everything about hermeneutics has been resolved. Behind each of these definitions there lies a complex theory, or theoretical dispute that I need not detail here. Again, my aim here is to supply a working conception of hermeneutics that will lend itself to the task at hand: the exploration of the relationship between hermeneutics and educational experience. This collection of definitions is one way to begin. The majority of them identify understanding or interpretation, especially as related to language and text, as the subject matter of hermeneutics. If we characterize hermeneutics as a study or theory of interpretation, we should also note that the paradigm of textual interpretation dominates hermeneutical studies.

The interpretation of a written text is frequently offered as a model of the way that we come to attain understanding. The process of arriving at the meaning of a text is conditioned by a number of factors: factors built into the very act of reading, and conditions implicated in the situation of the reader and in the structure of the text. These conditioning factors constitute the limits within which the reader constructs an interpretation of the text. For example, the reader is defined by his or her own historical epoch, society and culture, educational background, linguistic ability, familiarity with a subject matter, and purpose or practical interests. The text is conditioned by its age, the culture in which it was produced, the language and talent of the author who produced it, and the author's intent. On one account the meaning of the text does not reside within the text alone, nor totally in the mind of the text's author; nor does it come to reside ideally in the mind of the reader. In the process of interpretation no one element—reader, text, meaning, and so on—exists in itself, in an isolated manner. Understanding a text involves building a complex series of bridges between reader and text, text and author, present and past, one society or social circumstance and another. These bridges have as their moorings the conditioning factors of interpretation; they are projected as possible interpretations defined by these conditions. One task of hermeneutics is to identify the different factors, including the epistemological, sociological, cultural, and linguistic factors, that condition the process of interpretation. Under the title of hermeneutics one might study, for example, the different factors that create a distance between the twentieth-century reader and a twelfth-century text: those factors that prevent the reader from attaining a complete or absolute understanding of it, as well as those factors that make possible an understanding of the text in question.

Language is a central concern of hermeneutics because of its importance in the process of interpretation. A number of the collected definitions emphasize this concern. Understanding is not an abstract mental act; it is a linguistic event. Language has a central role to play in understanding the world. Palmer nicely summarizes this hermeneutical principle.

> Language shapes man's seeing and his thought—both his conception of himself and his world (the two are not so separate as they may seem). His very vision of reality is shaped by language. Far more than man realizes, he channels through language the various facets of his living—his worshipping, loving, social be-

havior, abstract thought; even the shape of his feelings is conformed to language.[16]

Hermeneutics, however, is not linguistics. Habermas makes a clear distinction: linguistics "aims at a reconstruction of the system of rules that allows the generation of all the grammatically correct and semantically meaningful elements of a natural language, whereas a philosophical hermeneutic reflects upon the basic experiences of communicatively competent speakers."[17] Hermeneutics, in other words, is not the study of language as an objective entity; it is a reflection on the way language operates, such as, in the reader's interpretation of a text. A text is not simply a collection of grammatically constructed sentences arranged in a certain syntactic order. It is a totality of composition that bears within itself possibilities of meaning that overflow grammatical and syntactical arrangement. Language used by the author, language sedimented in the text, language employed in the event of interpretation will lead us toward or away from certain of these possible meanings.

Hermeneutics investigates the process of interpretation, the communication of meaning through a text, linguistic competence in conversation, and so forth. The phenomenon of the text and the interplay of interpretation, meaning, and language in understanding the text are matters complex enough for textual hermeneutics. But hermeneutics has moved beyond its concern with the written text and spoken word to a more universal conception. This move is reflected in definitions (4) through (8) cited above. These definitions indicate that hermeneutics also deals with nontextual phenomena such as social processes, human existence, and Being itself. Still, hermeneutics must deal with things through the medium of language. Gadamer's suggestion, that hermeneutics must make the things "speak," is reminiscent of Plato's proposal that the truth of things is arrived at by considering objects in the mirror of speech: "everything that is reflects itself in the mirror of language."[18] The human being encounters the world and everything in it through language.

In some cases the move to a more philosophical conception of hermeneutics, beyond a more narrowly defined textual hermeneutics, has, none the less, been based on an expansion of the concept of text. In a certain sense, insofar as the world has significance for the human being, the world is like a text which calls for interpretation. Paul Ricoeur, for instance, indicates in a clear manner this expansion of the concept of text: "the notion of text can be taken in an analogous sense. Thanks to the metaphor of 'the book of nature' the Middle Ages was able to speak of an *interpretatio naturae*. This metaphor brings to light a possible extension of the notion of exegesis, in as much as the notion of 'text' is wider than that of 'scripture'."[19] The accompanying claim is that the same kind of process involved in our understanding of a written text is involved in our understanding of the world. Accordingly, Gadamer's definition indicates the broader task and subject matter of hermeneutics. Hermeneutics examines human understanding in general. All understanding is linguistic, and nothing that involves knowledge or seeking after knowledge escapes the domain of hermeneutics.

The dependency of hermeneutics on the extended textual paradigm raises the question of whether the model of the text is appropriate in all cases. Textual hermeneutics has a long history, and prior to this century it constituted the conception of hermeneutics in toto. Schleiermacher's project to develop a "general hermeneutics" was a legitimate attempt to discover general prescriptives (canons) that would govern the interpretation of all kinds of texts—biblical, legal, classical. In this sense general hermeneutics is equivalent to textual hermeneutics as a whole. Dilthey, however, attempted to employ hermeneutical canons in social scientific *Verstehen*. This involved an expansion of hermeneutics beyond textual concerns. Yet Dilthey still relied upon Schleiermacher's textual hermeneutical canons. Heidegger, inspired by Dilthey, proposed that hermeneutics be concerned with all types of interpretation insofar as interpretation is a universal feature of human experience. In developing this universal, philosophical hermeneutics, which is not simply a textual hermeneutics, Heidegger attempted to work out phenomenological-existential principles which describe human understanding and which go beyond the textual paradigm. Following Heidegger's insights, one might say that the proper and essential subject matter of hermeneutics is not the text, but interpretation. Nonetheless, the historical primacy of textual hermeneutics has led, in most philosophical hermeneutical theory, to the use of the text as paradigm.

The word *textualism* has been used by Richard Rorty to characterize a general orientation in philosophy that may be stated as follows: there are only texts, and one text can only refer to another text. Rorty has in mind the work of poststructuralists like Jacques Derrida and Michel Foucault.[20] Poststructuralist textualism, which clearly involves the expansion of the notion of text, may find its precursor in the medieval notion of the *liber naturae*, although there are obvious and profound differences between the medieval and contemporary versions. I will use the word *textualism* in a more specific way. Within the context of hermeneutics the problem of textualism can be stated in the following way: by basing its model of interpretation on the expanded notion of text, hermeneutics reduces all forms of interpretation to one form. From this viewpoint interpretation, whether it is the scientific study of the natural world or the attempt to understand another person through conversation, is always a form of reading. Does this reduction involve a distortion of the kinds of interpretation which are not textual readings? In textual hermeneutics, regarded as a theory, textual interpretation is not a paradigm but is properly the subject matter itself. But insofar as the text becomes a paradigm in nontextual hermeneutics, insofar as textual interpretation becomes the model for all interpretation, then hermeneutics involves a specific kind of textualism. If this hermeneutical textualism does not say that "there are only texts," it does say, at least, that "everything that is is analogous to a text," or that all interpretation is analogous to textual interpretation.

Although I do not deny that there is a properly defined textual hermeneutics in which the concept of text plays a central role, I will suggest that textualism may present a serious problem if it is the chosen basis for the development of philosophical hermeneutics. I will contend that it is counterproductive to use the text as a paradigm in attempting to solve all hermeneutical problems. Moreover, I will argue that the problem of textualism is closely connected to the obscuring of the more general connections between education and hermeneutics. One of the aims of this book is to show that a nontextualist, philosophical hermeneutics is possible, precisely by employing the more inclusive model of educational experience in place of the narrow textual paradigm.

Beyond the issue of textualism, several other disputed questions or *aporiai* can be clarified by taking a hermeneutical approach to educational experience. Before moving on to an examination of these disputes within the field of hermeneutics, however, it may be useful to map out this field by distinguishing four contemporary but different hermeneutical approaches. For simplicity I will term these approaches conservative, moderate, radical, and critical hermeneutics.

(1) *Conservative hermeneutics* is based on the nineteenth-century hermeneutical tradition defined by Schleiermacher and Dilthey. It is clearly the approach taken by the legal historian Emilio Betti and the American professor of literature and educational reformer, E. D. Hirsch.[21] These theorists would maintain that through correct methodology and hard work the interpreter should be able (a) to break out of her own historical epoch in order to understand the author as the author intended, and/or (b) to transcend historical limitations altogether in order to reach universal, or at least objective, truth. The aim of interpretation is to reproduce the meaning or intention of the author by following well-defined hermeneutical canons that guide reading.

(2) *Moderate hermeneutics* is developed by theorists such as Gadamer and Ricoeur. They contend that no method can guarantee an absolutely objective interpretation of an author's work because, as readers, we are conditioned by prejudices of our own historical existence. These prejudices, however, are not simply a matter of time and place; rather, beyond that, they are embedded in language. They are the changing biases of various traditions which are not past and bygone but are operative and living in every reader and every text. Language does two things in the interpretive process: (a) it limits our interpretive powers and keeps us from gaining an absolute access to any textual meaning, even the meaning of our own texts (the author has no privilege in this regard); and (b) it enables *some* access to textual meaning. This enabling power can be defined in terms of a dialogical conversation, a "fusion of horizons," a creative communication between reader and text. Such communication is the positive basis of interpretation. As interpreters, however, we never achieve a complete or objective interpretation since we, limited by our own historical circumstance and by our own language, are inextricably involved in the interpretive conversation. This is in clear violation of conservative hermeneuti-

cal canons which seek for and promise objectivity. Theorists like Betti and Hirsch worry about the subjectivity they see implied in moderate hermeneutics. Moderate theorists respond that, since interpretation has a dialogical character, it is not purely subjective. No matter how we read Plato, for example, we never end up with Milton; the text itself constrains our interpretation. Subjective and objective interpretations, rather than being the only two possibilities, are two unattainable extremes of interpretation.

Moderate hermeneutics proposes a somewhat optimistic view of interpretation. Interpretation involves creativity and not just reproduction; the reader participates, just as much as the author does, in putting together the meaning, or in the case of poetry or literature, in creating the aesthetic experience. This optimism might be contrasted, on the one side, with what some would call the wishful thinking of the conservative school and, on the other side, with what might appear to be the nihilism of radical hermeneutics.

(3) *Radical hermeneutics*[22] is inspired by both Nietzsche and Heidegger, and is practiced by deconstructionists and poststructuralists like Derrida and Foucault. In contrast to conservative hermeneutics, this radical school would claim that reading is more a case of playing or dancing than a puritanical application of method. Interpretation requires playing with the words of the text rather than using them to find truth in or beyond the text. Through the use of deconstructionist techniques the text is played off against itself. In contrast to moderate hermeneutics, the radical reader is skeptical about creative interpretations that establish communication with original meaning; rather, for radical hermeneutics, original meaning is unattainable and the best we can do is to stretch the limits of language to break upon fresh insight. For Derrida, there is no original truth or being or *archē* beyond language itself. Moderate hermeneutics is too naively optimistic in this regard.

Deconstruction can only be performed within the language it attempts to deconstruct. Its aim is not to establish an authentic or even creative interpretation. Such an interpretation would simply be another text in need of deconstruction. Radical hermeneutics aims at deconstructing the meaning of a text, not in order to analyze it or to reconstruct a different meaning. It is not a replacement of one text with another, but a displacement of certain metaphysical concepts such as unity, identity, meaning, or authorship, which operate in and around the text. The hope is not to establish some other version of the world as the proper or correct version, but to show that all versions are contingent and relative.

(4) *Critical hermeneutics* has been developed in the writings of critical theorists like Habermas and Karl-Otto Apel, who find inspiration in Marx, Freud, and the Frankfurt School of social criticism. Critical hermeneutics can be characterized as a curious combination of radical and conservative elements. On the one hand, it is radical to the extent that its social and political aims continue a tradition that is rightly called "radical." The aim of critical theory is social and individual emancipation from the political power and economic exploitation found in advanced (capitalistic as well as communistic) class systems. Hermeneutics is employed as a means of penetrating false consciousness, discovering the ideological nature of our belief systems, promoting distortion-free communication, and thereby accomplishing a liberating consensus. On the other hand, critical hermeneutics is conservative to the extent that it promises to destroy false consciousness rather than to live within it, as radical hermeneutics contends we must. It is conservative to the extent that it expects actually to accomplish an ideology-free situation of consensus. This is like saying, with conservative hermeneutics, that an absolutely objective perspective can be gained, that, given the right method, we can escape the hermeneutical constraints of our finite, historical situation. From the point of view of deconstruction, critical theory shares the conservative and moderate, naive optimism that language, through ideal communication, will deliver something other than itself or that it will, if played rightly, effect significant nonlinguistic, material emancipation.

APPLICATIONS AND LIMITATIONS OF HERMENEUTICS: THREE APORIAS

This map of contemporary hermeneutical theory is oversimplified. But it serves as a point of departure from which we can begin to identify three major aporias which disrupt the contemporary hermeneutical field. These three impasses are well defined by three debates which concern the nature and scope of hermeneutics. The focus for each of these debates has been Hans-Georg Gadamer's hermeneutical theory. More than anyone else on the contemporary philosophical scene, he has attempted to work out the universal hermeneutics first broached by Heidegger early in the twentieth century. Gadamer's influential work, *Truth and Method* (1960), almost immediately sparked controversy. Emilio Betti, who represents what I have termed "conservative" hermeneutics, initiated an important debate with Gadamer concerning methodology and the possibility of valid and objective interpretation in the human and social sciences. In a second debate, Jürgen Habermas, representing "critical" hermeneutics, raised questions concerning Gadamer's claim for the universality of hermeneutics and proposed to define the possible limits of hermeneutical practice. Finally, in a third debate Jacques Derrida, developing a deconstructionist or "radical" hermeneutics, raised fundamental questions about the possibility of meaning and truth as it is proposed in Gadamer's theory.

The details of these debates, to the extent that they are relevant to educational issues, will be sorted out in later chapters. Here it is important to identify and briefly summarize the hermeneutical issues they raise. We will then be able to see that the aporias found in hermeneutical theory correspond in a remarkably significant way to related issues in educational theory.

Aporia I: Reproduction

According to Gadamer's moderate hermeneutics, interpretations are always constrained by the prejudices of the interpreter. An inescapable condition of any interpretation is that it is biased in some way. These prejudices may be productive or nonproductive aspects of the interpretation process. So Gadamer recommends that the interpreter ought to "raise to awareness those prejudices that guide and condition the process of understanding," neutralize those that "are of a particularistic nature," and preserve those "which enable veracious understanding." In hermeneutical practice the task, according to Gadamer, is to base interpretation on the productive prejudices and to eliminate the nonproductive ones (see TM 291ff). The idea of the biased nature of interpretation motivates a question concerning the objectivity and validity of interpretation. Given the prejudicial nature of interpretation, is it ever possible to achieve an objectively valid interpretation? There may be no problem arriving at what seems to be a correspondence or agreement between the subjectively conditioned (prejudiced) interpretation and the object of interpretation, but does this constitute objective agreement? In other words, is the interpretation correct? This is precisely the issue that had concerned Emilio Betti and that continues to define the difference between moderate and conservative hermeneutics.

According to Betti, the aim of hermeneutics is to prescribe how the process of interpretation should proceed so that we can successfully understand human forms of expression. Successful understanding is possible only if interpretation satisfies two seemingly contradictory requirements: it must achieve a degree of objectivity (that is, it cannot be arbitrary); but at the same time the requirement of objectivity must be met within "the subjectivity of the interpreter and his awareness of the preconditions of his ability to understand in a manner adequate to the subject-matter" (Betti 57). Interpretation is a dialectical process between these requirements. Hermeneutics works out the rules or canons that guide the dialectical process of interpretation. Betti, in contrast to Gadamer, insists on a measurable objectivity and a definable concept of validity in connection with interpretation.

The dispute between Betti and Gadamer, which has been called "the chief contest in philosophical hermeneutics,"[23] revolved around the problem of objective reproduction. Can the historian, for example, objectively reconstruct the original meaning of past events? Indeed, what would an objective interpretation consist of? The notion of objectivity here is not the same as that found in the natural sciences (see Betti 63). But Betti claims that a form of objectivity corresponding to the historical evidence can be and must be achieved if the interpretation is to be successful. The historical fact must remain autonomous; the interpretation must take account of its otherness. Betti agrees that historical interpretation depends on the historian's perspective, and that different perspectives are possible, but this element of subjectivity ought not touch the objectivity of the interpretation. The concept of objectivity employed by Betti does not signify an absolute and ultimate truth. The hermeneutical task is in fact never complete, and this means that "the meaning contained within texts, monuments, and fragments is constantly reborn through life and is forever transformed in a chain of rebirths" (Betti 68). Nonetheless, Betti insists, the historical text speaks to us in a nonarbitrary way: it says something that has some degree of objectivity. As the dialogue between the subjective element (interpreter) and the objective one (text), the interpretation is always determined to some degree by the objective element. Objective reproduction is accomplished and arbitrariness avoided with the help of controllable, consciously employed, historiographical-methodological guidelines.

In Betti's view, Gadamer emphasizes the subjective factors of interpretation too much, and this results in a "loss of objectivity" (Betti 78). For Betti the prejudices involved in interpretation are subjective conditions and should not be allowed to undermine the objectivity (nonarbitrariness) of the interpretation gained by a methodically defined set of hermeneutical canons or procedural rules.

This debate has raised issues, not only with respect to the objectivity of interpretation and the autonomy of the object, but also in regard to the nature and application of hermeneutics. In Betti's conception hermeneutics is a method employed by the human and social sciences to guarantee the objectivity of its conclusions. For Gadamer, on the other hand, hermeneutics is not intended to "elaborate a system of rules to describe, let alone direct, the methodological procedure of the human sciences." Gadamer's concern has been philosophical; for him "the methods of the human sciences are not at issue" (TM xxviii). The question that Gadamer sets out to address is: How is understanding possible? "At any rate," he responds to Betti, "the purpose of my investigation is not to offer a general theory of interpretation and a differential account of its methods (which E. Betti has done so well) but to discover what is common to all modes of understanding" (TM xxxi). Gadamer's concern has not been with empirical descriptions or with rules of procedure, but with hermeneutical principles, not with "what we do or what we ought to do, but [with] what happens to us over and above our wanting and doing" (TM xxviii). Gadamer has thus protested that Betti attempts to make him answer a question that he (Gadamer) never intended to ask (see TM 512).

E. D. Hirsch, who joins the debate on the side of Betti, is also concerned about validity and objectivity. In Hirsch's view, to the extent that Gadamer has disregarded the question of the author's original intention, he has foreclosed on the possibility of a determinate objective meaning. None of Gadamer's principles can save him from the "indeterminacy of textual meaning." Gadamer, who, for his part, holds that such a position would lead to an "untenable hermeneutic nihilism," nonetheless, on Hirsch's reading, ends up in just that untenable position.[24]

Ricoeur calls this debate over methodology and validity "the central *aporia* of hermeneutics" (HHS 47). We note, for future consideration, that the general terms of this debate are repeated within the context of educational theory. One way to pose the impasse defined by the Betti-Gadamer debate is to ask whether it is possible to *reproduce* the original meaning of the object of interpretation. Betti and Hirsch have maintained, not only that such reproduction is possible, but that it ought to be the aim of interpretation. Within the context of educational theory, conservative theorists, including Hirsch, argue that education must be based on a similar reproduction of meaning, whereas others, using the critical hermeneutical approach, provide normative arguments against reproduction. We will see (in Chapter 7) that a third argument in educational theory can be formulated on the basis of Gadamer's approach to the hermeneutical question of reproduction, namely, every attempt at reproduction involves a production of new meaning, and thus, strict reproduction is not possible. This approach would undermine both the conservative and the critical normative positions.

Aporia II: Authority and Emancipation

A more developed and more complex debate has taken place between Gadamer and Habermas, and to some extent it continues in various commentaries. In his review of Gadamer's *Truth and Method* and in subsequent essays, Habermas has raised a number of questions concerning language, scientific knowledge, reflection, authority, tradition, and the operation of political and economic power. For example, Habermas has pointed out that a number of hermeneutical problems originate in the process of scientific communication, because discussions within the community of scientists must take place in natural language. Hermeneutics is "called upon in one area of interpretation more than in any other and one which is of great social interest: the translation of important scientific information into the language of the social life-world."[25]

According to Gadamer, the necessary translation from scientific and technological studies to practical knowledge understood in natural language is conditioned by the universality of language itself. In effect, specialized scientific language always remains related to ordinary language. "The findings of science, travelling through modern channels of information and then, after due (many times after unduly great) delay, via the schools and education, become at last a part of the social consciousness."[26] Gadamer maintains that this translation and communication process is possible because the "universality of human linguisticality" is unlimited and carries everything understandable within it, including the entire procedure of science and its methodology. No less than practical and political consciousness, scientific consciousness is conditioned by various traditions and conducts itself according to the universality of human linguisticality.

Habermas questions this claim of universality. The fact that scientific activity is dependent on natural language communication, which has a *dialogical* structure, does not solve the problem of translation between the technical field and everyday life. Simply put, the technical language of science and the everyday language of communication are quite different. The sociologist Anthony Giddens explains it in this fashion: "The technical language and theoretical propositions of the natural sciences are insulated from the world they are concerned with because that world does not answer back."[27] Science arrives at its conclusions by using *monological* interpretation. In such cases, "linguistic expressions appear in an absolute form that makes their content independent of the situation of communication."[28] Habermas contends that in such cases hermeneutical processes do not apply. This indicates a problem with the claim of universality made by hermeneutics. Precisely here, Habermas argues, hermeneutics discovers its own limitations.

> Hermeneutic consciousness does, after all, emerge from a reflection upon our own movement *within* natural language, whereas the interpretation of science on behalf of the life-world has to achieve a mediation *between* natural language *and* monological language systems. This process of translation transcends the lim-

itations of a rhetorical-hermeneutical art which has only been dealing with cultural products that were handed down and which are constituted by everyday language.[29]

The dispute between Habermas and Gadamer, then, concerns whether there is a universality, based on language, that bridges the dividing line drawn by Habermas between the monological language systems of science and dialogical natural language. If Gadamer is right, then hermeneutical principles are universal and apply across the board. On the other hand, if Habermas is right, then hermeneutics has run into one of its limitations.

Two different conceptions of language operate within this dispute. For Habermas, language is always limited by extralinguistic experience. Moreover, a type of interpretation (critical reflective interpretation) which escapes the constraints imposed by language systems is always possible. In contrast, Gadamer maintains that even extralinguistic experience, if it is to have any significance or effect, must always be mediated by language. All interpretation falls under linguistic constraints. "There is no societal reality, with all its concrete forces, that does not bring itself to representation in a consciousness which is linguistically articulated."[30]

Habermas challenges the universalization of hermeneutics in another important way, helping to move the discussion more deeply into social and political contexts. He charges that Gadamer's position remains politically naive to the extent that Gadamer fails to recognize the elements of distortion and deformation of interpretation imposed by force, compulsion, and coercion, that is, by extrahermeneutical factors. An adequate frame of reference for the interpretation of meaning must include not only language and its corresponding hermeneutic but also economic facts of labor and class and political factors of domination. If, as Habermas admits, language is a "metainstitution on which all social relations are dependent," language itself is dependent on extralinguistic social processes of domination, organized force, modes of production, scientific-technical progress, and so on.[31] Thus, the objective framework of social action is not exhausted by language. "The linguistic infrastructure of a society is part of a complex that, however symbolically mediated, is also constituted by the constraint of reality," that is, by economic, political and technical relations which "behind the back of language . . . also affect the very grammatical rules according to which we interpret the world."[32] Extralinguistic factors always distort language, and therefore they distort ordinary interpretation and communication.

Distorted communication may be the result of consciously perpetrated falsities—the product of political rhetoric or propaganda—or unconsciously enforced determinations—the result of economic arrangements beyond the present control of social groups. Habermas has brought this viewpoint even to the level of the individual psyche by citing the psychoanalytic realization concerning the repression and conversion of socially unacceptable behavior or expression. In both the political-economic and the psychoanalytic models, the key concept is power. Insofar as philosophical hermeneutics ignores or denies the dimensions of power in interpretation, by focusing exclusively on language as meta-institution, hermeneutics remains inadequate to its task.

In place of a trusting interpretation, Habermas proposes a "depth hermeneutics" in the service of the critique of ideology. In a critical or depth hermeneutics, hermeneutical reflection is supplemented by metahermeneutical explanation. Through critical reflection depth hermeneutics uncovers and attempts to neutralize built-in distortions operative in understanding in order to promote emancipation through self-reflection. For Habermas, Gadamer's philosophical hermeneutics remains limited insofar as it fails to recognize or deal with extralinguistic elements that shape ideology and misshape the contours of communication.

In response, Gadamer clearly objects to a conception of critical reflection that claims to dissolve or neutralize the process and force of tradition. In response to Habermas, who contended that Gadamer had failed to recognize the power of reflection, Gadamer states: "My objection is that the critique of ideology overestimates the competence of reflection and reason. Inasmuch as it seeks to penetrate the masked interests which infect public opinion, it implies its own freedom from any ideology; and that means in turn that it enthrones its own norms and ideals as self-evident and absolute." In Gadamer's view, a critical hermeneutics can only be accomplished in an ongoing communication which "always demands a continuing exchange of views and statements" but never claims a privileged ideological neutrality.[33]

This impasse concerning language, power, and the universality of hermeneutics constitutes a second *aporia* within contemporary hermeneutical theory. It can be expressed in terms of the following question: Does hermeneutics, even when conceived of as depth hermeneutics, actually move us beyond constrained communication to a reflective emancipation, or is such critical reflection itself bound by hermeneutical constraints? In other terms, to what extent are traditions (and various authority or power structures) necessarily assimilated or *reproduced* in understanding, thereby lending themselves to forces of domination, or to what extent are traditions (authority or power structures) *transformed* in hermeneutical experience? This *aporia* is also reflected in the conflict between moderate and critical approaches to educational theory. To what extent are traditions and established power structures reproduced in educational experience, or to what extent can they be transcended by critical work? Those who take the critical approach to education will insist upon the power of reflection to break up structures of power and authority in educational processes and institutions. Those who take an approach to educational theory consistent with a moderate hermeneutics will insist that structures of power and authority are inevitably embedded in educational experience. These are issues to which we return in Chapter 8.

Aporia *III: Conversation*

What we have termed "hermeneutics" up to this point is contested by Derrida's deconstructive approach to interpretation, which is sometimes viewed as an attempt to get beyond hermeneutics. Derrida offers the following definition of hermeneutics: "By hermeneutic, I have designated the decoding of a sense or of a truth hidden in a text. I have opposed it to the transformative activity of interpretation."[34] The contrast made here between interpretation as decoding meaning or truth and interpretation as transformative activity is the contrast between traditional hermeneutics and radical deconstruction. Derrida acknowledges that such a transformation was first explicated by Heidegger.

The concept of deconstruction comes originally from Heidegger's early work (see BT, section 6). Heidegger there defines a "destructive" interpretation of the Western metaphysical tradition as a "transformation" (*Verwandlung*) of that which has been handed down to us. This seemingly violent rereading of tradition which aims at getting out from under the domination of traditional categories does not pretend to be able to escape traditions or to think in a vacuum. Heidegger's description is somewhat more moderate: "Deconstruction means—to open our ears, to make ourselves free for what speaks to us in the tradition."[35] Deconstruction, in Heidegger's terms, is more of a listening; it allows the release of a meaning different from the usual interpretations of reality.

Derrida perceives a tension or conflict within Heidegger's conception of deconstruction.[36] If Heidegger sets out to disrupt the domination of traditional metaphysical thinking, he ends up simply repeating that thinking to the extent that he seeks to listen to a truth or origin which he terms "Being" (*Sein*). Derrida contends that the categories of truth, origin, and Being belong to traditional metaphysics. He proposes a different regime of deconstruction: "The hermeneutic project which postulates a true sense of the text is disqualified under this regime. Reading is freed from the horizon of the meaning or truth of being. . . . Heidegger's reading subsists, throughout the near totality of its trajectory, in the hermeneutic space of the question of the truth (of being)."[37]

So, for Derrida, there are "two interpretations of interpretation," and thus two hermeneutics. One "seeks to decipher, dreams of deciphering a truth or an origin." In this sense, hermeneutics is always oriented toward an original text which requires explication—and thus is oriented toward a hidden truth, origin, being, or presence. Its role is to conserve, reproduce, and flourish within the tradition of metaphysics and its traditional interpretation of human existence as "man" (that is, humanism). On the other hand, radical deconstructive hermeneutics, "which is no longer turned towards the origin, affirms play and tries to pass beyond man and humanism."[38] Derrida sees elements of both interpretations in Heidegger but appropriates only the radical, disruptive, antihermeneutical approach. In Derrida's view, Gadamer embraces the more conservative search for truth.[39]

The differences between Gadamer and Derrida can be discerned in the "encounter" which took place between the two thinkers in Paris in 1981. The contrast in their styles reflected a fundamental disagreement in interpretive approaches. One difference clearly manifested itself in regard to language: for Gadamer, the essential nature of language is to be found in the event of conversation, and his style of discourse reflected an attempt to bring Derrida into a conversation about hermeneutics. Derrida, on the other hand, understands language to work as a play of signifiers with indeterminate meaning, and his style reflected the attempt to disrupt the very concept of conversation which Gadamer was theorizing about and practicing. Their minimal debate centered on the concept of trust or "good will" which Gadamer proposed as a prerequisite of conversation. Distrusting the very concept of "good will," Derrida attempted to show its metaphysical roots in Kant, and thus to show the metaphysical background for the notion of the primacy of conversation.[40]

Given the terms of this encounter, we can make good use here of Paul Ricoeur's distinction between a "hermeneutics of trust" and a "hermeneutics of suspicion" in order to clarify Derrida's critique of hermeneutics—a critique that is leveled against conservative, moderate, and critical approaches. According to Ricoeur, a hermeneutics of trust involves the restoration of meaning. Hermeneutical recollection or restoration of meaning requires a trust placed in language, in the text at hand—a trust that, through interpretation, meaning can be found in the text. To the extent that this faith or trust in language remains naive, hermeneutics remains more conservative than critical.

At the other extreme of hermeneutics Ricoeur places "the school of suspicion"—Freud, Marx, and Nietzsche. These three thinkers have in common a profound suspicion of the obvious, of what purports to be truth. "If we go back to the intention they had in common, we find in it the decision to look upon the whole of consciousness primarily as 'false' consciousness."[41] If conservative hermeneutics expresses an implicit faith in what consciously controlled methodology accomplishes, the school of suspicion expresses a deconstructive doubt, a radical distrust of consciousness and language. The task of the hermeneutics of suspicion is to decipher, decode, or unmask the "reality" or "truth" of consciousness, capitalism, and Christian (= Western) metaphysics in order to show the contingency and relativity of these systems. According to Ricoeur, each member of the school of suspicion aimed at the inversion or the deconstruction of the dominant Platonic, meta-physical dualisms which prevailed in his respective field. This radi-cal version of hermeneutics as the suspicious and destructive deciphering of morals, of social institutions, and of conscious life contrasts starkly to the conservative hermeneutics associated with Betti and Hirsch.

If hermeneutics is generally conceived to be seeking meaning, truth, or consensus through interpretation modeled on conversa-tion or dialogue, it reflects an optimism or trust that in some sense truth will be found. Conservative hermeneutics may disagree with moderate hermeneutics concerning the nature of truth, but for both approaches there is some kind of truth to be found in the process of interpretation. Critical hermeneutics, as we have seen, points out that what usually passes for truth is ideologically dis-torted. Thus, following lines first drawn by Marx and Freud, one needs a hermeneutics of suspicion, a depth hermeneutics, a harder-working and distrustful hermeneutics in order to accomplish truth or arrive at a true, undistorted consensus. But even this critical approach optimistically promises that we will really be "on to something" in the end, that we are moving toward an ideal consen-sus and an emancipation from false consciousness. Within the school of suspicion, Derrida befriends Nietzsche but leaves Marx to Habermas and critical hermeneutics. Marx, and to some extent Freud, as well as critical theorists like Habermas, are all too trust-ing, not suspicious enough for Derrida. They think that there can be some resolution to the hermeneutical situation: communism, psychoanalytic cure, ideal consensus, the suspension of her-meneutical communication, and so on. They all promise eman-cipation from false consciousness, and thereby a liberation of truth.

In contrast, radical or deconstructive hermeneutics, following Nietzsche, would argue that the only truth is untruth, that all interpretations are false, that there is no ultimate escape from false consciousness, that the whole metaphysical concept of truth re-quires deconstruction. In opposition to hermeneutics in any tradi-tional sense, Derrida proposes a Nietzschean "active interpreta-tion, which substitutes an incessant deciphering for the disclosure of truth as a presentation of the thing itself in its presence."[42]

Gadamer contends that in following Nietzsche's radical ventures both Heidegger and Derrida have been led away from the primary aspect of language: conversation. Indeed, in Gadamer's view, the concept of deconstruction was originally meant to defrost the frozen language of metaphysics—technical words emptied of living conversational sense and thus alienated from their original experience of being. Deconstruction was originally designed by Heidegger to enter into conversation with these alienated words, to make the words speak again and to rediscover the experience of being. Gadamer understands his own philosophical hermeneutics as an attempt to follow this kind of deconstruction. Derrida's path, from Gadamer's point of view, involves a "shattering of metaphysics," a destruction of conversation.[43]

For Derrida, Gadamer is too trusting of and in conversation. When Gadamer states that fundamentally, in conversation, "both partners must have the good will to try to understand one another," Derrida interprets *good will* to involve a modern, Kantian metaphysics of subjectivity with the implication that conversing subjects maintain (or will) a degree of control over the words of the conversation.[44] Derrida wants to know what happens to trust and "good will" in cases of distorted communication which demand suspicion, as in the psychoanalytic situation.

The "conversation" which occurs between Gadamer and Derrida in Paris embodies a third *aporia* within hermeneutical theory: the *aporia* of conversation itself, which is caught between trust and suspicion. This *aporia* concerns the possibility or impossibility of truth, conversation, and transformation. This impasse is expressed in the differences between the "transformative activity" which Derrida opposes to a hermeneutics of trust, the transformation (*Verwandlung*) which Heidegger identifies as the aim of deconstruction, and the transformation which, according to Gadamer, is at the same time the preservation (*Anverwandlung*) of tradition (TM 281).

Here, again for future reference, we note that this same hermeneutical *aporia* of conversation is repeated within the context of education. Some theorists would argue that education is possible only as some kind of transformative activity. The nature of education depends upon the nature of this transformation. If transformation, in principle, goes beyond reproduction and thus breaks with conservative theory, does this mean that transformation must involve the radical suspicion of all conversation? Or is education a transformation within the larger framework of what some theorists call the "conversation of mankind," an ideal sometimes taken as a metaphor and model of education? We return to these questions in Chapter 9.

THE RELEVANCE OF HERMENEUTICS TO EDUCATION

If the essential connections between *hermēneía* and ancient *paideía* have been obscured in modern and contemporary theory, still, it does not require an historical or genealogical analysis to discover the relations between contemporary hermeneutics and education. The very same issues raised in the aporias of hermeneutical theory are raised again in educational theory. Reproduction, authority, and conversation; objectivity, distortion, and transformation: these are issues that both hermeneutics and education must deal with. If education involves understanding and interpretation; if formal educational practice is guided by the use of texts and commentary, reading and writing; if linguistic understanding and communication are essential to educational institutions; if educational experience is a temporal process involving fixed expressions of life and the transmission or critique of traditions; if, in effect, education is a human enterprise, then hermeneutics, which claims all of these as its subject matter, holds out the promise of providing a deeper understanding of the educational process.

The various approaches to hermeneutics just outlined, and the contemporary aporias that distinguish them, constitute a framework within which the contemporary relevance of hermeneutics to educational theory and practice can be discerned. In fact, each of the approaches to hermeneutical theory—conservative, moderate, critical, and radical—can be associated with respective approaches in educational theory. Moreover, we find similar aporias defining the educational field. What we fail to find, in most cases, is any attempt to explicate the hermeneutical background of educational theory.

Hirsch, for example, has recently proposed the concept of "cultural literacy" as an educational ideal.[45] This concept clearly conforms to his conservative hermeneutical theory insofar as it is based on the reproduction of traditional values and cultural information. Although Hirsch likes to contrast cultural literacy with certain aspects of "critical thinking" as an educational ideal, it can be shown that the extremely influential critical thinking ideal also reflects certain conservative principles of hermeneutics. In almost every case, however, the hermeneutical principles which inform these educational ideals remain unexplicated in educational theories.[46]

At the other end of the hermeneutical and educational spectrum are educational theories which have direct correspondence to critical and radical hermeneutical approaches. Habermas's critical theory and associated neo-Marxist approaches have inspired the development of critical educational theory by such thinkers as Apple, Giroux, Bowles and Gintis, Bourdieu and Passeron, and Young.[47] Despite the often admitted connection between these educational approaches and critical theory, the hermeneutical dimension of critical theory remains far in the background. Few attempts have been made to consider or justify critical educational theory in terms of critical hermeneutics.[48] In even fewer cases critical hermeneutical principles have been questioned in light of educational processes.[49]

Radical views on education have been developed by a number of theorists, including Derrida and Foucault.[50] More so than others, these theorists explore the connections between their radical (anti-)hermeneutical theories and their proposed educational reforms. Yet, to the extent that they deny the hermeneutical nature of their radical theories, they do not help in any direct way to explicate the connections between hermeneutics and education.

In contrast to the previous approaches, very little has been done in the area of an educational theory that would correspond to moderate hermeneutics. I need to add a qualification, however: very little has been done *in any explicit way*. My intention in this book is to help fill this gap, and to show that there are some existing educational philosophies that can be interpreted as having a moderate hermeneutical background. With respect to the explicit correspondence between educational theory and moderate hermeneutics, however, Elaine Atkins makes the relevant point very clearly: "Very few writers within the hermeneutic tradition deal with pedagogical issues. And those who do often do not go far enough to give us concrete guidance."[51]

The grouping of these theories, which reflects a correspondence between hermeneutical theory and educational theory, is more than coincidental. It indicates the essential connections between hermeneutics and education, which are, at the same time, obscured by the way these theories are generally developed. These connections will be clarified if we consider that the three aporias which help to distinguish hermeneutical theories find a close correlation to three aporias which define contemporary educational theories. As we have noted, the *aporia* concerning reproduction, expressed in the Betti-Gadamer debate, is related to a corresponding set of problems in educational theory involving cultural reproduction. Should interpretational and educational practices be viewed as instruments for cultural reproduction? Is reproduction desirable or even possible? If the tradition that education wants to reproduce includes a tradition of critical thinking, is it reasonable for conservative theory to assert the authorial intention theory of meaning, encourage the acceptance of teacher expertise and authority, the memorization of objective fact, and the lecture approach to teaching?

The *aporia* concerning authority and emancipation, which represents a central issue in the Habermas-Gadamer debate, also corresponds to questions raised in educational theory. Do educational practices and institutions promote or prevent domination by the authority of traditional social structures and ideologies? This critical *aporia* comes close to what R. Graham Oliver has called the paradox of authority and autonomy. "Briefly stated, it is that it seems impossible for a child to develop into a rationally autonomous person unless, in the course of the developmental process, there is a substantial deference to other persons as authority. Yet such deference appears to be in opposition to what was sought, namely, personal rational autonomy."[52]

Finally, the problem of trust versus suspicion in interpretation, the *aporia* concerning the practice of conversation, which is the focus of conflict between radical and moderate hermeneutics, corresponds, in the context of education, to the question of whether education as transformation, understood on the model of the "conversation of mankind," for example, should be or can be deconstructed. Because the conversation of education is suspected of reproducing the metaphysical framework of Western thinking and of prolonging heteronomous authority relations, radical theories of education challenge its appropriateness as a metaphor for education.

Since the three aporias which define the hermeneutical field make their appearance in the educational field as well, it should be clear that if some resolution of these aporias could be gained in either field, resolutions in the other field might also be advanced. Indeed, by viewing these aporias within the context of educational experience we can see that the three are closely related and that, in some sense, they are three sides of a central issue, namely, the issue of transformation in both educational experience and interpretation. So, by suggesting that hermeneutics has a relevance to theoretical problems in education I do not want to rule out the converse proposition. If a hermeneutical exploration of educational experience suggests any resolution to the central issues in educational theory, hermeneutics may in the process help itself to a resolution of its own *aporiai*.

In the course of the following investigations I show not only that hermeneutics has relevance for educational theory, but that the analysis of educational experience has import for hermeneutical theory. Hermeneutical principles are not simply applied in a mechanical fashion to educational experience. Rather, in the encounter with educational experience, hermeneutical principles are themselves opened up for inspection and revision. The hermeneutical analysis of educational experience not only helps to provide a basis for understanding the nature of education, but also helps to clarify some of the difficult issues involved in hermeneutical theory. Indeed, rather than a specialized hermeneutics, or one application of hermeneutics among others, the analysis of educational experience may count as a paradigmatic analysis of interpretation, one that is even more revealing than the paradigm of the text which guides so much of contemporary hermeneutical theory.

This book is guided by two aims. First, I propose that by exploring the relation between hermeneutics and education we will come to a better understanding of the aporias that define both fields. In this understanding we will also be able to clarify the nature of education, specifically with respect to its interpretational character, and the nature of hermeneutics, specifically with respect to the possibility and limitations of a universal hermeneutics. Second, I propose, to the extent that it is possible, to develop a moderate hermeneutical approach to education that will answer the objections raised by conservative, critical, and radical theories. This moderate approach will not be identical with Gadamer's philosophical hermeneutics in every detail, but will approximate it in general terms.

In the first part of this book I work out the details of a moderate hermeneutical approach to education. I begin by introducing some preliminary conceptions of educational experience and interpretation (Chapter 2). I then propose and explore a hypothesis concerning the interpretational nature of educational experience. The implication of this hypothesis is that by pursuing a theory of interpretation we are also developing a theory of learning. I examine this thesis first by describing the principle of the hermeneutical circle and its relation to educational experience (Chapter 3). Chapter 4 involves a detailed explanation of the constraining roles played by language and traditions in the processes of interpretation and learning. In Chapter 5 I show that, even within these constraints, interpretation and educational experience are productive rather than reproductive. The moral dimension implied in the processes of interpretation and self-understanding is also explored with relevance to educational experience. Part 1 concludes with the attempt to explicate the implications of this moderate hermeneutical approach for understanding the nature of education (Chapter 6). In this regard I review a number of traditional theories of education, including one expressed in Plato's dialogue, the *Meno*. I contend that Plato's theory in the *Meno* comes close to a moderate theory of education.

In Part 2 I return to the hermeneutical debates and aporias mentioned in this chapter. In Chapter 7 I show how several contemporary theories of education correspond to the tenets of conservative hermeneutics and how, within a theory of education formed on the principles of moderate hermeneutics, the *aporia* concerning reproduction can be better understood. In Chapter 8 I describe how the *aporia* concerning authority, raised in the Habermas-Gadamer debate, finds a correspondence in the educational context, and how the moderate approach must come to deal with the concerns raised by the critical theory of education. Chapter 9 proposes the moderate response to radical (deconstructionist) views of education. In response to the *aporia* concerning conversation, the moderate approach suggests that the practice of deconstruction itself reflects the very nature of education as conversation. In the concluding chapter I develop the implications of my analysis for hermeneutics itself. I suggest that the concept of a universal hermeneutics, although legitimate, is limited and requires the supplement of a "local hermeneutics" which is inadequately modeled on the textual paradigm, but finds a better model in educational experience.

Part 1

CHAPTER 2

Interpretation and Educational Experience

A PRECONCEPTION OF EDUCATIONAL EXPERIENCE

It is clear that I must provide some preliminary and provisional indication of the subject matter to be studied, namely, educational experience. Even if the aim is to develop a fuller understanding of such experience, a certain conception of it must already operate within the projected design of the following study. This preconception of educational experience will function as a guide in subsequent discussions, and the explication of it here constitutes an attempt to clarify our presuppositions and prejudices about education.

We have at our disposal two sources that inform us of our subject matter: (a) our own experience of education; and (b) a set of traditions which define, correctly or incorrectly, the nature of education. No doubt some of these traditions already operate in our approach and in our very experience. I want to begin closer to experience than to theory, however, although I admit that such an approach can never claim to discover experience in itself, free of theoretical presuppositions. Given this qualification, I set out to explicate our preconception of educational experience in two steps. First I attempt to provide a provisional characterization of educational experience that is based, for the most part, on experiences familiar to us. Second, given this characterization, I formulate a hypothesis about educational experience that will act as a guide throughout the remainder of this study.

Most of us are familiar with different varieties of educational experience. Educational experiences are found in both formal and informal settings, from the formal structure of a classroom situation with well-defined teacher and student roles in place, to the informal self-discovery of the child at play. Three forms of educa-

classroom reading play

tional experience should be familiar to all of us: classroom experience, reading experience, and play experience. One can learn in the classroom situation as student or as teacher; one can also learn by reading texts or by participating in play activities.

From the viewpoint of traditional hermeneutics it seems obvious that the experience of learning involved in reading and interpreting texts would be the most promising place to start in order to see the relations between hermeneutics and educational experience. Such a start, however, would almost beg the question. If textual interpretation is cast as the educational model, that is, if learning is viewed as a process of reading to understand or acquire knowledge, then it seems self-evident that the study of the process of textual interpretation is also the study of learning. This is not something that we can deny. Textual interpretation is an important way to learn. Indeed, this fact in itself is a quite direct way to establish the relevance of hermeneutics to education. Learning itself, however, is the experience that we want to focus on. Although learning can take place in textual interpretation, it is clear that not all learning takes place in textual interpretation. In fact, since one must *learn* how to read and interpret texts, a certain priority must be given to a kind of learning other than learning by textual interpretation. To take textual interpretation as the paradigm for all learning would be to distort learning processes that do not depend upon texts. Moreover, one of my concerns, as outlined in Chapter 1, is to move hermeneutical analysis away from distortions that may be introduced by textualism. For these reasons I will focus on the other two models of educational experience mentioned above: classroom experience and play experience.

formal classroom structure

There are many classroom models. The conception of educational experience that we find in one of the more traditional models involves a formal structure. A teacher presents a particular subject matter to a group of students. Educators and students are familiar with many of the elements of this model: teacher, teaching method, material presented, classroom circumstances, student, student's background and preparation, and so forth. All of these elements condition educational experience in the classroom. For example, the physical appearance and layout of the classroom, as well as the psychological dispositions of the students, will foster or hinder or bias the learning process. Our concern, however, is to ask about the nature of educational experience itself, and that directs us to the teacher-student relation, for, as we shall see, within the interchange between teacher and student, learning either occurs or fails to occur. Some, of course, would want to locate learning specifically within the student. It might be said that the teacher teaches and it is up to the student to learn or not learn. Teaching does not guarantee learning. Moreover, an individual can learn in an isolated fashion, through experience or reading, without a teacher. But it is misleading to say that in the classroom situation learning takes place within the student. If we are seeking a "location" for learning in this circumstance, then we should say that learning takes place in the situation, in the interchange, or between the student and another person, where the other person may be the teacher or another student.

Remember that here we are sketching a preliminary characterization of educational experience. This preliminary characterization, which is neither developed nor justified here, will count toward an explication of the preconception of educational experience operating in this study. It will also lead us toward developing a particular hypothesis that will be tested out in subsequent chapters of this book.

In the traditional classroom model learning involves an interchange. If we take this as a preliminary characterization of educational experience, then two questions arise. First, can we further explicate this interchange? Second, does this interchange characterize educational experience in general, or is it limited to the classroom situation? Specifically, can isolated learning or informal learning also be understood as an interchange?

By explicating the interchange of learning in the classroom situation we will be led directly to the hypothesis that will make our analysis of educational experience hermeneutical: the interchange of learning in the classroom situation is an interchange of interpretations. Consider what these interpretations are in the most traditional model of classroom experience. A teacher has some knowledge that she wishes to communicate to the student. The student, in turn, attempts to grasp the knowledge that is presented. Of course, this is an oversimplification. The teacher is not passing knowledge to the student as one might pass a ball to a teammate. We can begin to see the more complex picture if we consider the following qualifications. When we say that the teacher has some knowledge, we mean that the teacher has interpreted some particular material or subject matter. Let us call this aspect of teaching simply the teacher's "understanding" of the subject matter. Traditional hermeneutics would describe it in terms of the *subtilitas intelligendi* (the subtlety of understanding). The teacher understands the material in a certain way, but also wants to communicate this understanding to the student. We will refer to the means of doing so as the "pedagogical presentation." The traditional description would involve the *subtilitas explicandi* (the subtlety of explication).

In communicating to the student, the teacher may not present precisely or explicitly her own understanding of the subject matter, but may create a way for the student to come into that understanding for himself. The teacher's understanding and her pedagogical presentation may, and usually do, differ. Israel Scheffler explains this difference in the following example. "A parent's sophisticated understanding of sexuality is of the utmost usefulness in helping him to discuss the issue with his children, though he would generally be ill-advised simply to recount such understanding to them."[1] The teacher, likewise, is in the position of an "insider" familiar with the subject matter, who must translate or interpret for an "outsider" who may lack any specific knowledge in that area. For example, if the teacher is an accomplished scholar and has spent a great deal of time studying the French Revolution, this understanding of that complex historical period may be characterized by a high degree of sophistication. The teacher's presentation to a group of students who have never studied history before may have to be so simplified that it would actually amount to a distortion of her own understanding. The presentation may serve the purpose of drawing the students closer to the teacher's own understanding, but it itself constitutes a different interpretation from the teacher's own. There is certainly in this case a lack of coincidence between the teacher's understanding and her pedagogical presentation. And obviously there are good reasons for this. Chladenius, who equated interpretation with teaching, put it in general terms: "In constructing an interpretation, one must consider the insight of the pupil and use this or that interpretation in accordance with the pupil's lack of knowledge. Since there is no one interpretation of a book suitable for all readers, there may be as many as there are classes of readers grouped according to knowledge and insight. To be precise, almost every person needs a special interpretation."[2]

Of course, one could suggest that the teacher's understanding and pedagogical presentation might in fact coincide. One could say that in a more advanced course with a group of advanced students the teacher may try to express and even succeed in expressing her understanding in her presentation. On the level of interpretation, the coincidence would mean that there is only one interpretation. Whether or not such perfect communication between the teacher's understanding and the pedagogical presentation is possible is a topic that will be addressed later. Here I only suggest that if the teacher herself is to learn something through her teaching, there must be some kind of interchange between her understanding and her presentation. In that interchange the teacher's understanding might govern her presentation, or, in a special sense of discovery, her pedagogical presentation might lead her to a new understanding or at least open up to question her current understanding. The necessary condition for this interchange of learning on the side of the teacher is some degree of noncoincidence between her understanding and her presentation. At the very least, the presentation is, as Derrida would put it, "an extra text" which complicates the original understanding, an interpretation modifying an interpretation.[3]

There is, of course, another interchange at work in the classroom, one that might be considered more essential to the classroom situation. The student must in some way deal with the pedagogical presentation. Here a number of options present themselves. The student can be drawn toward the teacher's own understanding through the presentation, or can be inspired in a different, unintended direction by the presentation, or can question the presentation, or can be misled by the presentation, and so forth. In any case the student is always involved in *interpreting* the pedagogical presentation. The teacher's presentation becomes, for the student, the material or subject matter that he must come to understand. On the student side, this interpretation of the material involves a learning process. Again, this interpretation—let us call it the student's "comprehension"—may be precisely what the teacher wanted, or it may be a complete misunderstanding, or something in between. As Gadamer suggests, "meaning can be experienced even where it is not actually intended."[4] How or why the student's comprehension is close or not close to the meaning intended by the teacher is a topic that will be discussed later (Chapter 5). The important point here is that there may be varying degrees of noncoincidence between the student's comprehension and the pedagogical presentation. It is precisely the degree of non-coincidence that allows there to be an interchange which is irreducible to a simple transmission of information between teacher and student. The interchange is an interchange of interpretations rather than an exchange of information.

This interchange of interpretations is a dialectical give and take between one interpretation and another, and it characterizes precisely the process of learning. The interchange is an ongoing movement in which, ideally, the student continually revises and enlarges his comprehension as the teacher modifies, adapts, and builds her presentation. Here we could not object to Piaget's terminology: the process is one of "assimilation" and "accommodation" on the part of both the student and the teacher.[5] The student assimilates the pedagogical presentation to his own comprehension, or allows his comprehension to accommodate itself to the presentation. A similar process takes place on the side of the teacher. On the basis, perhaps, of her interpretation of how the student is grasping the material, the teacher may decide at various times to modify her presentation by drawing it closer to her own understanding of the subject matter or by accommodating her presentation to the student's comprehension.

These adjustments to pedagogical presentation, adjustments which may be based upon the teacher's perception of the student's progress, complicate the issue and provide some indication that we are still working with an abstract and oversimplified model. Adjustments to the pedagogical presentation are based on another kind of interpretation made by the teacher, an interpretation not of the subject matter but of the student's comprehension and progress. Here we could distinguish between "material interests," which guide the pedagogical presentation with respect to the subject matter being presented, and "formal interests," which guide the presentation with respect to the communicative concerns of the teacher. Even further, if in the process of attempting to ascertain the student's progress the teacher calls upon the student to explicate his comprehension of the subject matter, that explication may not coincide fully with the student's comprehension but may in fact be guided by what the student interprets to be what the teacher wants to hear. To indicate more of the interpretational complexity that we here leave unexamined, we can note that we have not mentioned another kind of interpretation associated with the teacher's understanding of what it means to be a teacher, or interpretations associated with what the student understands about the teacher's role and about his own role as student. Nor have we mentioned anything about the "hidden curriculum," which involves a complex of interpretations that are not easy to characterize. I think I have said enough, however, to indicate that the classroom model leads us to characterize educational experience as a complex interchange of interpretations in which each interpretation may itself be complex: an interpretation conditioned by and conditioning other interpretations.

This characterization leads directly to the hypothesis that I intend to explore in the following chapters. Educational experience is always hermeneutical experience. Put another way, learning always involves interpretation. If at this point this proposition seems trivial, I contend that its implications are not trivial. By exploring the meaning of this proposition we will discover a sense of education that is not only not clearly expressed in contemporary educational theories, but is opposed to many of the current conceptions of education.

To begin testing this hypothesis we need to look at informal educational experience. Perhaps the characterization of education as an interchange of interpretations only applies to the formal classroom model. But before we examine informal educational experience in terms of the concept of play, we need to clarify the concept of interpretation which operates in our hypothesis.

THE RANGE OF INTERPRETATION

The concept of interpretation which guides our hermeneutical analysis of educational experience is opposed to the narrowly defined, epistemological notion of cognition. Interpretation is not to *interpretation*

be construed as fundamentally an intellectual activity which happens only in the mind, or only when our cognitive faculties are exercised. Rather, interpretation is a universal feature of all human activity. We can find a similar universality associated with the term *rational* in the Western philosophical tradition, especially prior to the modern era initiated by Descartes. In the Aristotelian tradition, for instance, the human being, conceived of as "rational animal," was thought to be rational throughout, not just to the extent that the human being used mental capacity. Aquinas, for example, held that the human soul is rational only to the extent that the human body is rational.[6] The human being grasps things rationally with the hand as well as with the intellect. All human activities are permeated by a rational dimension, and such rationality specifically makes such activities human. If we take up this thought and realize also that human rationality is finite, less than divine, we will come close to the conception that all activities specifically human involve interpretation. Human rationality is interpretive rationality.

This broad conception of interpretation has been developed within the history of hermeneutical theory. Its development can be traced through the writings of the Romantics, Dilthey, Husserl, Heidegger, and Gadamer. In these writings the term *understanding* gradually takes on a wider significance than in the epistemological tradition, which is sometimes contrasted with hermeneutics.[7] In epistemology the word *understanding* usually signifies a mental process which takes place in the mind (the soul or consciousness). It is an intellectual process whereby a knower gains knowledge about something. This is explained in terms of a straightforward linear, dualistic relationship between the subject (the knower) and the object (the known). Quite often in epistemology understanding is said to depend on a representation, a mental image that mediates between subject and object.

For Romantic hermeneutics, in contrast to epistemological models, interpretation and understanding were considered problematic primarily within the context of textual reading or, by extension, in interpersonal communication. If epistemology has been oriented by the question of how we come to know *things* as objects, hermeneutics was oriented by the question of how we come to know *others* as persons, and their expressions. Reading and the proper comprehension of another person's speech, it was thought, involved interpretation which should be guided by certain rules. The "historical school" (Droysen, Ranke, Boeckh) expanded this problematic into a set of questions about historical method, and Dilthey carried it over to a more general conception of understanding as methodology for the human and social sciences.

For Dilthey, interpretation and understanding (*Verstehen*) are concepts that have special status as part of the methodological procedure of the human and social sciences. For Edmund Husserl, who offers a critique of Dilthey's historicism, one does not escape the problematic of interpretation simply by calling interpretation a method, as Dilthey does. In other words, if the question is how we actually understand another person, culture, historical epoch, and so on, the question is begged by the response Dilthey proposes: that we understand by the special method called "understanding." The reason interpretation remains problematic, even in the wake of Dilthey's concept of *Verstehen*, is that the most fundamental of conscious acts—perception—itself involves interpretation. Any attempt to define interpretation as a special kind of perception of the other fails to explain its genuine nature since it fails to explain perception itself as interpretational. This is Husserl's insight, even as early as his *Logical Investigations* (1900–1901).

Perception itself is interpretational. Husserl explains this in terms of a schema in which perceptual meaning itself is constituted in an informing act of consciousness which "interprets" the sense content ("hyletic data") of consciousness.[8] Furthermore, perception itself has a certain primacy in consciousness in the sense that all other modes of consciousness are built up on a perceptual foundation. Not only conscious acts of memory, imagination, judgment, and expression, but also emotional and volitional acts of consciousness are founded on acts of perception. In effect, this means that human consciousness in all of its forms, from logical cognition to love and hate, involves interpretation.

The hermeneutical importance of Husserl's insight, that perception and therefore all forms of consciousness involve interpretation, is recognized and developed by Heidegger. Heidegger, influenced by twentieth-century neo-Kantian philosophy, accepts what is revolutionary in Kantian epistemology, that is, that the knowing subject shapes the object of knowledge, at the same time that he rejects the dualistic metaphysics which underlies it. Existence rather than knowledge is Heidegger's starting point, and his analysis is hermeneutical-ontological rather than epistemological. Understanding is not, fundamentally, a mental or intellectual operation; nor can it be adequately explicated in a Husserlian phenomenology of consciousness. For Heidegger, understanding is essentially a way of being, the way of being which belongs to human existence.

Heidegger broadens and deepens the concept of understanding. Although intellectual comprehension is one kind of understanding, understanding itself is an existential characteristic of human existence which can find expression in a number of ways. Understanding is the disclosure of meaning or the opening up of the "world" which belongs to being human. Human existence by its existential structure of understanding is "in-the-world." The world, disclosed through existential understanding, is not an objective entity that stands in epistemological opposition to a knowing subject. Rather, human existence is so much constituted by being-in-the-world that the world and human existence can be discriminated from one another only abstractly and post factum.

For Heidegger, we are in-the-world in all essential aspects of our existence. Being-in-the-world is not primarily a cognitive relation between subject and object, although being-in-the-world is a way of existing which allows there to be cognition. Human existence discloses the world, or is in-the-world by way of an understanding that functions on all levels of behavior, conscious or unconscious. Thus, Heidegger contends, understanding is "a basic determination of [human] existence itself."[9] We can refer to this aspect of understanding, that it is involved in all human behavior, as its "existential comprehensiveness." In all human behaviors, not just intellectual ones, human existence is involved in an interpretive relation with meaning. Consider, for example, the relationship between a carpenter and his or her hammer. One can say that the fundamental meaning of the hammer is disclosed to the carpenter when it is in use, unconsciously integrated into the matrix of the carpenter's performance. Certainly the carpenter does not have to think about the hammer, or turn it into a thematic object present to consciousness in order to use it. Indeed, thinking about the hammer may get in the way of hammering. The carpenter understands the hammer best with his or her hand, in the hammering process, rather than in mental cognition of the hammer as an object. Interpretation, according to Heidegger, "is carried out primordially not in a theoretical statement but in an action" (BT 157/200).

Gadamer agrees with Heidegger that understanding "is not an isolated activity of human beings but a basic structure of our experience of life. We are always taking something *as* something. That is the primordial givenness of our world orientation, and we cannot reduce it to anything simpler or more immediate."[10] This hermeneutical "as" means that understanding is always interpretational. Gadamer, following Heidegger, can explain interpretation in the following terms. In understanding, human existence projects its possibilities before itself. As a human being I plan, proceed, pursue goals, dream, anticipate consequences, expect results, and so forth only because, as human, I am essentially orientated toward that which I am not yet. Existential understanding, always oriented toward the future, is a projection of meaning, the projection of my own possibilities, and a projection of my own self into the world, on the basis of what I have been. Given the finitude of human existence, that is, given its temporal limitations, its incompleteness in the sense that it is a constant projection or transcendence toward its possibilities which it is not yet, then understanding is never absolute *sub specie aeternitatis*. A divine, absolute intuition of the world lies beyond human understanding. I do not intuit the thing-in-itself, I interpret it *as* something. Human understanding is always interpretational.

The concept of "practical interests," common to both hermeneutical and educational theory, may serve to indicate, in a partial way, the nature of interpretational experience. Our everyday life is guided by any number of practical interests. We set practical goals, long-term and short-term, and we are motivated by needs of various kinds. We may even structure our activities by a priority list of concerns. Whether these interests are kept consciously in mind or operate unconsciously, they tend to determine, in some measure, the way we understand the surrounding world.[11] The direction of our interests will determine, to some extent, what we will look for and what we will see in any environment. In principle, hermeneuticists argue, there are no disinterested perceptions or interpretations. Indeed, perception itself is interpretational precisely on this account.

A similar conception is explicated by John Dewey with respect to education. We tend to adopt the interests of our social group in such a way that they come to bias our interpretation of the world and of others. "In accord with the interests and occupations of the group, certain things become objects of high esteem; others of aversion. . . . The way our group or class does things tends to determine the proper objects of attention, and thus to prescribe the directions and limits of observation and memory."[12] Dewey argues that practical interests are formed through informal educational experience, communication, and community life. They are pervasive throughout experience but remain for the most part unconscious. The hermeneutical point is that such interests condition and bias interpretation. Dewey confirms this view: "we do not anticipate results as mere intellectual onlookers, but as persons concerned in the outcome, we are partakers in the process which produces the result."[13]

Interpretation is the "laying out" (*Auslegung*) of meaning. By the time our cognitive apprehension arrives on the scene, the scene has already been laid out, structured, for example, by unconscious interests; the interpretation, Heidegger says, "has already decided for a definite way of conceiving it" (BT 191/150). For example, if I cognitively reflect on why I automatically, without conscious decision or thought, take a shower every morning, I would be able to make some sense out of it. I would be able to explain certain concepts of hygiene that I grew up with, certain psychological benefits that accrue from this practice and that prepare me for the day ahead. This meaningful context that makes sense out of my habit of showering, that shows it to be a meaningful act, is not something that only and suddenly becomes operative in the event of cognitive reflection. It is a context that operates at the level of my existence. I live within this usually unexplicated context. It is a meaning that is built into my act of showering before I do any cognitive reflection. I understand my showering, I project meaning into it, it fits into a context that defines my everyday practices, in a way that is prior to my intellectual decisions and yet beyond blind animal instinct.

The concept of interpretation, as it is developed by Heidegger and Gadamer, includes three characteristics that are of immediate importance for our preliminary account. (a) Interpretation is existentially comprehensive, in the sense explicated above. Interpretation is not something than can be limited to cognitive performances; every human activity involves interpretation. (b) Interpretation is always constrained. There is never a presuppositionless or absolute interpretation of the world; meaning is always constituted "under the guidance of a point of view" (BT 191/150), conditioned by practical interests, and within the constraints of human finitude. (c) Interpretation is a process that we already find ourselves in. It is a process that is larger than subjectivity, and, to some extent, it is a process that we do not entirely control.

The analysis of interpretation in Heidegger and Gadamer recalls Dilthey's remark about the traditional epistemological conception of understanding: "No real blood runs in the veins of the cognitive subject that Locke, Hume, and Kant constructed."[14] The living human being understands the world as he finds himself already in it, not as an anemic egological entity eruditely confronting an opposing objective entity. Interpretation is not something that I (the epistemological ego) do, but something that I am involved in. As with human rationality, I am not rational because I decide to act in a rational way; rather, I can only act in a rational way because I am involved in a rationality that goes beyond me and which I cannot choose even though it is the foundation of all my choosing.

PAIDIÁ AND *PAIDEÍA*

Our preliminary characterization of educational experience, which suggests the hypothesis that learning always involves interpretation, is based on observations about one classroom model. Does educational experience in general involve interpretational interchange, or is our hypothesis limited to the classroom model? To answer this question, and thereby to explicate our hypothesis further, we will now consider the concept of play as an example of informal educational experience.

Since the time Plato suggested that man was the "plaything of the gods" and urged men and women to make of the noblest games the real content of their lives (*Laws* 644d–e), the concept of play has claimed an important although peripheral place in theoretical studies of both ethical and aesthetic value. It is of more central importance, both practically and theoretically, in the field of education. Werner Jaeger, in his analysis of the connection between *paidiá* (play) and *paideía* (education) underscores some traditional distinctions.

> In Greek, the two words have the same root, because they both originally refer to the activity of the child (*pais*); but Plato is the first to deal with the problem of the relation between the two concepts . . .

> Plato is anxious to include the play-element in his *paideía*: the guard's children are to learn their lessons through play, which means that *paidiá* helps *paideía*. Dialectic, however, is a higher stage. It is not play, but earnest. Since many modern languages have taken over this classical contrast of the two concepts, it is difficult for us to realize what an effort of abstract philosophical thinking created it.[15]

Here Jaeger names two distinctions: the first between play and education; the second between play and seriousness. In the following analysis we explore these distinctions to see how strictly they can be maintained. I focus initially on two theories concerning the nature of play developed, respectively, in the fields of ethics and aesthetics. These theories will help to reveal the essence of play and its relevance to our characterization of educational experience as an interchange of interpretations.

The two theories of play discussed here appear in certain respects to be diametrically opposed. The first, an ethical theory proposed by Jean-Paul Sartre under the title of *existential psychoanalysis*, centers play around the concept of subjectivity; the second, an aesthetic theory described by Gadamer, attempts to decenter subjectivity precisely by the concept of play. I begin with a brief outline of each theory.

Sartre frames his analysis of play within the general categories of authenticity and inauthenticity which he had found in Heidegger's early works. Sartre equates inauthenticity with what he terms "bad faith" or "the spirit of seriousness" and associates authenticity with a "self-recovery" or radical conversion of self that can be effected through play. In contradistinction to Heidegger, Sartre recognizes these concepts to have an ethical import. Thus, as Sartre indicates, the concept of play belongs to the realm of ethics.[16]

Sartre contrasts play to the spirit of seriousness (bad faith, inauthenticity). Seriousness takes its orientation from the world, so that the serious person attributes more reality or value to the world than to himself. Thus, in bad faith one might measure one's worth in terms of the world, as, for example, one might measure a person by his clothing or financial status. The serious person, in this way, turns himself into an object and loses himself in the world. This means, according to Sartre's ontology, that the serious person hides his subjectivity, his freedom, and his possibilities from himself and reduces himself to a substantial and objective thing. On the other hand, play involves putting into effect one's freedom, which strips the real world of its reality and "releases subjectivity" (BN 580). For Sartre, human subjectivity is the source of and the end of playful activity. "What is play indeed if not an activity of which man is the first origin, for which man himself sets the rules, and which has no consequences except according to the rules posited" (BN 580). And so, according to Sartre, "the first principle of play is man himself" (BN 581). Play involves the recognition that the meaning of the world finds its source in human subjectivity. In play reality and value are transferred from the world to human existence, and human existence is rediscovered in its authentic freedom. "The function of the act [of play] is to make manifest and to present to *itself* the absolute freedom which is the very being of the person" (BN 581). Play effects a recovery of authentic existence and thereby allows an escape from bad faith.

It is clear that in Sartre's conception of play human subjectivity maintains control, consciously chooses, freely enters or exits the spirit of play, and is therefore responsible for recovering or losing authentic existence. Gadamer offers us a contrasting conception of play, one that is purged of all aspects of subjective control.

Gadamer claims that the "players are not the subject of play; instead play merely reaches presentation (*Darstellung*) through the players" (TM 103). Starting from the use of the word *play* (*Spiel*) in such phrases as *the play of light, the play of the waves, the play of forces*, and so forth, he contends that the essence of play is "movement as such" which has no goal but constantly renews and repeats itself.[17] Play is an impersonal movement in which subjectivity loses itself. Thus, "play fulfills its purpose only if the player loses himself in play" (TM 102).

Play is not to be contrasted with seriousness. According to Gadamer, play includes "its own, even sacred, seriousness" so that "seriousness in playing is necessary to makes the play wholly play" (TM 102). The seriousness, however, belongs not to the player but to play itself. Furthermore, "the actual subject of play is obviously not the subjectivity of an individual who, among other activities, also plays but is instead the play itself" (TM 104). There is a primacy of the game over the players, a primacy of play over the consciousness of the player. The player does not play the game; rather, the game plays the player: "all playing is a being-played. The attraction of a game, the fascination it exerts, consists precisely in the fact that the game masters the players" (TM 106).

Gadamer uses this concept of play to describe the experience of the work of art. For the player, play itself is not something objective. It is rather something that draws the player out of herself, a force into which the player is lured and in which she is lost. Just so, "the work of art is not an object that stands over against a subject for itself. Instead the work of art has its true being in the fact that it becomes an experience that changes the person who experiences it. The 'subject' of the experience of art, that which remains and endures, is not the subjectivity of the person who experiences it but the work itself" (TM 102). Gadamer thus argues that the being of the work of art is of the same nature as play. Aesthetic experience is a playful experience, and yet a serious one in which human subjectivity loses itself.

In Gadamer's analysis of play and aesthetic experience human subjectivity is not the origin; man does not set the rules or keep control. If in Sartrean play human existence rediscovers the freedom that it is, in Gadamer's concept of play freedom is at risk because "the game itself is a risk for the player. One can play only with serious possibilities. Obviously this means that one may become so engrossed in them that they outplay one, as it were, and prevail over one. The attraction that the game exercises on the player lies in this risk. One enjoys a freedom of decision, which at the same time is endangered and irrevocably limited." (TM 106).

Sartre's conception that play effects a self-recovery, that it reveals possibilities to the player and thereby makes the player conscious of her freedom, is an essential moment of play which we will call "appropriation." But Sartre's contention that human subjectivity is totally in control, initiating and setting the rules of the game, or, alternatively, constituting in an absolute way the meaning of the world, cannot be maintained. Rather, Gadamer correctly points out that the player loses herself in the game, that at a certain point the game takes over, determining the possibilities that are presented to the player. This is an aspect of transcendence involved in play. We want to show that play involves both appropriation and transcendence.

Gadamer does not fail to mention that a transformed subjectivity survives the game, reappears after its disappearance, and takes something away from the process. Being at play, for Gadamer, is like being in a conversation. "To be in a conversation, however, means to be beyond oneself, to think with the other and to come back to oneself as if to another."[18] This transformation, which depends on the movement between appropriation and transcendence, is what makes play educational.

Play educates. This is an accepted principle in educational theory. The importance of play as a means of learning can be traced back through theorists such as Froebel, Pestalozzi, Rousseau, and Comenius to Aristotle and Plato.[19] Educational researchers know that in the process of play children learn about "the nature of materials and begin to form concepts of weight, size, texture, softness, hardness, plasticity, impermeability, transparency and so on." Of equal, if not greater importance, "children begin also to discover the possibilities and limitations of their own powers."[20] Piaget agrees that "the child when it plays is developing its perceptions, its intelligence, its impulses toward experiment, its social instincts, etc."[21] In playing a game I learn about myself as I learn about the world that I live in. I learn about others. I come to understand the different roles that are open to me. The player who participates in sports learns about her limitations, her potentials, her capacities, and therefore about herself, just to the extent that she learns about others, about team effort, accomplishment, and the resistance of situations. How does this educational aspect of play work?

An essential aspect of all educational experience, including play, involves venturing into the unknown, going beyond ourselves and experiencing the unfamiliar. Seriousness, if understood as Sartre understands it, as becoming fascinated with the world, is, as Gadamer rightly indicates, an essential part of play. The unfamiliar that we experience in play is first of all interpreted in terms of the world. In play we become so fascinated with the world that we move beyond ourselves, we transcend the limits of the self. What remains primary here, however, is play itself, not the world or the reality created by the game. If we become lost, we become lost in play; otherwise we would end up as Sartre's serious man who fails to discover his possibilities. The self-transcendence that is essential to play involves a projection toward one's own possibilities. So play also opens the world up to question or strips the real of its reality, as Sartre would have it. Play bestows reality on the unreal; it gives weight to that which is possible or fanciful.[22]

The fact that in play the player comes to recognize her own possibilities directs us to the other essential aspect of play: self-appropriation. The possibility of losing oneself or transcending oneself in play is attractive or alluring only because of the possibility of finding oneself again. I can let myself be taken up by the game, I can immerse myself in the spirit of play, only because I know that at some point I will reemerge transformed. The self lost in play does not disappear altogether. Play is productive for the self rather than destructive. Insofar as play is educational experience, the player risks herself to acquire an openness for new experiences. The result is self-transformation.

Gadamer notes aspects of transcendence and appropriation in the concept of education, *Bildung*. *Bildung* or self-formation (*Sichbilden*) is more than "the mere cultivation of given talents" (TM 11); it involves transformation. Gadamer, citing Hegel, remarks that in educational experience, as in the experience of work, "man gains the sense of himself. . . . he finds in himself his own frame of mind [*Sinn*], and it is quite right to say of work that it forms" (TM 13). This transformation is the result of recognizing "one's own in the alien," which is "the basic movement of spirit, whose being consists only in returning to itself from what is other." In this sense, "every individual is always engaged in the process of *Bildung*" (TM 14). Gadamer understands the essence of *Bildung* to include the dialectical movement of transcendence and appropriation. "Thus what constitutes the essence of *Bildung* is clearly not alienation [= transcendence] as such, but the return to oneself [*Heimkehr*, literally, the return home]—which presupposes alienation, to be sure" (TM 14). It would be more accurate to say that neither transcendence nor appropriation is more essential than the movement which encompasses them both. Precisely this movement or process of *Bildung* is the movement of play.

Sartre views the dialectical movement of transcendence and appropriation in terms of authenticity and inauthenticity. The self that the player loses in play is the everyday, "serious," or inauthentic self. In play we transform the serious attitude and transcend ourselves; we discover the possibility of our authentic existence. Experientially, this transcendence toward possibilities is a positive moment. Considered as part of the dialectical movement of play, however, it is the negative moment out of which emerges a reappropriation. The reemergence of the self, however, is neither a Hegelian synthesis of the old self with the new nor simply a repetition of the old, inauthentic self. The self that is reappropriated is the self that has undergone transformation.

To cast the explanation in terms of authenticity, however, is somewhat misleading because we end up with a conception of the "self" that both Sartre and Gadamer intend to discredit. Indeed, despite their apparent oppositions, these two theories of play can be viewed as complementary because they fundamentally agree in their rejections of traditional theories of the self.[23] Sartre's emphasis on self-recovery in his analysis of play is not inconsistent with his acknowledgement in various other contexts that subjectivity itself is always a self-transcendence, an ekstasis never coinciding with itself. For him, self-appropriation means a recovery of self-transcendence, that is, the realization of the persistent lack of coincidence which constitutes the freedom of subjectivity. When Gadamer contends that subjectivity is displaced in play and Sartre argues that subjectivity is recovered in play, they do not strictly disagree; for both philosophers the phenomenon of play destroys the traditional concept of self as substantial entity and reveals the self as an openness to various possibilities. The "self" involved in play is not a totalized self-identical essence, but a "self-narrative," a self-process which never stops being a process in play.

More importantly, the disfranchisement of the self is not simply a theoretical displacement or the discrediting of a metaphysical theory about the self. For Gadamer, the player who enters into the play of art is, in a very practical way, and not without ethical significance, lured out of herself into a possibility of truth. This experience of truth involves bringing human existence into its proper relationship with being. For Sartre, the traditional metaphysical theories of subjectivity are not merely mistaken theoretical constructs, but in very real terms are a source of the false consciousness of bad faith. They constitute the self-images of "serious" individuals. To think of oneself as a substantial thing is precisely what it means to be in bad faith. In play one frees oneself of that attitude and recognizes oneself as a free process of possibilities. This is why Sartre sees play as having an ethical import and why he also views play as a technique that is useful in existential psychoanalysis.

The self is not a substance that undergoes merely accidental changes in the experience of play; it is being undone and redone, or, more precisely, the self is nothing more than this undoing and redoing process. Transformation is neither an internal nor an external occurrence happening to the self; rather, the self is this process of change. In Ricoeur's terms, the self is a process of *déprise* (relinquishing) and *reprise* (recapture). The self is nothing other than this playful process of transcendence and appropriation taking place through the possibilities opened up for it in art, in action, in all educational experience.

The claim that play is this movement of transcendence and appropriation which expresses something essential to human subjectivity goes significantly beyond the usual connotation of play. But even Piaget, who adopts a concept of play closer to its usual connotation, suggests that "play is in reality one aspect of any activity. . . . Play is not a behavior *per se*, or one particular type of activity among others. It is determined by a certain orientation of the behavior."[24] Piaget, however, denies the aspect of transcendence. For him play is a type of assimilation of the world to the ego, a pure appropriation without accommodation. That both assimilation and accommodation, both appropriation and transcendence, are essential to human experience is verified in a theory familiar to both Sartre and Gadamer: Husserl's phenomenology of time-consciousness.

According to Husserl, consciousness is, fundamentally, a flow which unites itself in a retentional-protentional structure.[25] Sartre uses Husserl's concept of retention to justify a nonegological conception of consciousness (see BN 149). His emphasis on retentioning here mirrors his emphasis on appropriation in his analysis of play. The unity of subjectivity is not a substantial unity but a unity of process constantly recovering itself through its retentional structure. In contrast, for Gadamer, the temporal structure of play entails that the player gives herself over to the play. The player is taken up by a presence outside of herself and is thus involved in a self-forgetfulness which is a projection beyond herself (see TM 125–126). What Husserl shows in his analysis of time-consciousness is that *both transcendence*, or what in the context of his time analysis he would call "protentioning," a projection toward the not yet realized, *and appropriation*, the retentioning of what has already been realized, are integral aspects of the structure of human experience. Such is the dynamic structure expressed in the movement of transcendence and appropriation which characterizes the play experience.

This analysis of play suggests that we are constantly learning about ourselves in light of our experiences. If play is the dialectical interchange of transcendence and appropriation, then not only is play one kind of educational experience but it might make sense to say that all educational experience involves play in this fundamental sense.

But have we shown that play has the structure of interpretation? Can we say, without begging the question, that transcendence involves an interpretation of the world and that appropriation involves a reinterpretation of self, a new self-understanding? If so, we could simply claim that if play is the dialectical interchange of transcendence and appropriation, then play is an interchange of interpretations. What we will show, however, is not simply that transcendence and appropriation involve a process of interpretation, but that the transcendence-appropriation structure is interpretational in its nature. Play is interpretational because it shares the same structure as interpretation. In the tradition of hermeneutics, this structure is called the "hermeneutical circle." Accordingly, we can see more clearly what it means to say that transcendence is a projection of possibilities, and that appropriation is a retrieval of these possibilities as one's own possibilities by examining the notion of the hermeneutical circle. We will then understand in a more precise way that the dialectical interchange of transcendence and appropriation not only represents the interpretational structure of play, but also, as Gadamer suggests, of conversation, thought, and education in its general sense of *Bildung*.

CHAPTER 3

Interpretational and Educational Circles

Romantic hermeneutics, from Schleiermacher to Dilthey, defines hermeneutics as an art, that is, as a way or method of interpreting. In contrast, philosophical hermeneutics, as defined by Gadamer, consists of a reflection on the nature of interpretation and on the conditions of possibility which allow for the art of interpretation. For Gadamer, hermeneutics does not supply a specific method to be used in interpretation, but clarifies the conditions under which interpretation and the use of method can occur. The work of philosophical hermeneutics "is not to develop a procedure of understanding, but to clarify the conditions in which understanding takes place" (TM 295).

The contrast between the art of interpretation and the theory of interpretation is the basis for an extremely important distinction between normative and philosophical hermeneutics. Philosophical hermeneutics offers a theoretical description of the conditions which necessarily define how interpretation happens. Normative hermeneutics defines the aims and procedures of interpretation as it ought to be practiced. Philosophical hermeneutics produces descriptive hermeneutical *principles*, whereas a normative approach produces prescriptive *canons*.[1] Hermeneutical principles describe the various constraints and possibilities that belong to the nature of interpretation. They are descriptive statements within the discourse of philosophical hermeneutics intended to express how interpretation actually does work. Several principles which express the constraints and the possibilities of interpretation will be explored in this and the following chapters. Hermeneutical canons, on the other hand, are normative regulations (procedural rules, prescriptives) which specify how interpretation ought to be conducted.

Some examples of hermeneutical canons are offered by E. D. Hirsch in his work *The Aims of Interpretation*.[2] In textual hermeneutics a canon that had been explicated by Schleiermacher can be stated in this way: (a) "Everything in a given text which requires fuller interpretation must be explained and determined exclusively from the linguistic domain common to the author and his original public."[3] Hirsch contrasts this prescriptive to what he formulates as the implicit canon which guided medieval allegorical readings of pre-Christian classical texts: (b) "Everything in a given text which requires fuller interpretation need *not* be explained and determined exclusively from the linguistic domain common to the author and his public." These two canons reflect different value judgments: preferences for either "original meaning" (related to the author and his original audience) or "anachronistic meaning" (related, perhaps, to universal truth or to the interpreter's current situation).

Hirsch makes an important claim about the relationship between hermeneutical principles and normative canons. According to Hirsch, *canons* are a matter of value preference and are based on an "ethical" choice. For example, Schleiermacher's rejection of anachronistic allegory reflects a preference for what he thinks is a good or legitimate reading of a text. Hermeneutical *principles*, however, are based on logical analysis, empirical fact, or what Hirsch calls "metaphysics," and they belong to theories about the nature of interpretation. Hirsch claims that, not only is there a theoretical distinction between principles and canons, but there ought to be a practical divorce between them. He rejects any attempt to derive a normative canon from hermeneutical principles. He contends that any such attempt will end up importing the normative judgment into the descriptive fact. Furthermore, with specific reference to principles derived from metaphysics, he states: "I would argue that there is far less danger in ignoring metaphysics than in introducing it prematurely into the practical questions of interpretation."[4] To the extent that Hirsch would allow canons into his interpretive methodology, he prefers the ethical judgment ("the common sense of a practitioner who disdains theory to get on with his work") to be the only guide to their formulation.[5]

Is Hirsch's characterization of the relation between principle and canon correct? Is it not clear, rather, that principles have a priority over and govern normative canons? If a particular hermeneutical principle, for example, that all interpretation is anachronistic, does actually describe interpretation, then it would certainly undermine the legitimacy of Schleiermacher's canon, which expresses a preference for nonanachronistic reading. In other words, if, in principle, a twentieth-century reader cannot help but read twentieth-century concerns into a thirteenth-century text, then it does not make sense to say that the reader ought to read without those twentieth-century prejudices. Such a canon would be impossible to follow. If, according to its nature, interpretation actually works in a certain way, can I decide on normative grounds that it ought to work in a different way? The *is* constrains the *ought*, even if we think that it ought not to. The same constraining relationship between descriptive principle and canon would also hold for the relation of principle to any procedural rule. One cannot legitimately follow a procedural rule that would not be allowed by the very nature of interpretation.

On the other hand, the formulation of hermeneutical principles is always biased by normative choices concerning interpretation. We will discover this for ourselves when we attempt to formulate the principles of conservative hermeneutics (Chapter 7). In any principle there will always be embedded some normative aspect which identifies it as conservative, critical, radical, and so forth. Normative preferences and specific aims associated with interpretation will influence the definition of hermeneutical principles.

Those who maintain that seeking normative canons or procedural rules is a separate aspect of hermeneutics that can be carried on independently of consideration about hermeneutical principles ignore the constraining relationships between principle and canon or rule.[6] I am not proposing here the "Coleridgean argument" which Hirsch disputes: that canons are *derived from* principles. Indeed, even if direct derivation were possible, a canon so derived would not guarantee validity of interpretation.[7] Hirsch is not wrong to contend that canons are derived primarily from "ethical choices." Canons may depend on the chosen aim of a particular interpretation as well as on the peculiar ideological preferences of the interpreter. But whatever canon is chosen, for whatever intentional or ideological reason, it will be practical or impractical, realistic or idealistic, depending on its relation to principles that define the possibilities of interpretation. Hirsch is right to maintain that canons and principles should be kept conceptually distinct. But that there is a connection between them, namely, that specific principles will allow or disallow certain canons or procedural rules, and not vice versa, cannot be denied.

If educational experience is hermeneutical, then we should be able to employ hermeneutical principles to explicate the way in which learning involves interpretation. This procedure, however, is double-sided. The hermeneutical principles themselves, which are not absolute or unchanging but have their own history, are opened up to question in a unique way when they are used to interrogate educational experience. This double-sided process, in which we examine educational experience and hermeneutical principles simultaneously, offers us an opportunity to explicate and critically examine hermeneutical principles unconstrained by the textual model which dominates most contemporary discussions of hermeneutics.

THE PRINCIPLE OF THE HERMENEUTICAL CIRCLE

The hermeneutical circle, a central principle found in almost all works on hermeneutics, can be stated in its most general terms as follows: all understanding has a circular structure, but one which is not logically vicious. In this section I intend to examine, briefly, three different formulations of the hermeneutical circle: its traditional formulation as found in Schleiermacher and Romantic hermeneutics; its phenomenological conception as developed in Husserl, Heidegger, and Gadamer; and the concept of the "corrigible schema" as presented by Hirsch. In the next section, I will look to educational experience as a way to sort out these formulations.

Three Models of the Hermeneutical Circle

The traditional model of the hermeneutical circle is found in Schleiermacher. But even prior to Schleiermacher it was customary to discuss this aspect of interpretation in terms of parts and wholes. Gadamer traces the concept back to classical rhetoric but identifies the more proximate source for Romantic hermeneutics to be Protestant biblical hermeneutics (TM 174). To understand a particular passage in the Bible one is required to put it into the context of the whole bible. As Gadamer points out, this involves a dogmatic postulate, namely, that the Bible is a whole rather than simply a collection of separate texts. If the differences between the individual authors and their historical contexts were to be properly recognized, as Semler and Ernesti proposed in the eighteenth century, then the "whole" to which the biblical passage needed to be referred comprised not the dogmatic unity of the Bible itself but "the totality of the historical reality to which each individual historical document belonged" (TM 177). There is this historical dimension in the relation of part to whole proposed by Schleiermacher.

The essential circularity of understanding is expressed by Schleiermacher in the following way: the meaning of the part is only understood within the context of the whole; but the whole is never given unless through an understanding of the parts. Understanding therefore requires a circular movement from parts to whole and from whole to parts.

> When we consider the task of interpretation with this principle in mind, we have to say that our increasing understanding of each sentence and of each section [of a text], an understanding which we achieve by starting at the beginning and moving forward slowly, is always provisional. It becomes more complete as we are able to see each larger section as a coherent unity. But as soon as we turn to a new part we encounter new uncertainties and begin again, as it were, in the dim morning light. It is like starting all over, except that as we push ahead the new material illumines everything we have already treated, until suddenly at the end every part is clear and the whole work is visible in sharp and definite contours.[8]

The hermeneutical circle, therefore, is not a vicious circle. The more movement in this circle, the larger the circle grows, embracing the expanding contexts that throw more and more light upon the parts.

Dilthey, following Schleiermacher, describes the circle in similar terms.

> [Interpretation] starts from the apprehension of indefinite-definite parts and proceeds to the attempt to grasp the meaning of the whole, alternating with the attempt to take this meaning as a basis for defining the parts more clearly. Failure makes itself

known when individual parts cannot be understood in this way, this then creates the need to redefine the meaning so that it will take account of these parts. This attempt goes on until the entire meaning has been grasped.[9]

In both Schleiermacher and Dilthey, the hermeneutical circle is described in terms of the text and its objective historical context. The only subjective element admitted into this circle is the individuality of the author's subjective intentions or subjective uses of language. But for Romantic hermeneutics, the task of interpretation is to resolve these subjective elements through a comparative analysis of the objective historical context and common linguistic usages.

A different conception of the hermeneutical circle has been developed in hermeneutical theory which follows the phenomenological tradition. Husserl, concerned with a phenomenological description of experience, discusses something akin to the hermeneutical circle in terms of the "horizon structure" of experience. He writes: "It is not open to doubt that there is no experience, in the simple and primary sense of an experience of things, which grasping a thing for the first time and bringing cognition to bear on it, does not already 'know' more about the thing than is in this cognition alone."[10] This preknowledge (*Vorwissen*) is based on the fact that "every experience has its own horizon." This horizon structure means that everything comes to be known within a context and never in isolation. The context makes sense out of the "unknown" thing. Even the unfamiliar thing has some degree of familiarity. "Unfamiliarity," Husserl notes, "is at the same time always a mode of familiarity."[11] He calls this horizon structure a feature of "prepredicative experience." We are always already actively understanding the world even before we attempt to grasp anything in a thematic or cognitive fashion. The knowledge which we already have of the whole, constituted in our prepredicative experience, impacts on the constitution of the meaning of any particular thing, while the meaning of any particular thing adds to or reshapes our knowledge of the whole and will go on to condition our subsequent understanding.[12]

The importance of the concepts of horizon structure and *Vorwissen* to hermeneutical theory, if not fully grasped by Husserl, is clearly recognized by Heidegger and developed in his concept of *Verstehen*. For Heidegger, the hermeneutical significance of these concepts is to shift the centerpoint of the hermeneutical circle from the objective concerns about whole and parts to the transcendental conditions of interpretation.

In Heidegger's view, before we come to explicitly understand something we already have a preconception of it. We drive at an insightful and explicit understanding of something only on the basis of "something we have in advance," which Heidegger calls a "fore-having" (*Vorhabe*) (BT 191/150). This fore-having conditions and is conditioned by any "fore-sight" or "fore-conception" that we may have in perceptual or cognitive experience. Thus, Heidegger concludes, "an interpretation is never a presupposition-less apprehending of something presented to us" (BT 191–192/150). Rather, what is presented is already interpreted under the guidance of "the obvious undiscussed assumption of the person who does the interpreting" (BT 192/150). Human understanding rides on a projection of meaning even before it reaches an adequate interpretation. The projected meaning is either borne out or modified in further projections. This process is not something the interpreter chooses to do or consciously devises as a method of interpretation; it is part of the very structure of human understanding. The process of interpretation is the process of revising my fore-conception as I gather more information. I continue to project these meanings until the unity or adequacy of meaning becomes clear.

As Gadamer points out, there is an explicit contrast between Schleiermacher's conception of the hermeneutical circle and Heidegger's explication of the fore-structure of understanding. Schleiermacher believed that by means of the back and forth, circulating movement between parts and whole, the process of interpretation would eventually come to conclusion in a complete understanding. Gadamer questions the possibility of this completeness. Following Heidegger, but casting his discussion in terms of Schleiermacher's textual hermeneutics, he seeks to show that the circle never disappears in understanding; understanding never comes to closure or completeness. In opposition to Schleiermacher's theory that the circular movement of understanding runs backward and for-ward along the text, and ceases when the text is perfectly under-stood . . . Heidegger describes the circle in such a way that the understanding of the text remains permanently determined by the anticipatory movement of fore-understanding. The circle of whole and part is not dissolved in perfect understanding but, on the contrary, is most fully realized. (TM 293)

This lack of closure, which turns the circle into an unfinished spiral movement, is based upon the finitude of human existence. "The circular movement is necessary because [as Schleiermacher noted] 'nothing that needs interpretation can be understood at once'" (TM 191–192). Interpretation is an understanding that is neither absolute nor all at once. An interpretation that would understand "at once" would not be an interpretation at all, but a divine, absolute insight. Absolute knowledge or absolute truth, even if possible for a timeless God, is not possible for a human being. For Gadamer, human understanding involves a constant temporal pro-cess of revision; it is always finite, temporal, circular; an in-complete interpretation because of the existential temporal struc-ture of human existence.

E. D. Hirsch offers a critical appraisal of Heidegger's concept of fore-structure and suggests a third alternative formulation of the hermeneutical circle. He proposes that we view this phenomenon on the model of "corrigible schemata," a concept he borrows from Piaget, R. C. Anderson, and others.[13] Since this concept finds its way into a good deal of educational theory, it will be useful to provide a general sense of its use and development in contempo-rary cognitive psychology.

The concept of the schema follows more from rationalist epis-temology and *Gestalt* psychology than from empiricist and be-haviorist approaches, which explain human behavior in terms of atomistic sensory imputs and stimulus-response relations. On the epistemological side, the concept can be traced back to Kant's notion of schematism; on the psychological side, to Sir Fredric Bartlett, who was influenced by Sir Henry Head's work on the concept of body schema in neurology.[14] The concept of schema signifies that knowledge which we already have does not consist of disconnected pieces of information but is organized into patterns which we access and use in the acquisition of new knowledge.

Piaget, among others, has shown that such patterns or schemata can organize or "assimilate" new information, and that schemata themselves can change or "accommodate" themselves to new information. Anderson explains the assimilative use of schemata in terms of "constructing" an interpretation. Interpretations are constructed out of incomplete perceptual information. In an example that is reminiscent of Husserl's explanation of *Abschattungen* or perceptual profiles, Anderson notes that "people have no trouble visualizing that an object is a cube even though several of its faces are not in view. The schema which accounts for what is directly perceivable entails expectations about unseen features."[15] The schema functions in the same way as Husserl's notion of horizon, supplementing the missing profiles with a pattern of meaning, that is, constructing a perceptual interpretation. Anderson puts this in explicitly hermeneutical terms: "Text is gobbledygook unless the reader possesses an interpretive framework to breath meaning into it."[16]

Schemata, although playing a conservative role in the assimilation of new information, are also open to change. Hirsch calls this their corrigible aspect. In the context of reading, he suggests, for example, that "two-way traffic takes place between our schemata and the words we read. We apply past schemata to make sense of the incoming words, but these words and other contextual clues affect our initial choices of schemata and our continuing adjustment of them."[17] Although Hirsch indicates that the interpreter actively selects and adjusts appropriate schemata, he also acknowledges that "such adjustments are largely unconscious" (CL 52). Hirsch's main contention is that these schemata are "context sensitive" and adjustable.

This model works well to describe how the fore-structure of understanding operates. It does not, however, contradict anything Heidegger or Gadamer hold with respect to the hermeneutical circle, despite Hirsch's suggestion: "Unlike one's unalterable and inescapable preunderstanding in Heidegger's account of the hermeneutic circle, a schema can be radically altered and corrected."[18] Heidegger would not have said, as Hirsch construes, that the fore-structure is "unalterable." The fore-structure is continually being modified by experience; it can be radically altered and corrected as it proceeds to guide understanding. A fore-structure, like a schema, in Hirsch's sense, can accommodate itself to changing circumstances and experiences, or can be structured by the meaning of previous experience, and, in turn, can assimilate various meanings, can project its meaning over the circumstance to be interpreted. In the process of interpretation, the fore-structure, or schema, is "worked out," modified vis à vis "the things themselves" (BT 195/153). This constant modification is, according to both Heidegger and Gadamer, the "first, last, and constant task" of interpretation.[19] "Working out this fore-projection, which is *constantly revised* in terms of what emerges as [the interpreter] penetrates into the meaning, is understanding what is there" (TM 267; emphasis added). Every revision of the schema involves a recasting of meaning. "This constant process of new projection constitutes the movement of understanding and interpretation" (TM 267).

We should note that Günther Buck, influenced by both Husserl and Gadamer, contrasts the constant modification of the hermeneutical fore-structure to Kant's notion of the unchanging apriori. The fore-structure of experience

> is itself involved in the process of the formation of experience (*Erfahrungsbildung*) which it makes possible. It is not simply a precondition of particular experiences, which is itself independent of experience, as expressed in Kant's concept of the apriori. . . . The anticipations which guide experience do not remain uninfluenced by the occurrence which they make possible. Husserl speaks of "fulfillment" and "disappointment" of expectations. The expression "fulfillment" hits the mark precisely.[20]

If fulfilled, the preconception is reinforced and continues to condition our understanding; if disappointed, the preconception is forced to undergo revision, which in turn continues to condition our understanding.

Concerning this point of alterability, there is no fundamental difference between the concept of fore-structure and the concept of corrigible schemata. A *Vorhabe* is precisely a corrigible schema which "sets up a range of predictions or expectations, which if fulfilled confirms the schema, but if not fulfilled causes us to revise it."[21] But even in the case of fulfillment, we are never without a schema. If schemata are "escapable," as Hirsch suggests, this does not mean we can, in the fulfillment of a schema, retire it. If we interpret something, we always interpret on the basis of some schema. We may, of course, move from one schema to another, widen or complicate a schema, but we never can escape working within some schema.[22] Heidegger puts no stricter constraints on the concept of fore-structure. "What is decisive is not to get out of the circle but to come into it in the right way. This circle of understanding . . . is the expression of the existential *fore-structure* of human existence [Dasein] itself" (BT 195/153).

Hirsch, in a different context, cites what I think is an extremely clear and striking example of how the fore-structure of understanding operates. The example is provided by an experiment in the field of psycholinguistics conducted by Bransford and Johnson.[23] In the experiment three groups of readers were presented with the following passage.

> The procedure is actually quite simple. First you arrange the items in different groups. Of course one pile may be sufficient depending on how much there is to do. If you have to go somewhere else due to lack of facilities that is the next step; otherwise you are pretty well set.

The readers were then tested in the recognition of sentences from this seemingly obscure text. One group had been supplied with the title "Washing Clothes" prior to their reading; another group was given no title; and the third group was given the title after the reading. Only the first group of readers, who had the title prior to their reading, were later able to recognize sentences from the passage. In effect, the title served to call up a specific fore-structure or schema which helped to structure the interpretation of the passage. The lack of a specific fore-structure made interpretation and recall more difficult.

Is Understanding Ever Complete?

The question of whether an understanding can be complete, or the hermeneutical circle collapsed, has been a disputed question in the history of hermeneutics. Chladenius clearly asserted the possibility of a complete understanding. The completeness of understanding, in the case of comprehending a text, for example, depends, according to Chladenius, on properly grasping the intention of the author and learning "the concepts and lessons which can and should be extrapolated."[24] Schleiermacher was more ambiguous. Although he indicated the possibility of exhausting the meaning of a text, he also indicated that "the goal of technical interpretation can only be approximated. . . . Not only do we never understand an individual view (*Anschauung*) exhaustively, but what we do understand is always subject to correction."[25]

Philip August Boeckh pointed to a similar ambiguity in terms of the hermeneutical circle. On the one hand, the circle can be "broken" on the basis of the development of grammatical and lexical studies of language. "The further these descriptions are developed, the *more nearly complete* becomes the interpretation." But "nearly" complete does not mean entirely complete. "The circle which embraces the interpretive task cannot be resolved in all cases, and can never be resolved completely. From this fact comes the limits which are placed upon interpretation." On the other hand, Boeckh claimed that "in certain instances complete understanding is reached in response to a feeling."[26] Such a feeling, which Boeckh called "vivifying contemplation," would be the aim of what Schleiermacher had called the "divinatory method."

One might say, then, that for Romantic hermeneutics (Schleiermacher, Boeckh), when the proper procedures of grammatical interpretation are complemented by the right "divinatory" intuitions on the technical (psychological) side, complete understanding may be attained. Accordingly, the circular structure of understanding collapses when the object of interpretation is perfectly understood. But is the Romantic conception of completeness, which remains somewhat ambiguous, the same as the Enlightenment conception found in Chladenius? Dilthey shed some light on this question.

The issue of completion troubled Dilthey as well; he also remained ambiguous on this point. On the one hand, he held that the complete reproduction of an author's thoughts cannot be accomplished. On the other hand, he maintained that through a process of "comparison" or a methodical practice of empathy one might accomplish such closure: "The highest form in which the totality of psychic life operates [whether with a person or a work] in understanding," is reproduction based on empathy.[27] The aims of understanding remain, for Dilthey, the objectivity of scientific knowledge and universal validity. For Dilthey, however, the type of objectivity which belongs to the understanding is different from the objectivity of the natural sciences. The contrast between these two types of objectivity provides a clue to the ambiguity expressed in Romantic hermeneutics concerning the completion of understanding. In the Enlightenment hermeneutics of Chladenius, completeness is acquired by an almost mechanical explication of concepts, the elimination of contradictions, and a calculus of viewpoints. Such a concept of completion resembles a natural scientific concept of objectivity. For Romantic hermeneutics, on the other hand, completeness can be attained through divinatory method, feeling, or empathy, by which the interpreter comes directly to discover the author's intention. Gadamer suggests that, in contrast to Chladenius's Enlightenment conception of objective completeness, for the Romantics the completion of interpretation is more like the completion of a work of art. For Romantic theorists, "hermeneutics is an *art* and not a mechanical process. Thus it brings its work, understanding, to completion like a work of art" (TM 191). The completion Schleiermacher had in mind is expressed in his formula of understanding the author better than the author understood himself—a completion more artistic than logical or mathematical.[28] The greater degree of knowledge implied by this assertion constitutes a "reproductive completion" which is neither an identity nor an *adequatio* between understanding and object, but is *more* than adequate to the original.

Betti rejects the notion of completeness in the sense of an absolute and final understanding, and admits that the hermeneutical task can never be complete. "The task of interpretation, which depends at all times on the actuality of understanding, can, as a matter of fact, never be regarded as finished and completed because no interpretation, however convincing it may seem at first, can force itself upon mankind as the definitive one" (Betti 68). This, however, does not rule out the kind of satisfaction attached to a high degree of probability as found in scientific induction. The task of interpretation is to seek such satisfaction by the use of those canons which make it possible "for us to approach the meaning [of the object], since it is part of the human spirit and is, to speak with Husserl, born of the same transcendental subjectivity" (Betti 69). Betti, in terms of the objective circular structure of whole and parts, explains that "every speech and every written work can equally be regarded as a link in a chain which can only be *fully* understood by reference to its place within a larger meaning-context" (Betti 60; emphasis added).

Hirsch follows Betti in rejecting the conception of a complete understanding and in proposing a model of the hermeneutical circle based on induction.[29] He proposes that the hermeneutical hypothesis (fore-conception, schema) is tested for validity against the customs and conventions operative *in the text*. In the inductive process of testing the hypothesis, "a ruthlessly critical process of validation," one never reaches absolute conclusions (complete interpretations), but one does reach a certain degree of probablility, and this would count as a measure of objectivity.[30]

The questions of the possible completion of understanding or, on the inductive model, of the degree of probability that would signify the adequacy of interpretation are closely linked to the concepts of objectivity and reproduction as they are found in conservative hermeneutical theory. The question of reproduction could be thought out in terms of the contrast between Schleiermacher's contention that interpretation seeks to understand the author better than the author understood himself, and Gadamer's contention that understanding always involves understanding differently, although not necessarily in a superior way (see TM 297). We will return to the questions of objectivity and reproduction in later chapters. For now we need to turn back to the concept of educational experience to see how the hermeneutical circle actually operates and whether understanding can ever be complete.

THE ENCYCLO-PAIDEIA

The notion of the hermeneutical circle does not originate with Schleiermacher or his immediate predecessors. Indeed, it is one of the oldest and most influential philosophical concepts. Aristotle refers to it in its educational context: "All teaching and all intellectual learning come about from previously existing knowledge."[31] Aristotle, however, is truly pointing us back toward Plato. For Plato's theory of recollection, if viewed properly, can be considered a statement of the hermeneutical circle.[32] We can learn about the unknown only by recognizing it "as" something already known. This hermeneutical "as" emerges out of our ability to place the unknown within an already known context which bestows sense.

Consider the ancient sophistical paradox presented by Meno in Plato's dialogue about education (*Meno* 80d). The paradox states that it is impossible to learn anything new: if we already know it then we cannot learn it; and if we do not know it, then we will not be able to recognize it or come to know whether we genuinely understand it. Suppose, for example, that I show you something that you have never encountered before. Let's call it "X." You have no idea what it is. How would you go about trying to understand it? Assume that you are, at first, limited to visual inspection. Contrary to the traditional epistemological model of the straightforward cognition (which in this case must fail), understanding X would require some kind of cognitive maneuvering on your part. Perhaps your first operation would be to assign X to some already established and familiar ontological category: X is a physical entity, animate or inanimate, perhaps a living organism or a piece of machinery. In assigning X a general place within this familiar world, you *eo ipso* project upon X some meaning. In effect, learning about X, in either the short run or the long run, always involves a preconception of what any X could be, given the habitual or typical ways that, as humans, we perceive the world. Even before we are confronted by X, we have some preconception of the possibilities of what any X could be. For any X, X is either physical object, text, work of art, and so forth, and we know how such things "behave" given our past experience and the predictability of our world. X has a preconceived, although as yet indeterminate, place within our body of knowledge. A more determinate understanding of X is possible as we explore further. But all further explorations of X will be conditioned, positively (or negatively) by the success (or failure) of our earlier preconception. Further observations may confirm or destroy the initial preconception; the foreconception that began our learning process is either reinforced and developed into our present interpretation, or is revised, or is replaced by a different fore-conception. All further confirmation or reinterpretation is based on the initial or revised projected meaning.

Recollection, which Plato equates with learning, is not our connection with a bygone past or with an unchanging eternity; it is our projection of meaning based on our past experience. It is the creation of a context by re-collecting into a unity the experiences relevant to unlocking the meaning of the unfamiliar (see *Phaedrus* 249b–c). Plato proposes that "the whole of nature is akin" (*Meno* 81d); likewise Husserl suggests that unfamiliarity is always a mode of familiarity. In interpretation and in learning we simply bring forward the parts that we are familiar with so as to illuminate the part that requires understanding.

Of course Plato is responding to an exaggerated paradox. He is addressing an extreme case, the case where we have no conception whatsoever of what X is. According to Plato, to learn about X in these circumstances would require some preconception that would work to suggest a context into which X might fit. In less extreme cases we may be familiar with the subject matter that we are trying to learn. If, for example, I am learning a new piece of music, I interpret it on the basis of my familiarity with music in general, or on the basis of some other pieces by the same composer with which I am familiar. Or if I sit down to learn a new word-processing program I approach it based on what I know about other word-processing programs. In fact, the usual problem in learning is not that one is absolutely ignorant of the subject matter, but that one thinks one already knows. In Plato's dialogue, for example, Meno's familiarity with the various opinions or definitions of virtue gets in the way of his learning.

Whether we confront something totally unfamiliar or something that we think we already know, preconceptions, fore-structures, and schemas already condition the learning process. The hermeneutical circle and the fore-structure of our understanding are made most apparent in the cases where they tend to obstruct the learning process. In such a case the task might be to learn by unlearning. The task of the teacher might be to undo those preconceived ideas which prevent learning. For example, if I think that I know how to solve a particular mathematical problem, I may in fact be blinded to its real solution, whereas if my fore-conception is of a general nature I may work out the approach more easily. If, instead of following the procedure of finding a solution to an equation system by a process of successive elimination of variables through substitution, which involves a general process of breaking down the problem to its separable parts, I approach it already convinced that it is, at base, a quadratic equation, and therefore automatically apply the quadratic formula, I may end up in a confused state, or I may end up with a quick resolution. The outcome (problematic or resolved) will depend not only on the nature of the problem but also on the preconception with which I begin.

There are many theories about the nature of learning, and they may all express something true about the different situations of learning. Is it legitimate, however, to claim that the hermeneutical circle is involved in every case of learning? We can agree with Dewey, for instance, that in some cases learning involves problem solving. But does not problem solving involve a projection of meaning that, as it succeeds or fails, informs and reforms the fore-structure of one's approach? Dewey describes the various elements of problem solving in the following way:

> The first stage of contact with any new material, at whatever age of maturity, must inevitably be of the trial and error sort. An individual must actually try, in play or work, to do something with material . . . and then note the interaction of his energy and that of the material employed. This is what happens when a child at first begins to build with blocks, and it is equally what happens when a scientific man in his laboratory begins to experiment with unfamiliar objects.[33]

The model of learning as experimentation requires that a certain amount of the student's "energy" be invested with the promise of a return in the form of corrective "feedback." This give-and-take process of trial and error involves a circular movement between student and problematic situation. The "energy" of the student may take the form of an action or an idea. The significant thing, according to Dewey, is that the unfamiliar, hence problematic, situation is "sufficiently connected with existing habits to call out an effective response." Learning depends on what the student already has: the student's *Vorhabe*, which takes the form of a "resource" or "working capital." One's fore-conceptions are, in Dewey's terms, "luminous familiar spots from which helpful suggestions may spring." Learning involves a projection of the known onto the unknown; "an invasion of the unknown, a leap from the known."[34] Implicit in Dewey's account is the concept of a fore-structure which conditions one's initial approach and is refined or revised in the process of learning.

Learning as problem solving involves a hermeneutical circle in its very structure. For Dewey the experimental model of learning involves, in some cases, forming explicit hypotheses to be tested out. The hypothesis must be based upon prior experience, the structure of which may undergo revision as it is tested out. Of course, a methodological hypothesis will be more explicit and more defined than the fore-conception upon which it is based. This difference in determinacy is the point of distinction between the hypothesis and the horizon structure that guides its formulation.[35] Nevertheless, the hypothesis will always be an interpretation and will always depend on fore-conceptions. Thus, if we consider the procedure of hypothesis formation as one model of learning, then learning is clearly defined by the hermeneutical circle.

The concept of the hermeneutical circle harmonizes well with conclusions drawn in cognitive psychology and learning theory. Frank Smith, for example, developing in great detail the notion of schema, or what he calls "cognitive structure," concludes that "the only effective and meaningful way in which anyone can learn is by attempting to relate new experiences to what he knows (or believes) already. In other words, comprehension and learning are inseparable."[36] The more recent analyses of problem-solving heuristics and critical thinking in terms of cognitive schemata also bear this out. Problem solving depends not just on the use of skills, but on a certain amount of background information organized in corrigible schemata for easy and efficient access.[37]

Joseph Schwab implicitly suggests the circularity of learning in his concepts of "re-search" and "rectification." He suggests that "the discovery of error and incompleteness and their progressive rectification can also be shown as outcomes of the continuing enquiry [of learning]: the consequences of expanded study of the subject, leading to recognition of over-simplicity of first formulations, leading, in turn, to the search for new conceptions to embrace new data and thus render the whole interpretation more nearly co-extensive with the complexity of the subject."[38] Interpretation in the learning process approaches a more adequate understanding of the subject matter only by returning on the circle of its original projections of meaning, and correcting, re-viewing, revising them.

The notion of constant revision raises the issue of whether the

learning process is ever complete, or, in terms of the debate between Romantic and phenomenological hermeneutics, whether
one breaks out of the circle and attains complete, objective understanding, or remains, of necessity, within the circle, constantly
revising. The circularity of learning speaks against straightforward
appropriation of knowledge; does it also speak against the possibility of coming to conclusions, or the idea that learning leads to
something complete and definite? Let us consider this question in
terms of the classroom model, which we characterized as an interchange of interpretations.

According to one theory, the task of the teacher is to bring the
student to an identical understanding of a subject matter, that is, to
make the student's understanding identical to the teacher's. Implicit here is the notion that the teacher himself has a completely
closed or objective understanding of a particular piece of information. Thus Chladenius, convinced of the possibility of such objective understanding, distinguishes between understanding and interpretation. The latter is defined as a pedagogical explication of
the subject matter: "interpretation is, then, nothing other than
teaching someone the concepts which are necessary to learn to
understand or to fully understand a speech or a written work."[39]
Interpretation, according to Chladenius, is a tool used by the
teacher to bring the student to "full understanding." Thus, "an
interpreter should guide a person (let us say his student) who does
not understand a text to a true [= complete] understanding of
it."[40] Once "the student has the same knowledge as the interpreter," pedagogical interpretation is no longer necessary. For
Chladenius, if learning is to take place, the pedagogical presentation must disappear as the student's comprehension comes to coincide with the teacher's understanding. Chladenius's views were not
uncommon. Consider William Bryant's summary of *Hegel's Educational Ideals* (1896): "The direct aim which actuates [the stu-
dent] in this is to develop in his own mind what he discovers as
taking place in the mind of the teacher."[41] The concepts of imitation and reproduction are reechoed in the approach of conservative
hermeneutics and educational theory (see Chapter 7)—the intention of the author being equivalent to the intention of the teacher.

With Chladenius we agree that teaching does involve an act of
interpretation: the pedagogical presentation. Primarily it is an act

of interpretation-for-others. At the same time, however, the teacher interprets the subject matter for himself; that is, he has his own understanding of the subject matter. One assumption made by Chladenius is that a complete understanding already resides with the teacher. Even if we allowed, for the sake of argument, that both the student's comprehension and the pedagogical presentation coincided with the teacher's understanding, we would still have to show that the teacher's understanding of the subject matter was closed, complete, and objective. Such completeness would entail that the hermeneutical circular structure of the teacher's understanding would be collapsed or dissipated. Even if we allowed this idealized situation, then, by definition, to the extent that one interpretation coincided with another, there would be no learning going on; knowledge would already be had. To the extent that the circular structure of the teacher's understanding collapses, learning is closed off for him and he falls into a dogmatic slumber. Moreover, to the extent that he succeeds in getting the student's understanding to coincide with his dogma, he closes off the learning process in the student. In the process of indoctrination, the student's own fore-conceptions are repressed and are not allowed to operate. If learning is an interchange of interpretations, learning ceases when either the interchange collapses into an identity or, with respect to individual interpretations, the hermeneutical circle is broken. Learning involves an essential incompleteness of knowledge, a noncoincidence between teacher and student, a hermeneutical circularity that remains open.

Earlier we characterized play (and the very nature of experience itself) as a dialectical interplay of transcendence and appropriation. This is precisely the dialectical movement that we find here in the classroom situation. Learning requires (a) a dialogue or circulating relationship between an individual learner's fore-structure and the subject matter; and (b) a dialogue between the teacher's understanding and the pedagogical presentation. These two kinds of dialogue or interchanges are not unrelated; as parts, they enter into a third dialectical interchange which constitutes the whole of the classroom situation—(c) the give and take of discussion, the interchange of interpretations between teacher and student.

In the classroom the first kind of dialogue, between fore-structure and subject matter, may, for example, depend upon the second one, between the teacher's understanding and his presentation. The circle of understanding in the teacher remains open to the extent that there is an ongoing dialogue between his understanding of the subject matter and his presentation to the class. Etienne Gilson, favoring Aquinas's view, indicates that in teaching the teacher is required to go through the whole process of interpretation again: "unless he is actually thinking aloud and engaging his own intellectual activity in his lecture, the teacher does not really teach."[42] Of course, the *subtilitas intelligendi* will generally govern the *subtilitas explicandi*, although it may happen that by working through the pedagogical presentation the teacher's original understanding will be opened up to question and be recast. Teachers often claim to understand something better after having taught it. In light of this, one might say that the teacher's understanding of the subject matter functions as a fore-conception relative to the pedagogical presentation. From the perspective of the teacher, teaching is, in part, a dialogue with himself, a sorting out of interpretations which are in a constant process of revision. The teacher's understanding of the subject matter governs his presentation just as fore-conceptions govern understanding in general. And the teacher's presentation may recast his understanding, just as fore-conceptions are constantly undergoing revision in the process of learning. At least, this would be the case if in his teaching he was also learning. Moreover, it seems to me that this would be the case if the teacher was properly involved in the other, third dialogical structure that characterizes the classroom situation: the interchange of interpretations between teacher and student.

The interchange of interpretations should not be viewed as an exchange of finished products. The communication occurring in the classroom is itself hermeneutical in nature; the interchange itself, in its communicative aspect, is interpretational. The give and take of the play of discussion involves the hermeneutical circular structure. The circular, dialogical structure of the teacher-student communication is maintained by the difference between the fore-structure operating in the student's comprehension and the fore-structure which conditions the pedagogical presentation. Precisely this difference, along with the maintenance of this dialogical circle in the learning process, argues against Chladenius's attempt to collapse the circle of the teacher-student interchange, or to see teacher's understanding, pedagogical presentation, and student comprehension as coinciding and complete.[43]

There is an important breakpoint in educational experience which is instructive in regard to this issue of the completeness or incompleteness of understanding. The teacher first teaches the student what she (the teacher) knows. At some point the student is prepared to move on to a more important aspect of learning, which begins, as Lyotard notes, when the teacher confides to him what she *does not know* (see PMC 25). The student is introduced to the incompleteness of the teacher's understanding and is thus given the opportunity to make his own way in that regard. This is an essential part of educational experience if education is to be successful. In this regard, we might say that teaching can never be reduced to the transmission of information but is the attempt to bring the student into a conversation precisely where the conversation is uncertain, indeterminate—where the teacher cannot answer the question—where the question remains a question.

To what extent is the hermeneutical circle evident in the informal educational experience of play? That aspect of play which we called "transcendence" involves venturing into the unknown, going beyond ourselves to experience the unfamiliar. But transcendence does not begin from a zero-point; it starts from that which is known. I only venture into the unknown from out of the known. The unfamiliar that we experience in play is, as we indicated, first interpreted in terms of the world. But the world is precisely that with which we are most familiar. The world is the context within which we find ourselves in a prereflective or prepredicative way. The world, in its phenomenological sense of life-world, is the store from which we borrow our schemata, *Vorhaben*, preconceptions, and so forth. There is no experience of play that exists outside of a prereflectively constituted context which bestows meaning on our activities. Our playful activities reveal the meaning of *our own* possibilities. They are not alien or meaningless possibilities precisely because they find their place within a meaningful context projected by the fore-structure of our understanding. They do not emerge out of nowhere; they emerge on the basis of past experience.

We can refer to an example in the field of physical education. Practice is required in most sports. If a game requires a certain physical movement that outside of the game would not normally belong to the potential player's repertoire of bodily movements, she must begin by practicing that movement. In such practice the player must count on a body schema that defines what the body is normally capable of. This schema is precisely the physical capability which forms a *Vorhabe* of movement which conditions the practice of any new, unfamiliar movement. In learning a new dance, in learning to catch a baseball, in the case of a child learning to clap hands, certain schematic bodily movements are already in place and must be modified in practice. As practice continues, bodily performances become more proficient and this proficiency in turn becomes the basis for any further development of capabilities. The body schema, now modified, enables the development of further possible practices. Schemata, on the level of physical movement, just as fore-conceptions, on the level of cognitive performance, condition learning in play experience. Transcendence is limited by what our present capabilities allow us to project as our possibilities.

One can also see that to the extent that these schemata, *Vorhaben*, fore-conceptions, and so forth, are modified in play experience, play involves appropriation. The player transforms herself, educates herself, precisely to the degree that a transformation of the fore-structure of understanding takes place. The reforming of a schema or fore-conception, based on the "feedback" or the reevaluation of one's experience, is precisely the aspect of self-formation involved in play. But again, self-appropriation is not a recovery of some substantial, identical ego or substance. It is, as Sartre might indicate, a self-recovery of self-transcendence. To the extent that play is the dialectical interchange of transcendence and appropriation, it reflects the circularity found in all learning. If this circularity collapses, if the lack of coincidence which characterizes subjectivity is suddenly transformed into coincidence, then subjectivity congeals into substance, play ceases, "seriousness" or "bad faith" sets in, and learning comes to an end.[44]

The hermeneutical circle is another way to express the openness that is necessary for learning. If the openness is closed off, if the circle collapses into its center, learning ceases. The analysis of play as educational experience shows that the hermeneutical circular structure conditions and maintains the possibilities of self-formation. The fore-structure of understanding qualifies, sets limits to one's own possibilities. Without operative schemata or preconceptions of what is possible, our possibilities would be limitless and therefore meaningless.

The finitude of human understanding is expressed in the hermeneutical circularity of educational experience. Whether in play or in the teacher-student interchange, learning is never an all-at-once phenomenon. There is no instantaneous learning. Rather, learning is a temporal process that always has a dimension of pastness and a dimension of futurity and incompleteness. Indeed, the futurity is evidenced by our experiences of the incompleteness of learning. The more we learn, the more we are aware of how much we do not know, and of how much our current conceptions change as we learn more. No matter how many times we read a classic, we always discover new possibilities in it. But the finitude of the learner not only means that he is unable to acquire an absolute understanding in the manner of an unmediated, instantaneous occurrence. It also means that the learner is not a tabula rasa. The learner is neither all-knowing nor totally ignorant. He always has his own preconceptions about the subject matter conditioned by his past experience.

Consider, for example, the young child who is given a first lesson in mathematics, a field in which it is often thought that interpretation comes closest to absolute understanding. If in a classroom situation the child is presented the equation $1 + 1 = 2$ for the first time, this is not totally unfamiliar to him. Disregarding the child's previous acquaintance with numbers, he is prepared for this lesson in a more fundamental way. The teacher acknowledges this in her communication. She uses two apples to demonstrate the equation, which means she uses a familiar, nonformal addition that the child is already familiar with. Rudimentary arithmetical equations are present in a virtual and nonformal way in childhood perception. One task of the teacher is to formalize the already familiar. The child is prepared for this lesson because he has already experienced nonformal, unformulated perceptual addition. He already has mathematical fore-sight. As mathematical education continues the child's first formal understanding of basic arithmetical functions will, in turn, prepare him for the higher order, more abstract functions. The teacher's method uses the fore-structure of the child's understanding, which defines the context in which arithmetic may be learned. If the context of learning is not set up on the basis of the child's preconceptions, the communication fails. For example, the teacher may be able to foresee possible confusions based on the student's fore-conceptions, and she sets out to avoid them by saying what something is not, so as to define what it is. For instance, a social science teacher may begin her explanation of the concept of "ideal type" by stating that the term *ideal* does not mean, in this context, *best* or *perfect*, and so on. The teacher makes an effort to enter into, in order to expand or reroute, the hermeneutical circle of the student's understanding.

This last consideration suggests that the pedagogical presentation is governed not only by the teacher's understanding of the subject matter, but by her understanding of how the subject matter can best be articulated for the student concerned. The educator must be concerned with the processes by which the subject matter may be passed on. She must not only understand these processes but try to implement them through her presentation. The pedagogical presentation, therefore, is neither something identical nor something less than the teacher's understanding of the subject matter, but something more, for it encompasses not just the subject matter but also the educational concern with the facilitation of learning. This element may be hidden from the student, or it may present itself, along with the material, as the teacher's concern. This element also helps to explain the difference between the pedagogical presentation and the student's comprehension, and why they can never coincide. I indicated before (p. 38) that the factors which condition both student comprehension and teacher understanding are of two kinds: first, those factors that relate to fore-conceptions about the subject matter, which I called "material" interests; and second, those factors that relate to the different roles or tasks that belong to teacher or student—"nonmaterial" or "formal" interests. Precisely because the material and formal interests that condition the student's comprehension are different from those that condition the teacher's understanding, there is no possibility of the coincidence that Chladenius speaks of.

From the student's perspective, fore-conceptions must of necessity be present for learning to take place. When educational theorists define certain developmental stages in which children are predisposed to learn certain lessons, they are describing something related to the concept of fore-structure. Learning functions on the basis of a prepared understanding. This is not a reference to the student's preparation of lessons, but to prior learning or the instruction of experience. This preparation is not simply the accumulation of information, but includes the development of abilities to project certain schemata which translate the unfamiliar into the familiar. These preconceptions or schemata guide the student's attempt to understand. They guide but also limit, as Plato, or Piaget, or any teacher will attest.

Teaching, in part, requires the ability to open up these schemata or preconceptions to new possibilities of understanding. The teacher's task is not solely to inform these preconceptions, but to allow the student to reform, reshape, and revise his preconceptions so as to come into the subject matter in an appropriate way. Thus, the aim of teaching cannot be to make the student think precisely as the teacher thinks or to attain the coincidence of interpretations, but to foster the hermeneutical relations which constitute learning. As Augustine suggests, the teacher's task is to foster the student's recollection.[45]

The hermeneutical circle, sometimes expanding, sometimes shrinking, in the dialectical interplay between fore-structure and reality, between transcendence and appropriation, keeps open the possibilities that define our experience as educational experience. Taken to the extreme, however, a dogmatic fore-structure may close off possibilities almost altogether. Without the openness, and thereby the possibility of recasting, revising, or reforming our preconceptions, our possibilities would reduce to an overly narrow range, and, at the extreme, experience would no longer be educational. We discover in the following chapters that an *absolute* dogmatic interpretation, that is, one in which the hermeneutical circle completely disappears, is never possible. A closed and completely reproductive interpretation is as impossible as a *completely* open and *absolutely* unconstrained interpretation. Educational experience is always found between the ideal extremes of complete coincidence (identity between teacher and student, dogmatism, reproduction) and complete openness (lacking any fore-structure).

I have been arguing against the conception that one aim of education is to bring the student's comprehension to coincide with the teacher's. Rather, I am proposing that learning, in the classroom, takes place only when various dialectical interchanges of interpretations are maintained: first, in each individual involved (teacher and student) the dialectical interplay between foreconception and subject matter which constitutes the hermeneutical circle of interpretation; second, the dialogical relations between the teacher's understanding and pedagogical presentation; and third, the dialogical circle which encompasses the partial interchanges of the classroom situation. All of these circles of interchange are hermeneutical and productive. To the extent that learning is ongoing, they are never completely closed off. On this, Gadamer and Habermas agree: Gadamer writes that this "is the inexhaustible power of experience, that in every process of learning we constantly form a new preconception." Habermas reinforces this thought: in the process of learning, the student "merely develops a new pre-understanding, which then guides him as he takes the next hermeneutical step."[46]

CHAPTER 4

Hermeneutical Constraints

Various aspects of the hermeneutical circular structure impose constraints which both limit and enable the processes of interpretation and education. These constraints will be outlined in terms of two hermeneutical principles, which can be stated as follows: (a) All interpretation is governed by a tradition process, and (b) All interpretation is linguistic. These two principles describe how we, as interpreters, already have at our disposal some familiarity with those things that present themselves as unfamiliar or alien. They describe, therefore, a relatedness or "belongingness" of the interpreter (learner) to a process of tradition and to a linguistic context. In brief, and simply put, the fore-structure of understanding is shaped by certain biases (preconceptions, prejudgments, prejudices). These biases are derived from traditions to which we have access through language. Language, however, involves a dialectical turning: we not only have language, but language has us. For this reason, we not only have access to traditions, but traditions have a certain power over us. They exercise what Gadamer calls an historically effected (*wirkungsgeschichtlich*) hold on our interpretive abilities.

TRADITIONS AND PRECONCEPTIONS IN INTERPRETATION

The hermeneutical import of the principle of tradition might be made manifest by considering the project conceived by the seventeenth-century philosopher and mathematician Descartes in his *Meditations*. Descartes' project sets the stage, in a number of ways, for the emergence of modern scientific rationalism. It also represents the diametrical opposite to the conception of interpretation advanced by the philosophical hermeneutics of Gadamer, and represents a concept of education that stands opposed to the one expressed in our hypothesis.

83

Descartes set out to attain a beginning point for his philosophy that would avoid any presupposed belief. He sought to build the edifice of his thought on unshakable bedrock, the most certain foundation that he could acquire. He convinced himself that this zero-point beginning could be found through a methodical procedure of doubt: the systematic dismissal of anything that could be doubted. He would not let his beginning point be compromised by any belief or opinion accepted secondhand or on hearsay evidence from other thinkers. Such ready-made opinions, the prejudices of past philosophical traditions, which were clearly embedded in book learning, were to be excluded. Thus, he indicated in his *Discourse on Method*, "I thought that book learning—at least the kind whose arguments are only probable and unproved—had developed gradually by the accumulation of so many different opinions of so many different persons, and is therefore not as close to the truth as the simple and natural reasonings of a man of good sense, laboring under no prejudice, concerning the things which he experiences."[1] He further indicated how educational systems, with their built-in prejudices, tend to corrupt original ideas, and he proposed the method of doubt as a way to dismiss all ready-made opinions and prejudices. For example, Descartes was most anxious to escape the tradition of metaphysical disputations, which seemed to him to provide all of the convoluted categories responsible for leading our thought astray. This escape from tradition, as one part of his methodical doubt, was not an attempt on Descartes' part to justify a philosophical skepticism. On the contrary, his aim was to build a positive, presuppositionless, and certain philosophy that would approximate mathematics in rigor and clarity.

Descartes' project failed, and what this failure shows is the impossibility of escaping traditions. It becomes obvious, while reading the *Meditations*, that traditional logic and metaphysics are still at work in Descartes' philosophy, despite his attempt to methodically detach himself from them. Having resolved, in his first Meditation, not to trust his reasoning abilities because of the possibility of error, he allowed, and if he was to make any progress he had to allow, the use of reason and the rules of logical inference in subsequent meditations, without ever justifying their use. Moreover, having sent packing all metaphysical opinions at the beginning of his enterprise, metaphysical categories no less than 'substance', 'accident', 'form', 'matter', 'causality', and 'reality' continued to sneak in through the back door of his meditations. What we learn from Descartes is that no matter how much of a conscious effort we make to walk away from the traditions that define us, those traditions always walk with us. Descartes remained trapped in the very traditions from which he set out to escape. In the hermeneutical view, Descartes' language played the important and not so evil role of what he, following Augustine, called the "evil spirit," precisely to the extent that, unbeknownst to Descartes, his language carried within itself the metaphysical tradition.[2] I will discuss in detail the role that language plays in Descartes in the following section.

For the Cartesian project to work, a tradition would have to be something external, objective, and past. Indeed, this is Descartes' concept of tradition. Heidegger offers a different view. If in some sense traditions are past, this does not mean that they are temporally removed from us. According to Heidegger, human existence *is* its past: "and this is so not only in that its past is, as it were, pushing itself along 'behind' it . . . Dasein [human existence] 'is' its past in the way of *its* own Being. . . . Dasein has grown up both into and in a traditional way of interpreting itself. . . . Its own past—and this always means the past of its 'generation'—is not something which *follows along after* Dasein, but something which already goes ahead of it" (BT 41/20). Of course, we are capable of studying a tradition as a historical object, but this is not the primary relation that we have to it. Descartes mistook the ability we have to explicitly study a tradition to be the only kind of relation which exists between ourselves and our past. Heidegger indicates that such an attitude only leads to an implicit domination by the tradition. Human existence

> falls prey to the tradition of which it has more or less explicitly taken hold. This tradition keeps it from providing its own guidance, whether in inquiring or in choosing. . . . When tradition thus becomes master, it does so in such a way that what it 'transmits' is made so inaccessible . . . that it rather becomes concealed. Tradition . . . blocks our access to those primordial 'sources' from which the categories and concepts handed down to us have been in part quite genuinely drawn. Indeed it makes us forget that they have had such an origin. (BT 42–43/21).

An operative but concealed tradition, in this way, fooled Descartes, and modern consciousness in general, into thinking that we have escaped the old world and joined the radically modern one. Thus, the "seemingly new beginning which Descartes proposed for philosophizing has revealed itself as the implantation of a baleful prejudice." (BT 46/25).

If a tradition has become, implicitly, a dominating force because of the naiveté of our explicit objectification of it in historical study, then, according to Heidegger, a new attitude is called for. This new attitude would recognize the power of tradition for what it really is, treat it accordingly, and in that way would attempt to destroy its artificial domination. Heidegger calls this new attitude a "destruction" of tradition. But this "destruction" is positive rather than violently negative. It involves discovering "the positive possibilities of that tradition, and this always means keeping it within its *limits*. . . . To bury the past in nullity is not the purpose of this destruction; its aim is *positive*" (BT 44/22–23). The destruction of a tradition, which he characterizes as a conversation "with that which has been handed down to us," "is not a break with history, no repudiation of history, but is an appropriation [*Aneignung*] and transformation [*Verwandlung*] of what has been handed down to us. . . . Destruction means—to open our ears, to make ourselves free for what speaks to us in the tradition as the being of being."[3]

Gadamer sees several important hermeneutical implications in this concept of tradition.[4] He maintains that the process of tradition is a living force that enters into all understanding. It is not, however, an external force that totally determines how we understand the world. Nor is it a bygone past, or a finished, lifeless mass. Rather, we ourselves live through the process of tradition and provide it with its force.

> At any rate, our usual relationship to the past is not characterized by distancing and freeing ourselves from tradition. Rather, we are always situated within traditions, and this is no objectifying process—i.e., we do not conceive of what tradition says as something other, something alien. It is always part of us, a model or exemplar, a kind of cognizance that our later historical judgment would hardly regard as a kind of knowledge but as the most

ingenuous affinity [preservation, *Anverwandlung*] of tradition."
(TM 282)

The process of tradition is, in effect, within us. In this process we
do not deal with traditions objectively, as external and bygone
phenomena. They shape what we are and how we understand the
world. The attempt to step outside of the process of tradition
would be like trying to step outside of our own skins. The preten-
sion to escape the process would lead to a misunderstanding of
both the world and oneself. A genuine understanding of the world
involves, not the attempt to escape traditions, but a participation
in the happenings of traditions (see TM 290).

Tradition, as a process and a force, conditions all interpretations, whether scientific, artistic, literary, historical, or philosophical. The power of tradition appears impotent, dead, and inoperative
only when it is made objective in the explicit study of a particular
tradition. We are tempted to say that through such studies we
understand a tradition and have control over it. But this objectified
tradition is not the phenomenon that we seek to explicate in hermeneutics. Rather we understand tradition as a power process that
operates within and governs all our interpretations. All interpretation is shaped by the traditions in which we stand; interpretations
originate within and by traditions, and they continue traditions. To
get a preliminary understanding of how traditions operate within
our interpretations, Gadamer provides us with an explication of the
concept of prejudgment (bias, preconception, prejudice).

To delineate the hermeneutical principle of prejudgment in interpretation, Gadamer focuses on the modern thinkers of the Enlightenment. The Enlightenment inherited Descartes' dream: the
attempt to escape from the confinement of traditions and to base
all knowledge on a purified unprejudiced reason. But this, as
Gadamer points out, is precisely the prejudice of the Enlightenment: the prejudice against prejudice which was built into their
conception of method.

The Enlightenment made a distinction between two different
kinds of prejudice: prejudice due to authority and prejudice due to
overhastiness (see TM 271). In identifying authority as a source of
prejudice, the modern philosophers, from Descartes to Kant, were

concerned with avoiding a dogmatic metaphysics. The Enlightenment turned its back on the dogmatic beliefs of the medieval schools and turned toward reason as the timeless and ultimate justification of belief. In this way reason became the new authority. And the new authority became the judge of the old authority: the written word—specifically the texts of the ancients—became subject to the tests of reason. "It is not tradition but reason that constitutes the ultimate source of all authority. What is written down is not necessarily true. We can know better: this is the maxim with which the modern Enlightenment approaches tradition and which ultimately leads it to undertake historical research" (TM 272). A tradition thus becomes the object of a scientific criticism. The belief in the absolute authority of reason manifested in both the natural and the historical sciences is part of the "basic discrediting of all prejudices." But this belief that reason stands outside of the process of tradition and thereby offers human understanding a way to escape all prejudice is itself a prejudice. The case of the "prejudice against prejudice" provides the clearest evidence that no interpretation escapes prejudice.

The Enlightenment dream continued in the philosophy of positivism and transformed itself into the modern enterprise of science. The scientific researcher, through the proper use of the scientific method, pursues complete objectivity, free from the prejudices of traditional beliefs and superstitions. Upon entering his laboratory or field the experimenter attempts to shed, like a cloak, all of his own prejudices, personal biases, and pet theories in order to enter into the search for objective truth. Scientific knowledge attempts to completely exclude prejudice. "In adopting this principle, modern science is following the rule of Cartesian doubt, accepting nothing as certain that can in any way be doubted, and adopting the idea of method that follows from this rule" (TM 271). As Gadamer shows, this approach itself involves following a tradition which embraces its own prejudice against prejudice and traditional authority. Unless the scientific researcher follows the tradition of science and the authority that defines a scientific inquiry, the work he does is not scientific. Tradition and authority, and the positive preconceptions involved in following a rational method, rather than undermining reason, enable reason to pursue its task in an orderly way.

The Enlightenment distorted the notion of authority by opposing it to reason. According to Gadamer, however, the concept of authority is not opposite to that of reason; rather, authority is based on reason. It "rests on acknowledgment [*Anerkennung*] and hence on an act of reason itself which, aware of its own limitations, trusts to the better insight of others. Authority in this sense, properly understood, has nothing to do with blind obedience to commands. Indeed, authority has to do not with obedience, but rather with knowledge" (TM 279).

One may be better able to see that both reason and freedom are at work in this relation between authority and interpretation by referring to a similar observation, albeit in a different context, made by John Stuart Mill. Mill's rule-utilitarian ethics recommends that in the process of coming to a moral decision we should first attempt to do our own reasonable calculations, but if, because of lack of experience, for example, we are unable to come to our own decision, we must look to others. The others who would act as authorities in such matters would be those whom we recognize as being "competently acquainted" with the options that we face. Thus Mill suggests that a certain authority which is found in "the judgment of those who are qualified by knowledge of [the various options], or if they differ, that of the majority among them, must be admitted as final."[5] Mill also recognizes that the reason of utility is generally at the basis of law and custom and that throughout history "mankind have been learning by experience the tendencies of actions."[6] Traditions, objectively expressed in laws and customs, maintain an authority based on human experience and reason. What Mill prescribes for moral interpretation Gadamer holds to be a general descriptive principle of all interpretation. Interpretation is based, to some extent, on individual experience, but such experience is embedded in traditions which find their way into interpretation in the form of authoritative prejudices.

The hermeneutical principle developed here is that all understanding involves preconceptions; all interpretation is informed, in some way, by the tradition process. Gadamer calls this the principle of "historical effect" (*Wirkungsgeschichte*), which states that "understanding is, essentially, a historically effected event" (TM 300). This means that through the biases of traditions the past plays an efficacious role in our interpretations. Understanding is always under the influence of history. Gadamer explicates this important concept as follows: historical effect means "that we cannot extricate ourselves from the historical process, we cannot distance ourselves from it in such a way that the past becomes completely objective for us. . . . We are always situated in history. . . . I mean that our consciousness is determined by a real historical process, in such a way that we are not free to simply juxtapose ourselves to the past."[7] Even the enterprise of scientific research, which, as we have seen, inherits its spirit from modern thinkers like Descartes, does not escape this force. Any claim to unbiased, neutral, and objective knowledge is itself a prejudice that determines what counts as good science. The experimenter enters the laboratory with a general preconception of what she is looking for and what might count for valid results. If the laboratory's ceiling plaster falls into the middle of an experiment, the experimenter will count the experiment ruined rather than proclaim this a fantastic scientific discovery, because her understanding of the event is guided by the scientific tradition which tells her what kinds of questions to ask and what may count as scientific method and evidence. In all scientific reasoning certain traditions are at work in various ways: "in choosing the theme to be investigated, awakening the desire to investigate, gaining a new problematic" (TM 282).

Philosophical hermeneutics shows, in contrast to the spirit of the Enlightenment, that one cannot escape traditions and the preconceptions they foster; at most one can explicate the preconceptions that are built into any interpretation and see how the past operates in the present. Hermeneutics shows that no matter how hard one tries to escape all preconceptions, being biased constitutes the historical reality of human understanding. Preconceptions are conditions of even the most reasonable understanding. All meanings are projected on the basis of prior knowledge. That prior knowledge, even if in the form of an inexplicable hunch or unconsciously motivated intuition, enters into understanding in the form of preconceptions. The fore-structure of understanding is shaped by the biased knowledge that reflects our immersion in various traditions. Thus Gadamer writes that such preconceptions "are biases of our openness to the world. They are simply conditions whereby we experience something—whereby what we encounter says something to us" (PH 9). Understanding, even if in the form of sudden insight, does not develop from out of nowhere, without basis; its ground is always prepared in a past which we carry around with us.

It should be noted that not all preconceptions come in the form of prior knowledge or prejudgments, in the sense of controllable and conscious presuppositions. Many of them remain unconsciously embedded in our understanding. "The prejudices and fore-meanings that occupy the interpreter's consciousness are not at his free disposal. He cannot separate in advance the productive prejudices that enable understanding from the prejudices that hinder it and lead to misunderstandings" (TM 295). This does not mean that we cannot become aware of and circumvent a particular bias; we can, through reflection, revise and reform our preconceptions. Indeed, the hermeneutical canon that follows from this principle encourages us to try to escape those that are not productive. The hermeneutical task is to identify, in any interpretation, which preconceptions are productive, (ones that further interpretation) and which are nonproductive (ones that perpetrate misunderstanding). The way in which we sort out and jettison nonproductive preconceptions is not by appeal to some independent criterion of truth, however. Such a criterion does not exist. Whatever criteria we use to identify nonproductive preconceptions must be worked out within the hermeneutical situation.

We will refer to the hermeneutical operation of tradition as having an "anterior" relation to the interpreter. We always find ourselves with a past that does not simply follow behind, but goes in advance, defining the contexts by which we come to interpret the world. Despite the fact that traditions operate for the most part "behind our backs," they are already there, ahead of us, conditioning our interpretations.

THE PROCESS OF TRADITION IN THE EDUCATIONAL CONTEXT

Aristotle recognized the importance of memory for learning. Even more fundamentally, he noted that experience itself is "produced" from memory (*Metaphysics* 980b). But Plato, Aristotle's teacher, specified the type of memory essential for learning. In Plato's dialogue, *The Meno*, Meno is good at memorizing various opinions and definitions. Yet, if he is capable of memorizing he seems incapable of understanding what he memorizes. Meno is unable to learn because of the attitude he takes toward traditional authority. He accepts without question, and memorizes the prejudices of a tradition. This is a use of memory that blocks the possibility of learning. The proper use of memory, which fosters learning, is expressed by the term *recollection* and is reflected by the attitude taken by Socrates toward various traditions. Plato's Socrates allows a tradition to inform and guide the learning process. The dialogue begins by allowing the traditional answers to set the stage for inquiry. The purpose of inquiry is not to make the tradition an object of study, but to interrogate it for the purposes of throwing light on the matter at hand. Recollection is thus shown to be, not a passive acceptance, but an active interchange or dialogue with traditions which orients inquiry and learning. Plato clearly recognizes that learning is possible only through re-collecting what is already known, allowing the informing power of traditions to work.

In more contemporary terms, Scheffler tells us that "to become rational is to enter into traditions, to inherit them and to learn to participate in the never-ending work of testing, expanding, and altering them for the better."[8] The educational process is, he notes, "central to this fundamental process of human renewal." To achieve rational and truly human life one must enter into these "multiple evolving traditions."[9] To "enter into," "to inherit," "to participate in" traditions: this is what we do in any interpretation, whether we are conscious of it or not. In educational experience, traditions are not necessarily the objects of study or the resources to be retrieved by straightforward memorization or critique, but they are always such that they allow learning to take place and condition the way that education is accomplished.

In the formal classroom situation traditions determine the course of learning, even if the teacher has complete academic freedom and absolute control over curriculum. They define, to some extent, what is teachable and how it might be taught. Just as a tradition of science informs the scientist concerning what counts as a genuine scientific pursuit, so in any discipline some tradition plays an informative role. The authority based in various traditions determines the very concept of academic discipline, the actual divisions of subject matter, and the proper biases under which the subject matter can be learned. If a teacher decides to teach mathematics rather than literature, the terms of his choice have already been outlined in advance. Traditions enable the choice to be made, precisely because the meaning of the choice is governed by the authority of traditional definitions. If the teacher decides to teach geometry rather than algebra, he does not create geometry ex nihilo; it has been handed down to him as an inheritance. This is a figurative way of saying that he has learned geometry himself within a context governed by a scientific tradition. In teaching as well as in learning, the teacher and student are participating in traditions that have long, and often obscure, histories. But no matter how remote and obscure the beginnings of geometry are, they reside within the teaching and the learning. One might see this in the way that the term *teaching* refers not only to an act of teaching but to what is taught. *The teaching* refers to the content of a tradition which is taught, that is, delivered or handed over in trust. In teaching, the tradition is entrusted or "commended to the keeping of someone."[10] The word *learning* can also be used as a noun in a similar fashion.

Even if a teacher attempts to present the subject matter in a radically innovative way, the innovation is guided by both the traditional delineation of the subject matter and the tradition of academic teaching which defines the formal aspects of what counts as pedagogy. To teach means to show something or to communicate with the student in some way. But the tradition of teaching specifies acceptable means of communication. Supposedly, these means are acceptable precisely because they are thought to be the most reasonable or effective ones. The authority of the tradition here is not based on empty belief or superstition but, for example, on the trial-and-error experimentation of past teachers. Innovations that succeeded have been retained; ones that failed were forgotten. Any present innovation will be judged according to the same authoritative criterion of success, which, in the teaching tradition, has won out over style, for example, as the primary test of innovation. If innovations are to some extent guided by criteria set within a teaching tradition, then it would not be the complete truth to call such innovations "nontraditional."

Learning, as much as teaching, is possible only on the basis of traditions. In learning, the student is brought into certain preconceptions which serve to orient her toward the subject matter. The fore-structure of the student's understanding is conditioned by those traditional preconceptions which are offered under the sign of authority. The student never creates an interpretation ex nihilo. Her fore-conceptions are derived from past experience; they are based on some prior knowledge which determines the parameters of what she can expect to find in the world. Her fore-conceptions never lie outside of the framework provided by the past. The fact is that as learners we are all historians in a peculiar way. Whatever we try to learn has its own history embedded in the subject matter or practice. In learning about X, I implicitly learn the history of X, even if I do not learn, explicitly, "about" the history of X. In this sense, what Gadamer calls the principle of historical effect applies not only to explicit historical study, but to all study. Past experience is something that the student is constantly in touch with; it is something that she consistently makes use of in her interpretations and learnings. This past is not past in an objective sense; it is a past that is continually lived. The past experience that the student "consults" in forming her fore-conceptions is not a list of events that she has studied in an objective manner. In some sense it is part of herself, although it is not in any simple sense strictly personal or private, belonging only to her. Just as I might say, for example, that this is my country, or that I am an American, without meaning that this country belongs only to me or that I am the only American, so I could say that this is my experience, and when I understand it I understand myself, without implying that this experience is totally unique to me or that in understanding myself I do not also understand others. The past experience that I live and depend on in my present learning is larger than my own personal experience; it is, in fact, the experience of traditions which belongs to all learners.

To the extent that the principle of historical effect describes educational experience, it is clear that part of the task of the teacher must be to become aware of the force of tradition. Gadamer calls this awareness "hermeneutical reflection," which is a reflection on "historically effected consciousness." "Reflection on a given preunderstanding brings before me something that otherwise happens 'behind my back'. Something—but not everything, for what I have called the *wirkungsgeschichtliches Bewusstsein* [historically effected consciousness] is inescapably more *being* than *consciousness*, and being is never fully manifest."[11] That a good part of teaching and learning requires such reflection seems clear. Gadamer makes explicit reference to the proper relation to traditions which characterizes educational experience. The proper relation is a *transformative* relation. Only through hermeneutical reflection "do I learn to gain a new understanding of what I have seen through eyes conditioned by prejudice. But this implies, too, that the prejudgments that lead my preunderstanding are also constantly at stake, right up to the moment of their surrender—which surrender could also be called a transformation."[12]

Hermeneutical reflection also includes the ability to allow a tradition to work. The teacher, as well as the student, must remain open to the inexhaustible possibilities presented by traditions, and must do so by recognizing how traditions work to present these possibilities. From the perspective of pedagogy, an ignorance of historical effects, or worse, a belief that tradition is controlled in historical objectification, could lead to the closing off of learning and the domination of dogmatic interpretations. Gadamer correctly states that "a person who believes he is free of prejudices, relying on the objectivity of his procedures and denying that he is himself conditioned by historical circumstances, experiences the power of the prejudices that unconsciously dominate him, as a vis a tergo. A person who does not admit that he is dominated by prejudices will fail to see what manifests itself by their light" (TM 360). This is especially critical for the teacher because, if he fails to remain open to and aware of the effective force of tradition, he runs the risks of being captivated by dogmatic interpretations and of closing off the possibility of learning in both himself and his students.

According to Karl Jaspers, education is a dialectic between authority and freedom.[13] But one should not identify authority too quickly with domination and violence, as critical hermeneutics tends to do. According to Gadamer, the essence of authority is acknowledgment (*Anerkennung*) rather than obedience. "Thus, acknowledging authority is always connected with the idea that what the authority says is not irrational and arbitrary but can, in principle, be discovered to be true. This is the essence of the authority claimed by the teacher, the superior, the expert. The prejudices that they implant are legitimized by the person who presents them" (TM 280). The authority of the teacher in the classroom situation, for instance, rests, not on fear, if learning is to genuinely take place, but on the reasonableness of that which is taught. When students enter a classroom, or open a book, or when they are shown how to perform some task in the field, they are confronted by authority. Even in the apparent isolation of self-reflection, we do not confront ourselves without the intervention of authority in the form of those socially determined categories by which we conceive of ourselves. Many times manifest, but most of the time latent, authority is embedded in every educational experience. Gadamer insists that "all education depends on this [authority], and even though, in the case of education, the educator loses his function when his charge comes of age and sets his own insight and decisions in the place of the authority of the educator, becoming mature does not mean that a person becomes his own master in the sense that he is freed of all tradition" (TM 280).

Authority and freedom should not be conceived of as opposites: "To be situated within a tradition does not limit the freedom of knowledge but makes it possible. . . . The fact is that in tradition there is always an element of freedom and of history itself. Even the most genuine and pure tradition does not persist because of the inertia of what once existed. It needs to be affirmed, embraced, cultivated" (TM 361, 281). Educational experience is not only conditioned by traditions, it conserves traditions. This conservation is an aspect of freedom in educational experience, but not a freedom that involves freeing ourselves from traditions. Descartes does not supply us with the proper model of education. The task of education is not to overcome tradition, since learning takes place only through a structure supplied by traditional preconceptions. A totally unprejudiced interpretation could be found only in a godlike, absolute knowledge which is beyond the possibilities of human understanding.

If, for example, in self-reflective meditations I attempt to learn about myself, I find that I must use certain categories that have been already provided to me. I do not make up such categories ad hoc, as I go along. I inherit the categories by which I understand myself from others, from society, from traditions. The categories are forced upon me; at least I do not choose them in absolute freedom. Nor is it possible for me to have an unconditioned, "purified" reflection by which I capture a genuine transcendental self. A pure reflection (whether for Kant, or Husserl, or Sartre) remains only an ideal, again the godlike absolute insight that is impossible for human understanding. My self-reflection is always prestructured according to the various categories that I employ in reflection. These categories bias my view of myself; they are given to me with all of the authority of society and tradition. Moreover, these categories are preserved by me in my experience. I am forced to grant to them the legitimacy that they demand when I fail to conceive of myself in any other way. Traditions are conserved, and authority finds legitimacy in such educational experience.

This does not mean that the structure provided by such preconceptions is always right, true, or unchallengeable. Indeed, there is a fundamental ambiguity involved in our relation to authority structures. In this regard we can cite Mill once again. Not only does he describe a legitimate role for authority in his rule-utilitarianism, but he also warns us of the threat authority poses to our freedom. If our attitude is one of blind obedience to a tradition or custom, its authority turns into a tyranny, the famous "tyranny of the majority," "the tyranny of the prevailing opinion and feeling."[14] In opposition to such tyranny Mill places experience and free critical discussion: "Not by experience alone. There must be discussion to show how experience is to be interpreted. Wrong opinions and practices gradually yield to fact and argument."[15] Conversation and the practice of listening, which Mill prescribes as guards against the dangers of authoritative tyranny, are in principle embodied in educational experience. Indeed, if learning is not simply the passive acceptance of information, but involves interpretation and hermeneutical reflection, then authoritative structures are constantly challenged within educational experience. The very authority of the structure (preconception, tradition) stands or falls through this challenge. Productive preconceptions, ones that facilitate understanding, will survive the challenge of interpretation. They will be shown to be legitimate structures that make sense and are reasonable. Unproductive preconceptions, which lead to misunderstanding, will ultimately fail the challenge. Thus, learning involves the sorting out of productive from unproductive preconceptions. Learning challenges the authority of traditions which make learning possible. Through educational experience preconceptions stand or fall, authority is constituted or destroyed. Interpretation not only preserves traditions but also transforms them. So we may say not only that there is no learning without authority, but that there is no authority without learning. Authority is constituted within educational experience.

To say that authority will find its legitimacy through educational experience is not to say that authority does not sometimes dominate the educational process or that unproductive preconceptions do not sometimes persist. In such cases, however, educational experience is distorted; it becomes indoctrination, and learning does not take place. Dogmatic interpretation originates in and is transmitted by an indoctrination that fails to challenge traditional learning. The problem with dogmatic interpretation is that explicitly it appears to be educational experience while implicitly it is just the opposite. In Plato's dialogue Meno is so convinced that he already knows the answer that he stops listening, he fails to genuinely participate in the conversation, and his conviction gets in the way of genuine learning. Dogmatic interpretation blocks our access to understanding. Dogmatic interpretation itself becomes an unproductive preconception which constantly reproduces itself; it perpetrates a vicious circle which can be broken only by educational experience.

Gadamer stresses the fact that through historical effects our interpretations carry the past into the present. "Understanding is to be thought of less as a subjective act than as participating in an event of tradition [Überlieferungsgeschehen], a process of transmission in which past and present are constantly mediated" (TM 290). The idea that understanding is not so much an action of subjectivity reminds us of Gadamer's analysis of play, which for him involves primarily a transcendence of subjectivity. But with respect to play we saw that transcendence was only one dimension, and that the concept of appropriation was also required for a complete picture. Likewise, in the context of historical effect, it is not enough to speak of a simple "transmission" of the past into the present. Gadamer is right to say a "mediation" of past and present. It is true that a great deal of the past is carried forward even in the most innovative interpretations, and that interpretation both transcends and appropriates traditions, or in other terms, that interpretation both "assimilates" and "accommodates" traditions. Innovation builds on the past, but it also extends beyond the past. Even if, as Gadamer holds, the past, in the form of a living tradition, is operative in and helps to shape the interpreter's present, and in this way allows the present to emerge in a meaningful continuity, this does not mean that the past strictly determines the present.

Of course, as Heidegger indicates, when a tradition comes to dominate, there may be a concealed transmission of the past into the present that is difficult to break or overcome (BT 43/21). More importantly, however, he also indicates that if a tradition is to be operative in the proper way, so that it fosters interpretation rather than dictates dogma, then a proper disposition is required of the interpreter. The principle is one of conversation instead of dictation, participation instead of transmission. Again, in naming this disposition a "destruction" of the tradition Heidegger does not want to signify a violent overthrow. In fact, Descartes' failure shows us that such an overthrow is not an option. But if we are careful to note that the destruction of the tradition does not mean breaking with the past, we must also be careful to avoid reducing it to just the transmission of the past. Heidegger uses the word *transformation* (*Verwandlung*).[16] This transformation, which is not unrelated to the self-transformation of *Bildung*, involves an active challenging of the tradition. In the learning process we are involved in a transformation which takes us beyond what our relationship to tradition has already supplied.

In educational experience, traditions are continued, not as a reproduced past, but as a transformed past, insofar as they are challenged and questioned, and insofar as they take on new meanings in our present interpretations. Traditions are transformed in educational experience insofar as learning is a dialectical interchange of transcendence and appropriation. The learner, in transcending himself toward his possibilities, also transcends tradition toward *its* possibilities. The transcendence and appropriation of tradition do not constitute a serial give and take, but a give that is also a take. There is an ambiguous dialectic in which tradition operates as both a constraint and a liberating force which the learner must play along with if he is to form himself. Educational experience involves an active transformation that leads always to an ambiguous interplay of overcoming and recovering, of transcendence and appropriation. Scheffler comes near to the truth: to learn is to enter into traditions, to inherit them, and "to participate in the never-ending work of testing, expanding, and altering them for the better."

LANGUAGE AND INTERPRETATION

"Every word is a prejudice"
Nietzsche

If, as I have indicated, the way that traditions constrain our interpretations does not depend on their objectification in explicit historical studies, then it seems necessary to ask how this anterior constraint operates. In other words, if in our interpretations we do not always consciously interrogate a tradition about what our foreconceptions should be, how is it possible that some tradition always conditions our interpretations? If we were working in a physical science we would ask what the "mechanism" is that accounts for effective history. But the question here is more difficult to pose because we are not looking for a mechanical apparatus. Moreover, the process happens, for the most part, "behind the back" of the interpreter. Even to gain a reflective consciousness of effective history does not mean that we objectify or neutralize the process or come to fully realize the effect of a particular tradition. The covert entry of a tradition into our interpretations needs to be explicated in a more precise fashion, without mitigating its covert nature or reducing it to a mechanistic functioning.

Fortunately, we have almost unanimous agreement that language plays the role of medium or vehicle by which traditions enter interpretation. As early as Schleiermacher, it was recognized that "language is the only presupposition in hermeneutics, and everything that is to be found, including the other objective and subjective presuppositions, must be discovered in language."[17] Unfortunately, however, the concept of language is like that of happiness, in that, as Aristotle long ago pointed out, everyone is willing to agree that happiness is the proper goal of life, but everyone is also willing to argue for a different conception of happiness. In the same fashion, there is no universal agreement about the nature of language or specifically how and to what degree it works to condition interpretation.

It is clear, however, that the essence of language in its hermeneutical performance cannot be grasped through a study of linguistics, whether from an empiricist or a structuralist point of view, because such approaches objectify language and distort its genuine performance in interpretation. Language at work, or in use, is something that inescapably encircles interpreter and interpreted, and hermeneutically encompasses even the linguistic scientist in her attempt to interpret language as a problem. One can only attempt to understand language from within language and with an understanding that is shaped by language.

Let us try to clarify the issues by again returning to the example of Descartes. Descartes, in his attempt to escape the effect of tradition by the employment of radical doubt, placed the traditional metaphysical notions of substance, reality, degrees of existence, causality, and so forth into doubt. He dismissed these concepts as traditional prejudices in order to gain his presuppositionless starting point—the *cogito*. However, without any justification whatsoever, every one of the aforementioned metaphysical categories found their way back into his meditations. For example, as part of his strategy of justifying his belief in his former opinions, Descartes set out to prove the existence of God. The problem, although Descartes failed to recognize it as a problem, is that he was only capable of setting up his proof in terms of substance, reality, degrees of existence, causality, and so on. His enterprise was invaded by precisely those metaphysical concepts that he thought were safely disposed of. The reason he could not escape the metaphysical tradition, and its conceptual categories, is that he was forced to use a language which carries this tradition within itself. His project was undermined by language, for language acts as the vehicle of those traditional metaphysical categories from which he tried to escape.

Both Friedrich Nietzsche and Bertrand Russell have pointed out that one of Descartes' most important discoveries, the *ego cogito*, is nothing other than the result of language, indeed, the very grammar of Latin.[18] Because Descartes was forced, through his own human nature, either to use language or remain silent in these matters, he became caught in a web of language. Language is not something that the interpreter has total control over; if it were, Descartes could have avoided taking up the metaphysical terms that undermined his project. Descartes was constantly bedeviled by language, which always operates, perhaps, in a fashion similar to his description of the evil demon which he thought he had neutralized by resolving to keep the possibility of such deception in mind.

But could Descartes have avoided these metaphysically determined words? Could Descartes have used language a little more carefully, as a tool under his complete command? It is the contention of philosophical hermeneutics that, in principle, Descartes could not have escaped the power which language exercised over his project, and hence could not have escaped the metaphysical tradition. The failure of Descartes' project indicates, at least, that, unavoidably, traditions and preconceptions enter into interpretation by way of language. Descartes' meditations may be viewed as an implicit dialogue, not simply one that takes place within Descartes' mind, but one which stretches over generations of thinkers, across a large tradition, via language.

At least one of the interlocutors who had a say in Descartes' conversation was Augustine. Augustine's attitude toward language found expression in Descartes. The certainty of thoughts, Descartes' *cogitationes*, corresponds to the certainty of what Augustine called the *verbum interius*, which belongs to no language.[19] In his view, the inner word totally escapes the constraints of grammar, syntax, or the diacritical multiplicity of the lexicon. In the realm of the *res cogitans*, or as Augustine would have said, "in the heart," language holds no sway; absolute and immediate understanding is possible. Of course, when we proceed to speak the word, when we attempt to express the thought, we find ourselves constrained by words that are the signs of our thoughts.[20] The possibility of error or deception comes only with the task of expressing our inner words. Descartes marveled at this: "for although I am considering these things within myself silently and without words, nevertheless I latch onto words themselves and I am very nearly deceived by the ways in which people speak."[21] But here, Descartes would contend, we must simply exercise caution and seek clarity of expression in order to avoid error.

Augustine, Descartes, and many others believed that language operates as an innocent instrument that, with some care, can be used in a nonprejudicial way to externalize thoughts that occur within a nonlinguistic *cogito*. From the viewpoint of hermeneutics, however, language is never innocent. It is laden with tradition; it embodies thought, not as a mere expression of thought, but in such a way that, without language, thought would be empty. Thinking is something that is carried on, not within an isolated *cogito*, but within language. Language limits or expands thinking, but always determines it. Within this determination we may choose to use language in a certain way, but our ability to use language is always conditioned by the larger and more comprehensive power that language has to determine our thinking. After all, as Gadamer points out, language is not something that we invent. Language is given to us and we must learn to play within it. The "language game" that twentieth-century philosophers often discuss is not a game that we humans set the rules for; it is a game that language plays with us, and that we necessarily participate in. Language sets boundaries to our understanding; but it also empowers our understanding.

Two of Heidegger's ideas on language are important here. The first is that language is so essential to human existence that it pervades all human activities. The second is that we do not control language so much as language controls us. In *Being and Time* Heidegger sets out to show that language is not just something that we use but that it belongs to human existence in an essential way. In an obvious way it is accomplished by the human body; it expresses the human spirit. Without the ability to use language—and this is not limited to speech but includes listening, keeping silent, and any form of communication—the human being would not be human. Language is a necessary condition for human existence.

In his later works, Heidegger emphasizes that language not only has this essential connection to the human being, but is essentially bound up with Being itself. Indeed, Heidegger calls language "the house of Being" wherein Being and all entities dwell.[22] This means that in the human use of language, language is the expression of something larger than human existence: the use of language by man is at the same time the use of man by Being. Language is not something that we have complete control over; language, in some sense, has control over us. Heidegger describes this as follows: "Man acts as though *he* were the shaper and master of language, while in fact *language* remains the master of man."[23]

The hermeneutical principle employed by Gadamer, that all interpretation is linguistic, derives from these Heideggerian ideas. Gadamer suggests that the model of dialogue or conversation captures the essentially linguistic relations we have to traditions. Tradition, however, "is not simply a process that experience teaches us to know and govern; it is language [*Sprache*], i.e., it expresses itself like a 'thou' [*Du*]. A 'thou' is not an object, it relates itself to us" (TM 358). We, as interpreters, are involved in our dialogical relationships with various traditions through the medium of language. Language, in such a relation, is not a means or mechanism used to make the connection to a distant tradition; it is the process of our communion with a tradition.

Gadamer's characterization of this relation as an "I-thou" dialogue is problematic. In this "dialogue," a tradition is not an object which confronts us, or even a "thou" whom we encounter face on; rather, traditions tend to locate themselves covertly behind our interpretations. If interpretation is a conversation, it is more akin to "the silent course of a conversation that moves us," suggested by Heidegger.[24] Gadamer's notion of an I-thou dialogue confuses the issue somewhat and fails to capture the genuine communion shared by interpreter and tradition. The important thing is to see that this relationship is, in all cases, an *anterior* relation: it operates not only "behind the back" but also out ahead of the interpreter. Only in specialized cases (as in historical studies) does the interpreter thematize traditions and make them the object of interpretation, or a "thou" to converse with. Even in these specialized cases, however, traditions still maintain their primary and universal anterior operations, placing constraints upon even our historiological understanding of tradition.

Consider the following example. My daughter receives a Christmas present, the utility of which is not immediately obvious. We are confronted by something that is unfamiliar. Our immediate reaction is to begin talking about it. Even if I am alone, perhaps inspecting presents on Christmas eve, my first reaction is to make some remark. The remark is not addressed to the thing, directly, but to myself. Yet within that "interior" discourse I include the thing. Even my monologue is dialogical, not in the sense of "talking with another," but in the literal sense of "talking something through": it includes reference to some object of interpretation. The language which forms my discourse, however, is not the object which I (or we) directly interrogate with questions about utility, safety, satisfaction, and so on, which reflect my (or our) particular circumstance as interpreter(s). We interrogate the unfamiliar thing. Of course, our questions, our fore-conceptions, could not even be framed without language. The influence of language is something already there—something that works to allow my discourse, or our conversation, to operate with its included reference to the thing. Language allows me to confront the unfamiliar. But if language-in-use is not the object of my interpretation, neither is it simply a tool which I use or manipulate in order to perform my interrogation. In a sense, I am my language. The transparency of language, the fact that language functions both "behind my back" and in an anterior way, the fact that I see through language, means that my essential relation to language and to the tradition which it carries is not an overt, "I-thou," "con-frontal" one. It can be overt and confrontal only in specialized cases where a tradition or a language is the object of interpretation. To turn the specialized case into the universal rule is to distort our usual and essential anterior relation to language and traditions.

For similar reasons, our relation to a tradition should not be conceived of on the model of translation. If one says, as Habermas once put it, that "the appropriation of a tradition through understanding follows the pattern of translation,"[25] and means that the tradition is the thing translated, this is true only in the specialized cases when a tradition is the direct object of interpretation. If one is involved in translating a foreign language into a familiar one—an unknown into a known—tradition is not the direct object of that translation, but again plays its anterior role, a role similar to the one played by the grammar of the familiar language. The "appropriation" of tradition is really an appropriation of our interpretational practices by what Habermas calls the "tradition-context of language." This appropriation is balanced against the "tendency to self-transcendence embedded in linguistic practice" and the correlative character of language as an enabling condition.[26] The tradition context of language comes into play, not as an explicit act of translation or as a frontal I-thou relationship, or only in special cases where tradition is the object of interpretation. All under-standing involves the "interplay of the movement of tradition and the movement of the interpreter" (TM 293), but in an anterior fashion. Conversation and dialogue are processes "which happen to us," rather than ones we conduct, only if we stand in this anterior relation to tradition and language.

I do not mean to reject the idea that interpretation can be modeled on conversation. In a conversation, however, language functions both as a medium between interlocutors and as the vehi-cle of a tradition. In this latter role, the essential hermeneutical function of a tradition is not to be an interlocutor, or a "thou" in the conversation. Rather, traditions function in a constraining rela-tion, operating in an anterior, yet "behind the back" fashion. If there is no direct dialogue between interpreter and tradition, I do not mean to deny an indirect, dialectical interchange between them. We should distinguish this indirect interchange from the other, more direct interchange that takes place in interpretation, that is, the dialogue (conversation) between interpreter and inter-preted, which we previously described in terms of the hermeneuti-cal circle. Direct and indirect interchanges are, of course, related: the indirect interchange (the anterior relation) with tradition in-forming the fore-conceptions upon which an interpretation is based, and the direct interchange, as a whole, feeding back to effect an adjustment of the interpreter's relation to tradition. The follow-ing diagram represents these two dialectical relations as a complex of hermeneutical relations.

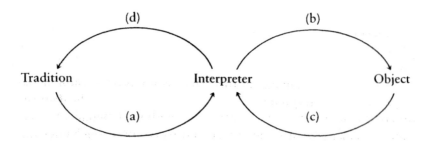

In this figure, the anterior operation of tradition (a) constrains (conditions, suggests) the fore-conceptions (b) which the inter-preter employs to interpret that which requires interpretation (the object, or an interlocutor). The feedback (c), or alternatively, the interlocutor's response in a conversation, will motivate a new projection of meaning. Thus, the relations (b) and (c) represent the hermeneutical circle, as proposed by Heidegger and Gadamer, or as explained by Hirsch's notion of the corrigible schema. In the process of interpretation, the interpreter's relation to a particular tradition can change (d). This change, which involves a transformation of the tradition, will be discussed in more detail below (Chapter 5).

Although language permeates all of these interchanges, the primary linguistic nature of interpretation can be traced to the first, anterior relation (a); in other words, language conditions our interpretations, and in so doing introduces the constraints of tradition. Only in certain specialized cases will we find that interpretation is linguistic in another, secondary way, that is, in those cases where the object of interpretation is language, for example, in an actual conversation or in reading a text. Often in such cases a tradition also turns out to be the object of interpretation, even while it never ceases to condition interpretation in its anterior fashion. In reference to the general principle, however, Gadamer is right to say that linguistic interpretation "is the form of all interpretation, even when what is to be interpreted is not linguistic in nature—i.e., is not a text but a statue or a musical composition."[27] His model of dialogue or conversation, however, sometimes confuses these relations— specifically by taking the specialized case as the model of the primary, hermeneutical relation. This is precisely what happens when Gadamer suggests that we encounter the tradition as a "thou."

Interpretation is linguistic; that is, interpretation occurs "from out of" language. Language conditions, sets limits to, yet at the same time makes possible our interpretations of the world. As Gadamer notes, language, in this sense, is not a possession at the disposal of the interpreter (see TM 378–379). Rather, the disposition of the interpreter is to be caught up within a language. Understanding emerges within language and works itself out under the influence of a language which transcends interpreter and interpreted. Gadamer cites Hönigswald: "language is not only a fact, but a principle" (TM 404, n.17).

The work of Piaget and his followers counts as an objection

against this principle and this view of language. Piaget contends that interpretive intelligence precedes language. Language is one among a number of semiotic or symbolic or representational functions, including imitation, symbolic play, drawing, and mental images, which are acquired after some ability to interpret has already developed in the child. Language is defined by Piaget as a symbol or sign system of "differentiated signifiers" which the child learns only after she already commands a system of prelinguistic "undifferentiated signifiers."[28] A signifier is undifferentiated to the extent that it is identical with or copresent with the signified, for example, the presence of food signifying it is time to eat. Differentiated signs emerge around the second year of childhood, when "certain behavior patterns appear which imply the representative evocation of an object or event not present."[29] According to Piaget, there is already a certain logic built into the undifferentiated signifiers of prelinguistic action which helps to structure linguistic behavior. He concludes that "language does not constitute the source of logic but is, on the contrary, structured by it. The roots of logic are to be sought in the general coordination of actions (including verbal behavior), beginning with the sensorimotor level, whose schemes are of fundamental importance."[30] Language, therefore, does not guide thought, but vice versa: language itself would not develop without prelinguistic cognitive processes.

In this view, the learning of language would depend on one's ability to interpret. The psychologist Hans Furth notes this in the following way: "In other types of symbol behavior [e.g., imitation or mental images] we speak freely of the production or formation of symbols; with language it appears to be first a problem of comprehension, followed only afterwards by expression or production."[31] In this view, language has no power of its own; it receives its power from the speaker who, out of his cognitive experience, decides how to employ signs proper to a situation.

Gadamer would argue that the system of undifferentiated signifiers which Piaget, in his early work on children's language, characterized as a "language of gestures, movement and mimicry" is genuinely linguistic in nature.[32] For Gadamer, it is language that acquires us rather than we who acquire language. More recent research on language acquisition would support Gadamer's view.

In their recent and exhaustive summary of this literature, Bates, O'Connell, and Shore state:

> Language development is a process that begins early in infancy. . . .

> Infants in the first few weeks of life can hear most and perhaps all of the phonological contrasts that are used by human language.

> In the first 2–3 weeks of life, infant sounds are restricted primarily to crying and a familiar set of "vegetative noises." Laughing and cooing begin at 2–3 months of age, and systematic play with speech sounds . . . [at 3 months] (when infants also begin to play games of reciprocal imitation or "vocal tennis" with their caretakers).

> Babbling does seem to indicate that children are "tuned in" to language in a new and very explicit way.[33]

If the recent research literature is right, then language plays a role in the infant's development long before it comes to the point of speaking. The infant's language may in fact be, as Piaget suggests, an ambiguous system of undifferentiated signifiers where the rule is one of identity rather than differentiation. The mother's voice, for example, does not represent the mother; it is identical with the mother.[34] This does not mean, however, that language is just one other object in the infant's environment. The central issue is not, as Furth would insist, to what extent language assists in the development of logical operations;[35] nor is the claim made, on the other side, that more language or a better grasp of language will necessarily lead to improved logical operations. Concerning the relationship between language and thought, the issue is whether thought develops outside of and independent of language. Intelligence can be given a priority over language only if language is understood in an objective and narrow manner. But speech is not learned by the child in an intellectual operation; rather, as Merleau-Ponty suggests, "what is involved is a kind of *habituation*."[36] We come to inhabit language; we find ourselves caught up in a "whirlwind of language"[37] before we know it.

If language is a more basic experience which acquires the child, sweeps the child up into a "linguistic whirlwind," and immerses the child in a linguistic world from the very beginning, then certainly all interpretation is linguistic. Even if no consensus can be reached concerning the definition of language, we do not have to understand the two views represented here as necessarily contradictory to one another. Could not the narrow definition of language given by Piaget fit within and add specification to the wider definition offered by Gadamer? Gadamer indicates as much. He states: "language is never separated from gesture. Also, it depends for its own elaboration on experiences which are more or less formed at a pre-linguistic age, as Piaget has pointed out. I have no doubt that this is true."[38] Some clarification of these hermeneutical issues may be found in educational experience and the role played by language therein.

LANGUAGE IN EDUCATIONAL EXPERIENCE

Language constitutes not only the earliest subject-matter, but also at every stage, the predominating medium of education.[39]

In spite of fundamental disagreements on the nature of language, all sides agree that language is an important aspect of educational experience. Piaget finds evidence that language can "increase the powers of thought in range and rapidity" and adds that "language plays a particularly important role in the formative process." He recognizes the obvious "positive contribution" made by language as "a kind of education of thinking."[40] Gadamer, referring us back to the concept of play, also indicates the importance of language in educational experience: "*Language games* exist where we, as learners—and when do we cease to be that?—rise to the understanding of the world" (TM 490). In order to follow out our exploration of the hypothesis that all learning involves interpretation, we need to clarify in more specific terms the linguistic nature of educational experience. Toward that end we pose two questions to guide our discussion: (a) Is language itself something that is learned? (b) In what way does language condition the learning process?

To the first question one may be tempted to immediately answer in the affirmative. Relying on one's own memory, one might say, "Yes, I remember learning grammar and vocabulary in primary school." Language is something that is studied and learned. No one will deny that we learn language in this sense. More precisely, we learn *a language*. But in doing so we study something that we already know; we learn to formalize, fine-tune, and expand what we already practice. Indeed, in order to learn grammar and vocabulary, we must employ a language that we already have. So this first answer really pushes the question back to the original acquisition of language.

Concerning the acquisition of language, we encounter several different views about whether the process of acquisition is a learning process. One answer, offered by Noam Chomsky, is that there are certain aspects of language that are innate rather than learned.[41] Chomsky argues that the deep-structure knowledge of linguistic universals, such as the categories of subject and predicate, is innate, whereas the surface structures of particular languages are learned. Piaget, on the other hand, responds that all aspects of language are learned on the basis of prelinguistic "symbolic functions."[42] In the first two years of life the child develops a prelinguistic understanding of language that prepares him to acquire his language skills. D. W. Hamlyn, for example, sides with Piaget, against Chomsky, by trying to show that the deep structures of language are learned in prelinguistic behavior, or specifically, prelinguistic communication. An understanding of language, he argues, eventually emerges in the child from communication with other people (especially the parents), and this prepares the child for the specific capacity of talking around age two.[43]

Those theorists that maintain that the acquisition of language is a learning process usually picture the child thinking about, considering, or conceptualizing certain phenomena which the child then comes to recognize as language or grammatical structure. When the child is prelinguistically prepared, she then recognizes language as something worth learning. According to Hamlyn, before the child actually acquires language, she must form the ideas of subject and predicate, as well as other deep-structure grammatical conceptions. The child will also have an understanding of what language is, that is, "the use of sounds as a means of communication" (p. 104). The child will have a "growing consciousness" or "awareness of communication as an aim" (p. 106), and an understanding and/or use of symbols (p. 109). Only then is the child ready to acquire language in the proper sense.

I focus on Hamlyn's account because I agree with most of the empirical observations he cites, although I view his interpretations of them to be incorrect. Consider the following empirical observations cited and interpreted by Hamlyn. (a) "It is well known that many children jabber away, before learning to speak in the proper way, in sounds that have something linguistic about them" (p. 104). Hamlyn interprets this to mean that the child has some primitive understanding of what language is. (b) "Parents communicate with pre-linguistic children by gestures, actions and expressions, as well as by talking to them" (p. 104). Hamlyn interprets: the child comes to understand what language is through her experience of such communication. (c) Even before the child talks or knows anything about language, (1) there is something propositional about the child's thought (pp. 76–77, 105ff.); and (2) the child has "some understanding of, and perhaps use of, symbols" (p. 109). Hamlyn's interpretation: despite what appears to be cognitive activity with a linguistic nature, these characteristics of the child's behavior are prelinguistic and remain prelinguistic until the child gains an understanding of truth and falsity, concepts that are at the center of language (p. 112).

What Hamlyn treats as accessory behavior I consider to be essential. The point overlooked by Hamlyn and other theorists is that language acquisition is not identical with the acquisition of speech. The acquisition of language does not begin at age two, when the child begins to speak. It begins at birth, or even in prenatal experience. The "jabbering" of children is, in fact, linguistic behavior, but does not mean that the child knows anything about language. The fact that parents do not wait for the child to begin speaking before they speak to the child, or the fact that in some cultures they speak to the child even before his birth, is essential in understanding that the child is born into a linguistic environment that begins to condition his behavior from the very start. If the child begins to perceive the world in an organized way, if the child's primitive thought patterns are somewhat propositional, and if the child is capable of symbolic behavior, it is not because the child understands what he is doing, or understands anything about language, but because, from the very beginning, the child begins to find himself in a world that is organized linguistically. As Merleau-Ponty expresses it, "the whole of the spoken language surrounding the child snaps him up like a whirlwind, tempts him by its internal articulations, and brings him *almost* up to the moment when all this noise begins to mean something."[44] The acquisition of language is similar to the development of motor coordination; it is not something that the child takes over, but something that takes over the child. It is more like the unintentional formation of habit; we fall into it rather than learn it. The one who is snapped up by the whirlwind of language "does not hold before himself the words said, understood as objects of thought or ideates. He possesses them only by a *Vorhabe* which is of the same type as the *Vorhabe* of place by my body that betakes itself unto that place."[45]

We are led back to the distinction between language as the system of differentiated signifiers (Piaget) and language as a way of being (Gadamer). Language as a system of differentiated signifiers is learned, but language as a way of being is not learned. But in saying this, we do not have to adopt Chomsky's viewpoint, that certain aspects of language are innate. Rather, we can borrow Piaget's distinction between development and learning,[46] and say that language as a way of being is developed rather than learned. Language as a way of being is not, in the original acquisition, an object of study. It is not something alien to the child because from the very beginning he finds himself immersed in it. His own developing self-concept is cotemporal with his progressive immersion in language. In more dramatic terms, we could say that language acquisition is not the acquisition of language by the child, whereby the child first learns what language is and then learns to use it. Rather, language acquisition is the acquisition of the child by language.

If language as a way of being is not something that is learned, but something that develops within us, or we in it, this does not mean that later on we do not learn language as a system of differentiated signifiers. But in making language an object of study and practice, we are already using language. And this points to the more general fact that in learning anything we depend on language. In a rough way this is the implication of the hermeneutical principle under consideration: all interpretation is linguistic. Language conditions all learning. Educational experience is linguistic experience. Moreover, the result of this linguisticality is that the boundaries of learning are set up by the various traditions embedded in our own particular language. Our educational experience, as Gadamer says, commits us to a direction of thought that "comes from afar and reaches on beyond [us]" (TM 548).

The linguistic nature of educational experience may seem clear. As we noted in the beginning of this section, even Piaget and his followers recognize the important role played by language in the learning process. The teacher lectures and the student listens and takes notes. Or the teacher elicits discussion and the student participates through words. From the primary-school recitation, to the secondary-school discussion; from the college lecture to the educated person's ability to express herself and articulate a point of view, language seems to be the conduit of education. Learning ability might even be characterized as the ability to translate what one hears or reads into what one can say. Obviously, the interpretation of linguistic events (lectures, texts, conversations) plays an important role in learning. But these observations do not tell the whole story. Several questions remain: Precisely how is language able to conduct learning? And, in this educational process, how does language act as the vehicle of tradition?

It is important to distinguish between "language-in-use" and language taken as an object. The former has hermeneutical significance and is what conditions and enables learning. When we make language into an object in, for example, the study of grammar or vocabulary, we still depend on the use of language which remains outside of our focused object. There is a transparency to language-in-use which Michael Polanyi nicely summarizes: "when we use words in speech or writing we are aware of them only in a subsidiary manner."[47] Language-in-use is like the windowpane that, without calling any attention to itself, or getting in the way of our vista, allows us to focus on objects outside. But language is not only transparent. It also structures our interpretations in a way that we usually remain unaware of. Language, like the windowpane, has a certain shape of its own which, outside of the user's awareness, may magnify or diminish the objects seen through it. Like the windowpane, language can have a distorting effect. But even more than this, and here the analogy with the window fails, language is not only an aperture to an already made world, but helps to constitute that world. It would be as if the window played a part in designing the objects that could be seen through it.

This hermeneutical view of language, as transparent, as structuring interpretation, and as helping in some degree to constitute that which gets interpreted, does not fit into the traditional view of learning. Augustine, for example, argues that the teacher does not convey knowledge through language.[48] In his view realities represented in knowledge must be present to the mind independently of language. Language does not function as a signifier of reality; the teacher's words function to merely "prompt" the student to seek realities on his own. If the student only appropriated words from the teacher, he would end up with what Plato calls a belief or opinion, but would not genuinely know or understand the subject matter. Thus, for Augustine, knowledge does not rest on the authoritative employment of language; the student must find out for himself within the interior of his own mind. Learning requires something more than words; it is a matter of insight rather than verbal communication.

Scheffler opposes Augustine's views about language and learning, but only in some respects. He agrees that learning is not simply the assimilation of linguistic information and that knowledge requires something more. But Scheffler contends that the information communicated by the teacher is a necessary condition for the student to be able to go further on his own. Thus, for Scheffler, language has an essential role to play in the educational process. Specifically, language carries information, and although this is not knowledge, it is necessary for knowledge to come about. Still, for Scheffler, language amounts to "external suggestion," and learning requires more. Thus he states, "One cannot convey new knowledge by words alone. For knowledge is not simply a storage of information by the learner."[49] It requires "personal engagement with reality." But here Scheffler is not so distant from the Augustinian tradition. For both thinkers, language, even if it contains information, is empty of genuine thought.

Neither Augustine nor Scheffler gives language its hermeneutical due. In Augustine language has no essential role to play in education; in Scheffler language is simply a container of information. If, however, we press Scheffler further by asking what he means by a "personal engagement with reality," the hermeneutical significance of language becomes apparent. "To initiate the child into the rational life is to *engage* him in the critical *dialogues* that relate to every area of civilization."[50] Personal engagement with reality is not some dumbstruck prelinguistic confrontation between student and raw nature. According to Scheffler, the model to be used to describe engagement is not Platonic vision (as in Augustine) but is one that must emphasize "the processes of deliberation, argument, judgment, appraisal of reasons *pro* and *con*, weighing of evidence, appeal to principles, and decision-making."[51] Moreover, none of this takes place in a mind isolated from the public practices of civilization. Tradition, Scheffler notes, "is a better guide here . . . than appeal to the innate structure of the human mind."[52]

The implications of Scheffler's descriptions give to language a more essential role in educational experience than Scheffler might want to admit. To engage ourselves with reality is to engage in a dialogue; to learn is to engage the language that surrounds us. Reality itself is interpreted by an understanding conditioned by language. We do not come face to face with brute fact; in our hermeneutical projections, we encounter a meaningful world which is not independent of the language we use to express it. To deliberate, to argue, to judge, to appraise, and so on—these are all ways that we enter into dialogue with the world. Such dialogue is made possible by language and itself constitutes the learning process.

The thought contained in language should not be conceived of as neutralized bits of information which can be retrieved from language and put together to construct meaning. Language carries the process of tradition in its thought. As Descartes' daemon teaches us, tradition is something within us rather than a collection of external bygone facts; moreover, it does not institute itself within us by some magical osmosis. It institutes itself, and has its instituting power by way of the language that we find ourselves immersed in. Traditions are embedded in language through the history of words, in the development of their meaning, and thus find their way into the categories of our thinking. Learning is not the collecting of information in an isolated mind; it involves the dialectical interplay between ourselves and traditions which we find within ourselves because we are linguistic beings.

The relationships between language and learning can be further clarified if we return to the concept of play as educational experience. It has been shown, in a variety of theoretical approaches, that language involves play. Wittgenstein, for instance, explores the idea that our uses of language can be characterized as a collection of language games and that words play different roles in different contexts so that a word cannot be employed univocally across a number of different circumstances. Words involve a play of usages in a "multiplicity of language-games."[53] Exploring language from a different perspective, the structuralist tradition, from Saussure to Derrida, has shown that linguistic signs have meaning only in a play of diacritical differences, an unending play which lacks a transcendental signified.[54] Nor does Heidegger fail to call attention to the play of language: "If we may talk here of playing games at all, it is not we who play with words, rather, the essence of language plays with us."[55] Gadamer, in agreement, suggests that "word and dialogue undoubtedly include within them an aspect of the game," so that language not only preserves but also alters, involves not only appropriation but also transcendence.[56] Gadamer refers to this as the "speculative" structure of language by which an infinity of meaning is played out in finite language games (see TM 456ff.). Sources as varied as Freud and Piaget join the chorus to indicate that in some aspect language involves play or constitutes a "field of play."[57]

Although the analyses underlying these insights have implications for educational theory, the question that we are concerned with at present is not whether and how language involves play, but whether and how play, as a form of educational experience, involves language. If it is clear that language is a necessary condition for formal learning situations (such as classroom experience, lectures, writing, reading), can we make the more comprehensive claim that language is a necessary condition for all learning, even the most informal experience of play?

There are some obvious ways in which play involves language. Certainly, one might appeal to a list of empirical examples of the more advanced games that could not be played without language operating either in interpersonal communication among players or in the formal establishment of rules which not only regulate play but establish gaming traditions. In this regard it is notable that in some cases the preservation of tradition is the only or the main reason that the games are sustained. One could also cite consciously formulated verbalized play used in educational settings.[58] But what about less formalized play? There are two clear and common cases of play in infancy that require language. The first involves the infant's playing with the voice and pronunciation. The second case includes play which involves the infant with others. The classic example here is the game of "peekaboo" in which vocalization is initially required. If the need for vocal stimulation later declines, it is only because it has been internalized by the infant.[59]

If we understand language to include undifferentiated signifiers, then even the most primitive sorts of human play activity must have a linguistic dimension. Piaget, for instance, in an early essay on language and the child, maintains that "the language used in the fundamental activity of the child—play—is one of gestures, movement, and mimicry as much as of words."[60]

Even if we establish, on the basis of empirical observation, that language is involved in all forms of human play, this does not demonstrate its hermeneutical significance, or the fact that language is a specific conditioning factor of play as educational experience. To do this we need to pursue the idea that play as educational experience always follows the play of language. More precisely, as we have already seen, language helps to constitute that which gets interpreted. In other words, language helps, in an essential way, to create meaning. But play can be considered educational experience only to the extent that it involves us in a meaningful world. So to the extent that play involves us in meaning, it must be conditioned by language.

One could turn to any number of theorists to find support for the proposition that meaning requires language, or that meaning is linguistic. Both Heidegger and Gadamer could help us here. But let's look for confirmation from a different quarter. John Dewey, for example, proposes precisely this view. He argues that meaning is primarily a property of linguistic behavior, and that in our language use we bestow meaning on our environment. "When we name an event, calling it fire, we speak proleptically; we do not name an immediate event; that is impossible. We employ a term of discourse; we invoke a meaning, namely, the potential consequences of the existence."[61] In effect, events acquire meaning through a projection of language, a linguistic anticipation of certain possibilities in the situation; "meanings do not *come into being* without language."[62] Dewey does not mean this relation to be an external or causal one. For him there is an intrinsic connection between language and meaning.

Play, like any educational experience, opens up our possibilities for us as already structured with a particular meaning or set of meanings only from within language. Language, like play, in its own play, involves transcendence—it carries us outside of ourselves so that we are always more than the Augustinian *verbum interius*. Moreover, being within language involves a transcendence of language. This transcendence depends on the transparency of language. In using language I do not maintain a "verbal image" before my mind, or represent words to myself as I use them. "The more language is a living operation, the less we are aware of it" (PH 65). This transparency of language allows for the appearance of meaning. When we read, for example, normally our thematic concern is not for the words but for what the words deliver—meaning. When we listen to another person, unless her words get in the way, we listen through her words in order to understand *what* she is saying. Language works behind the back of the speaker, or listener, or reader, outside of his or her conscious control, and allows meaning to manifest itself "out front."

Meaning requires language in order to manifest itself. If through language we are set up in an order of meaning, this does not mean that meaning is reducible to language. For the hermeneutical tradition from Schleiermacher to Gadamer, the play of language involves a shifting ambiguity, a lack of fixity between language and meaning. "Language as language never allows the ability of meaning to shift to terminate completely. . . . The real life of language takes place in such fashion that every repetition not only preserves but also alters, so that original meanings fade out of language through new fixation of meaning and yet are present in it."[63] The preservation and alteration, the recovery and transcendence, involved in the play of language allows for both the constitution of meaning and the instability of meaning. There can be an interplay of language and meaning (as in metaphor, metonymy, puns, and so on) only because there is no coincidence between them: language always transcends meaning, and meaning always transcends language. It is precisely for this reason that interpretation is required.

Interpretation is the attempt to get to the meaning of something. In the same sense, learning also involves meaning. Whatever is learned is meaningful. Even if one sets out to memorize nonsense syllables, meaningless series of letters, the learning takes place within some context which bestows meaning on their meaninglessness. They may be nonsensical precisely in order to have significance for psychological testing, and in that learning situation one is aware that the meaninglessness of the series is precisely its meaningfulness. In general, no matter how meaningless a lesson looks, one learns it only by putting it into a context of meaning. Even if the meaningful context is not apparent to the learner, she will guess at one or invent one and only in that way learn the apparently meaningless facts. This is simply another way to explain how we go about learning the unfamiliar—that is, by putting it into a familiar context.

One aspect of a meaningful context is its coherent structure. The world hangs together; it is collected together in such a fashion that the familiar throws light on the unfamiliar, the meaningful gives meaning to the meaningless. The coherence or structure of meaning is an open structure that allows for the assimilation or accommodation of the unfamiliar.

Play, insofar as it involves learning, involves meaning. Play takes its orientation from a meaningful context which is structured by our own possibilities; play involves us in a transcendence toward the world, toward our own possibilities. It is an intentionality, a reaching out for meaning even in our confrontation with the unfamiliar, or in the appropriation of unexpected possibilities. Coherence or structure is granted to the world in the dialectical interplay of transcendence and appropriation.

Gadamer speaks of the concept of structure with reference to play and the work of art, specifically theater. When play becomes *a play*, for example, a theatrical production, a transformation takes place. Gadamer calls this "the transformation into structure" in which play takes on the characteristics of a work, an *érgon*. Abstracting from this focus on theatrical play, we can characterize structure in more general terms. In these general terms we would say that play leads us to a transformation of meaning. Just as there is a transformation of the self in play, so also there is a transformation of meaning. "Above all," Gadamer writes, "what no longer exists is the world in which we live as our own. Transformation into structure is not simply transposition into another world" (TM 112). In play we do not simply move from one preconstituted world into another; rather, our existing world is transformed into a new one, one which was potentially there in our "undecided possibilities." The transformation in(to) structure takes place when what is unfamiliar or meaningless is finally integrated into the meaningful. But this integration not only transforms the unfamiliar; it transforms the familiar. The world of meaning opened up by play "is in fact a wholly transformed world" (TM 113).

Play involves the player in an original kind of "instruction." Originally, the Latin *instruere* meant, not simply to teach, but to put into order, to set up a structure, to build, to put into form. This involves more than simply passing along information. Instruction, in this original sense, is the very process of formation that can be found in the play situation. What is it that allows for such instruction or formation to take place? Gadamer indicates a general answer: "It is in language games, for example, that the child becomes acquainted with the world. Indeed, everything we learn takes place in language games."[64] More precisely, language conditions the instruction that occurs in play because meaning requires language. If the linguistic condition is missing, if play does not involve this linguistic dimension, it is reduced to meaningless movement. It is quite possible to speak of the "play of light," or the "play of physical forces," and to say that in themselves such movements have no significance, no meaning, until they become integrated into a human world, that is, until they become interpreted, which is only possible on the condition of language. So to be precise, we should say that the play of language is the necessary condition for every educational play, that is, for every play that involves human understanding and meaning.

It follows as a general conclusion that all educational experience, whether formal (in classroom relations, lectures, writing, reading, and so forth) or informal (in play), is linguistic. Language is a necessary condition for learning. Whether we set out to learn music or dance or to appreciate a work of art, we do not do so simply by mute staring; we find ourselves immersed in a linguistic universe that orders our interpretations. Learning takes place "by way of" language; it is accomplished, in the first place, in language.[65] Learning involves a hermeneutical "listening" ordered to language itself. This listening, as an instruction, a process of formation, is also the informing process of tradition. In learning we participate in the authority of the tradition, we "obey" it, which means that we open our ears to it, or harken to (*obedire*) tradition, insofar as we hear (*audire*) in our listening to language.

CHAPTER 5

Hermeneutical Possibilities

Hermeneutical constraints, although they are in some sense limitations, are not detriments to learning; they do not imprison our understanding but allow it to flourish. Language and the process of tradition are enabling conditions for learning because they provide the context of familiarity by which we can approach the unfamiliar. They operate as the necessary conditions for the acquisition and advancement of knowledge. As Gadamer remarks, "in tradition there is always an element of freedom and of history itself" (TM 281), just as language "means at once both constraint and freedom for the individual."[1] The fore-structure of understanding limits, but also opens up, hermeneutical possibilities.

Because the hermeneutical situation is never closed off, the learning process does not issue some ready-made or finalized product that is simply passed on from teacher to student. In exploring this lack of closure we will see that even though the authoritative power of tradition biases educational experience from the very beginning, learning still includes the possibility of challenging authoritative frameworks. Traditions are not simply reproduced or accommodated, but are advanced and reformed in the learning process.

In a different context Michel Foucault suggests that hermeneutics operates in the manner of an economic welfare function. It attempts to react to "enunciative poverty, and to compensate for it by a multiplication of meaning."[2] A different kind of multiplier effect is seen if we change the economic metaphor, and employ the principle of "the gains from trade." This principle, which is not uncontroversial in economic debate, states that one economic unit (such as, a nation) is always better off if it enters into trade with another unit than if it remains autarkic or self-sufficient. In a similar way, we can suggest that there will always be gains from interpretation—someone is always better off if he enters into her-

123.

meneutical processes of interpretation and educational experience than if he remains closed off to those possibilities. On this metaphor we can ask about the conflict between principles of *autárkeia* and interdependence, about what it means to be "better off" in the context of interpretation and learning, and about a hermeneutical sense of *trade* which explores the various meanings of this term: a course, a passage, a practice, an application, a calling, mutual communication, a schooling, a familiarization, a conversation.[3]

THE PRINCIPLE OF DISTANCIATION

The unfamiliar always calls for interpretation. This has been a constant theme of hermeneutics. But it is also the case that the familiar requires interpretation. At the very least, the familiar depends upon an interpretation which makes it familiar. Consider that, as philosophers often point out, the familiar is sometimes the most unfamiliar, or as Rousseau puts it, "experience of the strange leads us to examine the familiar."[4] That which is taken for granted is that which calls for the most philosophical questioning. We might say that an object of interpretation is never *absolutely* familiar or *absolutely* unfamiliar, but rather is located between these extremes. Thus Dilthey writes: "Interpretation would be impossible if the expressions of life were totally alien. It would be unnecessary if there was nothing alien in them. [Hermeneutics] thus lies between these two extreme opposites. It is required wherever there is something alien that the art of understanding has to assimilate."[5] If educational experience is primarily directed to the unfamiliar it also involves the possibility of throwing the familiar into question.

The hermeneutical situation involves not an imprisonment within a process of tradition which makes everything familiar, but what in German is called a *Spielraum*, literally, "room to play," or figuratively, "freeplay." Interpretation requires some clearance (*Abstand*) in which to play. Gadamer refers to this clearance as *Zeitenabstand*, "temporal distance." Interpretation, one might say, requires some room in which to move in its dialectic between the familiar and the unfamiliar. The context of the familiar, out of which we move toward understanding the unfamiliar, is supplied by the operations of tradition through language. The family resemblances among various language games provide the hermeneutical situation with a certain determinateness or perspective upon which our interpretations are based. But within this situation the unfamiliar must manifest itself precisely as unfamiliar and initially undetermined. The unfamiliar is not immediately overcome by familiarity; it does not spontaneously fit into the context set up by the fore-structure of understanding, but provides some resistance to understanding. The unfamiliar calls for interpretation only because it stands forth as the unfamiliar.

The principle of "distanciation" accounts for our ability to confront something as alien, unfamiliar. This principle is, as Ricoeur points out, the dialectical opposite to the principle of historical effect, and the counterpoint to the concept of appropriation.[6] Both Gadamer and Ricoeur discuss distanciation as a principle of textual hermeneutics. Gadamer is concerned primarily with the problem of historicism in Romantic hermeneutics (from Schleiermacher to Dilthey), and thus focuses on the reading of historical texts. In order to see how this principle works with regard to educational experience, we must try to move beyond the textual application and to see its more universal significance. To do this we begin with Gadamer's explanation and gradually abstract from it the essential and universal features of distanciation. We will then turn to Ricoeur to see if our abstractions can be verified in his discussion.

Gadamer begins by noting that despite the fact that the reader and the text may stand within a common tradition, the text must present itself as something in need of interpretation; it must present itself as something alien, in need of appropriation. "Hermeneutic work is based on a polarity of familiarity and strangeness. . . . Here too there is a tension. It is in the play between the traditionary text's strangeness and familiarity to us, between being a historically intended, distanciated object and belonging to a tradition" (TM 295). The description of this intermediate place (*Zwischenstellung*) is put in terms of a reader who is concerned to interpret a historical text. According to the Romantic hermeneutics of Schleiermacher, the reader should be able not only to *reproduce* the original intentions of an author, but also "to understand an author better than he understood himself." But Gadamer rejects this notion of "superior understanding" and suggests that the real dynamic that occurs in such reading is created by the historical (or temporal) distance that exists between the reader and the author. In an important passage, Gadamer explains that interpretation is always productive.

> Every age has to understand a transmitted text in its own way, for the text belongs to the whole tradition whose content interests the age and in which it seeks to understand itself. The real meaning of a text, as it speaks to the interpreter, does not depend on the contingencies of the author and his original audience. It certainly is not identical with them, for it is always co-determined also by the historical situation of the interpreter and hence by the totality of the objective course of history. . . . But this is of fundamental importance. Not just occasionally but always, the meaning of a text goes beyond its author. That is why understanding is not merely a reproductive but always a productive activity as well. (TM 296)

The historical distance between reader and author, between their relative circumstances and concerns, accounts for a difference of meaning, an interpretive productivity that goes beyond original intentions. Graham Nicholson, following Heidegger and Gadamer, rightly refers to this productivity as a transformation effected in an act of interpretation which is inescapably informed by contemporary interests. Even in the case of interpretation which is consciously intended to preserve tradition, a transformation of tradition takes place.[7]

We can easily see that this also applies to interpretation that does not involve reading a text. Gadamer notes, for example, that there is also a genuinely productive process going on in the interpretation of art (see TM 297). Following this suggestion, we can consider the case of the Vermeer forgeries. During the 1930s, Han van Meegeren, a Dutch painter, forged and sold a number of "Vermeers" in order to raise money. He was successful in selling these canvasses to several European museums. The experts and critics, honestly fooled by the forgeries, judged them to be authentic Vermeers. In 1945, van Meegeren, under the threat of prosecution for collaborating with the Nazis (he had sold one of the "Vermeers," and thus part of the Dutch national treasure, to Goering), disclosed, to the disbelief of the museum curators and art experts, that the "Vermeers" then located in various museums were not

Vermeers but forgeries. Only after a long and detailed scientific study of the alleged forgeries did the experts unanimously agree that they were painted by van Meegeren and not Vermeer.[8]

Why had the experts been deceived at first? Referring to the most famous of the forged Vermeers, Otto Kurz recounts that "when it turned up suddenly in 1937, the general chorus of enthusiasm was not broken by a single dissenting opinion. . . . In the extensive literature on the painting there was not a single word of doubt concerning the attribution to Vermeer, let alone concerning the authenticity of the painting."[9] Part of the reason for the deception was that it was a careful and brilliant forgery. But this is not the whole reason. We also have to consider how the interpretation, indeed, the perception, of Vermeer's work changes over time. Kurz gives an account of part of this change: "For the [nineteenth-century] Impressionists, Vermeer was the revolutionary painter of the 'View of Delft'. . . . For the twentieth century, Vermeer was no longer an open-air painter. Now he was admired for his quiet figures in interiors, those reticent human beings whose immovable, masklike faces refuse to communicate their inner thoughts by vulgar mimicry. Van Meegeren knew the ideals of the modern public, the 'arte non eloquente'."[10] Van Meegeren had painted a mid-twentieth-century forgery of Vermeer, one which could get by the mid-twentieth-century experts, but one which would not have gotten past the Impressionists, and, perhaps, not surprisingly, one which fails to get past graduate students today. For the past twenty years, in university art history courses, relatively inexpert students have easily determined the essential differences between the van Meegeren forgeries and original Vermeers.

How is it possible that a group of paintings can appear to be authentic at one time and dated forgeries at another time? Since the actual paintings did not change, except for some slight and imperceptible aging, it must be that either our perception of the paintings changed, or our interpretation of Vermeer's work changed, or both. Gadamer suggests that between interpreter and that which is interpreted there exists a distanciation that significantly impacts on understanding. Every age or generation understands a past work of art in its own way, for the work of art, although part of a tradition, is confronted from out of changing historical circumstances that guide interpretation. Whatever the significant aspects of Vermeer's work that served to guide van Meegeren in the production of his forgeries in the 1930s, those aspects no longer had the same significance for later generations. Later appreciation, informed by different interests, recognized that the forgeries lacked aspects that belonged to original Vermeers, as interpreted by the later appreciation. The meaning of any particular Vermeer as it appears to the interpreter does not depend entirely on the contingencies of Vermeer's own situation, or the situation of Vermeer's generation. Each generation, further removed in time from Vermeer's time, and always embedded in its own historical circumstances, interprets Vermeer differently. Every generation would define a "good" forgery in its own terms. What appears as essential in the meaning of Vermeer's work to a nation moving toward war perhaps appears as unessential in postwar times. The newness of each age's concerns redefines Vermeer and introduces an element of strangeness into the familiar.

Interpretations, therefore, never simply repeat, copy, reproduce, reconstruct, or restore the interpreted in its originality. Interpretation produces something new. A forgery is not a copy of an original work, or a simple imitation of an original style; it is an interpretation, and thus, a production of a new work. The distance between interpreter and that which gets interpreted is therefore something that positively affects interpretation. "Hence, temporal distance is not something that must be overcome. . . . In fact the important thing is to recognize temporal distance as a positive and productive condition enabling understanding" (TM 297). Productive interpretations, of course, if they are not acts of reproduction, are not pure acts of creativity ex nihilo either. Interpretation is always tempered by the process of tradition and by the object to be interpreted. It would be wrong to place too much emphasis on what is lost through time, for example, the irretrievable truth of the original intentions of author or artist. The text or the work of art does express the genius of the originator even while it elicits a creativity that goes beyond the originator. There is, thus, a *tension* between interpreter and that which is interpreted which Gadamer identifies as the "true locus," the intermediate position in which interpretation functions (TM 295).

One can discern in the above discussion several features that define the notion of distanciation in general.

(1) Distanciation involves *objectification*. That which is to be interpreted becomes an object, standing on its own: a "distanced objectivity" (*abständige Gegenständlichkeit*), as Gadamer says. It is something which confronts the interpreter as alien, other than the interpreter, unfamiliar. This, at least, is one moment of the "tension" which characterizes the hermeneutical situation.

(2) Distanciation involves *transcendence*. Here, if Ricoeur is correct in characterizing distanciation as a dialectical opposite to appropriation, we can see, from our previous discussions of play, that distanciation must in some way include transcendence. Gadamer points to the fact that the meaning of the object of interpretation always goes beyond, surpasses its originator. But the meaning of the object is not, thereby, reducible to the interpreter's meaning. It also transcends the interpreter and can be encountered only when the interpreter transcends himself, opens himself up, and allows the object of interpretation to have a say.

(3) Distanciation allows for the *productivity* of interpretation. Neither the narrow subjectivity of the interpreter nor the subjective intentions of the originator absolutely rule interpretation. The distance opened up by these two subjectivities allows for something new to emerge. The productivity of interpretation is something between pure creativity ex nihilo and pure reproduction.

(4) Distanciation involves a *projection of possibilities*. Indeed, what is produced is equivalent to our own possibilities within a situation. The projection of possibilities enters into an essential tension with historical effects. Historical effect means that we find ourselves already positioned within a tradition, in a way that cannot be completely objectified. But through distanciation we are still able to project our own possibilities, objectify them, and thereby transcend ourselves toward them.

These are four essential features of distanciation that we need to verify and explore, and to do that we turn to Paul Ricoeur's analysis. Before proceeding, however, there are two other issues that we need to raise. The first concerns the historical dimension of distanciation. Although the temporality and finitude of human understanding implies that all objects of interpretation are historical objects, this does not mean that all interpretation is necessarily or explicitly historiographical or that distanciation is only temporal. On this issue we receive some help from Ricoeur. He explicitly points out that distanciation is more than temporal distance (HHS 244). We return to this issue shortly.

The second issue concerns the concept of originator. One implication of Gadamer's discussion is that distanciation involves an originator, in the sense of author or artist. Is this something that belongs to the essence of distanciation, or is it an accessory phenomenon connected to the fact that Gadamer's discussion takes its orientation from textual hermeneutics? Here Ricoeur's analysis will not help, since Ricoeur, even more than Gadamer, takes the *text* to be the paradigm of hermeneutical theory. His analysis of distanciation speaks of an essential connection with authorship. Only in the next section, when we jettison the paradigm of text and turn to educational experience other than reading, will we discover that distanciation does not require the concept of originator.

Ricoeur's analysis clarifies the issue of the historicality of interpretation and reinforces our explication of the essential features of distanciation: objectification, transcendence, productivity, and the projection of possibilities. Ricoeur uses the paradigm of the text to work out the antithetic relations between distanciation and historical effect, or what in general Gadamer refers to as "belongingness" (*Gehörigkeit*) (see HHS 131). The text, according to Ricoeur, "is much more than a particular case of intersubjective communication: it is the paradigm of distanciation in communication" (HHS 131), and distanciation is a necessary condition for all communication (HHS 91). Moreover, through the analysis of distanciation we come to recognize the various ways in which the text, as that which needs interpretation, is autonomous.

The text lives a life of its own, beyond the intention of the author, beyond the conditions of its origination, beyond its original audience. This autonomy certainly involves what Ricoeur calls "the positive and productive function" of an "alienating distanciation," a transcending of the factors involved in the text's origination, and an objectification of the text as something independent. We can see immediately how Ricoeur would confirm the essential features of distanciation noted above. Meaning always transcends the event of origination (HHS 134); discourse is objectified, undergoes an "intentional exteriorization" (HHS 135) in a structured work (such as the literary text) and calls for interpretation (HHS 138). The text is productive of its own world, or, more precisely, in reading a text a new world of meaning is opened up (HHS 141). In this respect Ricoeur contends that interpretation involves "the projection of our ownmost possibilities." "For what must be interpreted in a text is a *proposed world* which I could inhabit and wherein I could project one of my ownmost possibilities" (HHS 142). Thus, distanciation opens the text to "an unlimited series of readings," that is, to the unlimited possibilities of interpretation that come from reading (HHS 139).

All of this testifies to "the positive and productive function of distanciation at the heart of the historicity of human experience."[11] Undeniably, all interpretation is historically situated. Both the interpreter and the object of interpretation are situated in their historical circumstances. Moreover, in the strictest sense, everything that requires interpretation is already past. Any text, event, or activity that I set out to interpret is already there, having just occurred or having a long history. Attestations to this can be found both in modern physics, which acknowledges the time differential introduced into perception by the speed of light, the speed of sound waves, and so forth, and in phenomenology, which holds that even immediate reflection can only grasp a just-past consciousness. Even our understanding of the future, strictly speaking, is an understanding of a just-past conception or expectation of the future. In this strict sense we might say that all objects of interpretation are "covertly" historical objects and that there is always a *temporal* distanciation involved in interpretation. But this does not mean that every object of interpretation is something that comes to us as an explicit monument of the past, or as an overtly historical object. Distanciation is not simply a consideration important to historians. Ricoeur helps us to see this when he states that distanciation "is not only temporal distance, as in the interpretation of texts and monuments from the past, but positive distancing; a *consciousness exposed to the efficacy of history* can understand only under the condition of distance" (HHS 244). The principle of distanciation operates not only in the interpretation of artifacts and texts of the overtly past, but also in trying to understand what in general and in the most practical sense we call the present and the future. Ricoeur's analysis of human action offers some insight into this issue.

In his hermeneutics of human action Ricoeur again uses the

text as paradigm. In this case, however, the object of interpretation—the meaningful action of another human being—is not necessarily something that comes to us from the remote or overtly historical past, but can be, in a broad sense, contemporary with our attempt to understand it. Through interpretation, action undergoes the same kind of "intentional exteriorization" or objectification which allows for the fixation of meaning in a text. The meaning of the action transcends the event of the action, just as the meaning of the text goes beyond the circumstances and intentions of its origination. "In the same way that a text is detached from its author, an action is detached from its agent and develops consequences of its own" (HHS 206). By either their direct or indirect consequences, actions can have relevance and importance in contexts beyond the originating context. Thus, Ricoeur notes, "deeds and works [are] capable of receiving relevance in new historical situations" (HHS 208). Precisely here we see the correct ordering: interpretation does not involve distanciation because of the overtly historical nature of the object of interpretation; rather, objects are able to gain overtly historical significance because of the distanciation involved in interpretation. Actions are not reducible to only the realizations of an agent's potential, but can open up new possibilities of action for all concerned, including interpreter, since "the meaning of human action is also something which is *addressed* to an indefinite range of possible 'readers'" (HHS 208). This means that human action is productive; in going beyond its relevance to its originating situation, action can open up a new world of meaning (HHS 207).

Whether the paradigm of the text reveals more about the hermeneutics of human action than it hides, as Ricoeur maintains, or hides more than it reveals, Ricoeur's analyses do serve to verify the essential operations of distanciation in interpretation. The terms *transcendence, objectification, productivity,* and *projection of possibilities* all help to point to the advent of the unfamiliar even within the familiarity which conditions the hermeneutical situation through the tradition context of language. In the process of interpretation (of texts, of works of art, of human actions, and so on) a distance is maintained between interpreter and the object of interpretation which allows for the production of new meaning and new possibilities for the interpreter. Unfamiliarity (*Fremdheit*) is an essential aspect in the dialectical interplay between interpreter and the interpreted. As Ricoeur puts it, "*Verfremdung* is not only what understanding must overcome, but also what conditions it" (HHS 140).

All interpretation occurs at a distance, and because of that, all interpretation is productive. This seems evident, at least for a hermeneutics which takes the text as its paradigm. In effect, if all interpretation is like reading, then the principle of distanciation holds. However, when we turn to educational experience we find some examples of interpretation that cannot be adequately explained by the paradigm of textuality. It is only in considering such educational experience that we can further our exploration of the connection between hermeneutics and education, and indeed verify that the principle of distanciation is a principle of all interpretation.

PRODUCTIVITY AND LEARNING

It would be easy, and in some sense productive, to follow Ricoeur's lead and to model the formal relations of student, teacher, and subject matter on the paradigm of textual interpretation. The very word *lesson*, which has its root in the Latin *lectio*, a reading or text, seems to justify such a path. One could treat the student as reader-interpreter and the teacher as the author of a *lectio*. The principle of distanciation would be operative here to the extent that the discourse of the teacher produces a meaning that goes beyond the spoken word and transcends the intention of the teacher. The objectification of the teacher's discourse opens up a plurality of possibilities for the student's understanding. This transcendence is something the teacher herself experiences. Not infrequently the teacher comprehends that what she has presented as a lesson goes even further than she had expected. Often this is the case because of something the student might see and explicate, a particular perspective that had been hidden from the teacher. Or the teacher may surprise herself with either the clarity or the style of the presentation, or the coherence of the lesson; she may feel that she knows the material better after having worked it out through her lectures. Ulmer, in alliance with Derrida, rightly

distanciation

claims that "every pedagogical exposition, just like every reading, adds something to what it transmits" (AG 162).

The distanciation which allows the teacher to learn from her own teaching finds a parallel in the distanciation between the pedagogical presentation and the student's comprehension. The alienation from the teacher of that which is taught, rather than a failure or a negative result of misinterpretation, creates the possibility of a positive emancipation of the material for the student. Productivity in learning is the rule rather than the unusual thing. Indeed, what the student may learn could easily surpass the intention of the teacher. Following Gadamer, this "going beyond" would not necessarily imply "superior understanding," but just that the student, with his own experience-based fore-conceptions, understands differently than the teacher. Productivity may not always be productivity in the proper direction. A student could fall short or miss the point, and thereby understand differently. In so doing, he may find another, unintended meaning, or he may misconstrue the lesson entirely. But whether a particular learning instance is correct or not is not the issue here. The notion of productivity has to do with the difference, the lack of coincidence between teacher and student. This difference is not always "productive" with respect to learning what one ought to learn, but it is the necessary condition for any such productive learning.

For example, the teacher's call for an exact replication of some information by the student will not guarantee an exact correspondence of interpretation. Memorizing a text, such as a poem, does not constitute learning, and we would rightly say that it is better to understand something than simply to memorize it. Even if the task of memorization remains purely mechanical on the part of the student, the possibility of an interpretation is always present. Even if the memorization remains totally mindless, as in the case of the student who perceives a poem as a series of nonsense syllables, there will be some form of meaningful understanding on his part. But with even the faintest glimmer of comprehension the call of exact replication is undermined. The student's interpretation will always be something more or less than, but at least different from, the teacher's. The student, after all, is working out of a different horizon or situation. For the student as interpreter, the text or the teacher's presentation holds a multiplicity of possible meanings, even within the hermeneutical constraints of the tradition context of language. As interpretation, learning requires more than a receptive attitude on the part of the student. The distance between the presented material and the interpretive reading of the material by the student allows a leeway that is essential to the learning process.

Everything that we could discover about educational experience by using the text as a model for the teacher-student situation we could discover simply by analyzing the actual reading of written texts. After all, the interpretation involved in reading is itself an important form of educational experience. There is no doubt that by making the reading of texts the paradigm of educational experience we could initiate a hermeneutics of the learning process that would be revealing; but it would also be limiting. To recognize these limitations one needs only to consider certain learning experiences which, if they were reduced to the textual model, would be distorted since they are not essentially textual. For example, we learn about another person through interactions which cannot be understood by reducing the other person to an author of actions. We may be involved in a learning process when we gaze at the stars or listen to music; but such gazing and listening do not follow the same dynamic as reading. Learning a performance (musical, dance, wood-working) is essentially different from the learning that goes on in reading a text. Learning mathematics, for instance, is more like learning to do something than like reading a text. Even learning to write cannot be modeled on the act of reading.

Ricoeur, while propounding the paradigm of textual hermeneutics and promoting its revelatory powers, at the same time, and unintentionally, shows the limits of the textual model by delineating the specifications of textuality that are not shared, for example, by spoken conversation (for example, HHS 198ff.). If our intention is to show that the principle of distanciation applies to all interpretation, we cannot do it by reducing every interpretation to textual interpretation. The universality of the principle of distanciation can be established only by showing that forms of interpretation other than reading are also characterized by the features of distanciation. Toward that end, as well as to continue our exploration of the connection between hermeneutics and education, we turn to educational experience without the textual paradigm.

The situation of the formal classroom, as one setting for educational experience, can be shown to reflect the four essential features of distanciation. Moreover, a consideration of this setting can clarify the nature of each of these features.

Objectification.   Within the context of the familiar, which is constituted by the tradition context of language, a teacher is called upon to present something in a lesson which is, from the point of view of the student, unfamiliar. The teacher, more than likely, recognizes the subject matter as something familiar, and yet must present it in a way so that it stands out from the familiar. If the teacher treats the subject matter as something "all too familiar," he would be wrongly assuming a familiarity with the subject matter on the part of the student. But in any instance of teaching, even when the teacher can assume that the student is in some way familiar with the subject matter, he still must make something stand out as unfamiliar, and he must call the student's attention to precisely that which is unfamiliar. The teacher thus presents the subject matter, or one aspect of the subject matter, as an unfamiliar object for learning.

Correlatively, on the student side of this relation, that which is to be learned must stand out as an unfamiliar object. That there is always an object of learning, of course, is a feature of all learning experience, and we could refer to this as the intentionality of learning. There is always some potentially meaningful object to be learned. Here the word *object* does not necessarily signify a thing or entity; rather the intentional object of learning may be a meaning, a song, a movement, an aspect, a style, a relation, a mathematical problem, and so on. When we say that the object is "potentially meaningful," we want to call attention to the fact that the unfamiliarity of the object does not constitute it as absolutely meaningless. In effect, unfamiliarity is always a relative unfamiliarity. This is especially true of a classroom situation, where the object is always presented within the context of a familiar discipline. Thus, when the teacher sets out to teach a mathematics problem, it will usually be apparent, or assumed, or explained that it is precisely a mathematical (or even more specifically, an algebraic or geometrical) problem. As such it is provided with a context which raises specific expectations in the student. But even outside of the formal educational setting, the unfamiliarity of the object will be relative to where or in what circumstances the object is encountered, and some note of familiar context will be sounded. At the very least, and in the broadest possible way, the object will be encountered as falling under some familiar category: physical thing, song, movement, aspect, relation, and so on.

This throws some light on the nature of the objectification involved in interpretational distanciation. The distanciation is not captured by the exaggerated sophistical paradox raised by Meno (see above, pp. 69ff.). We are not absolutely unfamiliar with the unfamiliar object of learning, since it is an unfamiliar object that occurs in the familiar context of the world, or on a horizon of meaning that we project toward it. The objectification here is not like the Enlightenment model of scientific, detached objectivity. In such detached objectivity everything is distance without collusion. The objectification that we find in learning experience—and the objectification that is characteristic of all interpretation—involves distance plus a collusion with the tradition-context of language. Even scientific interpretation entails objectification with collusion; there are no genuinely detached objectivities, or if there are, we can never learn about them. Since interpretation is always situated, the concept of distanciation, and the objectification which is a feature of it, must always be "placed together and in tension with" historical effects. Both Ricoeur and Gadamer fight against the illusion "that 'distance' puts an end to our collusion with the past" (HHS 74). The objectivity of the subject matter for learning is one worked out in a dialectical interplay, not only between teacher and student, but between the familiar and the unfamiliar, between the context of learning and the object that is still being learned. We can see this aspect of distanciation reflected in John Dewey's prescriptive emphasis on creating a "problematic situation" to facilitate learning. "The perplexing situation must be sufficiently like situations which have already been dealt with so that pupils will have some control of the means of handling it. A large part of the art of instruction lies in making the difficulty of new problems large enough to challenge thought, and small enough so that, in addition to the confusion naturally attending the novel elements, there shall be luminous familiar spots from which helpful suggestions may spring."[12]

Learning can take place only if objectivity is of this nature: objectivity with collusion. Only on the basis of such objectivity do we get what Gadamer refers to as a "fusion of horizons." The horizons may be characterized as the distinct horizons of teacher versus student, or within the subject matter, horizons of the familiar versus the unfamiliar, but the fusion will be one enabled only by a *relative* autonomy of the intended object of learning. Here the answer to historicism is not the timeless objectivity proposed by the antihistoricist, but an objectivity fashioned in a temporal and dialectical interplay of interpretations.

Transcendence.   We have already noted (pp. 38–39) that the pedagogical presentation or lesson includes more than an explication of the subject matter. From the teacher's perspective, the lesson must include extramaterial concerns about communication, the overall project of teaching, student situations, and so forth. These are concerns which I have termed "formal" interests. The teacher is concerned, not simply to make the material stand out as something unfamiliar, but to do so in such a way that the student will see the unfamiliarity and begin to understand in terms of the familiar. To do this the teacher must try to go beyond his own understanding of the subject matter and attempt to project how the student might begin to understand. Any realization on the teacher's part concerning such formal issues of communication may call forth some alteration or adjustment of the presentation. For the teacher, then, an aspect of transcendence is built into the whole conception of presenting a lesson, and into each actual lesson. As teacher, he goes beyond his own horizon and attempts to penetrate the student's horizon. The presentation is designed with transcendence as one of its means and ends.

In a corresponding way, on the student side, learning depends upon the willingness of the student to transcend herself toward the meaning of the presentation. Transcending herself means moving beyond the horizon formed by her own preconceptions in a way that allows these preconceptions to be challenged. Learning entails opening up the fore-structure of her understanding and projecting the possibilities of meaning that will ultimately situate the object of learning in a more familiar context. This transcendence means going beyond the once familiar context; it means risking that familiar ground in order to allow the unfamiliar to find its place.

Thus, the transcendence involved in distanciation is not simply something that happens between teacher and presentation, as if the latter were a text transcending its author. Rather, transcendence in this dialogical classroom situation means, for both teacher and student, moving beyond their own narrow horizons toward an indefinite interchange that, on both sides, presents a challenge and a risk. At the same time this is a transcendence which does not work without some complicity from that which is transcended. In some sense the pedagogical presentation transcends the teacher, but this happens only in that the teacher attempts to enter the student's horizon and the student attempts to interpret the lesson for herself. So, in another sense, the pedagogical presentation carries the teacher's challenge to the student; it transcends the teacher and yet the teacher demonstrates a complicity in accomplishing this transcendence. On the student side, learning involves a movement of the student beyond herself, her horizon, her familiar world, and yet not totally. The fore-structure of the student's understanding is not abandoned but challenged and revised.

Objectification with collusion, transcendence with complicity—these are different ways of expressing what we have already seen in the case of play as informal educational experience: transcendence always involves a dialectical interplay with appropriation. This is precisely the "tension" which forms what Gadamer characterizes as the "place of hermeneutics," the *Spielraum*, the *Abstand*. This is a place of interchange, trade, a competitive marketplace which depends on both the capital of tradition, fore-structure, and historical effects, and the risk factors attached to the innovative interpretations that are produced. The exchange of ideas which takes place in this learning process is not a simple bartering of ready-made commodities. It involves transformations of perspectives, the opening of horizons, the expansions of meaningful worlds.

Productivity. In the case of learning and interpretation the concepts of production and consumption cannot be as clearly distinguished as their analogous counterparts are in economics of the non-Marxist variety. The Marxist claim that production and consumption are two moments of one dialectical process might serve as a metaphoric clue here. In the dialectical interchange of learning, the consumption of ideas is never simply consumption; it involves productivity. The idea of productivity calls into question any view that takes education to be simply a consumption process, or a prepackaged consumer product. Educational productivity is based on the distance which necessarily exists, in this case, between student and teacher or, more generally, between the familiar and the unfamiliar. In the learning process the unfamiliar is not simply consumed by a familiar context in a one-way fashion. The familiar is also changed in the process. It is readjusted, revised, restructured, reformed, or transformed by the unfamiliar; otherwise no learning takes place.

Dewey explains the productivity of educational experience in terms of "inventiveness." "What is suggested [as, for example, a creative solution to a problem] must, indeed, be familiar in *some* context; the novelty, the inventive devising, clings to the new light in which it is seen, the different use to which it is put. . . . The educational conclusion which follows is that *all* thinking is original in a projection of considerations which have not been previously apprehended."[13] In fostering such inventiveness the teacher is not there simply to provide information for consumption. If learning is to take place, the teacher must provide the occasion or opportunity for a transformation to take place. If the teacher herself is to learn anything, she must enter into and participate in this productive process of transformation. The teacher, rather than standing off and looking on, must, as Dewey also indicates, share in the experience. "In such shared activity, the teacher is a learner, and the learner is, without knowing it, a teacher."[14]

Learning involves the student in a productivity that goes beyond the intellectual genius of either the teacher or the student. The multiplicity of possibilities found within the teacher's presentation are not all put there intentionally by the teacher. Rather they are the result of a dialectical interplay operating under the hermeneutical constraints of language and tradition. The practice of note taking may serve as an example. The teacher lectures or presents the material; the student takes notes. In the very act of taking notes the student is required to make some decisions. If a note is to summarize or to outline the essence of the lesson, the student must excise the unessential. How does the student know what is essential and what is not essential? How does the student recognize what is important and what is not? Of course, in some cases the teacher will properly emphasize certain material by using a variety of techniques peculiar to discourse or pedagogy. Such emphases are dictated by the teacher's own understanding of the particular subject matter or discipline she is presenting. The lecture, already biased in this way by the teacher's own understanding, and by the constraints of language and tradition, enters into the notes of the students. The note taker, however, does not simply take what is presented. The student's own prior knowledge of the subject matter, his own practical interests, his perception of the usefulness and relevance of the subject matter, and his knowledge of what is expected of him, for example, on examinations, determine the import of what he hears. He interprets the lecture from the perspective of his own understanding, which is shaped by language and tradition and informed by his interests and by what the teacher expects. If the notes are to be workable, if they are to be sufficient enough to lead the student to an understanding of the lecture, the student, constrained by his own knowledge, must enter that knowledge into a dialectic with the presented material. He must project his own possibilities into the presented material in order for this meaning to appear.

The student proposes an interpretation that belongs not simply to himself, since he does not invent the meaning. But neither is the interpretation simply a reproduction of the teacher's presentation. The student's interpretation must find its way into a wider circle of meaning defined by the tradition context of language. In so doing, the limits of meaning are expanded, both for the student and in themselves. This implies a transformation, not only of the student, but of tradition itself. The "reality" of the material presented is subject to the possibilities projected by the student, possibilities projected on the basis of prior knowledge and within the changing constraints of the tradition context of language. The hermeneutical constraints are not dead absolutes that define truth once and for all. The boundaries of traditions and language are constantly being pushed outward as the student's interpretation enters the broader circle of meaning.

The productivity involved in learning, then, is partially a transformation of traditions and partially a transformation of the one who learns. In educational experience, whether the student is reading a text, studying his notes, hearing a lecture, discussing a problem, playing a game, listening to music, making a friend, or experiencing an emotion, learning is not simply the passive acceptance of transmitted information. Learning involves the transformation of the hermeneutical situation of the learner. Any definition of educational experience which equates learning with the simple transmission of information is inadequate. According to the simple transmission theory, the learner changes only quantitatively by way of accumulation. The teacher and student are pictured as storehouses of knowledge, and the teacher's task is to be concerned, for the most part, with the proper methods or techniques for transferring or reproducing knowledge. The concern in the classroom is one of management or of engineering to facilitate the flow of information. A simple emphasis on educational technology, which, in Scheffler's words, focuses on "the development of devices, programs and new curricula for the more efficient packaging and distribution of knowledge," and which therefore returns to "the old transmission model of education,"[15] ignores the nature of the hermeneutical constraints placed on the educational situation and fails to recognize the natural productivity of the learning process. There is, as Scheffler notes, no virtue associated with inefficient methods; but overemphasis on methodological procedures ignores the productivity that must come from the natural tension which constitutes the distance between the familiar and the unfamiliar.

The productivity involved in hermeneutical distanciation is genuinely a transformation. This transformation is not something that happens automatically or without effort, but neither is it something that can be manufactured or controlled in a methodical fashion. The student is not a passive receptacle or storehouse into which knowledge, as a collection of ready-made wares, can be inserted; rather the student plays an active role. This activity can best be described in terms of a projection of possibilities.

The Projection of Possibilities.   We can return once more to Plato's *Meno* to find some insights relevant to contemporary discussions of education. The kind of "knowledge" that Meno possessed, and which Plato associated with "opinion" (*dóxa*), was not a genuine knowledge, but a collection of facts and definitions that, by means of memorization, Meno had inserted into his mind. But even those Sophists who, through exceptionally clever rhetorical techniques, could compose such fine-sounding and memorable definitions, did not represent, for Plato, the ideal of education. The type of knowledge that education is concerned with does not exclude a collecting of information, but it cannot be reduced to such a collection. Moreover, although it does not exclude critical thinking, it cannot be reduced to a reproduction of techniques that tell us what to do with information. We will see later that critical thinking, which is often associated with rationality itself, is really only an expression of a certain kind of rationality that is not central to educational experience (see pp. 220–237). Rather, education involves understanding, which requires the projection of one's own possibilities.

The productivity of learning does not refer primarily to the production of new interpretations which would simply add to the surplus of information already around; nor does it refer primarily to the innovative use of scientific or logical techniques to manipulate environments or conversations. Primarily, what is produced in educational experience, in the tension between the familiar and the unfamiliar, or between student and teacher, is understanding which is self-understanding. To say the same thing in another way, learning involves the production of one's own possibilities. These possibilities are discovered, not as ready-made answers handed over to the student from the authority of an author, a teacher, or a tradition. They are produced in the encounters between the student and that authority. Correspondingly, the teacher's essential task is not simply to provide opinions, or insert information, but, working within traditional authoritative frameworks, to open up opportunities for such encounters, to help create the occasions in which the student will come into a challenging relation to a particular tradition. Through the pedagogical presentation of subject matter, the teacher can help provide the distance (objectification, transcendence) necessary for the student's reflection on that subject matter's relation to a tradition, and on ready-made answers provided within various authoritative frameworks. This reflection, however, is in every case a self-reflection for the learner. In discovering the possible connections between the unfamiliar and the familiar, the learner also discovers his own possibilities. The hermeneutical principle relevant here is that all understanding is self-understanding (see pp. 157ff.).

All distancing, Ricoeur states, is "self-distancing, a distanciation of the self from itself" (HHS 244). Educational experience is experience that expands my horizons as learner, reveals my possibilities as they are mediated through the unfamiliar. In confronting the unfamiliar, in coming to understand and to relate it to the world which defines me, I open up that world, I transcend that world in a production of possibilities that reveal myself to me. Here, as Ricoeur points out, Dilthey's conception, that I understand myself only in understanding the worldly objectifications of myself, has relevance. "What I am for myself can only be reached through the objectifications of my own life" (HHS 51). Ricoeur is in agreement: "To understand . . . is to receive a self enlarged by the appropriation of the proposed worlds which interpretation unfolds" (HHS 94).

This moment of self-understanding which comes through distanciation is something we have already seen at work in the informal educational experience of play. In play, learning takes place through a distanciation between the "real world" and "possible worlds." Play frees the player from ostensive reference to his or her everyday world in such a way that it becomes an occasion for a reinterpretation of the player's own self. Here there is no question of simply taking in bits of information about the world or about oneself. Everything depends on the player's ability to transcend himself toward his possibilities. The dialectics of transcendence and appropriation are mirrored in the formal relations of student and teacher. Only in the playful attitude, for instance, can the teacher or student objectify something as unfamiliar which otherwise would count as familiar. Through such an objectification the student/player transcends his established world, produces a new set of possibilities, and in doing so appropriates them as his own. Play is finished as soon as the learner thinks that he already understands. This "serious" posture, which takes everything as familiar and recognizes no other possibilities, this "Meno-type" ignorance or bad faith, signifies a foreclosure of learning.

In the informal educational experience of play, then, we have already seen the essential relations of these various features of distanciation. They function in both informal and formal learning, including learning which takes place through textual interpretation. Transcendence, whether it is the transcendence found in play, or in reading a text, or in classroom experience, is always transcendence toward our own possibilities, mediated by the objectification of something as unfamiliar. Furthermore, transcendence always leads to an appropriation, a self-understanding which is a self-formation. Learning is productive of the self. This is always a gain made in the interchange or trade of educational experience.

THE PRINCIPLES OF QUESTIONING, APPLICATION, AND SELF-UNDERSTANDING

We have seen that one does not escape the process of tradition by a Cartesian side step or by an interrogation that seeks only information and fact in an objectified body of past knowledge. But it is not impossible to become aware of and to isolate the preconceptions that govern our understanding. Any interpretational encounter creates an opportunity for becoming aware of and suspending particular preconceptions in order to let the thing itself (*die Sache*) "speak." Referring again to the phenomenon of play, Gadamer suggests that interpretation involves risking one's own preconceptions so that the unfamiliar gets encountered precisely as the unfamiliar. Insightfully, he points out that "all suspension of judgments and hence, a fortiori, of preconceptions [*Vorurteilen*], has the logical structure of a *question*" (TM 299). The structure of questioning is such that it opens up both the interpreted object and the interpreter. As long as the question remains, the dialogue never achieves final closure. Gadamer finds the model for this dialogical questioning in Platonic dialectic.

Plato, writing in the indirect discourse of his dialogues, shows that progress in understanding is achieved only through an incessant questioning of the sort done by Socrates. The Platonic attitude toward the process of tradition starkly contrasts to either Descartes' theoretical attempt to escape it or a technical approach which aims to simply gather information from a traditional body of knowledge. Plato realizes that he must deal with traditional ideas because they shape our opinions and set the stage for any inquiry. It is on the basis of Socrates' continued questioning of traditional answers that preconceptions are laid open and that a state of *aporia* (perplexity) is achieved. *Aporia* represents a condition in which the ready-made traditional opinions and one's own preconceptions come to be recognized as barriers to understanding rather than as the sought-for answers. *Aporia*, the beginning point of philosophical inquiry, is reached, not by ignoring the process of tradition, but by working through a tradition and by treating it, not as simply a source of information but as setting the frame of reference for interpretation.

Gadamer goes further than offering the model of questioning as a prescriptive canon. He proposes that interpretation always already reflects the structure of questioning. That all interpretation has the structure of questioning, and not simply that it ought to adopt this structure to be successful, is genuinely the hermeneutical principle of questioning that we are after, and Gadamer states it as follows: "It is clear that the structure of the question is implicit in all experience. We cannot have experiences without asking questions" (TM 362). We must note, because Gadamer's discussion may be misleading on this point, that the direct object of the question, which is implicit in interpretation, is not a tradition (except in the case of historical interpretation, which takes a tradition as its direct object—this is what Gadamer tends to focus on [see TM 369ff.]) but the *Sache*, the object that is to be interpreted, the unfamiliar object which calls for understanding. This does not mean that the question put forward is not connected with the process of tradition or not framed within language. It is on the basis of tradition's essentially anterior relation to interpretation that in every interpretational question a tradition is challenged, at least in an indirect way. To develop this insight we need to take up Gadamer's discussion of another principle: the principle of application, that is, that all interpretation is application. Finally, we want to show that what gets questioned through interpretation is not only and directly the object of interpretation, and indirectly a tradition, but also, and usually indirectly, the interpreter herself. This final principle states that all understanding is self-understanding.

The Hermeneutical Priority of Questioning

Interpretation is structured as a question. A question itself has meaning and direction. It opens up the subject matter to be investigated. As such the question is the Socratic answer to the sophistical paradox presented by Meno and related to the concept of Socratic ignorance: how can we know what we do not know? Socrates' response is: by questioning. Meno is unable to properly question because he thinks he already knows the answer. He is not involved in the process of interpretation at all. The process of interpretation begins when the unfamiliar is recognized as unfamiliar. In Plato, "there is a profound recognition of the *priority of the question* in all knowledge and discourse that really reveals something of an object. Discourse that is intended to reveal something requires that the thing be broken open by the question" (TM 363). Asking the question, that is, interpretation, always opens up possibilities of meaning.

Gadamer asserts that the "real and fundamental nature of a question [is] to make things indeterminate. Questions always bring out the undetermined possibilities of a thing" (TM 375). However, there is not an absolute, unlimited openness in questioning; the meaning of the question would disappear if this were the case. Rather, Gadamer indicates, every question has a horizon that is based on established presuppositions. Every question includes both positive and negative aspects, thereby defining the direction and horizon of what it asks about and what it does not ask about. A question does not ask everything but limits itself to a particular perspective. Every question is asked from a particular circumstance, within a specific hermeneutical situation. If the essence of understanding includes being able to allow a proper question to emerge between interpreter and the interpreted, then the projective fore-structure of understanding has precisely the structure of questioning, and questioning is limited by the same conditions that define the fore-structure as the hermeneutical circle—the tradition context of language.

A question cannot be true or false, in the sense of correct or incorrect. It does not make a truth claim. But the question does fall under all of the hermeneutical constraints. A question expresses a preconception in calling for a particular kind of answer. It is often the case, for example, that the form of a particular question entails a certain type of response. Even if neither true nor false, a question may be determined as "proper" or "improper" by a tradition, as when a scientific tradition defines the propriety of a question as scientific. A question is obviously linguistic since it is defined by a certain sentence structure. Questioning also participates in hermeneutical possibilities: it involves an open, productive projection which both transcends the familiar and appropriates the unfamiliar, the indeterminate, in a definite way.

How does the "proper" question emerge? Gadamer indicates that there is no method to asking questions. "The priority of the question in knowledge shows how fundamentally the idea of method is limited for knowledge, which has been the starting point for our argument as a whole. There is no such thing as a method of learning to ask questions, of learning to see what is questionable" (TM 365). Questions arise suddenly, like a "breach in the smooth front of popular opinion" (TM 366). Of course, this is only a seeming suddenness. The insightful question is framed only from out of an operative tradition which more or less strictly defines what counts as legitimate or appropriate questions. Questioning is not a technical method, although Plato and Gadamer might consider it an art. "As the art of asking questions, dialectic proves its value because only the person who knows how to ask questions is able to persist in his questioning, which involves being able to preserve his orientation toward openness. The art of questioning is the art of questioning ever further—i.e., the art of thinking. It is called 'dialectic' because it is the art of conducting a real dialogue" (TM 367). It may be more appropriate to refer to a "Socratic art" rather than to a "Socratic method."

In a genuine dialogue or conversation one remains open to the thoughts of the other and, in principle, attempts to stay with the subject matter. "To conduct a conversation means to allow oneself to be conducted by the subject matter to which the partners in the dialogue are oriented" (TM 367). Questioning is the way that interpretation lets the subject matter itself, rather than the interpreter's own ready-made opinion, stand out. Although in a Platonic dialogue Socrates may seem to ask his questions in order to confuse his interlocutor, this is the case only to the point of *aporia*, that is, only to the point of perplexity and Socratic ignorance.

Socratic questioning is primarily directed at the subject matter and aims at opening up the subject matter in the same way and at the same time that the interlocutor is opened up by Socratic ignorance. Eventually, both interlocutor and subject matter must stand on their own and do their own speaking.

The question is asked between the interpreter and the interpreted. It is asked from out of a particular hermeneutical situation enframed in a language which carries within itself one or more traditions. The meaning that the unfamiliar can have for us is based on our circumstance, our expectations, and our anterior relations to the particular tradition which informs the subject matter. Trying to understand something or some person does not mean merely that the interpreter, from out of his own subjective circumstance, poses the question that he thinks the object or interlocutor can answer. Indeed, that would amount to simply seeking information from the other, the unfamiliar, on the basis of an already presumed understanding. Such a procedure would be a technical quest for information, a one-way manipulation, similar to requesting data from a computer. Interpretation involves more than proposing a loaded question or calling for a familiar answer. In quoting or citing another author, for example (and here our own practice is an example close at hand), interpretation is served not if the quoting is done in order to reconstruct the other author's answer to his original question, but only if his work has motivated a question for us and we are attempting to apply that work in understanding, to draw it into a genuine process of interpretation.

Application and the Normative Dimension of Interpretation

Even in the most erudite circumstances, understanding does not take place without some practical effect. Understanding always involves application. This seems obvious enough if one considers the interpretation of law or Scripture. "A law does not exist in order to be understood historically, but to be concretized in its legal validity by being interpreted" (TM 309). The same is true of Sacred Scriptures; they are interpreted to be applied in particular situations. Consider several other examples offered by Gadamer: the interpretation of music and drama involves an application in performance; "translating texts in a foreign language, imitating them, or even reading texts aloud correctly, involves the same explanatory achievement as philological interpretation" (TM 310). In all of these forms of understanding, Gadamer notes, there is no separation between interpretation and application. In all of these cases there is a normative element that appears as a "tension" between remaining open to that which requires interpretation and being concerned about the stylistic relevance of the performance, translation, or reading to the present situation. In the hermeneutical situation two claims are made on the interpreter: one by the object of interpretation and one by the interpreter's own circumstance. One might say that there is a normative dimension opened up between the two claims made respectively by familiar circumstance and unfamiliar subject matter. Interpretation is an attempt to responsibly bridge these two demands, to resolve or in some way deal with the tension between them.

This normative constraint involved in interpretation is not summarized by prescriptive canons that specify how we ought to interpret. Rather, the specification of canons is required only because interpretation already has a normative dimension built into it. If there were not first the tension between circumstance and subject matter, there would be no need for canons of interpretation.

Interpretation always involves the attempt to remain true to our circumstances while we maintain an openness to the object of interpretation. This tension, which has been described in terms of distanciation (pp. 124ff.), is found in all interpretation. If, for example, in a legal circumstance we are seeking an answer to a problem, we do not consult the law without keeping in mind the particular problem which demands an answer. This tension, of course, conditions our search and our interpretation of the law. We approach the law with a question that is conditioned by our circumstance. If, in our search, we come upon a law that holds no relevance for our particular legal circumstance, it would make no sense to distort the circumstance to make it fit the law. Nor would it make sense to distort the law to make it fit our circumstance. Notwithstanding, it should be noted, in many cases, especially when the interpretation of law is at stake rather than a mechanical application of law to a relatively unquestionable circumstance, there is both a distortion of law and a distortion of circumstance: we "bend the law" to fit our case, or construe our case so that it fits the law. How far one can go in such creative uses of law without becoming unfaithful to the law or dishonest to the circumstance is a question for legal hermeneutics. To the extent that an interpretation is not absolutely faithful to the intent of the law, we may speak of the productivity of understanding. But this productivity must be weighed against the amount of distortion that could be considered a misapplication.

All understanding involves application in the sense that all interpretation is interpretation for some purpose defined by the situation. Understanding "that cannot be applied to the concrete situation remains meaningless and even risks obscuring what the situation calls for" (TM 313). I interpret in order to answer a question, or to raise a question, to solve a problem, to amuse myself or others, to accomplish a task, to learn, or to live a good life, and so forth. If there is such a thing as interpretation for the sake of interpretation, it is still done for the sake of something, for some purpose. Interpretation is not an end in itself; but neither is it a mere means. If interpretation is neither end nor means, if it does not fit into these traditional normative categories, we may be tempted to deny the normative dimension of interpretation. How, then, do we justify referring to application, this tension between interpreter and interpreted, as a normative aspect of interpretation?

Gadamer recalls an ancient insight into different kinds of knowledge. The ancient Greeks classified knowledge into three types: theoretical knowledge (*epistēmē*), moral knowledge (*phronēsis*), and technical knowledge (*technē*). Modern epistemology, however, so emphasizes the distinction between theoretical and practical knowledge that ultimately moral and technical knowledge are reduced to one: practical knowledge. The distinction between *technē* and *phronēsis* becomes blurred. In positivistic and pragmatic philosophies moral knowledge is often reduced to a form of technical knowledge, a knowledge of particulars that tells one how to do something. Dewey, for example, viewed moral knowledge as a form of technical know-how. He proposed that answers to moral problems require the employment of scientific method: the use of information gathered from circumstances, past experience, tradition, and society in order to formulate a testable hypothesis. Ethics is characterized, in effect, as a technology informed by scientific procedures. But modern theoretical or scientific knowledge, and technical knowledge, obviously interdependent in the modern world, share a certain type of attitude or approach. This attitude, which we shall call, for simplicity, the "technological attitude," can be explained by appealing to a distinction made by the French philosopher Gabriel Marcel.

Marcel distinguishes between a "problem" and a "mystery."[16] A problem is something that can be totally objectified and resolved in objective terms because the person confronting the problem can completely detach himself from it and view it externally. For example, my car breaks down. I can hire a mechanic or I can attempt to fix it myself by examining, cleaning, dismantling, and rebuilding the carburetor or pump, and so forth. This is a problem to which there is an objective solution. Things are relatively clear-cut. A mystery, on the other hand, is somewhat different. A mystery is something that involves the person in such a way that the person cannot step outside of it in order to see it in an objective manner. She is caught within the situation with no possibility of escape, and no possibility of clear-cut solutions. Indeed, ambiguity is the rule within a mystery. My car is a problem, but my existence is a mystery, not because I understand my car and I do not understand my existence, but rather because I can junk my car or send it to the shop, but I am inextricably immersed in my existence.

In the technological attitude everything is reduced to the status of a problem. Everything is objectified and there appears to be the possibility of a clear-cut solution to every problem. Dewey's attempt to reduce moral knowledge to a type of *technē* is *eo ipso* an attempt to understand all morally significant situations as "problematic situations" and to provide clear-cut solutions through the scientific manipulation of objective elements in those situations. This approach assumes, however, that the person involved in the situation can detach himself from it, can become totally scientific about his circumstances, can see things in a disinterested, objective way.

In the ancient Greek conception of moral knowledge (*phronēsis*) this type of objective detachment from the moral situation is impossible. In effect, a moral situation resembles a mystery rather than a problem. Gadamer makes reference to Aristotle: "For moral knowledge, as Aristotle describes it, is clearly not objective knowledge—i.e., the knower is not standing over against a situation that he merely observes; he is directly affected [*betroffen*] by what he knows [*erkennt*]. It is something that he has to do" (TM 314). Moreover, for the ancients, there is an indissoluble intertwining of theoretical and moral knowledge that "is not as simple everywhere as it is in the fields of technology."[17] In effect, the relation between theory and practice, the very notion of application, is oversimplified in modern technological understanding.

The difference between technical knowledge and moral knowledge, blurred in modern epistemology, is clarified by Gadamer. Perhaps the most important difference is that *phronēsis* (moral knowledge) involves a self-knowledge that is not required in technical know-how. Moreover, whereas technical knowledge is knowledge about means and in a sense is itself a means, *phronēsis* "in a curious way . . . embraces both means and end" (TM 322). Finally, in agreement with Aristotle, Gadamer points out that whereas technical knowledge requires cleverness in application, moral knowledge requires understanding. "Once again we discover that the person who is understanding does not know and judge as one who stands apart and unaffected but rather he thinks along with the other from the perspective of a specific bond of belonging, as if he too were affected" (TM 323).

The normative tension between the familiar and the unfamiliar, between the interpreter's circumstance and the object of interpretation, between a belongingness and a distanciation, is adequately captured in the concept of *phronēsis*. Faced with uncertainty and the unfamiliar, the person with *phronēsis* does not appeal to ready-made universal rules that would be applied in a mechanical fashion. Rather, action is to be guided by a finite understanding of the actual circumstance. Instead of classifying a specific circumstance under an already devised set of laws, *phronēsis* calls for an application in light of the existing situation within which the actor finds herself. In *phronēsis* one approaches an understanding of the universal in light of the particular, rather than the other way around.

The distinction between *phronēsis* and *technē* holds importance for hermeneutics in the following way. If all understanding involves application, the model for this application is not technical knowledge, but *phronēsis*. Interpretation operates in the same way that moral knowledge does, or, as we have said, interpretation has a normative dimension: (a) The interpreter is always within a hermeneutical situation in such a way that she cannot objectify it or escape from it; it is, in Marcel's terms, a mystery rather than a problem; it resembles a morally significant situation rather than a problematic one. (b) Because of the structure of the hermeneutical situation—that is, because there is a fusion or tension between the interpreter's circumstance (with its horizon conditioned by the tradition context of language) and the circumstances of the unfamiliar object of interpretation, all understanding involves self-understanding, just as moral knowledge involves self-knowledge. I will return to this point shortly.

Gadamer attempts to carry his insights concerning the normative dimension of interpretation one step further. He suggests that insofar as the interpreter attempts to meet the demands imposed by both the object of interpretation and the interpreter's own particular circumstance, a "dialogue," which can be modeled on the moral encounter, the interpersonal I-thou relationship, is initiated. With respect to this point, however, we need to recognize two limitations which we also found in his analysis of temporal distance (see pp. 125ff., 129ff., 135ff.): (a) his discussion (TM 358ff.) is oriented by textual hermeneutics so that his analysis pertains to reading a text; (b) his discussion is limited to the example of reading historical texts, with the result that his analysis may only have validity when a tradition itself is the object of interpretation. Again we have to emphasize that the primary and universal relationship between the process of tradition and interpretation is the *anterior* relation in which a tradition functions to constrain interpretation. Rather than taking up Gadamer's analysis of interpretation as an I-thou moral relation (which does, nonetheless, have validity for certain cases of conversation, reading, and critical reflection), we can explore the normative aspect of interpretation by developing further a related concept, namely, that the hermeneutical situation cannot be completely objectified.

In critical reflection (or what Gadamer calls reflection on historical effects) one could, for example, attempt to turn one's own hermeneutical situation into a problem, that is, thematize it objectively and thus attempt to remove oneself from it. Of course, this is not completely possible, specifically because of the anterior role which the process of tradition plays. In such critical reflection one does not remove oneself from the hermeneutical situation; one simply expands it, enlarges the hermeneutical circle. The tradition context of language still operates mostly behind the back of critical reflection. But this does not mean that such critical reflection fails to accomplish anything. Rather, a number of things undergo transformation. One thing that gets transformed is the tradition and its historical effect. By thematizing the tradition we do not automatically or fully escape its influence, but we do transform our relation to it, and in a sense we transform the tradition itself. To see how this happens, and to see that it occurs not only in the specialized case of a critical reflection which takes a particular tradition as its object of interpretation, we have to recognize that this same process takes place in every hermeneutical situation, and occurs precisely because every interpretation is also an application.

The interpreter always approaches the object of interpretation with a question built into her very approach. As we have just seen, the question is framed within the tradition context of language which conditions interpretation. Whatever answer is forthcoming will be to some extent shaped by the question; otherwise it will not count as an answer. The answer constitutes a response to the question, which in the process of interpretation changes by that answer. This dialectical interchange of question and answer does not remain neutral to either the interpreter's circumstance or the tradition context of language. As we expressed it previously, the interpreter's fore-conceptions are transformed in his confrontation or encounter with the unfamiliar. The overarching dialectic, which takes place between the anterior relation (of tradition-interpreter) and the "frontal" relation (of interpreter-object of interpretation), involves a changing adjustment across both. One might say that through the process of interpretation, the interpreter's relation, not only to the object of interpretation, but also to tradition, changes. These relations between the process of tradition, the interpreter, and the object interpreted are represented in the figure we used earlier.

In this figure, line (a), which is not a starting point, represents the hermeneutical constraint of tradition; line (b) represents the fore-structure of understanding, conditioned by (a) and projected in the structure of a question to the object of interpretation; (c)

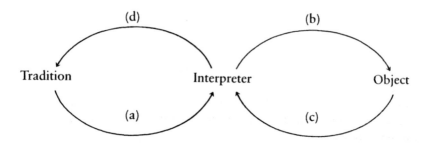

represents the response or feedback which causes a readjustment in the interpreter's fore-structure; and (d) signifies a readjustment in the interpreter's relation to a particular tradition.

Relation (d) is the one under discussion here. The point is that (d) does not signify merely a unilateral change in the interpreter's relation to a tradition, but a change in the process of tradition itself. In the interpretational process, a tradition itself undergoes transformation. Again, a tradition is not some bygone body of knowledge, or unchanging storehouse of information that is objectively arrogated in theoretical or technical appropriations; it is something that we take up and live in real applications to our circumstances. In such applications a tradition is added to, rearranged, and transformed.

The interpreter's relationship to the process of tradition, even if not an I-thou relationship, could be viewed in moral terms. The model here, however, is more like the moral concept of taking responsibility for our actions than like the morality of I-thou relations. Traditions do not coerce our interpretations; they do not lead us by the hand in a paternalistic relation. We are responsible for producing them. But again, the productivity of interpretation is not creation ex nihilo. To emphasize the dialectical character of this relation, the economic model of production and consumption might serve as a metaphor here. We are not just consumers of tradition, but in our consumption we produce it anew and in a new way. Marx's formulation is helpful here. Men and women not only make history, but history makes them; men and women not only transform the environment through technological invention; technology transforms human existence. Just so, we produce and transform traditions just so much as traditions produce and transform us. That this is a moral relationship of self-responsibility can be made clear by considering the principle that all understanding is self-understanding.

Self-understanding

Interpretation consists of a interchange that involves not only a questioning of subject matter between interpreter and the interpreted, but a self-questioning. The questioning is not just unidirectional or monological; it is reflective or dialogical. All understanding is self-understanding. Interpretation is a questioning of ourselves not only with respect to the subject matter, although the "person who thinks must ask himself questions" (TM 375); it is also a questioning of ourselves with respect to ourselves and our circumstance. Gadamer reminds us that "a person who understands, understands himself, projecting himself upon his possibilities" (TM 260). Ricoeur states this principle in terms of the interpreter's encounter with others: "It is thus the growth of [the interpreter's] own understanding of himself that he pursues through his understanding of the other. Every hermeneutic [interpretation] is thus, explicitly or implicitly, self-understanding by means of understanding others."[18]

For Plato, only by thinking for ourselves do we arrive at self-understanding. The contrast drawn between Meno, who is already convinced of his opinion, already closed to any further questioning, and Socrates who, seeking self-knowledge, admits to his ignorance, shows that Meno allows other people (the poets and sophists) to do his thinking for him, whereas Socrates attempts, as best he can, to think for himself. If we begin to think for ourselves only through questioning, then questioning itself is the most responsible form of thinking. We are genuinely responsible for ourselves only when we challenge the ready-made answers provided to us by others. This challenging is effected through questioning. Questioning, however, does not necessarily reject previously devised answers. We are certainly free to take up and live by the answers provided by others, but we do so responsibly only after having put them into question. But this is precisely what happens to some degree in any interpretation. The individual who understands and is capable of interpretation is the one who can think for himself.

Thinking for oneself, therefore, does not signify an internal monologue; it signifies the dialogue of interpretation. One might also say, along with Ricoeur, that all self-understanding involves an understanding of others and other things through dialogical questioning. For Ricoeur, interpretation results in self-understanding to the extent that interpretation involves application. In that case interpretation "culminates in the self-interpretation of a subject who thenceforth understands himself better, understands himself differently, or simply begins to understand himself" (HHS 158). But this is exactly the same process "by which one makes one's own (*eigen*) what was initially other or alien (*fremd*)" (HHS 178). His point is clear. Self-understanding comes about only in the dialectical interchange of distanciation and application (see HHS 94, 113). Self-understanding, however, is not to be equated to the epistemological "subject." Gadamer contrasts hermeneutical self-understanding to the modernist "primacy of self-consciousness."[19] To understand oneself does not mean, as in Descartes, to reflectively discover some central ego or transcendental source of personal existence within a *cogito* or mind. To understand oneself, Ricoeur suggests, is to understand oneself in one's relation to and application of that which gets interpreted (see HHS 113). Self-understanding is not the beginning point of interpretation, but the "terminal point" (HHS 132), the result of the interpretational process.[20] Interpretation is productive in this sense too. It produces self-understanding by producing a self. Self-understanding is a self-(trans)formation. We come to be ourselves only through the projection (which is a revelation and a production) of our possibilities in the interpretive process. Self-appropriation is effected only through self-transcendence. Ricoeur rightfully mentions play in this regard. To paraphrase: as interpreter I find myself only by transcending myself. The transformation of the world in play is also the playful transformation of the ego (see HHS 144). The concept of self-transformation leads us back to educational experience.

THE GAINS FROM EDUCATION

Does our review of the hermeneutical principles concerning questioning, application, and self-understanding add anything new to the already ancient discussion of these topics in educational theory? That there is such a long-standing discussion is apparent if we understand Plato to be putting forward a theory of education based on self-knowledge and the Socratic art of questioning. With respect to the issue of application, Dewey, in his educational philosophy, recognized it to be a traditional issue, "as old as Plato and Aristotle," and closely associated with the normative dimension of education.[21] Dewey referred to it as the problem of "interest"; it is sometimes characterized as the problem of relevance.[22]

For the most part discussion within the educational context has focused on the extremely interesting prescriptive side of these issues. Dewey, for instance, raises the question of interest (relevance or application) in prescriptive terms by contrasting two theories of what ought to be done by teachers or students. One theory asserts that the teacher ought to "make the material presented so interesting that it shall command and retain attention." We can refer to this as the *rule of interest.* The other theory asserts that it is the student's responsibility to put forth the effort "from within." This can be called the *rule of effort.* Dewey rightly points out that the rule of effort "simply substitutes one interest for another. It substitutes the impure interest of fear of the teacher or hope of future reward for pure interest in the material presented."[23]

The other issues of questioning and self-understanding are treated in a prescriptive manner as well. Self-understanding is often set up as an end or goal of educational experience; questioning is usually treated under the heading of "means" or methodology and often in terms of the "Socratic method." Here we must forgo following out these interesting prescriptive discussions to pursue the hermeneutical principles which are no less interesting; and in the context of forging a hermeneutical approach to education it is necessary and important that we do so.

We are given some direction in this regard by Dewey. He points out that the two prescriptive theories concerning relevance, summarized respectively by the rule of interest and the rule of effort, presuppose a common principle, namely, the "externality" of the subject matter. "It is because the object or end [of educational experience] is assumed to be outside self that it has to be *made* interesting, that it has to be surrounded with artificial stimuli and with fictitious inducements to attention. It is equally because the object lies outside the sphere of self that the sheer power of 'will', the putting forth of effort without interest, has to be appealed to."[24] Dewey offers an alternative descriptive principle: "the principle of the recognized identity of the fact or proposed line of action with the self; that it lies in the direction of the agent's own self-expression and is therefore, imperiously demanded, if the agent is to be himself."[25] For Dewey, of course, this principle of self-interest is cast in terms that are more psychological than hermeneutical. From our point of view, however, it has hermeneutical relevance.

On the principle of externality education is focused on the reproduction of external facts rather than the productive interpretation of material which effects a self-transformation. Dewey shows how an educational focus on reproduction can lead to a self-alienation, a "division of attention." Alternatively, Dewey's principle of self-interest is based on a genuine conception of interest in which "the self finds itself, is reflected back into itself" in the interpretational process.[26] This self-appropriation, Dewey suggests, poses no problem in the case of "immediate interest," that is, in the case where interest can be immediately fulfilled. However, it becomes problematic in the case of "mediate interest," which requires a longer time span for the interest to be fulfilled. Following the suggestion of Dewey's essay, we can examine "immediate interest" in the case of play.[27] We will then take the teacher-student relation as an instance of "mediate interest."

In the case of play, the hermeneutical principle that interpretation is application is clearly manifest. Heidegger, for example, suggests that "the 'because' disappears in play. Play is without a 'why'. It plays because it plays."[28] Gadamer reaffirms this: play is a movement which has no goal, but constantly renews and repeats itself (see TM 103). In the case of play there is no distinction to be made between means and ends as if interpretation were to be made practical in a particular application, or as if one particular action were to accomplish an external goal. The notion of self-transcendence in play indicates that the player is not in control of the play and therefore cannot set the game up as a means to an end. To the extent that play is more like a mystery than a technical problem, that is, to the extent that the player is directly, immediately affected in play and cannot attain objective detachment so as to stand apart and unaffected, or to the extent that the player is genuinely at play, there is no question at all of attempting to make the game interesting. Even the card player who suggests making the game "more interesting" in the sense of raising the stakes can do so only because the game already holds his interest. To find a game uninteresting means that one is not fully playing. If a player becomes involved in an uninteresting game, then he is not genuinely at play, that is, self-transcendence has not taken place. Play, then, is in principle always interesting; it always has immediate application. But such application cannot be measured in terms external to the play.

In the case of play the notion of interest or application cannot be equated to a pragmatic or mechanical application in a means-end framework. It is not the case, as it is in a technical knowledge, that we first possess or attain knowledge and then look around for a situation in which to apply it. The application involved in play as educational experience is not pragmatic in the cash-value sense. The value of play is not, as Dewey might suggest, that it prepares us to solve problems in situations more real. If the value of play is practical, it is practical in a more normative sense, understood within the framework of the projection of one's own possibilities and the self-appropriation of those possibilities. The application involved in play is precisely the self-appropriation in which the player becomes responsible for himself and his circumstance. In the context of self-appropriation, that which is relevant is practical in the sense of revealing our own self-responsibility in the process of play. This self-responsibility is not based on causality, as a technical practice might entail, but can be modeled as the responsibility of *phronēsis*: practical wisdom which involves self-understanding, rather than practical know-how. That which is genuinely relevant is not simply that which is useful to me in a particular problematic situation or that which allows me to carry on toward some self-proclaimed goal. Rather the genuinely relevant is that which pertains to the self-formation which makes play a form of educational experience.

This self-responsibility is part of the "seriousness in playing" noted by Gadamer (TM 102) but is not the "spirit of seriousness" which Sartre equates with bad faith or inauthenticity, a seriousness which hides responsibility in false consciousness. The seriousness in playing which characterizes educational self-formation contrasts starkly to the "serious" person's irresponsible spirit of being lost in the world. In opposition to an attitude that invests itself fully in worldly objects, play opens the world to question.

The structure or logic of play is the same as that of questioning, which we have called the most responsible form of thinking. By nature it challenges the real, and in so doing it opens up possibilities which form the player's own responses. All play has the structure of a question which interrogates not only the world but also the player's own preconceptions so that the unfamiliar gets encountered precisely as the unfamiliar. Play opens up both the interpreted and the interpreter. Thus one might say of play what Gadamer says of questioning: the real and basic nature of *play* is to make things indeterminate. *Playing* always brings out the undetermined possibilities of the player and the undetermined meanings of the world.

In a very real sense the logic of questioning is also at work in the formal situation of the classroom. Both teacher and student within the learning situation are involved in questioning in a primary way. Gadamer indicates that "deciding the question is the path to knowledge" (TM 364). We could say, in the context of educational experience, that involvement with a question or with the questioning process is the path or course of learning. Only the person who has questions can learn. But the question which allows learning must be a genuine question on the part of the learner. Gadamer contrasts this "learning question" to what he calls the "pedagogical question," which is "a question without a questioner" (TM 363). The genuine learning question is the question into which both teacher and student must enter, the question that guides the learning process.[29]

In a classroom situation the confrontation with subject matter can always be put in the form of a question. A question is implicitly raised even if not explicitly iterated. The teacher, of course, may express the question in defining the theme of the lesson. However, unless that question is or becomes real for the student, learning will not take place. How that question can become real for the student, or what method the teacher should use to make it relevant for the student, whether it should be introduced dishonestly or allowed to emerge in an exploration of subject matter—these are prescriptive issues. The principle, however, is that learning essentially involves the structure of questioning, and that given this structure—that is, given that the student has a question—the student will be interested, the subject matter will be relevant, and learning, as a form of interpretation, will involve application.

Learning does not take place on the basis of a rhetorical or pedagogical question posed by the teacher unless that question seriously and playfully opens up both the student and the subject matter to an indeterminacy. The learning question is a necessary condition of educational experience. But, as both Plato and Gadamer contend, it is not something itself that can be taught (TM 366). The situation with the "learning question" is similar to the situation with virtue if we follow Plato's analysis in the *Meno*. Virtue, which is associated with *phronēsis* and contrasted with *technē*, is not something that can be taught. But it can be learned. Plato agrees with Theognis: "from the good you will learn goodness," but "never by teaching will you make a bad man good" (*Meno* 95e). Virtue, Theognis suggests, like understanding, is never something that can be methodically instilled in the student. Gadamer suggests a similar case for questioning. It is the case that a question "'occurs' to us, that it 'arises' or 'presents itself' more than that we raise it or present it" (TM 366). Questioning, he says, is more a passion than an action. Of course we should not say that virtue or the art of questioning is the result of a passive acceptance. Even if a question "comes to us" or overtakes us, we must be capable of responding, not in the sense of answering the question but in the sense of making the question our own, responding to the call of the question. Virtue, which is a *habit*, a *practice*, requires *effort* on the part of the one who would learn it. Acquiring virtue is something more than learning by osmosis or from didactic teachings. Practice and habituation are also the ways into the art of questioning. Questioning is more a habit, disposition, or practice than a passion or action.

The distinction between teaching and learning, at work in Plato's discussion of education and virtue, is the basis for the prescriptive theories of interest and effort outlined by Dewey. But, as Dewey's analysis suggests, these theories are based on the principle of the externality of the subject matter. In contrast we must try to see the distinction between teaching and learning reflected within the hermeneutical principle of application. Dewey indicates that this is difficult to do because application becomes problematic in the case of "mediate interest." But to characterize classroom learning as a case of "mediate" interest is to ignore the hermeneutical principle that all interpretation involves application. Dewey is still concerned about the "practical" in the sense of technical application within the means-end framework. Thus, for Dewey, thoughts and ideas must be explicitly tested in experimental situations. "Till they are applied in these situations they lack full point and reality. Only application tests them and only testing confers full meaning and a sense of their reality."[30] Hermeneutical application, however, maintains a more primary place even within instances of technical application in experimental situations. Learning is practical, applicable, relevant, or interesting in this primary hermeneutical sense, because in learning the student's own possibilities are at stake. If this is not the case, then even in the well-designed experimental situation, learning will not take place.

This is not to deny that there are psychological or motivational problems involved in bringing students to the point of learning. Nor is it to deny the importance of well-designed learning situations. Certainly prescriptive theories of learning must provide guidance with respect to motivational problems and the technical manipulation of learning situations. Hermeneutical principles, however, describe the conditions sine qua non of learning. The best-designed experimental situations and the best attempts to motivate the student will not lead to learning unless the student experiences his own possibilities in interpretational application.

It may be justifiable for prescriptive purposes to characterize the teacher-student relationship in terms of an I-thou dialogical mediation. Gadamer and others suggest that such a model would be preferable to the authoritarian domination of the teacher over the student.[31] But again, for reasons outlined in the previous section, even if an I-thou model is relevant to the teacher-student relation, it is not the precise model required to capture the hermeneutical situation of educational experience. To focus on an I-thou teacher-student dialogue alone is to fall back into the principle of externality because such a focus explicitly leaves the subject matter outside.

That learning can take place without the presence of teacher or text attests to the fact that learning cannot be reduced to the dialogical encounter between teacher and student. The essential moment in learning is an encounter between the student as learner and that which is to be learned. But this is not an objective confrontation. Rather, it is a meeting on the basis of a question so that the unfamiliar is made to stand out by the question itself and thereby gain the possibility of attaining objective status. The learner approaches the subject matter with a question built into his very approach. The question, framed within the tradition context of language, may, of course, be posed by a teacher in her attempt to facilitate the encounter with subject matter. Such a pedagogical question would be iterated in language that, with varying degrees of success, would attempt to draw the student into questioning the subject matter for himself. The subject matter itself, however, not the teacher, is the thing that must elicit interest and demand effort in the form of a question.

If the learner is to gain from this questioning encounter with subject matter, then he cannot retreat. The questioning must be pursued. If we count the process of tradition and the subject matter, as well as teacher and student, as elements of the learning situation, then a student qua learner never reaches or retreats to an autarkic state. The learner, through questioning, is always involved in an interplay, a dialectical commerce with a tradition, a familiar context, a subject matter, an unfamiliar object. Here we return to our analogy with the principle of economic gains mentioned at the opening of this chapter. The modern principle of gains from trade states that more is to be gained from trade than from autarkic behavior. But this principle can easily be traced back to an archaic economic discussion. Notably in Aristotle, the relevant discussion of economic trade is linked to a discussion that has import for education. The term *autárkeia* (self-sufficiency) is one frequently used by Aristotle in both his ethics and politics. For Aristotle it has both an economic and a moral connotation. Morally it is associated with *theōría* and the virtue of wisdom, but not with *technē* or *phronēsis*. "What is usually called 'self-sufficiency'," Aristotle states, "will be found in the highest degree in the activity which is concerned with theoretical knowledge. . . . A wise man is able to study by himself, and the wiser he is the more he is able to do so. Perhaps he could do it better if he had colleagues to work with him, but he still is the most self-sufficient of all."[32] Notably, even within the emphasis placed on the self-sufficiency of *theōría*, Aristotle suggests that study might benefit from company. *Phronēsis* or practical wisdom, which is closely tied to politics, is less autarkic. Although in some senses *autárkeia*, as economic self-sufficiency, is viewed as an ideal goal of politics, it is always relative and only possible on the basis of an economic interdependence which for all practical purposes requires the ordering principle of *phronēsis* in the science of politics. The economic principle that would be Aristotle's, then, is that a limited independent economic unit would only be possible on the basis of the benefits gained from interdependent trade.

The gain involved in educational experience finds its model in a similar way in *phronēsis* rather than *theōría*. The learning process is one characterized by interrelatedness and interdependency rather than *autárkeia*. Even in the case of the wise man who studies by himself, there must be something to study, some context in which he finds himself and his subject matter. This involves an intentionality and a self-transcendence in educational experience. *Trade*, which, in its various connotations, archaic and modern, speaks of schooling, application, the course or path traversed, practice or habit, and the passage between learner and subject matter, always involves gain. But what precisely is the gain? The gain, based on the *applicatio* of educational experience, can be viewed in terms of self-understanding.

If we determine self-understanding as an outcome of the learning process, we should not limit it to simply an end product of education. Rather, like the happiness which Aristotle speaks of, self-understanding is part and parcel of the very process itself. The hermeneutical production of self-understanding is at the same time its consumption. All learning involves self-understanding, whether self-understanding is set up as a consciously determined goal or not. Ricoeur, who characterizes self-understanding as a "terminal point," does not hit the mark precisely. The self which gets understood is neither the self which stands prior to educational experience nor the self which stands at the end. If subjectivity is a dynamic structure, as I have tried to make clear in the discussion of play (pp. 45 ff.), then self-understanding is not an end state but is the process of transformation undergone in educational experience.

By self-understanding we do not mean a quiet and lonely reflective consciousness of self. On the contrary, self-understanding is always being tested out, challenged in the process of learning about the world. Self-understanding is not an autarkic state; it is a process interdependent with other persons and things that define the situation of educational interpretation. The teacher does not teach self-understanding to the student. By definition, self-understanding cannot be taught. But the student grows in self-understanding through his encounters with teachers, fellow students, and subject matter under study. Self-understanding involves self-transcendence as well as self-appropriation. The student moves beyond the narrow confines of his opinions by questioning and opening up the subject matter. This movement is simultaneously a questioning, opening up, and transcendence of himself. Again, the same interpretational dynamic involved in play is involved in all learning.

The learner is challenged in a process in which she challenges the subject matter. This is not a subject matter which remains external to the learning situation, but one that calls the student forth to an involvement beyond her established opinions or practices, to an involvement with her own possibilities. A subject matter has interest or relevance when it challenges the existing self-understanding—often a self-complacency—of the one who is involved in learning. Of course, this could be any subject matter, from poetic interpretation to mechanical technique—whatever provides the necessary resistance or leverage to challenge the student to think for herself or to project her own possibilities. In questioning the subject matter the student questions herself; in understanding the material she understands herself. The application of learning is always one in which both subject matter and learner are transformed.

This interplay between learner and subject matter also involves an indirect challenging of traditions. As traditions enter into and condition the learning situation, they do not operate in the form of passive and immutable information. They actively shape and structure experience, but equally are interdependent with experience.

The continued existence of traditions depends upon learning and interpreting processes. Traditions live only to the extent that they play themselves out in such situations, only to the extent that they are transcended and appropriated in this interchange which questions and transforms them.

The hypothesis with which we began, that learning always involves interpretation, has received confirmation in our investigations. At the very least it lends itself to a discourse which is edifying. We reasoned that if learning is or involves interpretation, then the hermeneutical principles which describe interpretation would also throw some light on educational experience. It seems clear now that, like interpretation, educational experience operates within the constraints of the tradition context of language and yet involves a productivity that enables it to transcend and modify those constraints. It remains to be seen what the implications of this hermeneutical approach to educational experience are, and how they have import for both educational theory and hermeneutics itself.

CHAPTER 6

The Nature of Education

The moderate hermeneutical approach to educational experience contains the rudiments of a theory of education that clearly contrasts with a number of contemporary approaches. In this chapter I will outline the "moderate theory of education" that can be associated with the moderate hermeneutical approach. This will not be a complete or absolute view of education. My intent is not to define education once and for all in order to close the book on further discussion. Rather, in what I would consider good hermeneutical practice, as well as good educational practice, my intent is to enter into the larger contemporary conversation about the nature of education. In subsequent chapters I will examine theories of education that are based on conservative, critical, and radical hermeneutics, and formulate responses that will help to further define the moderate position. My concern is not so much for what can be accomplished in the strictly moderate hermeneutical approach to these issues, but what can be accomplished in a dialogue among competing theories of education. In this regard it may be the case that the various *aporiai* found in educational theory may not be absolutely resolvable. It may be in the nature of the ongoing conversation that we all simply have to learn to live with the ambiguities at the root of these *aporiai*.

BEYOND THE MODERNISTIC CONCEPTION OF EDUCATION

The problem of finding a viable conception of education is not due to any scarcity of definitions. There are so many definitions that one can easily become lost or complacent in the multitude of them. Nonetheless, there is constant disagreement about what education is. Aristotle's ancient observation still holds true. Not everyone agrees about the nature or aims of education; whether it is meant to be training in "that which is useful for life," or "that which contributes to virtue," or "that which is exceptional" (*Politics* 1337a35–b3). Despite a long-standing plurality of views, however, most contemporary conceptions of education are formulated within one common discourse which betrays an affinity that is not often recognized. My intention here is not to provide an exhaustive inventory of contemporary definitions, but to examine a sufficient number of them to delineate the common ground on which the majority of theories stand.

Consider a group of definitions which equate education with a certain kind of learning. Education consists in learning to solve problems; or learning to inquire and conduct research; or learning to appropriate and test knowledge.[1] The model for these theories, which take their bearing from the influential pragmatic philosophy of John Dewey and are often referred to as "progressive," "instrumentalist," or "experimentalist" theories of education, is to be found in modern scientific knowledge and its emphasis on method. Even for those theories that emphasize content rather than technique, the content is often evaluated from a methodological standpoint. Dewey's definition of method, for example, is one that makes overt reference to content. "Method means that arrangement *of* subject-matter which makes it most effective in use. Never is method something outside of the material."[2] For Dewey the content of education lacks value *in itself*; it receives its value only when it is ordered to the solution of a problematic situation. Finding resolutions for problematic situations according to the scientific method is often described by Dewey as "reconstructing" experience or the environment. Thus he contends that "education must be conceived as a continuing reconstruction of experience"—a reconstruction "which increases ability to direct the course of subsequent experience" and which adds power and control.[3]

In many cases the focus on utility, whether one expresses it in terms of an art or technique or in terms of useful content or knowledge, is explicated in terms of learning how to manipulate, control, or deal with the environment.[4] Similar discussions reflect a concern for "application," where application is considered to be a technical ability distinct from logical or theoretical understanding.[5] Alfred North Whitehead captures the progressive ideal in his concise definition: "Education is the acquisition of the art of the utilization of knowledge." He cautions educators against useless or "inert" knowledge and recommends "applications" that are immediately relevant to life. The "golden rule of education" is that "whatever interest attaches to your subject-matter must be evoked here and now." Whitehead also explicates an alternative but familiar way of expressing this concern for relevance. "There is only one subject-matter for education, and that is Life in all its manifestations."[6] This is another way of saying that the knowledge imparted by education must be useful or relevant to the real world or "successful living," and, as R. S. Peters has pointed out, this "can be interpreted as a way of trying to fit the generality suggested by 'educated' into an instrumental type of mold."[7]

Tellingly, even those who criticize the progressivist ideal because it plays down the value of cultural heritage often end up reinforcing the progressivist ideal by justifying their own position on the basis of the utility value of such knowledge. One such critic neatly ties together the concepts just mentioned.

> Although all parts of a cultural heritage are significant, in the sense that they are potentially not neutral with respect to our efforts toward successful living, nevertheless it may be said that those parts of the culture which inform us concerning the probable character of the universe, and concerning what kinds of actions within a foreseeable range of events will produce what kinds of results, are to be called cognitive, or are to be designated as knowledge. From this definition it becomes obvious that knowledge is that part of our cultural heritage which is most directly useful to us in making such predictions as will enable us to gain control over our relationships with environment and thereby increase the likelihood of success in living.[8]

Formalism, to the extent that it represents an attempt to get away from progressivist ideas, gets no further away from the scientistic and technical focus. The new formalism, noted by Scheffler and Hirsch, continues to predominate in schools of education today. Scheffler notes that "unlike the old formalism rooted in classical studies, [the new formalism] pushes hardest for the scientific, mathematical and technical studies within the academic complex." Moreover, the new formalism emphasizes "educational technology, the development of devices, programs and new curricula for the more efficient packaging and distribution of knowledge."[9]

It is clear that the same scientistic and technical focus found in progressivist and formalist ideas about what ought to be taught is even more pronounced in ideas concerning how one goes about the process of teaching or of organizing school systems. Along these lines behaviorism represents the extreme reduction of education to a "branch of scientific technology."[10] In this context the term *behaviorism* is used to signify an educational theory which proposes a conception of education that "is consistent with our conception of other areas of applied science."[11] Here one would also have to consider various educational practices concerned with the training of students, such as programmed learning, instructional objectives planning, and competence-based instruction. These practices take the form of filling minds with information, programming them to think in certain ways, or placing disproportionate emphasis on attitudes about the acquisition of job-related skills.

A similar focus can be appreciated in certain familiar administrative practices. For instance, what Bruce Romanish calls "the preoccupation of the current system with what can be standardized and measured, [which] reduces teaching and learning to prescribed, measurable outcomes with accompanying formulas for reaching them," is reflected in William J. Bennett's official attitude toward reform in education. "*Fundamentally, education reform is a matter of improved results. It aims directly at bringing about measurable improvements in the knowledge and skills of American students. Education reform looks first to output, not input.*"[12]

To conclude this brief and incomplete inventory of contemporary conceptions, let us consider several of the more recent attempts to characterize education from a humanistic standpoint. In the tradition of British analytic philosophy John Wilson offers the following analysis: " 'Education' and 'educate', in what I take to be their primary senses, mark a particular kind of *human enterprise*, a certain mode of *activity* directed towards producing certain kinds of *results* or goods: roughly, those goods gained in or by learning."[13] Wilson, in this humanistic vein, considers the activity of education to be a *praxis* which must be part of an overall plan or "policy," and must be intentionally controlled. Thus, something counts as education only when the teacher or parent views what she is doing "as contributing to the child's serious learning and intend[s] it as such."[14] Frankena, admitting a certain ambiguity to the term *education*, explicates the same idea of deliberate methodological control by identifying education's primary connotation to be "the *activity of educating* carried on by teachers, schools, and parents (or by oneself)." In this sense, he explains, education "is the use of certain kinds of methods to foster excellences or desirable dispositions."[15]

From a different, although nonetheless humanistic perspective, J. Gordon Chamberlin, working in the phenomenological tradition, offers the following definition: "Education is a *consciously selected* set of *activities* in which an individual or a group *intentionally* presents *selected* ideas or actions to particular individuals in a particular setting by a *controlled process* that seeks the student's understanding and his *conscious choice* of response."[16]

Finally, consider the current emphasis on critical thinking in the curriculum. This movement promises that with a proper and complete education in critical thinking techniques "the individual becomes the owner and arbiter of his or her own existence, enabling the individual to intervene in the affairs of life on terms that give meaning and context. . . . [Critical thinking] *empowers* and equips a person *to confront the world* in all its dimensions, to understand it, and participate in it."[17]

Scheffler carefully distinguishes between stipulative, descriptive, and programmatic definitions of education.[18] For our purposes, however, it matters little whether the cited definitions and conceptions are descriptive, programmatic, or even stipulative. Nor does it matter in this context whether these definitions or discussions are correct or incorrect, adequate or inadequate. Our contention is that each of these definitions, and most of those that are to be found in contemporary philosophy of education, regardless of their status, are indicative of a certain thinking about education that we will call "modernist."

R. S. Peters insightfully shows the roots of contemporary modernist conceptions of education. He suggests that, prior to the advent of industrialism, the term *education* had a very general meaning. For example, it applied not only to human formation but to the rearing of plants and animals. "With the coming of industrialism, however, and the increasing demand for knowledge and skill consequent on it, 'education' became increasingly associated with 'schooling' and with the sort of training and instruction that went on in special institutions."[19] In this modern use of the term a number of connotations are excluded. Not only is it restricted to a totally human enterprise, but even the informal sense of raising children is excluded. Education becomes equated with the formalized didactics of "literacy, numeracy, knowledge, and skill" and becomes valued "because it has become the royal road to better jobs and to getting on in the world." In the modernist reduction of education to its instrumental connotation, by which "governments see it mainly as the source of trained manpower and . . . the average man sees it as the vehicle of social mobility," something essential to an older sense of education is left out. Peters refers to this as the Socratic-Platonic conception of "knowledge of the good." "This consists in seeing things under certain aspects which constitute intrinsic reasons for engaging in them. . . . It is, as Socrates and Plato argued, intimately connected with caring about something and does not seem to be a case either of 'knowing how' or of 'knowing that' which are the usual alternatives offered."[20] To this point we shall return shortly.

Peters is pointing in a certain direction that we can follow a little further. Contemporary definitions of education are modernistic in two ways. First, the common underlying concepts that determine these definitions, whether they are blatantly scientistic or tend toward the humanistic or cultural, are the modern concepts of power and control. Modernist theories of education share a conception of knowledge similar to the one described by Bacon at the beginning of the seventeenth century: knowledge is power. Education, as the acquisition of knowledge (whether "knowledge that" or "knowledge for," whether content or technique), constitutes the acquisition of power to control nature, the environment, society, life, oneself, and so forth. Second, contemporary definitions are modernistic to the extent that they are cast in terms of the modernist notion of subjectivity. The individual, either as independent subjective substance (ego, mind, consciousness) or as political individual working with others in social groupings, demonstrates a conscious and complete control over self, environment, and nature. In the humanistic accounts the concept of control is expressed in terms of will, intention, and conscious decision. We need not go back as far as Descartes' attempt to consciously control the influx of thoughts in his meditations to find appropriate examples. We can find the same leanings in Chamberlin, Wilson, the new formalists, and others: the notion of the "consciously selected set of activities" intentionally presented in a "controlled process" within a planned-out framework or "policy," the outcome of which will be to empower the individual to "gain increasing control over life."[21]

(handwritten margin note: control over life)

But what would motivate us to think differently about education? Here we will rely on some of Heidegger's suggestions concerning the nature of modern thought, its effective domination and pervasiveness, its danger, its reduction of all other forms of thinking. If any of his insights are correct, or even if he only raises doubts about the modernist way of thinking, then we have some motivation for trying to think about the essence of education in a different way.

Not long before Dewey noted the intrinsic connection between method and subject matter Nietzsche clearly pointed out the domination of method over knowledge. "It is not the victory of science that distinguishes our nineteenth century, but the victory of scientific method over science."[22] Although this realization led Nietzsche to the insight that "knowledge works as a tool of power," his proposition is completely different from Bacon's aphorism: knowledge is power. Nietzsche intimated something that was to be worked out in greater detail by Heidegger.

> In the sciences, not only is the theme drafted, and called up by the method, it is also set up within the method and remains within the framework of the method, subordinated to it. The furious pace at which the sciences are swept along today—they themselves don't know whither—comes from the speed-up drive of method with all of its potentialities, a speed-up that is more and more left to the mercy of technology. Method holds all the coercive power of knowledge.[23]

(handwritten margin note: method)

Heidegger, even more than Nietzsche, was in a position to perceive something that had been, for thinkers like Bacon or Descartes, impossible to see.

What Heidegger attempted to explicate concerning the nature of method and technology is true in microcosm of Descartes and in macrocosm of the entire modern, industrialized *Weltanschauung*. Descartes, who thoughtfully considered the methodologies he employed, was blind to the fact that his method, which stipulated his beginning point, also determined the results of his meditations. He failed to see this because he considered method, much like language, to be a simple instrument under his control; one which gave him complete control over his thinking. It did not strike Descartes that the method itself might end up undermining his well-defined intentions. Heidegger wanted to point out that in much the same way modern thought is shaped under the direction of scientific method and that even if modern thinkers are frequently conscious of employing scientific method, they do not truly see the broader implications of its use. To the extent that we regard method as something neutral, it controls our thinking. It determines the way that we view the world and understand ourselves. The result of this subordination to "the framework of the method" is a technological understanding of the world and of ourselves.

Heidegger questions the modern instrumental conception of technology as "a means and a human activity."[24] Technological thinking sets nature into a certain order of power, utility, and expediency, which Heidegger calls the "standing reserve" (Bestand). Whoever thinks that technology is merely an instrument fails to see that technology places human existence itself under its ordering principle. If human existence becomes part of the standing reserve of technology, and if modern man is not entirely passive in this process ("man drives technology forward" to the extent that he participates in a technologically oriented understanding), still, this is not simply something that humanity does to itself.[25] Heidegger calls this technological understanding "enframing" (Ge-stell). Enframing sets upon man himself, forms his understanding of everything and provides his standards for ordering.

The danger in all of this might be put most simply in terms of Gabriel Marcel's distinction between mystery and problem (see p. 152). Technological understanding reduces everything to the status of the problematic and therefore abolishes all mystery. Mysteries are dismissed in the same way that Descartes and modern science dismissed final causes. Mysteries, among which Marcel classifies human existence itself, are reduced to objective problems or elements of the standing reserve. As Allan Bloom most recently put it, "the search for solutions, easy or difficult, to problems is the stamp of modernity, while antiquity treated the fundamental tensions as permanent."[26] By reducing everything to a solvable problem, and by denying the permanency of certain fundamental ambiguities, the modern individual's own self-understanding is endangered. Our modern understanding falls prey to the illusion that our control is complete, that we are independent and self-empowered subjects who order the objective world. This illusory understanding is what closes off the possibilities of human self-understanding.[27]

The modernist (Cartesian) conception of human subjectivity, based on the metaphysical categories of substance and identical subject, is, according to Heidegger, closely tied to the illusory self-understanding or false consciousness of technological thinking. The modernist subject is characterized as a selfsame, underlying substance, ego, mind, or consciousness in control of its transparent, transcendental self. This conception is reinforced as the product of a socialized false consciousness (*das Man*, the "they," the anonymous "public opinion" operative in modern mass media) which thinks of the human subject under metaphysical-technological categories as something objectively "present-at-hand." Even if Descartes and the older humanistic tradition bestowed a special dignity on the human subject, their descriptions were still cast in terms of objectivity and causality. In effect, human existence comes to be understood in terms of nonhuman, externalized, and demeaning categories. Subjectivity is characterized as an objective entity with special causal powers. In this regard, "the highest determinations of the essence of man in humanism still do not realize the proper dignity of man."[28] Under the determinations of technology human existence is easily reduced to the status of standing reserve, and continues to suffer under a false sense of complete, technologically proficient control.

We need not follow Heidegger's path any further at this point to see its relevance to education. His analysis exhibits the connections between the modern concept of *technē*, the division of disciplines, and *humanitas*, the humanistic concept of education based on those disciplines. Heidegger, in contrast to Peters, pushes his analysis back to Plato. The basis for the concept of man as *homo humanus* was the ancient conception of *paideía*. Even ancient humanism was based on a metaphysical concept of education that had already been developed under the sway of a technological thinking about truth and the division of the sciences.[29] Out of this original humanistic determination of man as *animal rationale* arises the determination of *anima* (soul), *animus sive mens* (mind), and the modernist notions of subject, person, and spirit.[30]

We note that in Gadamer's return to the ancient distinctions among *technē*, *epistēmē*, and *phronēsis* (see p. 151) he is following a path similar to Heidegger. Gadamer argues that in modernist thinking, both *epistēmē* and *phronēsis* are reduced to forms of *technē*. We have seen evidence of this reduction in the definitions of education considered above. According to the instrumental, technological paradigm, theoretical knowledge (*epistēmē*), that is, "knowledge that," has value only if it can be used in practical contexts, whereas moral knowledge (*phronēsis*) is reduced to a form of problem solving or technical know-how. Gadamer's analysis also supports Peters's suggestion that in the industrialized world the concepts of knowledge and education have been narrowed to an instrumental connotation and have excluded a Socratic-Platonic conception of "knowledge of the good."

In a similar vein, George Grant, in his discussion of the technological "paradigm of knowledge" which defines modern reason, remarks that

> "modern reason" is the summoning of anything before a subject and putting it to the question, so that it gives us its reasons for being the way it is as an object. A paradigm of knowledge is not something reserved for scientists and scholars. Anybody who is awake in any part of our educational system knows that this paradigm of knowledge stamps the institutions of that system, their curricula, in their very heart, in what the young are required to know and to be able to do if they are to be called 'qualified'.[31]

Grant clearly indicates that our political, moral, and educational justifications concerning the orders, systems, and institutions in which we live are close to incapable of questioning the technological paradigm precisely because they themselves embrace and are embraced by the technological paradigm. There is no other paradigm, "no other language available which does not seem to be the irrational refusal of the truths of scientific discovery."[32]

Whether one agrees with the details of these analyses or not, they clearly provide all the motivation we need to question the various conceptions of education that we have been reviewing in this section. These conceptions, from the progressivistic to the formalistic to the humanistic, seem to reflect the same technological understanding pointed to by Heidegger, Gadamer, and Grant. But if we want to think in some way beyond these modernist conceptions, we find ourselves with a hermeneutical problem. The tradition of technological thinking so dominates that any attempt to think "outside" of it tends to find itself on the "inside." For example, the critical attempt to bring it into objective view so as to escape it is itself a modernistic, Cartesian, technological move. To ignore this complicity would be to fall into Descartes' naiveté concerning his escape from tradition. Even if we cannot completely escape it, however, can we not transform it by thinking of it in a different way? Can we not, even if ultimately guided by technological understanding, think in opposition to it in order to think of it as a whole?

I would suggest that if we are motivated to think of education differently, beyond or in opposition to (even if still within) the modernistic categories of humanistic subjectivity and technological control, then we must think of it according to the hermeneutical approach developed in the previous chapters. We should conceive of education not as a deliberate human enterprise, but as a process that happens to the human enterprise; not as a process that is consciously achieved within human culture, but as a process that achieves culture. Within education both individuals and traditions are formed and formulated. In opposition to those theories that equate education to certain technical forms of learning or methodological activities of teaching, or to the development of an individual's power over her environment, or to the transmission of what Bacon referred to as a "rich storehouse" of knowledge, we are motivated to question whether education is something under our control, or something that has its own power in which we must learn to participate.

A MODERATE THEORY OF EDUCATION

Education as hermeneutical, as interpretation, does not constitute the most familiar or automatically acceptable theory of education. But to say that education is irreducible to the controlled activities of human subjects or to the methodologically defined framework of educational institutions does not require a return to a nonempirical or speculative metaphysics of education. To speak of "mystery" as distinct from "problem" is not to become involved in an irrational mysticism about the educational process. To declare education to be a process "larger" than any particular individual or society does not necessarily lead to the Hegelian conception of an absolute Spirit that accomplishes its formative development (*Bildung*) in a dialectical journey through ever more perfect forms. Rather, a conception of education which is neither metaphysical nor mystical nor absolutist can be developed on the basis of the moderate hermeneutical approach proposed in the previous chapters. This moderate conception, which maintains that education is essentially a "larger" process than that defined by student-teacher relationships or the usual conceptions of teaching and learning, does not exclude the essential and necessary participation of individuals, be they teachers, students, or institutions. If I may borrow a phrase from R. S. Peters, then we might say that a moderate hermeneutical approach makes explicit how individuals are "put in the way" of educational experiences; how teachers and students find themselves in a process that encompasses them and that cannot be reduced to their individual efforts.[33]

A first approach to this moderate conception can be made by considering three aspects of educational experience previously described. Educational experience, to the extent that its nature can be defined as interpretation, is, on one side, conditioned by the tradition context of language and, on the other side, is opened out in a productivity that goes beyond all intentions. In both of these aspects education is a movement that transcends the complete control of those involved, while still requiring their participation. Participation or involvement in education means entering into "the way" or the movement of this process. Moreover, such participation requires a self-transcendence which projects the learner beyond a narrow subjective appreciation for subject matter and allows the subject matter to "speak" for itself. These three aspects of educational experience—its tradition context, self-transcendence, and productivity—manifest the irreducibility of education to a modernistically-conceived, humanly determined enterprise.

Tradition

All learning, as Aristotle pointed out, comes about on the basis of previously existing knowledge. Previously existing knowledge, organized in traditional disciplines, is not something bygone and unavailable. It remains existing and available within language. In the educational process, even when a teacher or institution attempts to control the student's access to information or historical fact, or to guide the student's use of language, there are aspects of the process of tradition and language at work which cannot be brought under control. Even the teacher's project to control the process is something defined or justified in a larger tradition which, though operative, may very well be exterior to the teacher's conscious intentions, although not external to the process of education. We have seen that the same forces of tradition and language form the fore-conceptions that operate in the student's understanding. A tradition is not something like a collection of information so that once it is entered into a program of education it is under the control of the participants, or neutralized with respect to the process. The educational process does not close around tradition. Rather, tradition is something that conditions the process. Like understanding, learning should be thought of "less as a subjective act than as participating in an event of tradition . . . in which past and present are constantly mediated" (TM 290).

To whatever extent the influence of traditions is excluded, the learning process is closed down. But this cannot happen as long as finite human understanding has a fore-structure that depends on previous experience. It cannot happen as long as learning something unfamiliar requires its relation to a familiar context. A *fore-structure,* a *context,* a *tradition*—these are all terms that signify necessary requirements for learning, and they cannot be reduced to explicit conscious control. We do not, for instance, invent a fore-conception ex nihilo in each case of learning; we do not create the context or tradition that we need in order to make sense out of the unfamiliar. These "fore-havings" are the always already constituted conditions for learning. To formulate this in an extreme way, we might say that they are not "possessions" of the epistemological subject; rather the subject is possessed by them, subjected to their power.

We saw this, too, with respect to language. Language is not a possession at the free disposal of the learner. Rather, the learner's disposition is to be caught up within a language which is "larger" than both learner and that which is to be learned. Precisely because of the nature of language educational experience moves in a line "that comes from afar and reaches on beyond [us]" (TM 548). Language carries us outside of ourselves, opens up a world which is already structured with meaning, and presents us with the possibilities which both transcend and belong to each of us.

Self-transcendence

Fore-structures, contexts, and traditions guide and place limits on learning. Yet, as we have seen, they do not, in a strong sense, determine the learning process. In any case of learning they are challenged, revised, renewed, opened up to question. Education is not the mere reproduction of tradition any more than it is an escape from tradition. The truth lies somewhere between these two extremes in the notion of a "transformation" of tradition. But what accounts for this transformation? Is it the individual power of the subjective consciousness faced with a quantity of information to manipulate? Just the opposite. Learning requires a self-transcendence which displaces subjectivity. In this regard, it is not so much the self which, under its own power, displaces itself, but the subject matter, the unfamiliar, which initiates the challenge to the fore-structure of understanding, and thus to familiar context and tradition. If self-transcendence starts from the self, it is not a "self-start." It is more the case that the self is startled out of itself in its encounter with the unknown.

Self-transcendence is an opening out toward one's own possibilities, a venturing into the unknown. But this is not a venturing completely within our own power. Nor do we create our possibilities ex nihilo. Something other is required to lure us out of ourselves; the *Atopon*: "that which does not 'fit' into the customary order of our expectation based on experience."[34] Richard Rorty refers to this as "the power of strangeness" (PMN 360). This strangeness, however, is not something that we, as learners or as societies of learners, project out in front of ourselves. We project our understanding in order to tame the unknown. The power of strangeness is transcendent to the limits of the self and only as such can it draw us into a playful, educational self-development of possibilities. We, as learners, find our own significance, our own sense of ourselves, only through a process that is both a transcendence and a submission to and participation in the play of experience.

In any case self-transcendence involves a movement into a larger experience, an experience that belongs to the self, not as a possession, but only as a possibility. Gadamer calls this experience "participation," which is not simply a "taking part," but a way of being taken up into the whole. Participation has an essential connection to productivity: "by our participating in the things in which we are participating, we enrich them; they do not become smaller, but larger. The whole life of tradition consists exactly in this enrichment so that life is our culture and our past . . . always extending by participation."[35]

Productivity

Is it possible to understand the notion of productivity, not in the narrow technical or economic sense, where "production is subordinated to utility,"[36] but in the way that Aristotle understood the concept of productivity as belonging to wisdom and *phronēsis*? Wisdom "produces happiness, not in the sense that medicine produces health, but as healthiness produces health" (*Nicomachean Ethics* 1144a4–5). Just so, the productivity of education is not concerned with an exterior outcome, the end result of a controlled production process, but is involved in the very experience of education. In familiar and popular terms, the university is not (and should not be) a factory; a curriculum is not a production device. The productivity of education is not the result of a planned-out curriculum which, with minor adjustments, could increase (or decrease) the outcome. Nor is it correct to equate the notion of educational productivity with the idea that education or its institutions produce a certain type of individual or class or society. A productivity of this type could be objectively measured and controlled. But the fact that the process of tradition and language, the same aspects that constrain and limit educational experience, also act as enabling conditions for it, gives us some indication that educational productivity is not entirely measurable or controllable.

The productivity of educational experience is akin to the creativity of the poet who, in composing poetry, does not always find herself in control of its composition. Language, or the poet's unconscious, or something beyond both language and the unconscious plays a role in the poet's productivity. In a similar way, with respect to interpretation, neither the narrow subjectivity of the interpreter nor the subjective intentions of the originator (of text, artwork, and so on) absolutely rule. Something new emerges, not as a product of a technically controlled process, but as a result of the tension or distanciation between interpreter and interpreted. The newness that emerges is not equivalent to what we termed the "strangeness" involved in self-transcendence. Rather, it includes what the encounter with the strangeness does to that which is already familiar. The familiar context, or our relation to tradition, is also changed in the process. There is a readjustment, revision, restructuring, reformation, renewal, or transformation of the familiar which accompanies the transformation of the unfamiliar into the familiar. The production of understanding is also a consumption and a renewed production (not re-production) of tradition.

Learning, then, involves the student in a productivity that goes beyond the intellectual genius of either teacher or student. It goes beyond what can be set up within the framework of educational institutions. It is as if we put to work all of our resources in a new, productive environment and found that we had produced not only educated individuals beyond our expectation but educated individuals who totally redefine our resources and environments. Rather than an economic multiplier effect, there is a transformation effect in education that gives us, not necessarily a quantitatively larger outcome, but an outcome qualitatively different from the one planned. Just as the interpretation of a text is not necessarily a better understanding than the author's own, but a different understanding, so education will not always signal progress, but it will signal something different from what educators might expect. History attests to this.

These three aspects of educational experience lead us to a conception of education that is not reducible to a modernist definition. We have already noted, however, that we cannot leap outside of the modernist, technological understanding but can only think further, within it, perhaps in opposition to it, as one might throw up a resistance within an oppressive political state. Thus, in our explication we still find ourselves using categories like power, subjectivity, and productivity which have been conditioned by a technologically oriented understanding. At most we can say that the moderate theory of education offers a conception that cannot be reduced to a modernist definition. In this sense, even if it cannot exclude certain modernist aspects, it does transform them.

Consider, for example, the progressivist emphasis on problem solving and critical thinking.[37] The principle of rationality which underpins these approaches is not as comprehensive as hermeneutical rationality. A theory of rationality that makes Enlightenment claims about escaping prejudice or ideology does not represent a broader conception of rationality than a hermeneutical one, which admits its human limitations; it represents an idealized extreme. The same idealized rationality is consistent with the narrow modernist emphasis on *technē*. Kant, as the central figure of modern thought, demonstrates this consistency when, in the Preface to the second edition of the *Critique of Pure Reason*, he characterizes reason in Baconian fashion.

> Reason has insight into that only, which she herself produces on her own plan . . . she must move forward with the principles of her judgments, according to fixed law, and compel nature to answer her question. . . . Reason, holding in one hand its principles, according to which concordant phenomena alone can be admitted as laws of nature, and in the other hand the experiment . . . must approach nature, in order to be taught by it: but not in the character of a pupil, who agrees to everything the master likes, but as an appointed judge, who compels the witnesses to answer the question which he himself proposes.[38]

Dewey's conception of reconstruction reiterates this Baconian conception of rationality in precisely the same terms.[39] In this fashion, his concept of reconstruction in education, which includes problem solving and critical thinking, represents a narrow, technical application of reason.

A moderate conception of education does not exclude the concepts of problem solving or critical thinking. Rather, only because in its essence educational experience involves interpretation, can we say of it that it can be viewed as problem solving, critical thinking, and so forth. For a hermeneutically based account of education, technical problem solving is only one part of a larger rationality that is never unprejudiced or unlimited by the constraints of human understanding. By such an account the reconstruction of experience involved in problem solving would be viewed as essentially a transformation of the type which takes place within a hermeneutical situation. Here the notion of application is different from the modern view of the relationship between theory and practice, in which a neutral theory is applied in an objective fashion to a particular problematic situation. Instead, the hermeneutical notion of application, related to the concept of *phronēsis*, requires a situated, less than objective response. In this view there is never anything like a pure problem unrelated to the more ambiguous or "mysterious" (in Marcel's sense) dimensions of human existence. In this moderate conception, problem solving or critical thinking takes place by means of a questioning that does not simply approach the situation from the outside or forget that the questioner herself, with her preconceptions and convictions, is involved. Such questioning is not totally under the control of an autonomous, prejudice-free, pure subjectivity which, by means of an idealized scientific method, approaches a problem in an absolutely disconnected and objective way. Rather, as I have indicated (p. 163), questioning is more a habit, disposition, or practice within a process larger than the individual subjectivity. It cannot be reduced to either pure passion or pure action or pure method. Questioning, in this sense, is a *praxis* informed by self-understanding.

If it is not too disconcerting to Greek translators, we could say that questioning is an art based on *phronēsis* rather than a method based on *technē*.[40] This linking of art and *phronēsis* suggests something other than the modernist ordering. Rather than reducing *phronēsis* to a form of *technē*, we would propose that *technē* should be actually practiced under the guidance of *phronēsis*. If in the modernist conception *phronēsis* is viewed as impoverished, if educational situations are constantly conceived of as problematic or nonhermeneutical situations, or if that which is technical is usually thought to be value neutral, so much the worse for education and *praxis*.

The concept of *phronēsis*, then, has an important place in the moderate conception of education. Specifically, in the way that we are *involved* in the educational process and to the extent that educational experience involves a *self-understanding*, we can say that educational practice should not be equated with a simple *technē*, but resembles more a practice guided by *phronēsis*. Educational experience depends on our involvement; without our involvement there would be no such experience. However, this involvement cannot be equated with instrumental attempts to control the educational process as a means to a certain end. Involvement does not mean that we are in contact with educational experiences in an external, objective way, or that we technically manipulate them for explicitly defined purposes. Educational experience is not *essentially* connected with the fact that educators and administrators construct institutions, set up explicitly defined goals, and design curricula. Such external dealings with educational phenomena do not constitute the involvement required for the one who would teach or learn. Educational involvement means that the student and teacher are in a hermeneutical situation, rather than what Dewey would call a "problematic situation." The hermeneutical situation is more of a mystery in which we are essentially involved than a problem which we simply confront. In Gadamer's terms, educational involvement is a form of hermeneutical belongingness.[41]

Involvement is clearly one of the characteristics of *phronēsis*. It can be positively characterized in terms of self-transcendence. In self-transcendence subjectivity is not maintained within itself and opposed to its object. Rather, subjectivity is drawn out of itself toward its possibilities. It is dispersed out of itself and exists as totally involved in the experience. Education does not occur if one stands back and acts as an external observer. Nor is education simply a gathering of information that does not affect the student. To be educational, experience requires self-transcendence, an involvement that gives education its moral dimension.

Self-understanding is another aspect of *phronēsis* or moral knowledge, one which can be viewed in terms of self-appropriation. In learning anything, we learn about ourselves; in a projection toward possibilities we come to understand ourselves. Self-appropriation is always effected through self-transcendence. To understand oneself does not mean to take an objectifying reflective view of some centralized, transcendental ego, but to interpret oneself in light of one's involvement in that which gets interpreted. The subject matter, in the end, is not something external to an inner process. To the extent that we are involved in it we must find ourselves in it.

The hermeneutical principle of application in educational experience has its model in moral rather than technical knowledge. It is not equivalent to a pragmatic or instrumental application in a means-end framework. Rather, its sense must be related to the projection and self-appropriation of possibilities. It is thereby connected to the dimension of self-responsibility implicit in self-understanding. Self-responsibility is the result of a practical wisdom rather than a practical know-how. It is not that the subject, after standing back from itself and viewing its actions in an objective manner, then decides to take responsibility for those actions. As already indicated (pp. 166–167), the self which gets understood is neither the self which stands prior to experience nor the self which stands at the end. Self-responsibility, a particular sense of *phronēsis*, is not an end state, but is involved in the process of transformation undergone in educational experience. This is so because in the dialectical process of transcendence and appropriation, self-understanding is always being tested out, challenged. One who learns by transcending the narrow confines of her own opinions through a questioning which opens up the subject matter simultaneously questions and transcends herself and assumes responsibility for the self-transformation that takes place.

We can best summarize this moderate theory of education by drawing up a list of principles which correlate with the principles of moderate hermeneutics. Simply stated, the moderate theory of education would be defined by the following principles.

(1) *Educational experience has a hermeneutical circular structure.* Whether the educational experience consists of attending a formal classroom lecture, playing, reading a text, solving a problem, thinking critically about a social problem, or having a conversation, we have seen that it involves a hermeneutical circle. Most explicitly, the learner's attempt to understand that which is to be learned is always guided by a fore-conception that provides a context to which he can relate the unfamiliar. In other terms the learning circle can be described as the dialectical interchange of transcendence and appropriation.

(2) *Educational experience is always constrained by the process of tradition.* Whether we consider the notion of the disciplines which define subject matter, or the discipline of education itself, with all of its specifications for method and practice, or the hermeneutical situation in which the student finds herself, we find some specific tradition operating. In such hermeneutical operations, a tradition is never something bygone and left behind. It lives on and biases the learning process in both positive and negative ways. It functions in an anterior manner and plays a role in defining the authority structure of educational experience.

(3) *Educational experience is always linguistic.* In obvious ways education involves language. Language is the medium of education, whether by speech, writing, or signing; unless an individual first comes into language, learning is impossible. The work of language, however, is not totally apparent. Covertly it is the vehicle of the tradition process, and in that role it introduces bias and authority into educational experience. Education always happens by way of an understanding conditioned by language.

(4) *Educational experience is always productive.* Education is not the simple reproduction of traditions. It allows for the renewal of traditions whereby traditions, understood differently, are made "our own" or become the subject matter of novel interpretations. In educational experience the participants neither escape nor repeat traditions; they transform them. The productivity of education involves the transformation of traditions, subject matters, and, most importantly, individuals and societies. The individual is never merely reproduced but is drawn out of himself toward his own possibilities and is remade by his experience. One needs only to consult the historical record to see that society is always undergoing transformation. The advents of the industrial, the technological, and the electronic/computer ages were never divorced or independent of education and of new interpretations of our relations to the past. The transformations of moral, religious, and cultural values are obvious in their connections with educational experience.

(5) *The hermeneutical structure of educational experience is the same as that of questioning.* In the learning experience the unfamiliar and the familiar, the learner and a particular tradition, the possible and the real, are all challenged and opened up in a

process that manifests the same logic as questioning. Through educational experience all of these factors are made indeterminate so that the possibilities of the learner and the meaning of the world are opened to a restructuring. Involvement with the questioning process is the way into educational experience and constitutes its course.

(6) *Educational experience always involves application.* Application is meant not in the instrumental or external sense of practicality, but in the more fundamental sense of making something relevant to oneself. Learning is always "interesting"; it always has immediate application because it always involves the projection and appropriation of one's own possibilities and thus entails self-formation. If this is true, then it follows that one does not "get" education or become educated simply by attending school or by memorizing information. Education is more than literacy. Nor is education guaranteed by a teacher who attempts to make the material relevant to the concerns of the student. Even the most irrelevant (in the external or practical sense) and uninteresting material can provide the opportunity for "putting the student in the way" of learning.

(7) *Educational experience involves self-understanding.* Self-understanding is not simply the end result of education but a constant and renewable process that is ongoing in every case of genuine learning. In the movement of transcendence and appropriation, the self is tested out and challenged. In contrast to the modernist primacy of self-consciousness, educational experience involves, not an autarkic retreat into a private ego, but an interpretation of the world, a movement out toward possibilities that are made one's own. Self-understanding is a growing transformation effected in one's encounters with the unfamiliar, formal subject matter and fellow students.

(8) *Educational experience has a normative dimension.* Learning involves self-responsibility, modeled on *phronēsis*, to the extent that the learner becomes involved in the experience and finds herself within a process of self-understanding. This normative dimension is diminished or hidden to the degree that the sense of education is reduced to objective confrontations with problematic situations, or to a straightforward transmission of information or technique.

These eight principles summarize a theory of education developed from the viewpoint of moderate hermeneutics. This is what education is. It is an interpretational process. It has a hermeneutical circular structure akin to questioning. It is informed by the tradition context of language and is productive of self-understanding and the interconnected transformations of traditions, subject matters, individuals, and societies.

If the nature of education is as I have described, then any prescriptive formulae that would specify how educational institutions ought to be arranged, or how teachers and students ought to conduct themselves in their attempt to move into educational experience, must take into consideration this nature.

A HERMENEUTICAL RETRIEVAL OF PLATO'S CONCEPT OF *PAIDEÍA*

> We frequently use the words learning and understanding synonymously.
>
> Aristotle[42]

I began by claiming that there is an ancient connection between hermeneutical and educational experience. One way to see this connection is to view Plato's theory of *paideía* from the vantage point of the moderate theory of education just outlined. I want to explore the idea that Plato's concept of education, as it is developed in the *Meno*, comes close to being the educational theory which corresponds to a moderate hermeneutics. This exploration will help to do three things. First, it will help to tie down some of the fleeting references I have made to Plato in the preceding chapters. Second, it will serve to flesh out the moderate theory of education as I have developed it here. Third, it will help to show how this moderate approach, finding its roots in the more ancient connection between *hermēneía* and *paideía*, transforms the modernist definitions of both interpretation and education.

Questioning Tradition

In the first part of the *Meno* (70a–80d) Socrates and Meno explicitly pose questions about virtue. Implicitly, however, questions are raised about the nature of learning and about the proper relationship between the process of tradition and inquiry. Meno, as a student of the Sophist Gorgias, represents an educational system that is based on the memorization of poetry and impressive-sounding definitions. In challenging Meno's ready-made definitions, Socrates challenges an established orientation toward education.

The contrast between the concept of education represented by Meno and that represented by Socrates is captured by Plato in the opposition between two types of ignorance. Meno's ignorance, based on memorization, can be characterized as thinking that one already knows the answer, or is in control or possession of the truth, when, in fact, one has failed even to think through the proper question. Meno's attitude closes the door to the pursuit of knowledge, to learning, since he feels that he already has the answer. Socratic ignorance, on the other hand, as a knowing that one does not know, constitutes a motive for the pursuit of knowledge. It is an attitude of openness which is necessary for a genuine educational experience.

In contrast to Meno's inclination to rely on his memory of Gorgias's definition, Socrates calls for Meno to do his own thinking (71d).[43] That Meno insists on his remembered definitions, however, dramatically serves Plato's purpose in a double way. First, in a way intrinsic to the dialogue itself, it serves to show who Meno is and what he represents.[44] Second, and perhaps more importantly for our considerations, it serves to indicate a relation to the process of tradition that is proper for genuine educational experience. That Meno's definitions are first stated and then questioned, and that this leads to a state of *aporia*, indicate several essential ways that traditions operate in educational experience.

A particular tradition, statically represented by Meno's definitions, must be viewed as a starting point for inquiry rather than as a storehouse of knowledge. In contrast to a Cartesian presuppositionless beginning, Plato would insist that any inquiry has its origin in a prior tradition and that since traditions operate throughout inquiry they need to be made explicit in the very beginning. The process of tradition operates in a way that defines the problem and orients our thinking. Reflection on traditional answers thus represents a way into inquiry. Of course, this does not mean that Meno's reliance on and obedience to traditional definitions represents the proper attitude for learning. Indeed, if opinions are repeated and immediately accepted, learning is closed off and indoctrination rather than education takes place. We can see throughout the dialogue that Meno is not open to the possibility of learning because his indoctrination is complete and he attempts to hold fast to his fleeting opinions. The proper attitude toward the process of tradition is represented by Socrates, who is dissatisfied with Meno's statements and questions them.

Socrates' dissatisfaction with Meno is more than a dissatisfaction with the particular inadequacies of his definitions. For Socrates, the important issue is not whether a particular definition is correct but whether Meno is taking the proper attitude toward traditional definitions. Specifically, Meno fails to think for himself. Thinking for oneself does not mean either starting from scratch or coming up with a definition that is unique and nontraditional. Thinking for oneself means questioning a particular tradition. By questioning ready-made definitions and opening them up to inquiry, Socrates, as Gadamer suggests, participates in the tradition (TM 362ff). In the end one might find that a particular definition does reveal something of importance. But making a definition one's own involves thinking through the tradition for oneself, and this represents something more than Meno's reproductive obedience. Learning cannot be reduced to memorization, even the memorization of the correct answers. It essentially involves asking questions within an orientation that is guided by a process of tradition.

Plato's concept of the proper relation to traditions is located between blind acceptance or reproduction and Cartesian denial or escape. It is properly represented by Socratic questioning and the resulting *aporia*. The first step in thinking for oneself, or in learning something, is to admit to perplexity. *Aporia* helps to clear away false opinions which act as unproductive prejudices. The state of *aporia* is not, as Meno claims (80a–b), a paralysis of inquiry, but a starting point which has benefited from a questioning of tradition. The state of *aporia* is opposed to the kind of "knowledge" that Meno possesses, which later in the dialogue is associated with opinion (*dóxa*). Meno's opinion is not a genuine knowledge but a collection of memorized facts and definitions. For Plato, education is more than a collection of information. Meno is literate. He can recite the poets. But this does not mean that he is educated.

Recollection and the Hermeneutical Circle

Meno opens the second part of the dialogue (80d–86c) by suggesting the famous eristic paradox about learning. The paradox, which Socrates states in full, is as follows: a person cannot learn that which he knows, for if he already knows it he has no need to learn it; nor can a person learn what he does not know, for if he does not know what it is, he does not know what to look for (80e).

The paradox works for Meno only because he holds to a certain underlying preconception about the nature of knowledge. Meno's preconception is that when one sets out to know something, the something is an isolated phenomenon without relation to other things, and thus to know it one has to recognize it totally, all at once, for what it is.[45] In the extreme, then, Meno conceives knowledge as disconnected bits of information. John Sallis relates this conception of knowledge to Meno's conception of definition, which is that one must define something once and for all in an absolute fashion because to do otherwise would be to become involved in an infinite regress from one undefined term to another.[46] The paradox simply restates this alternative: either one knows absolutely or one is totally ignorant. In Meno's conception there is no mediation between these extremes.

Sallis interprets the fundamental theme of the *Meno* to be the relation between whole and parts.[47] His interpretation facilitates an insight into the connection between Socrates' answer to Meno's paradox, that is, the concept of recollection and the notion of the hermeneutical circle. As we have seen, the traditional model of the hermeneutical circle is explained in terms of parts and wholes. The meaning of a part is understood only within the context of a whole; the whole is never given without an understanding of the parts. Understanding thus requires a circular movement from parts to whole and from whole to parts. Meno has a problem seeing this relation. His definitions of virtue turn out to be a listing of parts of virtue without any notion of the whole (71e–72c). This prompts Socrates to admonish Meno to focus on the whole and to "stop making many out of one" (77a; see 74a).[48] By the paradox and its underlying conception of knowledge, Meno denies the relations of parts to whole and thereby denies the hermeneutical circular structure of understanding. In effect, the paradox would make understanding and learning impossible.

The myth of recollection is offered by Socrates as an answer to the paradox. Many aspects of the theory of recollection have already been adequately discussed by others.[49] There is, of course, an aspect of its dramatic purpose that expresses Socrates' moral concern (as teacher) for Meno (as student) and for the subject matter. Socrates feels that the inquiry is beneficial for both himself and Meno and ought to continue, just as he fears that Meno might fall prey to the permanent paralysis of skepticism if he maintains the paradox. Over and above this concern, however, the doctrine of recollection calls for an interpretation that goes beyond its literal rendition or its dramatic purpose.

The theory of recollection is based on a conception of knowledge different from Meno's. This conception is summarized in Socrates' phrase: "the whole of nature is akin" (81d). Things are not disjointed. Parts are parts of a whole. Learning does not consist of stumbling upon an immediate, absolute, and satisfying knowledge of something. Learning is rather a searching for understanding within a context.[50] Knowledge is a movement between ignorance and absolute insight which never comes in contact with either extreme. All of nature is connected. Thus our knowledge of parts throws light upon the whole, and our knowledge of the whole throws light upon the parts. This concept of knowledge as dialectic reasserts the hermeneutical circle which had been denied by the paradox. We can learn about the unknown only by recognizing it *as* something that fits into or challenges what is already known. The hermeneutical "as" expresses our ability to orient ourselves toward the unknown from out of a context already known. Learning about some unknown always involves a preconception of what that unknown could be, given our prior experience and the typical ways that we interpret the world. We know in general how physical objects, philosophical concepts, works of art, and so forth behave given our past experience and the predictable nature of the world. We make room for the unknown in a preconceived although as yet indeterminate place within the familiar world. Further exploration will verify or change our preconceptions and will design a more determinate place for the object. Recollection, then, as "giving an account of the reason why" (*aitias logismos*) of something (98a3–5), means to gather together parts into a whole, things already known into a context that will make sense out of that which is unknown. Recollection, which is learning, is not our connection with a bygone past or with an unchanging eternity; it is our projection of meaning based on past experience, past association (see *Phaedo* 73d), or on our familiarity with a tradition. It is the creation of a context by re-collecting into a unity or kinship the experiences relevant to unlocking the meaning of the unfamiliar. In this sense it is a denial of the extreme alternatives of absolute knowledge or total ignorance. With respect to the process of tradition, recollection is not passive acceptance or reproduction, but an active interchange or dialogue with traditions which actually form the context for learning.

Crombie suggests that recollection is something like an exploration or explication of what he calls "truisms," or what we have called preconceptions.[51] These are categories or beliefs that are taken for granted, "crude beginnings" of conceptual definitions that operate beneath the surface of the dialogue to inform Socrates and Meno about what they are discussing. The common ground which is taken for granted by Meno and Socrates is what makes their conversation meaningful and allows at least a minimal communication. Recollection, in one sense, is a gathering together of this common ground of traditional beliefs upon which they might pursue the unknown. In Sallis's terms, it is a gathering together of parts to make a whole out of which the unknown might be encountered, or into which it might be incorporated. Sallis equates these preconceptions with "an implicit knowledge of the original wholes" which really has the nature of opinion (*dóxa*). He further suggests that the Platonic notion that true opinion is dispensed by the gods (99c) counts as a mythical image related to the story of recollection.[52] We return to this point shortly.

The slave boy scene, in which Socrates teaches and a boy learns geometry, constitutes not "one of the great frauds in the history of education,"[53] but an instance of dramatic reinforcement. Here the reader learns what Meno fails to learn—that learning is possible in a process that demonstrates the operative meaning of recollection. The boy, who never encountered the problem of the geometrical square before and who does not, therefore, recall or remember a solution to it, is, in Meno's eyes, in a state of total ignorance. But

Socrates recognizes that the boy has a significant fore-knowledge of Greek (82b), of the square's appearance (82b), and of calculation (82d) to constitute a common ground for learning. Through his patient art of questioning, Socrates guides the boy to see and to think for himself. Here questioning drives the process of gathering together the relevant information for solving the geometrical problem. Learning is possible and is not equivalent to a literal recollection. It involves thinking for oneself. The boy is motivated by Socrates' questions to think for himself and to gather his resources into a context that, one day, if he has the opportunity to continue his lessons, will result in mathematical understanding.

Self-understanding and Phronēsis

In the third part of the dialogue Socrates reasons as follows: If virtue is knowledge, then it is taught. But there are no teachers of virtue, and thus it is not taught. Therefore, virtue is not knowledge. In raising this problem Socrates implicitly suggests the possibility that there is a type of knowledge that cannot be taught. The real question is directed at an earlier assumption, that all knowledge is teachable. Obviously some knowledge is teachable. Geometry can be taught to a slave boy. And certainly in a didactic or dogmatic manner information can always be passed on. As Socrates' discussion with Anytus shows, technical knowledge is also teachable (90a–94e). But is the heart of genuine education, virtue, something that can be reduced to *technē*? Given the lack of teachers of virtue, notwithstanding the sophists, who do reduce virtue to *technē*, it seems that virtue must be something different from *technē*, at least in the way that it is acquired.

   Technē, as Gadamer has pointed out, was associated with the "new *paideía*" of the sophists, and as a basis for education it was consistently criticized by Plato. On the other hand, Plato associated *phronēsis* with dialectic and proposed it as the basis of genuine education, although in itself it cannot be taught.[54] If, with Gadamer, we return to the threefold distinction between theoretical, technical, and moral knowledge, it seems clear that for Plato both theoretical knowledge (like geometry) and technical knowledge (like medicine and flute playing) are teachable. But on the question of whether moral knowledge (*phronēsis*) is teachable (Meno's original question), Socrates must return to an examination of traditional answers and, through questioning, push toward another *aporia*.

One traditional answer provided by the poet Theognis is that one might learn virtue although it is not teachable (95d–96a). This appears as a contradiction only if the distinction between teaching and learning is obscured. More precisely, the state of *aporia* is reached with respect to the question of whether virtue is knowledge or something else. If one could maintain that virtue is a form of knowledge which can be learned but not taught, then the *aporia* might be resolved. But the perplexity grows because Meno has no conception of what kind of knowledge that might be.

Socrates obliquely hints at the answer: "We are probably poor specimens, you and I, Meno. Gorgias has not adequately educated you, nor Prodicus me. We must then *at all costs* [language which is reminiscent of 86b–c] turn our attention to ourselves and find someone who will in some way make us better" (96d). Obviously, if I turn my attention to myself I will find only one person, me. Socrates suggests that one must look to oneself in order to become virtuous. In effect, the type of knowledge which one can learn but not be taught is self-knowledge. If virtue is knowledge, it is in some sense self-knowledge. There is no teacher who can tell me who I am in a way that is superior to my own possibility of finding out for myself.

Self-knowledge, which is intimately linked with *phronēsis* and thinking for oneself, is clearly contrasted, not only to Meno's reliance on memorized definitions, but to the type of knowledge offered by the Sophists. Even those Sophists, like Gorgias, who, through clever technique, could compose fine-sounding and memorable definitions do not represent for Plato the ideal of education. Education is more than rhetorical technique, as characterized by Plato. Rhetoric, as practiced by Sophists such as Gorgias, is a collection of purely formal techniques used to impress those who listen. As formal technique it does not manifest moral involvement and concern for student, subject matter, or truth. If we define *art* (a term that in English once signified "learning") as a practice that manifests such moral concern, then for Plato education has more to do with art than with formal, unconcerned *technē*. The notion that art or learning involves moral concern would not be irrelevant to the concept of virtue (*aretē*) or *phronēsis* under discussion in the *Meno*. Education cannot be reduced to an exercise of techniques which simply allow us to manage information. In this sense, and to the extent that Socratic questioning is an art rather than a technique or method, Plato does not fall on the modern side of a transition line defined by Heidegger.

Heidegger's Line

Heidegger, in his essay "Plato's Doctrine of Truth," locates Plato on a transitional line between older, premodern conceptions of truth and education and newer, more modern conceptions already influenced by an emphasis on *technē* as a form of knowledge.[55] In Heidegger's reading, the ancient concept of *paideía* already begins in Plato to break down into a division of disciplines just to the extent that the concept of truth as *alētheia* (unconcealedness) is transformed into a concept of truth as *orthotēs* (correctness, *adequatio intellectus et rei*). In pushing his analysis back to Plato, Heidegger shows that the late ancient conception of *paideía* constituted a humanistic, metaphysical concept of education that had already come under the sway of a technological thinking about truth and the specialized division of the sciences.[56]

Heidegger "speaks against" the modernist, metaphysical concept of education in the same sense that he "speaks against humanism."[57] Heidegger is against education to the extent that education has been associated with *technē* and the division of the sciences, and to the extent that education encourages us to cling "to what is readily available and controllable even where ultimate matters are concerned."[58] Education in this sense encourages us to assimilate the unfamiliar always in terms of familiar metaphysical standards. Is there a way, then, to think of education beyond the concept of education Heidegger speaks against?

Heidegger sees, in Plato's allegory of the cave, a genuine association between *paideía* and *alētheia*. Plato's notion is that *paideía* as "a turning around of the whole person in his or her nature or essence" results in a turning toward truth. Problematically, in the same allegory, the more modern conception of truth emerges: correctness, conformity to Idea, *adequatio*. Yet Heidegger carefully notes the ambiguity of Plato's doctrine. Furthermore, the fact that

Heidegger's thinking on this transformation of truth from *alethēia* to *adequatio* undergoes some revision[59] suggests that a rereading of Plato is in order.

The reading of the *Meno* which I have just offered locates Plato on the earlier side of the transition line drawn by Heidegger between premodern and modern conceptions. Consider that in the *Meno* Plato refuses to treat the notion of truth as *adequatio* as primary, and indeed sets himself against such an ordering. He does so by opposing the views represented by Meno, especially his conception of knowledge. Meno's idea that one either knows absolutely or is absolutely ignorant, his idea that a thing is what it is in isolation from anything else, and his idea that one either knows the isolated thing or does not, all reduce truth to *adequatio*, correctness, or the holding of correct opinion. But on the conception of knowledge which reestablishes the hermeneutical circle, that is, the one held implicitly by Socrates in the theory of recollection, the concept of *adequatio* cannot express the sufficient condition of truth.[60] In effect, the concept of *adequatio* applies to correct opinion rather than knowledge. On the one hand, opinion is either true or false in the sense of correct or incorrect. On the other hand, if questioning has a priority in the formation of knowledge and sets the stage for the answer, and if the question qua question is not subject to a verifiability as a fact or opinion might be—that is, we cannot say that a question is true (correct) or false (incorrect), but only that it is appropriate or inappropriate in respect to what it reveals—then knowledge, in Plato's sense, is not a matter of *adequatio* but of *alētheia*.

Adequatio is taken as an inadequate kind of truth. It does not constitute the truth that must be sought in the educational process. For Plato, education means always going beyond truth as *adequatio*. *Adequatio* is a characteristic of purely technical or intellectual—logical, mathematical, formal—knowledge, a knowledge that lacks a moral dimension, a cleverness without *phronēsis*. Plato is not ambiguous about this. Education cannot be reduced to *technē* or *adequatio*. It involves more than a literacy with respect to correct opinions. It involves a self-knowledge that changes the learner. In this respect Plato's theory of education is located on the earlier side of Heidegger's transition line.

Participation

In another important way Plato's theory is nonmodernist. Plato does not reduce education to an activity that is totally under the control of human subjectivity. We recall Sallis's suggestion that the notion of divine dispensation raised at the end of the *Meno* counts as a mythical image connected to the recollection story. How should we interpret this image? Divine dispensation or inspiration is said to be the source for true opinions. The latter act as preconceptions or "truisms" (Crombie) which are taken for granted, but which must be interrogated and "tied down," that is, re-collected into a context for learning and the production of knowledge. But the source of such truisms (for example, Meno's definitions) is obviously a particular tradition as it is handed down by poets, interpreters, and teachers. By using the concept of divine dispensation as a mythical representation of tradition's role in education, Plato indicates that something larger than human subjectivity is involved.

We can find some confirmation of this interpretation in the *Ion*, where we find Socrates speaking about precisely those who at the end of the *Meno* are considered divinely inspired: poets, truthsayers, and seers. "Poets are nothing but interpreters (*hermēnes*) of the gods, each one being possessed by the god who inspires him" (*Ion* 534e). The interpretation of the gods is equated with the traditions that are handed down from poets like Homer. The poets, and those who receive the tradition from the poets, do not receive it through any technique that would control reception, but are said to be divinely inspired or have a divine power (533d–e and 536c; see also *Phaedrus* 245a). The distinction between *technē* and divine inspiration defines the difference between that which falls under the control of human subjectivity and that which is beyond the boundary of control. Divine dispensation, the process of tradition which transmits authoritative opinions and which operates as a starting point or orientation for educational experience, is something that transcends the boundary of subjective control. The learner, like the interpreter, like the poet, does not attempt a technically controlled production, but willingly enters into a realm larger than that allowed by the modernistic conception of subjectivity.

Here also we note that the Platonic conception of participation (*methexis*) appropriately expresses our relation to the process of tradition. Regarding this concept, Gadamer remarks that "like the Latin *participatio* and the German *Teilhabe*, the word *methexis* evokes the image of parts. . . . That the part belongs to the whole is precisely what [Plato's] new word underscores."[61] *Methexis* cannot be reduced to an act of subjectivity. The process, as a whole, is something larger than the subjective players involved. Of course, the balancing conception of questioning defines our proper and responsible participation in the process of tradition and makes education something more than passive acceptance of traditional opinions. The transformation of *dóxa* into *epistēmē*, which requires recollection as the *aitias logismos* (providing account of the reason why), is effected by questioning, as Plato clearly indicates (86a7–8). The paradox of learning raised by Meno is answered most effectively by questioning it. Indeed, the very possibility of questioning it defeats it. Questioning, as is clear from the Socratic art, is the practice which drives the recollective learning process.

To question a tradition, to turn opinions to account, to interpret in the proper way, requires a participation, an active taking part, that is not a reproduction of tradition, but a transformation. If education cannot be equated with skill in discerning the correctness of traditions, neither does it start abstractly without traditions. Plato and Gadamer are in agreement. With regard to our relation to the process of tradition in educational experience, we must seek a "truth in conversation" (*Protagoras* 348a) which is, in Heidegger's terms, a "conversing with that which has been handed down," so that there is no "break with history, no repudiation of history, but . . . an appropriation [*Aneignung*] and transformation [*Verwandlung*] of what has been handed down to us."[62]

Part 2

CHAPTER 7

Conservative Hermeneutics and Educational Theory

We return in this and the following chapters to the disputations and aporias that characterize the contemporary fields of hermeneutics and education. The discussions in these chapters cannot be exhaustive, either in terms of hermeneutics or educational theory. With respect to the various hermeneutical approaches, I will not identify a complete list of principles, but will focus only on those that contrast with the moderate principles developed in the previous chapters. Since I cannot consider all of the variations that exist in the field of educational theory, I will focus on those that seem to be the most influential in their respective areas. Granted these simplifications, I have tried to avoid oversimplifications.

The most productive approach in the following discussions will not be by way of a frontal attack which attempts to show how or why various theories are wrong. Without doubt, clear disagreements exist between the moderate approach developed in previous chapters and those considered in the following chapters. In highlighting the various disputations, however, my aim will not be to dismiss a particular theory as unsound. Wherever I can, I intend to show how and to what extent the theory under consideration may be genuinely compatible with or supplementary to a moderate hermeneutics. My aim is not to defend the moderate hermeneutical approach through a critique of other approaches; it is not even to hold fast to the classification of theories which I propose. Rather, the following discussions should be viewed as a testing of the moderate theory which on its own principles remains open to the possibility of revision.

PRINCIPLES OF CONSERVATIVE HERMENEUTICS

In our endeavor to specify the hermeneutical principles implied by conservative prescriptive canons and procedural rules, it will become apparent that there is no clear way of purging philosophical-hermeneutical principles of normative content. The normative content embedded in these principles constitutes the flag or emblem which identifies them as conservative, although they are not necessarily accepted in the same way by all theorists of conservative hermeneutics. In the following discussion, then, we will try to identify the source of these principles as well as some variations in their statements. The considerations which guide our selection of principles are twofold: first, we are interested in defining the differences between conservative and moderate approaches. Thus, the principles identified are ones that contrast clearly with Gadamer's hermeneutical principles. Second, since we are interested in those hermeneutical principles which lend themselves to a discussion of educational experience, our selection is ordered to that end. On the basis of these principles we will be able to define the educational theories that correspond to conservative hermeneutics.

The Hermeneutical Circle

The first and most famous of hermeneutical principles can be found in both conservative and moderate approaches: all interpretation involves a circular structure. In the previous discussion (Chapter 2) we saw how Hirsch's concept of "corrigible schema" is not unlike the phenomenological concept of fore-structure. Yet there is not complete agreement between the conservative and moderate versions of this principle. In the conservative approach the hermeneutical circle is an objective relation of whole and parts. Thus Betti, citing Schleiermacher, and without reference to anything like the fore-structure of understanding, describes the circle as "that relationship of elements between themselves and to their common whole which allows for the reciprocal illumination and elucidation of meaning-full forms in the relationship between the whole and its parts, and vice versa" (Betti 59). This concept of the hermeneutical circle, which identifies the whole as the objective totality of customs, conventions, and historical circumstances which make up the author's situation, and includes as parts objective aspects of the text, is the basis for Betti's canon of totality: "The meaning of the whole has to be derived from its individual elements, and an individual element has to be understood by reference to the comprehensive, penetrating whole of which it is a part."[1]

In contrast to the "circle of understanding" described by Gadamer in terms of the fore-structure of the interpreter's understanding and the projection of meaning, Betti and Hirsch (following Schleiermacher) describe a circle located on the side of the object of interpretation in which meaning is already present. In this concept of the hermeneutical circle Betti and Hirsch are led to an important and convenient distinction between meaning and significance, originally suggested by Husserl.[2]

Betti warns against confusing the meaning which belongs to the object of interpretation with a completely different phenomenon: "its present *Bedeutsamkeit* (significance) and relevance in changing historical epochs" (Betti 68). On the one hand, *meaning* is objective; it is embedded in the text and the text's relations to its own historical context. *Significance*, on the other hand, is something that belongs to the present interpretation because of the interpreter's circumstances. Hirsch explains: "There is a difference between 'the meaning of a text' (which is unchanging) and 'the meaning of a text to us today' [its significance] (which changes)."[3] What changes from one interpreter to the next "is not the meaning of the work, but rather their relationship to that meaning. Significance always implies a relationship, and one constant, unchanging pole of that relationship is what the text means."[4] From the point of view of Betti and Hirsch, Gadamer places too much emphasis on significance, which depends on an interpreter and the interpreter's situation, and too little emphasis on meaning, which belongs to the text. On the basis of this distinction several other principles become clear.

The Principle of Reproduction

Perhaps the most important of conservative principles, and the one with the greatest amount of normative content, involves the concept of reproduction or reconstruction (*Nachbildung*).[5] We approach it through the canon which states that interpretation ought to reconstruct (reproduce) original meaning if it is to be valid. Meaning originates with the author of a text, the originator of a "meaningful form," cultural object, and so on. The author's intention, then, is set up as the criterion which measures the validity of the interpretation, which depends on the extent to which the re-construction of meaning (as distinct from significance) takes place. Thus Betti describes the task of the interpreter to consist

> in recognizing the inspiring, creative thought within these objec-tivations, to rethink the conception or recapture the intuition revealed in them. It follows that understanding is here the re-cognition and re-construction of a meaning—and with it of the mind that is known through the forms of its objectivation—that addresses a thinking mind congenial with it on the basis of a shared humanity. (Betti 57).

This reproduction is not a productive act by the interpreter; within the interpretive process, productivity is identified only in the origi-nal author who invests the text with meaning. Interpretation "is an inversion of the creative process: in the hermeneutical process the interpreter retraces the steps from the opposite direction by re-thinking them in his inner self" (Betti 57).

For Hirsch, the identity and unchanging stability of meaning is manifested precisely in its ability to be reproduced. "Now the meaning of a text is that which the author meant by his use of particular linguistic symbols. Being linguistic, this meaning is com-munal, that is, self-identical and reproducible. . . . Being reproduc-ible, it is the same whenever and wherever it is understood by another."[6] Verbal meaning is determinate, self-identical, and changeless. "Indeed, these criteria were already implied in the re-quirement that verbal meaning be reproducible, that it always be the same in different acts of construing."[7]

The canon which prescribes that the interpreter ought to re-produce the author's intention or the original meaning depends upon the very possibility of a recognitive, reproductive interpreta-tion. The relevant conservative principle of reproduction can be formulated as follows: reproduction is possible, and requires the recognition of the author's original intention.

The Principle of Application

Both Betti and Hirsch express concern about the possibility of the interpreter's situation interfering with the validity of interpreta-tion. From their perspective, Gadamer's principle of application describes the place of significance in interpretation but fails to account for meaning. They offer a conservative principle of application that makes room for meaning, deemphasizes the role of significance, and thus limits the concept of application. The conservative principle of application can be discerned at the basis of Betti's "canon of actuality," which states that "an interpreter's task is to retrace the creative process, to reconstruct it within himself, to retranslate the extraneous thought of an Other, a part of the past, a remembered event, into the actuality of one's own life; that is, to adapt and integrate it into one's intellectual horizon" (Betti 62). This involves a transformation of meaning into significance. But such a transformation is always an extra step added to recognitive, reproductive interpretation, and depends on it. One cannot discern the significance of something unless one first knows its meaning.

The relevance or significance of a particular meaning to the interpreter's situation can be restricted or expanded by means of analogy. But since analogy goes beyond reconstruction, it requires the employment of further canons to guide it (see Betti 61–62). Moreover, it is not the case that all interpretation involves application. According to Betti, the historical interpretation of ancient texts, for example, will not necessarily have relevance to present-day situations.[8]

The Principle of Objectivity

A major concern of Romantic hermeneutics is expressed in Schleiermacher's phrase "active misinterpretation"—the case of reading "something into a text because of one's own bias."[9] Droysen describes the problem in clear terms, and proposes a solution. "The greatest danger is that we involuntarily bring in the views and presuppositions of our own time and the present interferes with our understanding of the past. . . . It is only through cautious, methodical interpretation that we can gain concrete and assured results and so correct our notions about the past. This will enable us to measure the past according to its own standards."[10] The solution to the problem of active misinterpretation is the employment of the proper method which will allow the interpreter to step outside of the hermeneutical situation or dissolve the hermeneutical circle in order to know the past according to its own standards, that is, to achieve historical objectivity and interpretational validity.

The concept of methodological disengagement or disconnection required to gain historical objectivity introduces a certain perplexity into hermeneutics which might be termed the "dilemma of Romantic hermeneutics." On the one hand, to judge the past on the basis of its own standards requires a methodological *disconnection* of the interpreter from his own historical situation. On the other hand, a necessary condition for the interpreter to understand an Other, an author, or a past object or text is the interpreter's *connection* to the historical life (shared humanity, spirit, or language) which he shares with the Other—a life that the interpreter has only by virtue of being situated in history. The Romantic dilemma is aptly expressed by saying that the interpreter must be connected to his historical situation for understanding to be possible, but disconnected from his historical situation for understanding to be valid.

This dilemma is resolved by Betti into a tension between two canons: the canon of actuality (reproduction must be accomplished within the hermeneutical situation of the interpreter, the actuality of her own life) and the canon of the autonomy of the object. The latter states that objects of interpretation must be understood "in accordance with their own logic of development, their intended connections, and in their necessity, coherence, and conclusiveness; they should be judged in relation to the standards immanent in the original intention" (Betti 58). One cannot disconnect oneself from the hermeneutical situation, but, within the situation, it is possible to treat the object of interpretation as autonomous.

At the basis of the canon of autonomy lies the principle of objectivity, which can be phrased as follows: interpretation can be autonomous; it can occur entirely within the terms and properties of the object's own standards. This is more or less Hirsch's formulation: "understanding is autonomous . . . it occurs entirely within the terms and properties of the text's own language and the shared realities which that language embraces."[11] This principle has a corollary, a principle of methodology which states that there is a general set of hermeneutical canons or procedural rules that, if followed, will yield valid interpretations. If the interpreter is to gain understanding, according to Betti, she must seek access to the autonomous object, "not in an arbitrary way, but with the help of controllable guidelines" (Betti 68–69). Contrary to the Romantic dilemma, the proper method will not disconnect the interpreter from her situation, but will build on those aspects of her situation that are shared with the object. The Romantic dilemma is avoided by an appeal to transcendental (ahistorical) subjectivity. The object "is part of the human spirit and is, to speak with Husserl, born of the same transcendental subjectivity" (Betti 69). By disconnecting ourselves (in a Husserlian phenomenological reduction) from our historical being, we effect a phenomenological connection with a shared transcendental being.

For conservative hermeneutics both the concept of validity, as a normative concept which relies on a methodological control over the interpretive process, and the concept of originary meaning, on which validity is founded, depend on the modern conception of subjectivity. Hirsch makes the determinacy of original meaning depend on a determining will. The act of will on the part of the author or originator constitutes the "discriminating force which causes the meaning to be *this* instead of *that* or *that* or *that*, all of which it could be. That discriminating force must involve an act of will. . . . Determinacy of verbal meaning requires an act of will."[12] Correspondingly, on the side of the interpreter, reproductive interpretation is governed by the interpreter's act of will, which must be made subordinate to canons or procedural rules if validity is to be gained. Ultimately the validity of interpretation can be traced back to the free choice of a norm for interpretation. Schleiermacher could easily be invoked here: "understanding must be willed and sought at every point."[13]

Hirsch also employs Husserlian concepts to discuss objective interpretation. Despite the variety of perspectives an interpreter might take, the intentional object, that is, the meaning of the object of interpretation, remains identical.

> Verbal meaning, being an intentional object, is unchanging, that is, it may be reproduced by different intentional acts and remain self-identical through all these reproductions. . . . Since this meaning is both unchanging and interpersonal, it may be reproduced by the mental acts of different persons.[14]

An interpretation is objective when it reproduces precisely the verbal meaning intended by the author. The verbal meaning, however, may depend, not only on context, but on implications which the author may not consciously intend. The author's intention, taken as a whole, also includes such unconscious implications. Husserl calls this an "inner horizon" which belongs to the objective meaning of the object; Hirsch defines it as "a system of typical expectations and probabilities." To attain an objective interpretation, then, the interpreter needs "to posit the author's horizon and carefully exclude his own accidental associations."[15]

According to Hirsch, the interpreter can attain a certain degree of objectivity by following a set of procedural rules. The interpreter, by following such rules, can attain a correct interpretation, although never a certain interpretation. "No one can establish another's meaning with certainty. The interpreter's goal is simply this—to show that a given reading is more probable than others. In hermeneutics, verification is a process of establishing relative probabilities."[16] We have already discussed Hirsch's concept of interpretation as an inductive process (p. 68). The point here is simply to indicate that the concept of objectivity which he employs is one based on probability.

Inductive logic, or the logic of probability, and Husserl's phenomenology appeal to similar concepts of evidence to define adjudication. It is no surprise, then, to discover that the procedural rules proposed by Hirsch for the attainment of objectivity depend on the concept of interpretive evidence. To arrive at an objective interpretation the interpreter must consider all relevant evidence for the probability of his interpretation. The interpretive hypothesis, which is the basis for an objective interpretation, "is ultimately a probability judgment that is supported by evidence."[17]

The four principles we have specified as defining conservative hermeneutics do not constitute an exhaustive list. They are, however, sufficient to our purpose of showing the hermeneutical basis of several current educational theories. We can expect that, given the stress on methodological control and subjective will, conservative hermeneutics will support what we have termed a "modernist" conception of education (see pp. 174ff.). We can also expect that the central notion of hermeneutical reproduction is not unrelated to the concept of reproduction much discussed in educational theory.

CONSERVATIVE THEORIES OF EDUCATION

Currently, two educational ideals dominate discussions of educational reform: cultural literacy and critical thinking. These approaches are not without precedence. The current discussion of cultural literacy, however, has been focused by Hirsch's book of the same title.[18] The critical thinking movement is less focused but more widespread. We will explore its theoretical foundations by discussing research conducted by a number of theorists. My contention is that both of these movements, although they are different and in some senses even opposed to one another, are implicitly based upon a conservative hermeneutical approach.

Cultural Literacy

Education functions as a means for passing on to a new generation the cultural heritage of a nation. This is Schleiermacher's view. It has recently been taken up by Hirsch. The aim of education, according to Schleiermacher, is to "prepare the individual for common participation in the state, the church, free society, and academia."[19] *Bildung* constitutes the development of a people, a nation or *Volk*. Hirsch explains it as follows: "In an anthropological perspective, the basic goal of education in a human community is acculturation, the transmission to children of the specific information shared by the adults of the group or *polis*" (CL xvi). Only on the basis of this shared cultural information "can we learn to communicate effectively with one another in our national community" (CL xvii).

In this section we need to show to what extent this conception of education reflects conservative hermeneutical principles which describe interpretation as reproductive. In the following section we will ask whether the cultural literacy program is based on an adequate conception of educational experience.

Hirsch's program calls for the transmission of certain information. It is not our purpose to argue here about the specific information that he considers essential to American culture. We are more concerned with the nature of the transmission process, and what in his view constitutes literacy. "To be culturally literate is to possess basic information needed to thrive in the modern world" (CL xiii).

There are three conceptual elements in Hirsch's opening statement on literacy: (a) the concept of possession; (b) the concept of content or information; and (c) an instrumental concept which explains why we need to be literate, namely, "to thrive in the modern world." These elements are explicated further in his later statements. "Only by accumulating shared symbols, and the shared information that the symbols represent, can we learn to communicate effectively with one another in our national community" (CL xvii). The possession of information involves a process of accumulation. The content consists of shared meanings. The reason for having such information is to communicate effectively and to share in such things as economic prosperity, social justice, and effective democracy (see CL 1–2). Hirsch introduces a certain ordering into these elements. From the point of view of education, the most basic element is the accumulation of information which takes place in the transmission process. The information or shared meaning of culture already exists as a presupposition to the transmission process, and effective communication is a potential outcome of education. Thus Hirsch proposes that "a human group must have effective communications to function effectively, that effective communications require shared culture, and that shared culture requires transmission of specific information to children" (CL xvii).

It would be an oversimplification and distortion of Hirsch's theory to try to isolate the transmission process from its context of presupposed content and potential outcome, or to call these latter two elements external to the educational process. Clearly these elements all depend on one another, and we must see how they fit together in an essential way. It would not be an oversimplification, however, and it would help us to see how transmission, content, and outcome fit together, to recognize that Hirsch presents a conception of education which corresponds, in large part, to conservative hermeneutical principles.

The transmission of information, basic to the ideal of cultural literacy, depends on the concept of hermeneutical reproduction rather than hermeneutical transformation. The concept of reproduction undergoes an important expansion in meaning as we move from the narrow field of textual hermeneutics to the educational context. As a principle of conservative textual hermeneutics, reproduction means the act of reconstructing the original meaning of a text, the original intention of an author. In the educational context, reproduction signifies a larger process, inclusive of, and to some extent dependent on, the former process of textual reconstruction. The larger process is often referred to as "cultural reproduction," a process in which traditional ideas and values are passed on in educational experience. Cultures are transmitted from one generation to the next. The concept of cultural literacy clearly involves a particular form of cultural reproduction in which the form of transmission includes the hermeneutical reconstruction of literary texts.

For the most part, Hirsch conceives of the relation between education and culture as a stable, "steady-state" system. Cultural meaning is something that has autonomous and relatively stable existence. This does not mean that the content of cultural meaning does not change. Hirsch admits to such change while still maintaining the notion of stability. "The flux in mainstream culture is obvious to all. But stability, not change, is the chief characteristic of cultural literacy" (CL 29). The stability of meaning—its autonomous self-identity—a basic feature of cultural meaning—can be explained in terms of the hermeneutical distinction between changeless meaning and fluctuating significance. The object (the content) of cultural literacy is meaning rather than significance. Transmitting this meaning implies that it is taken up and passed on *intact*, without damage. Indeed, damage or distortion introduced by educational experience would destroy the reproductive goal.

The most basic and controlling element of cultural literacy is meaning. Any transformation of meaning into significance, that is, any application to the student's present situation, constitutes a step beyond the reproduction of meaning, although it remains dependent on that reproduction. One cannot get along in the cultural world without first possessing the essential concepts which constitute literacy. Yet, as Hirsch has always maintained, on the *practical* level, one cannot isolate meaning from significance, nor can one separate the reproduction of meaning from the relevant use to which it is put in current situations.

Earlier, I defined significance as any perceived relationship between construed verbal meaning and something else. In practice we are always relating our understanding [of meaning] to something else—to ourselves, to our relevant knowledge, to the author's personality, to other, similar works. Usually we cannot even understand a text without perceiving such relationships, for we cannot artificially isolate the act of construing verbal meaning from all those other acts, perceptions, associations, and judgments which accompany that act and which are instrumental in leading us to perform it.[20]

This holds true for educational practice as well. The cultural meaning which is transmitted to the student cannot be isolated from the significance it has for him in his life—that is, the practical outcome. Precisely here Hirsch moves from the concept of reproduction to the conservative principle of application. Once literacy is attained, it automatically has an effect on our ability to deal with the world, to communicate effectively, to pursue our personal and national interests.

To what extent does significance impose upon, determine, or distort meaning? Or to what extent do practical interests impose upon or determine or distort the content of culture? In answer to these questions, raised in either the hermeneutical or the educational context, Hirsch carefully avoids any concept of transformation and systematically defends the concept of reproduction.

Hirsch explains the effect of literacy on our practical dealings by using the concept of 'background information'. This is a concept he generalizes from the area of textual hermeneutics. "The comprehending reader must bring to the text appropriate background information that includes knowledge not only about the topic but also the shared attitudes and conventions that color a piece of writing" (CL 14). For Hirsch, cultural literacy consists of "the network of information that all competent readers possess. It is the background information, stored in their minds, that enables them to take up a newspaper and read it with an adequate level of comprehension, getting the point, grasping the implications, relating what they read to the unstated context which alone gives meaning to what they read" (CL 2). The hermeneutical circle is apparent here. Background information constitutes the appropriate knowledge one needs to fill in the context, construct the whole, into which a particular part will fit. Without such background knowledge, that is, without cultural literacy, the student would not be able to contextualize the object under study and would fail to understand.

So far, Hirsch's educational theory is consistent with his hermeneutical approach. We can see the principles of reproduction, application, and the hermeneutical circle at work in his theory of cultural literacy. But when he attempts to show how background information actually functions, not just in the practical outcome, but in the very process of learning, he cites certain research results which are not totally consistent with his conservative hermeneutical principles. The central concept of this research is the familiar notion of schema, a notion Hirsch had previously used to describe the hermeneutical circle (see pp. 62ff.). Moreover, just as we have seen in the case of the corrigible schema as model for the hermeneutical circle, Hirsch's reliance on this concept in the educational context introduces some conclusions which are more akin to a moderate approach.

Hirsch cites language research which shows that reading is much more an active, constructive process than a passive reception of information. "It brings to the fore the highly active mind of the reader, who is now discovered to be not only a decoder of what is written down but also a supplier of much essential information that is not written down. The reader's mind is constantly inferring meanings that are not directly stated by the words of a text but are nonetheless part of its essential content" (CL 33–34). The reader can supply the proper information only if she has the appropriate background knowledge. Background knowledge is structured into models, prototypes, and middle-level categories ("ones [which] children learn first in acquiring language; they learn *tree* before *oak*" [CL 49]), or what Hirsch in general terms 'schemata' (CL 51). The source of background knowledge is, of course, our past experience, or more pertinent in this context, what we can learn in school. "We are able to make our present experiences take on meaning by assimilating them to prototypes [schemata] formed from our past experiences" (CL 51).

What Hirsch describes under this concept of schema is much more akin to Gadamer's notion of the fore-structure of understanding than to the conservative principle of the hermeneutical circle.

> Two-way traffic takes place between our schemata and the words we read. We apply past schemata to make sense of the incoming words, but these words and other contextual clues affect our

initial choices of schemata and our continuing adjustment of them. . . . Thus, the reader is not just passively receiving meaning but is actively selecting the most appropriate schemata for making sense of the incoming words. Then the reader actively adjusts those schemata to the incoming words until a good fit is achieved." (CL 53)

If we play down the instrumental control which the subject has over the schemata in Hirsch's account, and play up the sense of active participation, we are closer to Gadamer's notion of fore-structure than to the objective whole-parts relation of conservative hermeneutics. What Hirsch cites as evidence for the assimilative nature of schemata, that is, that our learning will be constrained (as well as enhanced) by the schemata we have at our disposal, also counts toward the notion that our schemata are essentially conservative—in Piaget's terminology, assimilative rather than accommodative (see CL 222, n. 25)—and that they introduce biases and preconceptions into our interpretations. Thus, as Hirsch says with respect to memory, we introduce "elements from our normal schemata that weren't in the original event, and, by the same token, [we] are always suppressing some elements of the original event that don't exist in our normal schemata" (CL 55). Here Hirsch contrasts the constructivity of schemata to the ideal of reconstruction. Distortion in the direction of "habitual schemata" indicates a productive, transformative process rather than a reproductive one. Our schemata, to some extent, function in the learning process to make the content conform to them (assimilation). Thus the reproduction of content or meaning, which would involve the accommodation of our schemata, is undermined by the way schemata actually function.

Hirsch, however, would not be willing to give up his conservative principles so easily, and in order to reassert them in this regard he would have recourse to two responses. First, this application of schemata and the potential distortion or productivity they introduce is something which occurs *after* the original reproduction which supplies the schemata or background knowledge in the first place. Hirsch does not deny the notion of productivity as an outcome of educational experience. He aptly demonstrates that education, even education in the most conservative ideology, can lead to radical changes in society (see CL 22–24). Cultural revision, he says, "is one of our best traditions" (CL 101). The problem, however, is that Hirsch himself has already admitted that the distinction between meaning and significance, and thus between reproduction and production, is theoretical, and that it would be artificial to impose such a distinction in practice. In effect, one might say that Hirsch's theory is that *in practice* educational experience doesn't work as neatly as he thinks it does in theory.

A second recourse for Hirsch would be to emphasize that the corrigible nature of the schemata can lessen their distorting (or productive) effects. "We know that schemata overlap and get embedded in other schemata, that we treat them as provisional theories open to revision, and so forth" (CL 56). This would bring us back to the conservative principle of application, which asserts not only that constructing significance can only be subordinate to reconstructing original meaning, but also that one must use proper procedural rules or canons to control the construction of significance. In this regard, if schemata are open to the process of controlled revision, one must appeal to appropriate procedural rules to guide that revision. For example, if, as Hirsch contends, we are forming our schemata on the basis of shared meaning, then, to some degree, our schemata must conform to the schemata of others (see CL 64). One is literate if one has internalized *shared* schemata (CL 68). Such internalization does not rule out productivity, but does allow for the original reproduction to rule over productivity. Reproduction remains the basis of cultural literacy.

Finally, in order to see the connection between the hermeneutical principle of objectivity and the program of cultural literacy, we need only look at Hirsch's argument that the content of cultural literacy is value neutral. Hirsch is sensitive to those who would argue that by requiring the reproduction of specific cultural information, the cultural literacy approach would be preserving the ideological content of the dominant social class. Hirsch argues that our "national vocabulary" is value neutral in the sense that it is open to all classes and constitutes the instrument "used to support all the conflicting values that arise in public discourse" (CL 102). The term *vocabulary* means, for Hirsch, "cultural literacy—the whole system of widely shared information and associations" (CL 103). Such a cultural vocabulary does not advocate one class over another, but is the vocabulary of adjudication and communication among classes. "In fact, one of the main uses of a national vocabulary is to enable effective and harmonious exchange despite personal, cultural, and class differences" (CL 104). Cultural literacy is inherently classless, ideologically neutral, and nonexclusive.

Within the educational situation the cultural literacy approach claims to provide the basis for the communication of objective, value-neutral knowledge, rather than knowledge biased by ideology or political belief. We can come to valid conclusions about social, economic, and political arrangements in our society only if, educated as citizens, we share such ideologically neutral information. The unbiased nature of this knowledge—its objectivity—allows for what Hirsch specifies as the aim and outcome of cultural literacy, that is, effective communication in our national community.

It should now be clear how the conservative hermeneutical principles of the hermeneutical circle, reproduction, application, and objectivity tie together in a cohesive theory the transmission process, content, and outcome associated with Hirsch's conception of cultural literacy.

Critical Thinking

At first it may not seem surprising that Hirsch is critical of current critical thinking programs which emphasize the teaching of thinking skills. Starting with his discussion of Rousseau and Dewey and the content-neutral conception of educational development which emphasizes learning how to think critically (see CL xv, 59), Hirsch sets out to show that such programs are ineffective (CL 61). One needs "substantive schemata that are highly specific to the task at hand" in order to make cognitive skills work. The kind of cognitive skills provided in critical thinking programs are *not* transferable from one kind of problem to another (CL 61–62).[21] Hirsch opposes the equating of literacy with the possession of a set of formal techniques, and he contends that such an equation has dire consequences, not only for students but also for teachers (see CL 112–113). Hirsch rightly perceives that the critical thinking movement tends to be critical of any approach (such as cultural literacy) which emphasizes content over skill; thereby, the critical thinking approach "avoids coming to terms with the specific contents of literate education" (CL 132–133).

On this last point there can be little doubt. In a recent announcement of a major conference on critical thinking and educational reform we find statements which clearly dispute the cultural literacy emphasis on content. "Education is not a mere piling up of more and more bits and pieces of information."[22] The same source states: "Everywhere information is multiplying and at the same time becoming rapidly obsolete. Half the information that students are laboriously memorizing today will be out-of-date in about six years." This same point is made in numerous studies.[23] Theorists of critical thinking generally seem to be critical of approaches that are based on the mere transmission of information or blind memorization.

Despite this apparent opposition between cultural literacy and critical thinking, it is not difficult to show that the two approaches are operating on the same ground. Indeed, cultural literacy and critical thinking can be so clearly opposed to each other only because they share the same fundamental principles; the two movements emphasize only different aspects of educational experience which are not, at bottom, incompatible.[24] One obvious area of agreement concerns the purpose of education, that is, to prepare the student to live in the modern, technologically oriented, and fast-changing world. Hirsch argues that the student can avoid disenfranchisement from the fast-paced technological environment only by becoming literate (see CL 108); proponents of critical thinking argue that only the possession of transferable skills will allow the student and citizen to keep pace with change. Indeed, if one focuses on the proposed outcome of education, then cultural literacy and critical thinking appear to be complementary parts of a progressive ideal of education.[25]

We can begin to see more of the common basis for the approaches of cultural literacy and critical thinking if we move from the dimension of outcomes (aims, objectives) to more central questions concerning the nature of learning. One area of contention between the cultural literacy and critical thinking approaches seems to be the use of memorization. That memorization is a basic feature of the cultural literacy approach is cautiously admitted by most of its proponents. Hirsch argues that the use of memorization is justified because, realistically, it is almost instinctive in young children (CL 30, 131). Still, Hirsch and others recognize that cultural literacy must be more than the simple memorizing of lists.[26] Without denying the need for memorization, Hirsch and the proponents of cultural literacy do not want to reduce learning to *blind* memorization. In effect, memorization must be supplemented by a certain critical component. Indeed, this is the whole point of cultural literacy. For Hirsch, the benefit of cultural literacy is that it is not inert information, but *useful* information—it allows one to function well in modern society. This means not only that cultural literacy and critical thinking share the same goal, but that a certain form of critical thinking itself must be employed for cultural literacy to be effective. In Hirsch's hermeneutical terms, the reproduction and application involved in the cultural literacy approach must be guided by procedural rules, and this involves critical thinking.

The employment of procedural rules, central to Hirsch's hermeneutical approach, is the sine qua non of reproduction and legitimate application. The objectivity of that which is to be reproduced is guaranteed only if the interpreter (whether student or curriculum designer) follows the proper rules of evidence in learning or choosing the content of cultural literacy.[27] Even if, in the student, reproduction is accomplished, uncritically, by memorization, still in the application of that information the student needs to become critical. The student cannot properly ascertain the significance of the reproduced meaning without paying heed to logical principles or guidelines that legitimate application. Literacy is not limited to simply having information; if we are to succeed in the modern, technologically complex world, if we are "to communicate effectively with one another in our national community," then we need to test and to apply information. Precisely this testing of ideas is what Hirsch calls the critical function of interpretation.[28] How different is such critical testing from the critical thinking concept of evaluating or assessing statements? Robert Ennis defines critical thinking in precisely this way: "the correct assessing of statements," that is, weighing evidence in terms of logical, empirical, and pragmatic (contextual) criteria.[29] In terms even closer to Hirsch's hermeneutics, Joanne Kurfiss offers the following characterization: "A student offering evidence from a literary text to support an insight about the author's intentions is engaged in critical thinking."[30]

Not only does cultural literacy require critical thinking, but critical thinking requires cultural literacy. The idea that cultural literacy is an enabling condition for critical thinking qualifies the claim made by proponents of critical thinking that it is useless to have students pile up information which will soon be outdated. Hirsch's contention is that a great deal of information never goes out of date. One is then required to discriminate between highly changeable information (as typically found in the sciences and technology) and more or less unchangeable information (historical, literary, cultural facts). In this regard, a more balanced approach is not unheard of in critical thinking programs. Authors of a recent text on critical thinking write:

> In focusing on thinking skills, one need not deny the importance of acquiring knowledge. Indeed, we question whether a strong distinction between thinking skills and knowledge—a distinction that has sometimes been drawn quite sharply—is really defensible. At the very least, we would argue that the two are interdependent. On the one hand, thinking is essential to the acquisition of knowledge, and, on the other, knowledge is essential to thinking. . . . Clearly, thinking involves thinking about something.[31]

For the critical thinking approach it is clear that the possession of information is not enough; one also needs to know how to use or apply it. But it is also clear that many theorists emphasize the role of correct information in problem solving and critical thinking skills.[32]

If we have shown that, despite immediate appearances, there is a practical and perhaps necessary connection between cultural literacy and critical thinking, we have only hinted at how the critical thinking approach reflects specific principles of conservative hermeneutics. We still need to see to what extent this is the case.

If we focus on how information functions in educational experience, not only does an agreement between cultural literacy and critical thinking again become apparent, but a hermeneutical principle comes into view. On this point it is important to note that theorists of critical thinking often appeal to the very same model used by Hirsch to justify the cultural literacy approach, namely, the schema. The concept of the schema is used in critical thinking contexts to describe the organization and application of knowledge. Jonathan Baron, for example, suggests that "schemata can direct the search for evidence," and such employment of schemata can therefore be regarded as a critical thinking method.[33] In terms consistent with the conservative principle of the hermeneutical circle, Baron explains that the discovery of one piece of evidence motivates the search for other associated pieces, which in turn would count as evidence for the valid interpretation of the whole. "The relevance of a part would yield a weight of evidence, and would thus permit revision of the strength assigned to the possibility as a whole."[34] The schema, then, would be a model in which possible interpretations would be organized in terms of typical relations among parts. Having a schema, that is, knowing of various possible interpretations, would be not just a useful but a necessary component of critical thinking. For Baron, critical thinking would involve knowing how to use schemata and knowing when they are transferable, from context to context. To the extent that schema are general or transferable they can be taught as part of general heuristics or problem solving. Although schemata are usually context specific and "the teaching of schemata is therefore part of the teaching of specific subject matters, not the teaching of thinking,"[35] still, in any particular situation, critical thinking would involve the application of the appropriate schema. It is also clear that knowing when and how to transfer schemata from one context to another would involve a process of analogy and would require the application of procedural rules akin to the ones mentioned by Hirsch.[36]

In the strict critical thinking approach there is a clear emphasis on method rather than content, and it might seem that the concept of reproduction would not be relevant. Indeed, the focus seems to be on productive kinds of problem solving or critique; critical thinking involves challenging and analyzing rather than simply reproducing a fact or an argument. If the particular aims of critical thinking, variously listed as problem solving, evaluating arguments, weighing evidence, generalizing, using criteria, discerning and ranking alternatives, organizing and classifying data, recognizing fallacies, and so forth, are not directed per se at the reproduction of meaning, still, critical thinking is not incompatible with such an aim. Consider that reproductive interpretation may be one of the critical skills employed in critical thinking. Teachers of critical thinking may deem it important to distinguish carefully and clearly between what the author means and what we interpret to be the significance of that meaning relative to our own circumstances. They may also consider it important to distinguish between a fact, an opinion about a fact, and the use of a fact in a particular situation. In these cases critical thinking would include knowing and using skills, procedures, or methods necessary for the reproduction of meaning.[37]

The principle of reproduction could also hold for the learning of the skills and techniques of critical thinking. One could say that the critical thinking approach intends for the student to reproduce the skills demonstrated by the instructor. Many proponents of critical thinking, however, are careful enough to design their programs to foster a self-discovery process in which the student discovers for herself the required skills. Still, every critical thinking program will identify a variety of skills that the student needs to acquire and be able to replicate. If this is not the reproduction of meaning or content, it is not inconsistent with a reproduction of skills.

If it is difficult to make a clear case concerning critical thinking and reproduction, a stronger and more apparent connection can be shown to hold between the conservative principle of objectivity and critical thinking. Critical thinking, especially to the extent that it is modeled on scientific logic and problem solving, is conceived of as a way to attain objective and valid conclusions and solutions. There is a good deal of literature on different types of subjective and procedural biases and how to avoid them.[38] The analysis of procedural biases usually describes inadequacies in inductive procedures which limit or qualify the validity of the reasoning process. One tends to maintain one's own hypotheses, for example, by seeking only evidence which would confirm them and discounting evidence which might challenge them. Thinking critically means to avoid such biases and to be as objective as possible. Subjective biases, due, for example, to ideological beliefs that color our interpretations, can also limit the validity of our thinking, and critical thinking seeks to correct them.[39]

Not only is the analysis and avoidance of biases, and thus the concern for objectivity and validity, a specific aim of critical thinking, but, at least for some theorists, it is a definition of the critical thinking approach as a whole. Education, according to this approach, means literally being led out of one's own prejudices. For critical thinking this is what it means to achieve an objective understanding of subject matter. This is possible only if (a) the critical thinker avoids procedural mistakes and biases (this is a matter of proper technique and method), and (b) critical thinking itself is ideologically neutral. This last, rather controversial claim is argued by Harvey Siegel.[40] The argument he makes for critical thinking in this regard is similar to the argument put forward by Hirsch for cultural literacy, that is, that it is based on a value-neutral vocabulary.

Siegel argues against those who maintain that, since all thinking is conditioned by particular ideological perspectives, fundamental educational ideals like critical thinking must, of necessity, be based on a particular ideology and therefore cannot be ideologically neutral. In this view, Siegel notes, rationality itself would be a function of ideology. Siegel argues that rationality is more basic than ideology and must be "conceived of as autonomous from ideological constraints and indeed as providing the ground from which alternative ideologies can themselves be evaluated."[41] The very possibility of a true critique of ideology depends on the priority and autonomy of rationality. Critical thinking belongs to "enlightened rationality" rather than to any particular ideology, and thus, as an educational ideal, it is ideologically neutral. Such ideological neutrality, for Siegel, means that critical thinking operates in a way external to any ideology. In critically thinking about a particular ideology, we operate not only outside of that ideology, but outside of any ideology, in a realm of pure, enlightened reason. Even if we argue against a particular ideology from within our own ideological standpoint, we need to appeal to ideologically neutral criteria (such as logical consistency and validity) in order to construct a convincing argument. Critical thinking, much like conservative hermeneutics, claims to effect a methodological disconnection from ideological standpoints and thus to escape practical interests. Through critical thinking we can raise the question of the legitimacy of any ideology. We can criticize it "according to its own standards" or according to standards of a neutral rationality. We can examine it objectively because our own critical thinking escapes the bias of ideological beliefs.

If critical thinking clearly reflects the principle of objectivity, it also conforms to the conservative principle of application. Even within our own circumstances—ideological, educational, historical, social, and so on—we have recourse to a rationality that is independent of those circumstances. The validity of our interpretation is guaranteed by autonomous, rational criteria which we can find even from within our own situation. If, in conservative hermeneutics, objective meaning controls significance and thus defines legitimate application, in critical thinking the same autonomous, rational criteria which deliver objectivity will define what counts as legitimately significant, and likewise will control analogical interpretation.

The critical thinking approach thus translates conservative hermeneutical principles into an educational program, albeit not in precisely the same way as the cultural literacy approach. The latter emphasizes a literacy based on reproductive learning, an emphasis which is not central to critical thinking but one which is not incompatible with it either. Critical thinking shares with cultural literacy a central concern for ideologically neutral objectivity and validity in interpretation and for a controlled application of knowledge. Cultural literacy and critical thinking should not be viewed as essentially opposed to one another. They can function in a complementary fashion to provide a single comprehensive educational program.

A MODERATE RESPONSE: UNAVOIDABLE TRANSFORMATION AND THE BIAS OF LANGUAGE

Cultural literacy and critical thinking represent two programs for educational reform. As programs they are normative proposals which specify how educational experience ought to be conducted.[42] Our intention is not to dispute their normative conclusions or practical recommendations. Indeed, in some respects the complementary proposals of cultural literacy and critical thinking constitute viable and valuable approaches to educational reform. Our questioning and our discussion will focus more on the implicit principles of cultural literacy and critical thinking, and on the way in which their proponents understand the respective theories. Are their common assumptions about educational experience adequate to its interpretational nature? Do these approaches sufficiently capture the nature of the learning process?

Both the cultural literacy and critical thinking approaches reflect conservative hermeneutical principles. Such principles are contested by Gadamer's philosophical hermeneutics and the moderate hermeneutical approach to education worked out in previous chapters. In the moderate view, the hermeneutical circle involves a projection of a fore-structured understanding, rather than the purely objective relation of whole and parts; interpretation is not reproductive but transformational, both for the interpreter and the subject matter. The moderate claims that understanding cannot be complete, that the hermeneutical circle never collapses, that the student's comprehension never coincides with the pedagogical presentation, all speak against the concept of reproduction. In contrast to the strict distinction between significance and meaning, and the conservative ordering which places significance under the control of meaning, the moderate approach understands significance and meaning to be essentially connected in the hermeneutical situation. If anything, application always colors meaning with significance. Finally, the unbiased objectivity of interpretation is denied by the moderate principle of the unavoidably biased nature of interpretation. If, as we have contended, moderate hermeneutical principles genuinely describe the nature of educational experience, what does this portend for the cultural literacy and critical thinking approaches? If educational experience is not what cultural literacy or critical thinking claim it is, is it still something which enables both cultural literacy and critical thinking to be viable programs?

Although cultural literacy and critical thinking are not necessarily opposed to one another, their difference in emphasis is simply the theoretical distinction, writ large, between the reproduction of meaning and the production of significance. In practice, as Hirsch admits in the hermeneutical context, and ought to admit more clearly in regard to educational practice, one does not become literate without practicing critical skills, and one does not become a critical thinker without being literate. This essential and practical connection between literacy and thinking is made most clearly and carefully by the educational psychologist Robert Glaser.[43] Moreover, Glaser employs the concept of the schema in a way that leads us away from conservative hermeneutical principles and toward a more moderate hermeneutical approach.[44]

Schemata, Glaser explains, are prototypes based on previous knowledge, which learners use to interpret unfamiliar information. "In many situations in which they cope with new information, much is left out so that they could never understand the situation without filling it in by means of prior knowledge."[45] A particular schema may be compared with or projected upon a new situation; "if it fails to account for certain aspects of these observations, it can be either accepted temporarily, rejected, modified, or replaced." Such schemata may be overt or tacit, consciously employed or unconsciously functioning to shape our approach to knowledge acquisition. They play a central role in all thinking and understanding. "The strong assumption, then, is that problem solving, comprehension, and learning are based on knowledge [that is, prior knowledge organized in schematic form], and that people continually try to understand and think about the new in terms of what they already know."[46] Glaser thus makes a point which is not inconsistent with Hirsch's emphasis on knowledge (literacy) but which describes educational experience in terms of the fore-structure of understanding. Indeed, as we have seen, Hirsch's own account of schemata leads him in the same direction.

Because of the role played by schemata in learning, the learner does not passively receive meaning, but actively construes (constructs) it. According to both Hirsch and Glaser, the learner actively selects the appropriate schema for the construal of meaning (see CL 53). Learning will be constrained and/or enhanced by the schemata the learner has at her disposal. Such schemata are both assimilative and accommodative, both conservative and corrigible; but to the extent that they are assimilative, they bias our interpretations.[47]

The context provided by schemata, however, is neither purely subjective nor purely objective. The interpreter operates by construing the contextual horizon (schema) into which she attempts to place the intentional object to be understood, and then continuously makes adjustments until the object and context fit and make sense. This means that the hermeneutical process can never be described in purely objective terms. The process of construing, while guided by the object to be interpreted, and thus a process which is not entirely subjective, also depends upon a horizon of knowledge and prior experience which shapes the interpreter's understanding and constrains the possibilities of interpretation.

As Glaser notes, several pedagogical canons follow from the notion of schema. First, the teacher should "understand an individual's current state of knowledge in a domain related to the subject matter to be learned." Second, a teacher ought to educate toward a transformation of the student's schemata, that is, toward enlarging the student's horizon. Presenting new schemata, "different from, but close to, the [ones] held by the learner," would allow the learner to evaluate and modify her own schemata. "When dealing with individuals who lack adequate knowledge organization, we must provide a beginning knowledge structure. This might be accomplished either by providing overt organizational schemes or by teaching temporary models as scaffolds for new information."[48] The education of the student involves getting the student to explore and interrogate her own fore-conceptions, a critical "interactive inquiry" which, Glaser suggests, is similar to Socratic dialogue.[49]

The focus, here, on the transformation of the learner's horizon is quite different from the focus of cultural literacy on the reproduction of information. Yet it presents a way to justify a cultural literacy approach. Cultural literacy would expand a student's horizon and enable the student to build further upon that expansion. But this would be cultural literacy without reproduction. If schemata function as Glaser and others propose, then transformation is the rule and reproduction is ruled out.

Furthermore, the functioning of schemata involves a productivity which blurs the distinction between meaning and significance. If the learner is constantly supplying or supplementing information that is not present in the (theoretically) self-present and unchanging meaning, isn't that meaning shaped within a context defined by significance? As Hirsch puts it, "the reader's mind is constantly inferring meanings that are not directly stated by the words of a text but are nonetheless part of its essential content" (CL 33–34). If educational experience involves the employment of schemata (horizons, fore-conceptions), the reproduction of a self-identical and unchanging meaning would not be possible. What conservative theory calls "reproduction" is, from the moderate viewpoint, not reproduction at all, but something more inventive. The employment of schemata involves a process of assimilation and not just accommodation (see CL 51). "Thus, the reader is not just passively receiving meaning but is actively selecting the most appropriate schemata for making sense of the incoming words" (CL 53). "Making sense" implies the production of meaning; indeed, research on reading cited by Hirsch (CL 55) and research on mathematical problem-solving cited by Glaser indicate that the learning process is productive rather than reproductive.

The assimilative nature of schemata (that is, the projective nature of the fore-structure of understanding) undermines, not only reproductive interpretation, but also the objectivity of knowledge. Hirsch bases the notion of objectivity on procedural rules which define the proper criteria of evidence. One establishes the validity of an interpretation on the basis of the evidence one has for objective meaning. But clearly this simply pushes the problem back one step to the validity of one's interpretation of evidence. Procedural rules, the use of well-defined techniques and methods, do not solve the hermeneutical problem since they themselves fall under hermeneutical constraints. If I claim that my interpretation of "X" is valid because I have such and such evidence, on what basis do I claim the validity of my interpretation of the evidence? In the end, as Hirsch himself knows, one adopts a hypothesis which defines what will or will not count as evidence. But the nature of the hypothesis is a "guess," an interpretation—a projection of meaning based on past knowledge—a fore-conception that is constantly revised in light of the "evidence" and its interpretation. Baron rightly points out that the search for evidence is always directed by schemata (fore-conceptions).[50] An appeal to evidence does not get us out of the hermeneutical circle, but simply puts us into it in a different way.

Our discussions in the next chapter will examine the claims about the ideological neutrality of educational experience in some detail. Here, however, we need to take a closer look at the arguments of Hirsch and Siegel in this regard. Hirsch argues that cultural literacy is inherently classless, ideologically neutral, and nonexclusive. Thus, in principle, cultural literacy provides objective, value-neutral knowledge. Still, Hirsch does not try to deny that cultural literacy is culturally based. In defining the subject matter of cultural literacy, he seeks a "national vocabulary." Hirsch does not say that a national vocabulary is value free, only that it is value neutral. Clearly, this can only be maintained if the national vocabulary expresses, or is capable of expressing, all values. If, however, one moves to a more global, intercultural level of discourse, it will be difficult to maintain that national vocabularies are value neutral. Languages are always ethnocentric. National languages do conserve national values, worldviews, and traditions. The "necessary conservatism that exists at the core of the national vocabulary" (CL 107) is not just a linguistic conservatism. It is not just that vocabulary and syntax change with "glacial slowness"; old values are maintained against the intrusion of new values.

Richard Rorty argues that Hirsch's program of cultural literacy supports a pluralistic democracy precisely because of the neutrality of the cultural knowledge required for democratic communication.[51] But Hirsch's solution to cultural and political exclusion is not as clear-cut as either Hirsch or Rorty would like. Either (a) language is value neutral (as Hirsch would have it) and excluded groups need only become culturally literate to become included, while still retaining their own values, worldviews, and so on, or (b) language is not neutral but conserves established values and traditions, so that excluded groups, in becoming literate, must give up their own "un-common" values, worldviews, and so on, and adopt the established common ones. In the first case, Hirsch would have us believe that the original exclusion was based only upon the lack of literacy and that prejudices or differences in values and worldviews were not relevant to exclusion. In this sense Hirsch speaks of a pluralistic nation, but one conceived on a naively simple conception of political exclusion and communicative competence. In the second case, the excluded group would become included only by becoming the same as everyone else. As Hirsch indicates, "the specific contents of the different national vocabularies are far less important than the fact of their being shared" (CL 107). In this case, however, there is no pluralism, but only a nonpluralistic cultural leveling in which everyone would share and reproduce the same unchanging or slow-changing cultural meanings.

The claim that language is neutral in the educational process is opposed to the moderate hermeneutical concept that language carries within it the biases and preconceptions of various traditions. To what extent can we maintain one or the other of these claims? This is an important issue if educational experience is essentially linguistic. If we can show that language biases the knowledge acquisition process, both the neutrality of language and the objectivity of knowledge will have to be qualified.

The idea that literacy and schooling, to the extent that they rely upon language, lend themselves to "the construction of a *particular* form of knowledge that is relevant to a *particular* set of socially valued activities" has been demonstrated by David Olson.[52] Olson, citing empirical and cross-cultural studies, as well as the work of Piaget, shows that different means of instruction and different goals of education will bias the knowledge which is presented in a learning situation; furthermore, "knowledge is limited by the purposes for which it was acquired. . . . The information people acquire, whether written or pictoral, is selective. It is selected on the basis of its appropriateness to the task at hand." To the extent that knowledge is the consequence of various programs of instruction, such as cultural literacy and critical thinking, knowledge is not completely objective. Rather, "the types of knowledge that the school develops and the intellectual competencies that it fosters fit quite closely with the literate biases of the culture as a whole."[53] Olson's argument is based in part on the concept that written texts, used extensively in the educational institutions of Western societies, bias learning toward propositional logic and Enlightenment notions of knowledge.[54]

The low regard in Western literate culture for nonscientific (mythical, religious, superstitious) knowledge and the high regard for scientific knowledge is reflective of a Western Enlightenment bias. Hirsch himself suggests that the importance of scientific literacy for purposes of communication in a democracy is "closely tied to basic principles of the American republic" (CL 108). The very idea of cultural literacy itself reflects this same bias. In school instruction, the preferred language is one that emphasizes truth functions, validity, and objectivity in the service of logical description and explanation, rather than emotion, intuition, or authority. The emphasis placed on literacy and critical thinking testifies to precisely such a locutionary focus. In strict opposition to Hirsch's claim about the neutrality of common English (versus the biased nature of specific dialects) (see CL 105), Olson concludes that "'Standard English' is not a general model of the mother tongue but rather the specialized instrument of the description and explanation functions of literate prose."[55] The language of schooling, therefore, is biased in favor of a particular type of intellectual achievement.

This general conclusion reached by Olson is supplemented by sociological research which shows that the language of schooling fluctuates from one type of school to another, and that there are corresponding fluctuations in intellectual styles highly related to social class and background.[56] Further empirical research conducted by Olson and others puts in question the concept of the reproducibility, autonomy, or objectivity of the object of interpretation, and suggests the more moderate hermeneutical principle of productivity. Olson's research shows that if the teaching method, the presentation, or the proposed aim of the lesson changes, so does the content actually learned. If students "are taught the same content in two different ways, they are in fact not learning the same content but a somewhat different but related content."[57] Olson suggests that changes in the type of language used in instruction would reveal similar changes in content, and that language thus biases knowledge. The research of Olson and others thus challenges the idea that language is neutral in the educational process; it supports the moderate hermeneutical conception that language carries with it the prejudices of tradition.

Siegel, in a fashion similar to Hirsch, argues for the ideological neutrality of critical thinking. Critical thinking is conceived of as a pure instrumental rationality prior to and independent of any ideological commitment or prejudice. But even Siegel recognizes that pure reason is always embedded within particular traditions.[58] There is no getting away from this if, for example, Glaser, among others, is right about the essential connection between literacy (knowledge or information) and critical thinking. To think critically, within any particular discipline, one must be familiar with a traditional body of knowledge. Siegel cites Scheffler on this point. "The fundamental point is that rationality cannot be taken simply as an abstract and general idea. It is embodied in *multiple evolving traditions*, in which the basic connection holds that issues are resolved by reference to reasons, themselves defined by *principles* purporting to be impartial and universal."[59] Siegel argues strongly for the latter part of this statement. Reason may be embedded within traditions, but it transcends traditional prejudices and can be impartial and universal. Rationality is connected but at the same time is capable of disconnection. Isn't this the Romantic dilemma once again: an attempt to maintain the Enlightenment idea of instrumental reason together with the Romantic conception of embeddedness in tradition?

By introducing this dilemma, Siegel moves the discussion to the level of hermeneutical principles where we are confronted by a fundamental philosophical problem concerning the nature of rationality. If rationality always functions contextually, under the influence of particular traditions, then an appeal to a transcendental reason cannot be justified. Such a transcendental conception of reason is embodied in the conservative hermeneutical principle of objectivity and is defended by Siegel. He rejects the argument which reduces this conception of rationality itself to an ideology— the Enlightenment ideology.[60] Given the ambiguity inherent in the concept of ideology, it would be difficult to maintain this argument. But on hermeneutical grounds one could argue more generally that Siegel's conception of rationality belongs to an Enlightenment *tradition*. Gadamer's notion that the "prejudice against prejudice" itself operates as the Enlightenment prejudice defines the bias of this particular tradition. In the context of educational theory, Olson's work supports this view. Does not such bias limit the claim for objectivity in critical thinking? We return to this question for a fuller response in the next chapter.

The appeal to rational criteria which transcend any particular situation characterizes the notion of application in both cultural literacy and critical thinking. Even those who admit that the relevant rational criteria or operations depend on the particular context or discipline and are not generally transferable claim a particular sense of transcendence for them in order to guarantee objectivity and validity. As in conservative hermeneutics, the principle of objectivity overrules the search for subjective significance and defines the proper application to one's own situation. Does the call to objectivity within any particular hermeneutical situation, operating as a prescription for proper reasoning, accurately reflect the possibilities inherent in the actual hermeneutical or educational process?

In critical thinking, one clear prescription about how to control the interpretational situation and to guide thinking toward objective answers concerns the notion of metacognitive behavior.[61] The critical thinker must be able to step back from her thinking process to reflect on the procedure she is following and to measure her thinking in terms of transcendental procedures that guarantee objectivity. The model for this metacognitive check on reasoning is found in problem solving of the well-structured mathematical kind. It is a reflective technique which we can employ after or before the actual reasoning process in order to check results or plan out strategies. The modern concept of rationality at work in such critical thinking prescriptions is part of a tradition that can be traced back through Descartes and Leibniz to Plato and Aristotle: reason as *logon didonai*—providing reasons in support of one's assertions. But in Plato and Aristotle one can also find the beginnings of another tradition which considers rationality, not as strict *epistēmē*, but as *phronēsis*. The kind of deliberation involved in *phronēsis* concerns things that are not as well structured as mathematical problems but are ill structured or, as Aristotle says, "are susceptible of being otherwise than they are."[62] In educational experience the usual learning situation is ill structured. Here, the model of objective thinking, based on well-structured problems and sometimes offered as a model for critical thinking, is inappropriate and inadequate. A different model, more in line with moderate hermeneutical principles and with the rationality of *phronēsis*, would be more appropriate for the majority of educational situations. Critical thinking, to the extent that it incorporates the demands of cultural literacy and to the extent that it goes beyond the inadequate model of well-structured problem solving, requires a model consistent with moderate hermeneutical principles, a model more akin to the logic of question and answer, *phronēsis* and conversation, than the logic of syllogism.

In educational experience, in conversation and play, strict metacognitive control is not operative. In mathematical reasoning we may strategize from clear and distinct starting points to absolutely certain conclusions; in conversation, or in any play that is genuinely play, there is no such clarity or certainty. In metacognitively controlled problem solving, we already know the rules—we already understand prior to our cognitive operations. In educational experience, we are in the process of trying to understand something of which we are neither clear nor certain. Gadamer, following Plato and Aristotle, contrasts the certitude of mathematical *epistēmē* with the type of experience we have in *dialegesthai*, which is *to pathos tōn logon*, a coming and going of thoughts within the dialogue which is larger than any participant.[63] In the view of moderate hermeneutics, metacognitive processes are monological, but, as such, they are abstractions from the more original dialogue of educational experience.

Moderate hermeneutics tells us that critical thinking must in principle operate within the language context of tradition, within a literacy which is always biased one way or another, and therefore never in a pretentious disconnection from the hermeneutical situation. Critical thinking must begin, not by gaining objective control over the situation, but by opening up a question. Critical questioning does not raise questions to which the interrogator already knows the answers; nor does it question absolutely everything, as in Cartesian doubt. The focus of critical questioning must come from the hermeneutical situation itself: the language context of tradition, the learner's fore-conceptions, and the literacy which biases every question. In questioning the object is brought into a state of indeterminacy (TM 363), and this indeterminacy must be sorted out within a process more akin to Platonic dialogue, or in some cases jurisprudence (*dikastē phronēsis*), than to syllogistic argument (see TM 318). This is a logic of inquiry, or what Aristotle calls deliberation (*boúleusis*), guided by *phronēsis* and moving toward choice (*prohairesis*). Within this logic, procedural rules with respect to evidence gathering are not eliminated, but, given the hermeneutical starting point, and the fact that all evidence remains open to question and in need of interpretation, such rules are tempered with respect to claims about objectivity. Ultimately, educational experience is not susceptible to procedural rules. It remains open-ended, beyond control, beyond method, *to pathos tōn logōn*. Both cultural literacy and critical thinking, to the extent that they are made dependent on concepts of reproduction and metacognitive rules, propose to control experience instead of admitting the larger experience of education described by moderate hermeneutics.

CHAPTER 8

Critical Hermeneutics and Educational Theory

In those works that aim to establish a critical theory of education the concept of a critical hermeneutics remains far in the background.[1] My intention in this chapter is to bring forward the hermeneutical presuppositions of various critical theories of education by focusing on the work of Jürgen Habermas, who, as the foremost representative of critical theory, is frequently cited by educational theorists of this school.

Habermas grants to hermeneutics a place within the project of critique. His project is defined most clearly as the attempt to arrive at unconstrained communication. Hermeneutics, according to Habermas, "is designed to guarantee, within cultural traditions, the possible action-orienting self-understanding of individuals and groups as well as reciprocal understanding between different individuals and groups. It makes possible the form of unconstrained consensus and the type of open intersubjectivity on which communicative action depends" (KHI 176). As we have already seen, Habermas has in mind not a hermeneutics which, confined to the realm of philology, operates only on the literal surface of texts, but a "depth hermeneutics" which, modeled on Freudian psychoanalysis, uncovers and undoes the deception and distortion involved in communication (see KHI 217–218). A "depth hermeneutics" is part of a critical reflective procedure which is articulated in the context of "a self-formative process" (KHI 197), which, for our purposes, we will associate with educational experience.

In the discussion of the Habermas-Gadamer debate I defined the *aporia* which distinguishes the critical approach from Gadamer's philosophical hermeneutics, namely, the *aporia* which concerns the interpreter's ability or inability to escape the constraints of power and authority structures. Does hermeneutical practice, conceived as a depth hermeneutics, actually move us be-

239

yond constrained communication to a reflective emancipation (as claimed by Habermas), or is such critical reflection itself bound by hermeneutical constraints (Gadamer's position)? Ultimately we want to examine whether an answer to this *aporia* is to be found on the level of educational experience. We need, first, to clarify the terms of this *aporia* by clearly identifying the principles of critical hermeneutics and understanding how they apply to educational experience.

PRINCIPLES OF CRITICAL HERMENEUTICS

From the viewpoint of critical theory, hermeneutics should be placed in the service of critical sciences such as the critique of ideology. Critique calls for a special and suspicious interpretation of those ideologies and institutions which support and maintain ruling power structures. It requires a type of understanding that dispels and transcends an ideologically prejudiced understanding. In its most idealistic form, critical theory requires a hermeneutical ability to escape from the domination of repressive traditions and to attain an ideologically neutral, tradition-free, prejudice-free communication. Critical hermeneutics thus attempts to get to the objective truth behind the false consciousness of ideology. This cannot be accomplished by either a traditional philosophical escape from the cave or by a positivistic dependence on science. Although philosophy and science tend to be suspicious of appearances, they are not suspicious enough for the process of critique. Even if one can trace the origins of the notion of critique to the critical and suspicious attitude of seventeenth-century science[2] and see its development through figures such as Kant, Feuerbach, and Marx, critical theory in the twentieth century stands on more radical ground. The hermeneutical dimensions of that ground may be outlined in the principles of critical hermeneutics, of which I will discuss four. The first two (reproduction and hegemony) are constraint principles. They describe precritical interpretation. The last two (reflection and application) describe critical interpretation and might be termed "principles of possibility."

Reproduction

As we saw in the discussion of conservative hermeneutics, it is difficult to clearly separate principles from normative canons. Perhaps it is impossible to define a principle without some normative aspect being embedded in it. We see this again in the case of critical hermeneutics. The following principles trace a path from what critical theorists consider normally distorted interpretation to an undistorted interpretation which results from a critical or depth hermeneutics. This distinction between two types of interpretation reflects the normative framework of critical hermeneutics, which, to put it succinctly, prescribes suspicion rather than trust. This suspicion can be seen in the first principle, which describes normal, everyday interpretation. Interpretation, to the extent that it is not critical, that is, to the extent that it is naively unreflective and ideological, is reproductive interpretation. A noncritical understanding simply continues, reiterates, and reproduces tradition, cultural values, ideology, and power structures.

This principle is quite different from the one with the same name found in conservative hermeneutics. Habermas explicitly rejects the conservative principle of reproduction.[3] The difference is twofold. First, there is a difference in the normative dimension. The intent of conservative hermeneutics is to move, methodologically, toward reproductive interpretation; the aim of critical hermeneutics is to move away from reproductive interpretation. For a conservative hermeneutics of trust, to fail to reproduce the object of interpretation is to invalidate the interpretation and to fall into subjective relativism. In contrast, for the critical hermeneutics of suspicion, to reproduce the object of interpretation is to legitimize the traditional power structures associated with it and to fall under the spell of false consciousness. The reproduction of meaning is also the reproduction of ideological distortions.

This leads us to the second difference, which concerns the scope of reproduction. The concept of reproduction in the conservative principle involves the reconstruction of original meanings, original intentions of texts and authors. To apply this principle in the educational context, one needs to show how this principle can be generalized to include cultural reproduction. For critical hermeneutics, however, the principle of reproduction already includes the sense of cultural reproduction. In other words, for critical hermeneutics, reproduction is not the conscious result of a methodological procedure of interpretation but, for the most part, an unconscious, unreflective transmission of the authority and power structures of tradition.

Hegemony

All interpretation is linguistic, but, critical theorists would maintain, also more than linguistic. The linguistic aspect of interpretation is not exhaustive. The principle of hegemony can be formulated as follows: normal interpretation is distorted by extralinguistic, extrahermeneutical factors: material and hegemonic factors such as economic status and social class. These factors constrain interpretation and communication just as much as language and particular traditions do. Indeed, these nonhermeneutical factors determine one's relations to the hermeneutical factors of language and tradition. The acquisition and use of language are always conditioned in some degree by the social conditions and power relations in which they happen. Language, in effect, serves a larger master, a cultural and social system that tends to reproduce itself. Language is a "medium of domination and social power [that] serves to legitimate relations of organized force. Insofar as the legitimations do not articulate the power relations whose institutionalization they make possible . . . language is also ideological."[4]

Extralinguistic forces distort interpretation. This is a central point of debate between Gadamer and Habermas. Habermas holds that language is dependent on social processes that cannot be reduced to language. He rejects Gadamer's principle of the universality of language—"that linguistically articulated consciousness determines the material practice of life"—as idealistic, and states that

> the objective framework of social action is not exhausted by the dimension of intersubjectively intended and symbolically transmitted meaning. The linguistic infrastructure of a society is part of a complex that, however symbolically mediated, is also constituted by the constraints of reality. . . . [B]ehind the back of language, they also affect the very grammatical rules according to which we interpret the world. *Social actions can only be comprehended in an objective framework that is constituted conjointly by language, labor, and domination.*[5]

Interpretation is thus determined and often obstructed by social forces ("material relations") unexpressed but implicitly concealed in linguistic behavior. It follows that interpretation, to the extent that it is not critical, involves false consciousness. Interpretation is not aware of its social prejudices or the forces that operate to dominate it "behind the back" of language. Habermas remarks, "Force acquires permanence, moreover, only through the objective appearance of forcelessness in a pseudo-communicative consensus."[6] A critical or depth hermeneutics reveals that extralinguistic forces prevail in interpretation to deform and systematically distort communication. Every interpretation is thus under suspicion of being induced by such forces.

Critical Reflection

The principle of reflection leads us away from everyday distorted and reproductive interpretation toward critical interpretation. It states that critical reflection can neutralize the language context of tradition, as well as the extralinguistic forces which distort interpretation. This principle is the basis for what Habermas calls "depth hermeneutics." If language, traditions, and extralinguistic forces operate anonymously, "behind the back" of the interpreter, critical reflection must bring them forward, must make the anterior operations apparent, and thus change our relations to them. For Habermas, "the reflected appropriation of tradition breaks up the nature-like [*naturwüchsige*] substance of tradition and alters the position of the subject in it."[7] Critical reflection puts the interpreter in charge of those conditions which he had been passively and unconsciously suffering. If reflection does not allow the interpreter to "leap over" his relations to a tradition, "it does not follow that the medium of tradition is not profoundly altered by scientific reflection."[8]

The debate between Habermas and Gadamer also finds a focus here. Whereas Gadamer insists that all interpretation is constrained by the process of tradition, Habermas proposes that this constraint can be lifted or at least loosened by reflection. "Gadamer fails to appreciate the power of reflection that is developed in understanding. This type of reflection is no longer blinded by the illusion of an absolute, self-grounded autonomy and does not detach itself from the soil of contingency on which it finds itself. But in grasping the genesis of tradition from which it proceeds and on which it turns back, reflection shakes the dogmatism of life-practices."[9] In contrast to conservative hermeneutics, the critical approach does not claim a methodological disconnection or absolute escape from the anterior relation of tradition. "Criticism is always tied to the context of traditions which it reflects."[10] Yet it does claim that by becoming aware of this relation through critical reflection, ideological and cultural domination and the social biases of traditions can be neutralized, and interpretation can be freed of distortion.

The principle of critical reflection here brings critical hermeneutics close to the conservative principle of objectivity. Reflection, in making the process of tradition and other nonlinguistic forces transparent, helps to neutralize them and moves us toward an objective (ideologically neutral) interpretation. "A structure of preunderstanding or prejudgment that has been rendered transparent can no longer function as a prejudice."[11] The objectivity sought for in depth hermeneutics, however, belongs first to the interpreter and only then to the object of interpretation. If in conservative hermeneutics the primary aim of interpretation is to attain a valid and objective understanding of the object, in critical hermeneutics the aim is to define the objective situation of the interpreter. Hermeneutics can claim an "impartiality of understanding" only by first reflectively identifying the objective constraints and power structures within which the interpreter operates, so that eventually they may be brought under control. Habermas thus proposes that "hermeneutical understanding can arrive at objectivity to the extent that the understanding subject learns, through the communicative appropriation of alien objectivities, to comprehend itself in its own self-formative process. An interpretation can only grasp its object and penetrate it in a relation in which the interpreter reflects on the object and himself *at the same time* as moments of an objective structure that likewise encompasses both and makes them possible" (KHI 181).

The purpose of critical reflection is to assist in the achievement of emancipation. The objectivity of interpretation is seen either as a tool to be used in the pursuit of emancipation or as a result of emancipation, but not as an end in itself. The aim of critical hermeneutics, then, is to modify the hermeneutical situation. If, in Gadamer's view, understanding is always and inexorably situated and so constrained by language and the process of tradition that no privileged disconnection is possible, for Habermas, reflection has the power to create a positive perspective from which to evaluate the constraints of situated interpretation.

To identify and dissolve hermeneutical constraints and extra-hermeneutical power structures, critical hermeneutics requires a depth-hermeneutical procedure which includes the use of critical reflection as well as scientific explanation. The aim of this procedure is to control interpretational and communicative experience. Scientific explanation must play a role in depth hermeneutics, along with hermeneutical reflection, because the nonhermeneutical constraints that condition interpretation require such explanation. If understanding aims at the "what" (meaning), explanation aims as the "why."[12] According to Habermas, both the critique of ideology and psychoanalysis operate according to such a procedure. We will see that it also plays a central role in the critical educational context. Habermas suggests, in this regard, that through a depth-hermeneutical procedure, interpreters "turn back on themselves in reflection in order to make sure of their own educative process: in self-reflection we make our own individual or collective life-history transparent to ourselves at any given time, in that we, as our own products, learn to penetrate what first confronts us as something objective from the outside."[13]

Application

Emancipation, as the aim of depth hermeneutics, may be associated with a principle of application summarized in Habermas's words: "in a process of enlightenment, there can only be participants."[14] Interpretation, if critical enough, always has a positive application with respect to emancipating the interpreter from authority structures. Practically speaking, critical interpretation moves us closer to hermeneutical situations in which the interpreter enjoys the possibility of unconstrained communication and autonomous action. The idealized conditions of "unlimited and control-free communication" in an "unlimited interpretive community" or "ideal-speaking situation" operate as a "regulative principle of understanding," a measure of truth obtained in rational discourse.[15] Such an ideal hermeneutical situation may not be attainable, but as a regulative idea it is anticipated in every interpretation, in every conversation, and operates as a measure of validity.

In conservative hermeneutics, application is second to reproductive interpretation; *significance* is subordinate to *meaning*.
Correct interpretation places the interpreter properly under the
rule of a proper tradition and authority. For Gadamer, one could
say, interpretation is always already application so that significance
always constrains meaning. Significance is always biased because
the interpreter is always constrained by her anterior relation with a
particular tradition. For Habermas, however, application, which is
the result of critical interpretation in the sense that it always comes
along with the practice of depth hermeneutics, involves an escape
from prejudice, a radical modification of the anterior relation with
the tradition process. The "deep" meaning discovered by the critically suspicious interpretation is not only enlightening but also
emancipating for the interpreter.

Habermas explains that, in contrast to empirical science or
"hermeneutical-historical" science, critical science is governed by
an interest in emancipation. Only the interpretations of the critical
sciences can make a claim to such application. They are productive, not only of valid interpretation and true consensus, but of
emancipation. To the extent that depth-hermeneutical interpretations move us toward ideal, unconstrained hermeneutical situations, they are not merely erudite or theoretical cogitations; they
are enlightening and have a practical impact on the hermeneutical
situation.

CRITICAL THEORIES OF EDUCATION

In an essential way critical theory is concerned with educative
processes. Not only could one count the critical theory (and practice) of education as a critical science, along with the critique of
ideology and psychoanalysis, but one could contend that all of the
critical sciences are themselves educative to the extent that they
aim at enlightenment and emancipation. Education ought to be
critical, just as critical science is educative. This is a position that is
developed in a variety of ways by a large number of theorists. In
order to limit and organize our examination of this large body of
developing theory, we will focus on a specific question: To what
extent and in what ways are critical theories of education dependent upon or consistent with the principles of critical hermeneu-

tics? To answer this question we will examine a representative group of theorists under the headings of each of the previously identified critical principles.

Reproduction and Beyond

The claim made by most critical theorists of education is that to some extent education as actually practiced, that is, noncritically, tends to be reproductive. This claim clearly reflects the constraint principle of reproduction in critical hermeneutics. In contrast to conservative theorists of education (such as those who advocate cultural literacy), who worry that education is not reproductive enough, critical theorists worry that education is primarily reproductive along class, race, and gender lines. Their claim relies on empirical, sociological studies, of which the one most frequently cited is Pierre Bourdieu and Jean-Claude Passeron's study of cultural reproduction in the French educational system, *Reproduction in Education, Society and Culture* (RE).[16]

Focusing on the concept of "pedagogic action," defined as "the action of teaching or educating considered as a general social process, neither limited to the school nor even necessarily perceived as education," Bourdieu and Passeron identify inculcation or reproduction (the transmission or "imposition" of cultural and social structures) as the "essential function" (or "transhistorical" feature) of education (see RE xiii, 26, 171, n.17, 194, 197, 214, n.18). Pedagogic action is "the imposition of a cultural arbitrary by an arbitrary power" (RE 5), and thus it attempts to reproduce the arbitrary (that is, not deduced from any universal principle) cultural schemata (ideas, values, ways of thinking) of a particular social class. The power ("symbolic violence") expressed in pedagogic action is based on "the power relations between the groups or classes making up a social formation." In general, what gets reproduced in educational experience is the dominant culture, and thereby "the power relations within a social formation in which the dominant system of education tends to secure a monopoly of legitimate symbolic violence" (RE 6). Cultural reproduction includes ideological, class, and political reproduction. In effect, educational experience reproduces society.

Reproducing society, education also reproduces the conditions for its own reproduction, that is, "the conditions in which the reproducers were produced." This self-reproduction of educational systems involves a "slow tempo" of pedagogic change and the inertia of educational institutions, the function of which is always to conserve "inherited traditions" (RE 32). The reproduction effected by education is longer lasting than political coercion because, in contrast to the latter, which is an external force, the traditions inculcated by education are internalized to form a "habitus" ("a durable and culturally determined set of schemata") (RE 31ff.). The primary habitus, the one which is inculcated in the earliest phases of upbringing, does not exclude the acquisition of other, different schemata but will always determine such acquisition (RE 42–43). In other words, our first, culturally determined understanding of the world, our outlook, viewpoint, or *Weltanschauung*, the result of reproductive, primary educational experience (in the family or the earliest school years), will always govern the acquisition of alternative schemata (for example, in the study of other cultures). Reproduction is not only the primary educational phenomenon, but also the controlling one which transfers to all subsequent experience (see RE 36). The controlling habitus is more assimilative (conservative) than accommodative (corrigible). "Because learning is an irreversible process, the habitus acquired within the family forms the basis of the reception and assimilation of the classroom message, and the habitus acquired at school conditions the level of reception and degree of assimilation of the messages produced and diffused by the culture industry, and, more generally, of any intellectual or semi-intellectual message" (RE 43–44).

The conclusions of Bourdieu and Passeron are based on empirical studies which show complex correlations between certain social factors (origin, class, gender, corresponding degrees of linguistic competence), factors of educational practice (such as selection, streaming), and degrees of success. For example, these studies show the following: (a) To some degree, "social origin predetermines educational destiny" through the mechanism of initial streaming and selection based on prior academic record (RE 80). (b) There is a high degree of correlation between educational opportunity and success, and parent's occupation (RE 74, 91–93, 221ff.). Working-class children are ensnared in "a truncated educational destiny" (RE 158, 174, n.29), whereas, for example, "the evolution of the structure of educational opportunities between 1962 and 1966 consecrated the cultural privileges of the upper classes" (RE 227). (c) There is some degree of correlation between class and gender factors and the choice and success rate in particular disciplines (RE 76–77). (d) The educational system translates or reinterprets external constraints of social class and order into technical selection processes like the examination. It thus reproduces social hierarchies as academic hierarchies (RE 142–153, 158, 162, 175, n.37).

The educational theory of reproduction, as presented by Bourdieu and Passeron, leaves little room for other possibilities within the educational context. The social order and its individual citizens are determined in a process that seems to lack any possibility of transformation. Not all critical theorists, however, are willing to follow such strict deterministic lines within the theory of reproduction. Critical theorists do accept the general conclusion of reproduction theory in education—that "schools have operated to support and legitimate the dominant cultural, social, and economic order"—while at the same time they admit "important limitations to the work of reproduction theorists."[17] Henry Giroux outlines the accomplishments and failures of reproduction theory:

> Reproductive theory and its various explanations of the role and function of education have been invaluable in contributing to a broader understanding of the political nature of schooling and its relation to the dominant society. But it must be stressed that the theory has not achieved its promise to provide a comprehensive critical science of schooling. Reproduction theorists have oversimplified the idea of domination in their analyses and have failed to provide any major insights into how teachers, students, and other human agents come together within specific historical and social contexts in order to both make and reproduce the conditions of their existence. . . . Indeed, human subjects generally "disappear" amidst a theory that leaves no room for moments of self-creation, mediation, and resistance.[18]

Thus the limitations of reproduction theory include the absence of a notion of human agency and specific accounts of how the process works or how it could be changed. Critical theorists of education, who depend on the theory of reproduction to describe in general terms the social consequences of noncritical education, are required to move beyond reproduction theory in order to pose a solution.

Critical theorists have accepted the general conclusions of reproductive theory concerning the actual state of education but have rejected its deterministic descriptions and have proceeded to formulate "resistance theory." Resistance theory shows "how students not only accept, but often reject, mediate, or ignore the message of schooling."[19] Reproduction is never absolute or complete even if it is a basic fact of precritical education. Educational experience, Giroux explains, allows the school to be a contested terrain, "marked not only by structural and ideological contradictions but also by collectively informed student resistance." Still, as reproduction theory shows, educational conflict and resistance are always constrained by "asymmetrical relations of power which always favor the dominant classes."[20] Resistance would be unnecessary unless there already existed hegemonic relations.

It seems clear that for these theorists an adequate critical science of education requires both reproduction and resistance concepts. In other words, the constraint principle of reproduction in precritical educational contexts must be supplemented by other principles of possibility that would outline resistance theory. Before moving on to the principles of possibility, however, we need to examine the "asymmetrical relations of power" which are implied by both reproduction and resistance theories.

Hegemonic Relations

That educational experience is constrained by asymmetrical relations of power might be enunciated by reversing a statement made by Antonio Gramsci: "Every relationship of 'hegemony' is necessarily an educational relationship."[21] Critical reproduction theory maintains that every educational relationship is necessarily a hegemonic relationship. Power relations constitute the "precondition for the establishment of a relation of pedagogic communication" (RE 6). Indeed, for Bourdieu and Passeron, pedagogic action operates as "the chief instrument of the transubstantiation of power relations into legitimate authority" (RE 15). There is, of course, something that seems unavoidable about hegemonic relations in the educational context. The relation between teacher and student seems to be precisely asymmetrical and to involve an authority-power structure. Power and tradition operate on the side of the teacher; the student is caught in a struggle between authority and autonomy. But this *aporia* has larger dimensions than the teacher-student model. Critical theory makes it clear that typically the asymmetrical power relations involved are the relations of domination of one class, race, or gender over another.

For strict (deterministic) reproduction theory, the individual's subjective expectations are always produced in a framework of objective relations that operate "behind the back" of the subject. The notions of the "hidden curriculum" or "implicit pedagogy" account for the efficient mechanisms of translating social power relations and ruling economic interests into educational contexts.[22] The teacher, who has unconsciously internalized class, race, and gender prejudices, unconsciously transmits these same prejudices to students. According to the critical view, the transmitted prejudices are thus anonymous and concealed in a false consciousness which masks the "objective truth" of the reproduction. Because educational institutions are ordered within a hidden framework of power relations, they have a concealed function of reproducing the cultural capital of the established order.[23] Having translated social advantages and disadvantages into academic and technical ones, the educational system translates these academic advantages and disadvantages back into social ones in the labor market.

This concealed function of educational institutions is reflected in the fact that conservative theorists of cultural literacy, for example, conceive cultural capital to be "jointly owned property of the whole society" (RE 11). Hirsch maintains that the best way for disadvantaged or disfranchized groups to claim their rightful culture is to acquire cultural literacy in the free school system. In reality, according to reproduction theorists, the inherited culture corresponds to the economic and symbolic interests of those groups already advantaged within the existing power system. The claim that such knowledge is "jointly owned property" is simply a cover-up of the inequities that already characterize and will continue to characterize the system (see especially RE 24). Thus programs like cultural literacy are utopian and demonstrate a naive faith in "the inherent neutrality of our institutions."[24]

There are various ways to approach the phenomenon of hegemony. One could focus on class, race, or gender problems, or on the reproduction of dominant ideology. One could also develop a general argument about the dominance of technocratic rationality in schooling which serves the interests of corporate business. In this context technical and economic rationality become equated with critical thinking, theory (conception) becomes separated from practice (execution), and school knowledge comes to serve the economic interests of corporate business.[25]

In this, and various other ways, it has been argued that hegemonic factors—power relations, economic interests, class, race, and gender prejudices—operate to constrain educational experience. Michael Apple explains in succinct terms:

> We do not confront abstract 'learners' in schools . . . instead we see specific classed, raced, and gendered subjects, people whose biographies are intimately linked to the economic, political and ideological trajectories of their families, to the political economies of their neighborhoods, and—in an identifiable set of connections—to the exploitative relations of the larger society.[26]

Apple, who moves beyond strict reproduction theory toward resistance theory, sees the hegemonic nature of relations as a foundational phenomenon of educational systems. Hegemony "isn't an already accomplished social fact, but a process in which dominant groups and classes 'manage to win the active consensus [of those] over whom they rule.'"[27] Apple recognizes, however, that the concept of hegemony may be overplayed. This is especially so if "hegemony" becomes the too-ready answer to numerous questions concerning cultural reproduction, rather than that which needs to be explained.[28] To explain how relations of dominance and subordination are embodied in educational institutions, critical theorists have analyzed these relations in curricula, in research practices, in textbook design and marketing practices, in "management pedagogies,"[29] and in the practice of redefining teachers' roles.

One of the most developed of these critical analyses focuses on the way that hegemonic relations are reflected in school language and text. We have already discussed David Olson's research into the biased nature of the language of schooling (see pp. 233ff.). Critical theories of education embrace similar research conclusions. The first principle of such analyses is that the linguistic nature of educational experience is not exhaustive.[30] Bourdieu and

Passeron, for example, show how academic discourse embodies a certain pedagogical authority which makes education something more than mere communication.

> The mere fact of transmitting a message within a relation of pedagogic communication implies and imposes a social defini- tion . . . of what merits transmission, the code in which the mes- sage is to be transmitted, the persons entitled to transmit it or, better, impose its reception, the persons worthy of receiving it and consequently obliged to receive it, and finally, the mode of imposition and inculcation of the message which confers on the information transmitted its legitimacy and thereby its full mean- ing. (RE 109)

The *full* meaning of the lesson, embedded in the language itself, includes both a microcosm of power relations (those between teacher as authority and student as dominated) and a reflection of the macrocosm of power relations in the larger society.

The reception of information by students depends upon their linguistic competence, which in turn is determined to some extent by their social class. The emphasis on textual and literate knowl- edge in schooling, on the one hand, combined with correlations between social class and "legitimate" linguistic competence, on the other hand, guarantees effective hegemony within educational in- stitutions.[31] Critical theorists tend to agree that "the unequal social-class distribution of *educationally profitable linguistic capi- tal* constitutes one of the best-hidden mediations through which the relationship . . . between social origins and scholastic achieve- ment is set up" (RE 116). Various aspects of bourgeois language ("abstraction, formalism, intellectualism and euphemistic modera- tion") indicate a certain relation to language which reflects bour- geois social position and power. The academic use of language is simply one part of—perhaps an essential part of—the propagation of extralinguistic constraints upon educational experience. Lan- guage, as Michael Ryan suggests, is just one other material force in the hegemonic system.[32]

Given the educational situation as critical theorists describe it, given the constraints defined by reproduction and hegemony re- flected in curriculum and textbook design, research practices, teacher performance, and the language of schooling, is it possible to actualize a critical pedagogy and thereby create an educational situation in which enlightenment and emancipation are possible?

Critical Reflection

Critical theorists propose to lead us away from educational situations characterized by hegemonic distortions by employing critical pedagogical practice, the educational equivalent of depth hermeneutics. If language, the process of tradition, and extralinguistic forces operate systematically and anonymously in educational institutions, critical reflective pedagogy promises to reveal the hegemonic and reproductive character of such institutions and thereby change educational practice. Critical pedagogy allows educators to recognize and control those conditions which distort and constrain educational experience.

How can we define the reflection which is characteristic of critical pedagogy? Does critical reflection in educational contexts neutralize hegemony and disrupt the reproductive cycle? Can the reflective process be effected by following a set of critical scientific procedures? To answer these questions we need to look at the models of reflection found in critical pedagogies. In a way that resembles conservative theory, critical theorists propose two models of reflection in the educational context: critical thinking and critical literacy. We need to ask how the conceptions of critical thinking and critical literacy are similar to or different from conservative models of critical thinking and cultural literacy.

Critical Thinking as Critical Reflection.   With respect to using critical thinking as a model of critical reflection, some preliminary questions are in order. First, is the word *critical* used in the same sense in the phrases *critical theory* and *critical thinking*? The initial answer is "no." The concept of critique, as appropriated by critical theory, has a political and (anti)ideological connotation absent from the word *critical* in *critical thinking*. But things are not really as simple as that. Some critical theorists embrace critical thinking approaches, claiming that critical thinking is essentially political because it challenges the given status quo and contributes to emancipation.[33] Other critical theorists condemn critical thinking approaches because, as an educational ideal proposed by conservatives, they perceive it to be political and ideological. Harvey Siegel's defense of critical thinking as an educational ideal argues against this latter position of some critical theorists. Critical thinking, according to Siegel, is an ideologically neutral instrument, and is thus an important tool for the critique of ideology.

Second, doesn't the fact that critical thinking is employed or prescribed by both conservative and critical theorists prove Siegel's point, that it is politically and ideologically neutral? The obvious answer here appears to be "yes." But, again, things are not so simple. The very idea of a neutral, pure instrumental rationality is the product of the Western Enlightenment tradition. To return to our first question, the term *critical* in both *critical thinking* and *critical theory* can be traced to their common roots in the Enlightenment tradition of scientific critique. Is it not that same modern Enlightenment tradition which, standing behind critical theory and critical thinking, biases these approaches in favor of the conceptions of neutrality, scientific objectivity, and the power of reflection? Critical theorists tend to be aware of this question as they appropriate critical thinking for their own purposes.

Siegel's defense of critical thinking as an educational ideal shows how this appropriation is possible. If critical thinking is ideologically and politically neutral, it does not rule out the political use of critical thinking precisely in the service of the critique of ideology. In the educational context Aronowitz and Giroux show how this is done. They clearly indicate that their critical theory of education can also be called a "liberal" theory which adopts elements of the "progressive" approach to education. Specifically, they call upon Dewey for inspiration. Progressive education as developed by "its leading theorists, John Dewey and the Columbia School . . . contains a language of possibility for fruitful intervention into contemporary educational battles, because it poses the relationship of power and knowledge in a positive as well as critical way."[34] Not progressive education as it has been practiced, but progressive education as Dewey had theorized it, presents a model of "reflective experience" relevant to critical pedagogy. In educational experience, "the child must *understand* the consequences of what has been undergone for reflective experience to come into play. For Dewey, the aim of education is to help the student gain conscious direction and control of the learning process."[35]

How precisely does Dewey's progressive approach fit into critical pedagogy? He does not offer any help on the constraint side—

he does not recognize the reproductive and hegemonic aspects of educational practice[36]—but he can play a role on the possibility side; specifically he describes a concept of reflection in educational experience. Critical pedagogy begins with a reflective experience which provides two things: (a) "increased power of control" and (b) increased meaning, "the experienced significance attached to an experience." For critical theory a reflective understanding of where student and teacher stand within the hegemonically distorted communication system of education allows them to gain control over their experiences.

What precisely is reflective experience, and how do teachers bring themselves and their students into such experience? For Aronowitz and Giroux the answer is unequivocal. Reflective experience is equated with critical thinking. "Thus Dewey's philosophy of education is to direct schools to devise curricula that orient around critical thinking." Critical thinking as part of "the enlightenment tradition of reason and critical theory," and as "the fundamental precondition for an autonomous and self-motivated public or citizenry," offers a model of critical reflection appropriate to critical pedagogy.[37] Critical thinking here means, not simply the acquisition of logical or rhetorical skills (although the critical power of such skills is argued for by both Gramsci and Wood), but the critical interrogation of culture and mass media as to their political and ideological content, and the critical examination of structures of family, schools, workplaces, and other social institutions, with particular attention paid to "concepts, abstractions, arguments, evidence, and the other categories of critical thought."[38]

Critical reflection also involves a hermeneutics of suspicion to the extent that it recognizes that "things are not what they seem to be." Students, using a depth-hermeneutical approach, "must learn to examine their own lives, the ways in which they have been part of the system of social reproduction."[39] Critical thinking as a model of reflection also involves getting a "critical distance" from those things that are interrogated. One must view them objectively in order to see how they objectively shape our lives. In order to demystify popular cultural forms, for example, we must reflectively distance ourselves from them in our analysis, giving up "the pleasure one gets from them."[40] This distanciation can never be absolute or complete, however. As noted in our discussion of Habermas's depth-hermeneutical principle of reflection, a reflective distance cannot be a methodological disconnection or escape from hermeneutical or extrahermeneutical constraints. Aronowitz and Giroux reassert the partial nature of reflective distance and the limitations of objective reason, again noting that "the enlightenment conceptions of truth, objective reason, etc., are themselves part of the partial discourses of historical actors, situated in specific times and places."[41] Here they fault Habermas for overemphasizing the possibilities of distortion-free communication. "By positing the autonomy of reason and the possibility of freeing knowledge from its ideological presuppositions, [Habermas] has merely reasserted the ideology of modernity in which science as a value of neutral discourse is possible and depends for its realization on such categories as undistorted communication, reflexive understanding and autocritique."[42] The partiality and ambiguity involved in this issue of reflective distance (and the ambiguity to be found in both Habermas and Aronowitz and Giroux on this issue) come close to the heart of the second *aporia* in educational theory. We will return to this issue in the next section.

Critical Literacy as Critical Reflection.   Critical thinking, as it is incorporated into a critical pedagogy, is not opposed to critical literacy. In contrast to the supposed opposition of cultural literacy and critical thinking in conservative theory, critical thinking and critical literacy are essentially related. The use of critical thinking is a constituent part of what it means to be critically literate. Michael Katz contrasts critical thinking with "rote memorization, routine drill, and passive, unquestioning acceptance of everything said by the teacher or written in textbooks," and holds that critical literacy means taking critical thinking seriously.[43] If critical literacy is the employment of a critical thinking approach, it is also something more than that. It includes gaining certain kinds of knowledge which enable critical thinking to operate in a political and ideological context, knowledge about oppressed groups and cultures, racial minorities, women, working-class culture, and so on. "Put another way, critical literacy interrogates the cultural capital of the oppressed in order to learn from it."[44]

Critical literacy involves an essentially different approach than cultural literacy. Critical theorists point out the hegemonic and utopian nature of cultural literacy despite its profession of ideological neutrality. Although cultural literacy is represented as "merely presenting a previously agreed upon and generally resolved cultural heritage, it is, in fact, doing cultural violence to the diverse traditions children bring to school."[45] The difference between cultural literacy and critical literacy might best be seen by examining Paulo Freire's distinction between the "banking" concept of education and a conception of literacy which involves critical reflection.[46]

In Freire's view, the concept of literacy should not be reduced to skills of reading and writing. Rather, it ought to include "reflecting critically on the process of reading and writing itself, and on the profound significance of language."[47] The approach taken by cultural literacy, which conceives of literacy as the transmission of information, turns students into "containers" to be filled by the teacher. "Education thus becomes an act of depositing. . . . The teacher issues communiques and makes deposits which the students patiently receive, memorize, and repeat. This is the banking concept of education" (PO 58). The banking concept of education mirrors oppressive society as a whole and maintains (reproduces) oppressive practices by suppressing critical thought. Freire proposes a critical pedagogy guided by an interest in liberation. "Authentic liberation—the process of humanization—is not another deposit to be made in men. Liberation is a praxis: the action and reflection of men upon their world in order to transform it" (PO 66).

Freire adopts an existentialist (Sartrean) view of consciousness as intentional and reflective to justify a "problem-posing" concept of education (PO 66–67). The "critical thinking" (PO 81) or reflection (PO 100) of problem posing takes place within a framework of dialogue between teacher and student. If liberation is to be accomplished in educational experience, teachers who are also students and students who are also teachers must communicate in a situation free of hegemonic authority but full of "the critical reflection of both teachers and students" (PO 68). The teacher "does not regard cognizable objects as his private property, but as the object of reflection by himself and the students. In this way, the problem-posing educator constantly reforms his reflections in the reflection of the students. The students—no longer docile listeners—are now critical co-investigators in dialogue with the teacher" (PO 68). The concept of critical literacy thus turns language (as dialogue) into an instrument for liberation.[48]

Freire's concepts of reflection, problem-posing education, and dialogue constitute the elements of critical literacy. The principle of critical literacy is transformation rather than reproduction. "In problem-posing education, men develop their power to perceive critically *the way they exist* in the world *with which* and *in which* they find themselves; they come to see the world not as a static reality, but as a reality in process, in transformation," and they begin to perceive themselves as engaged in "creative transformation" (PO 71). In Freire's Sartrean ontology, critical pedagogy grants to human subjectivity a transcendental control over the situation. A transformation of human consciousness implies a transformation of the world, a constitution of a world that allows for humanizing action and emancipation (see PO 74). Genuine dialogue, communication that leads to emancipation, is based upon a transcendental word: a word free from real distortion and under the control of critical speakers who use it to dominate, not other speakers, but the world.

Application and Emancipation

Critical education, as Freire indicates, involves transformation rather than reproduction. Both the student and the school (the interpreter as well as the hermeneutical situation) are transformed toward an emancipatory situation, measured in terms of true communication. Critical theorists seek "a literacy process which is dialogical, a pedagogical engagement among equals in a community, characterized by social relations of equality and liberation and reflecting the values of trust and respect for persons."[49] In the educational process we are moved along toward a situation of trust only through a hermeneutics of suspicion, a critical reflection which enables us to gain control over the situation. The controlled situation is one in which communication is free of distortion and each participant has an equal chance to speak.

The movement toward an ideal educational situation is accomplished in the critical educational process itself. Critical theorists are thus able to define education as "the practice of freedom" (PO

69). Critical reflection is productive of self-understanding and re-sponsibility, and involves an ethical dimension defined in terms of freedom or autonomy.[50] Just as Habermas recognizes the quest for emancipation as an *a priori* interest built into the communicative process, so the critical educational theorists find the same interest in liberation built into the educational process. Can this liberation ever be absolute? If Freire, for example, adopts Sartre's ontology of consciousness, does this mean that he would accept Sartre's phi-losophy of absolute freedom? Does critical reflection, like Sartre's Husserlian concept of phenomenological reduction, deliver us to an idealized hermeneutical situation, free of hegemonic distortion?

Critical theorists are careful in describing the move toward a situation of autonomy. It is a move from a pseudo freedom to a genuine critical freedom. For this reason one must be cautious about what one identifies as freedom. The case of "academic free-dom" is often a focal point in this regard. In the first instance, what passes for academic freedom is really a distorted idea which serves the reproductive design of the educational system (see RE 125–126). One might discern this distortion in statements like the following from a Carnegie Commission Report on Higher Educa-tion: "The price of academic freedom is eternal vigilance" against those who would exercise it too freely, that is, outside the "struc-tures of [good] citizenship, and . . . [good] scholarship."[51] As Der-rida's reading of Nietzsche suggests, and the critical theorists would not disagree, behind the concept of academic freedom "one can discern the silhouette of a constraint which is all the more ferocious and implacable because it conceals and disguises itself in the form of laisser-faire. Through the said 'academic freedom', it is the State that controls everything."[52] The task of critical pedagogy is to move toward a more genuine academic emancipation.

If critical educational practice moves us away from distorted situations, however, it also moves us closer to what Graham Oliver called the paradox of authority and autonomy. On the one hand, critical theorists admit that the educational process "can only be directed, as it were, from without by persons (teachers) who share the goals of the students."[53] But even if the teacher shares in the student's interest, we do not have an ideal educational situation in which equality is the rule, for, as George Wood admits, "schooling, regardless of its master, is always a form of imposition."[54] This is especially true when students have not yet reached a developmental stage equal to critical reflection. In this case it is not possible for them to thematize in reflection the limitations placed on the classroom situation by the authoritative status of the teacher.[55] On the other hand, rational autonomy can only be accomplished in rational participation. Habermas contends that in "the collective process of education the vindicating superiority of those who do the enlightening over those who are to be enlightened is theoretically unavoidable, but at the same time it is fictive and requires self-correction: in a process of enlightenment there can only be participants."[56] Thus, "emancipation cannot be delivered from the outside."[57] Since critical educational theory requires that the student act on his own autonomy and not just passively receive information, it cannot be the case that, as R. S. Peters suggests, children "enter the Palace of Reason through the courtyard of Habit and Tradition."[58]

The ideal educational situation, like the ideal speech situation, seems to be a regulative idea which serves to measure the transformation away from reproductive, hegemonic, authoritarian structures toward an educational process of participation in dialogue which moves beyond systematically distorted communication. Beyond reproduction, beyond hegemony, through reflective transformation, participation, and dialogue, toward emancipation, critical education moves according to the principles of critical hermeneutics. But if the paradox of authority and autonomy remains unresolved, do we not end up back at the *aporia* which defines the difference between critical and moderate approaches?

A MODERATE RESPONSE: CRITICAL CONVERSATION AND THE INCOMPLETENESS OF EMANCIPATION

From the viewpoint of a moderate theory of education both strict reproduction and critical emancipation are extremes which never happen. Reality always falls somewhere in between. Socrates, in Plato's *Meno*, wonders precisely at the inability of fathers to teach their sons, at their inability to effect a reproduction where it really counts. How does it happen that the son or daughter of a conservative figure of established culture ends up a revolutionary? How is it possible to get the worst of children from the best of parents, or the best of children from the worst of parents? This is not a phenomenon confined to ancient times. One of the constant complaints of contemporary society concerns the failure of reproduction, especially in education. This is precisely the motivation of conservative theorists who attempt to design methods for cultural reproduction. But isn't one generation always complaining about the neighboring one; and hasn't this been the case since ancient times?

Reproduction theorists may say, however, that social and economic reproduction operates in a framework larger than can be measured by a younger generation's counterculture movements. After all, in America the 1960s counterculture has seemingly given way to the older, conservative values of the good life measured in terms of materialistic accumulation. Reproduction has, in the end, worked; capitalism has triumphed again. There is no doubt that the larger social and economic framework is entrenched and slow-changing. In the long term, however, and relative to the larger framework, the rule is gradual transformation rather than reproduction: generations are never exactly the same; race and gender relations are understood differently; even the nature of social classes changes. At certain times such gradual transformations speed up, as the recent and dramatic innovations of democratic processes in traditionally nondemocratic nations attest.

Transformation, however, does not necessarily imply absolute emancipation or progress. Emancipation is always relative. We can emancipate ourselves from something, but never from everything. Transformation simply substitutes one set of constraints for another as revolution substitutes one regime for another. One tradition can be critically abandoned only by moving into or setting up another one. Even the concept of autonomy, often associated with anarchy, reflects the rule of subjectivity, a concept developed within the Enlightenment tradition on idealistic assumptions about the nature of the human being as an essentially asocial animal. Given the hermeneutical situation, which is always social, linguistic, and tradition bound, pure autonomy or absolute emancipation is impossible.

These are easy and often polemical arguments which respond to oversimplified versions of critical theory. Indeed, the critical theorists have already advanced beyond these arguments to the extent that they move beyond strict reproduction theory and to the extent that they define the "ideal speech situation" (or ideal educational situation) as a regulative idea rather than as a real situation. We need to look closer and consider in more realistic detail both the strengths and weaknesses of critical theories of education.

Beyond Reproduction

A moderate approach to hermeneutics and education maintains that interpretation is transformative rather than strictly reproductive. Even in those cases where the aim is to preserve a particular tradition, it can only be preserved differently. Habermas admits something like this with respect to the process of translation. Translation does not permit the reproduction of statements of one language system into statements of another. "Rather, the act of translation highlights a productive achievement to which language empowers those who have mastered its grammatical rules: to assimilate what is foreign and thereby to further develop one's own linguistic system."[59] Thus, and just so, interpretation ("the structure of which is similar to translation") does not permit a reproduction; it is always a productive achievement which not only makes the unknown known, but transforms that which is already known. In educational experience too, the process is a complex one of both assimilation and accommodation. If assimilation takes place under the constraint of a tradition-informed schema, the schema itself is modified in the process of accommodation. In the educational process a tradition never survives entirely intact. In educational experience assimilation plus accommodation never add up to reproduction.

David Olson's experiments tend to support this conclusion. Unless we are willing to maintain that every generation of teachers teach in the same way, then we have to say that what gets learned changes across generations. The same applies to different school systems, different schools within a system, and even to different classrooms. The "unintended consequences of a particular form of instruction" indicate that it would be extremely difficult to effect a reproductive experience.[60] In addition, even if we cannot allow Dewey's identification of content and method, we at least must see their interdependence. As we have seen in prior chapters, changes in the teacher's understanding will entail changes in her presentation. *Subtilitas intelligendi* and *subtilitas explicandi* never entirely coincide; on hermeneutical principles *what* is taught is modified by *how* it is taught, and how something is taught is determined by the teacher's understanding of it. If there are these differences between teacher's understanding, teacher's presentation, and what the students actually learn, then the transformation of knowledge rather than the reproduction of knowledge must be the rule.

How would reproduction actually work in the classroom? A teacher asks or demands or coerces (by soft or hard approaches) the student to recite or memorize a poem—in effect, requires the student to reproduce a verse. Granted the complexity of the situation—that a certain cultural meaning and value are bestowed upon the poem, that the student comes from a certain social class and is prepared or unprepared by that fact, that a certain arbitrariness may characterize the situation, that the presentation rebiases an already biased content, and so forth—can reproduction actually occur? Granted the complexity, admitted by reproduction theorists, can this be a simple imposition, the outcome of which is a reproduction of everything the same? Only by discounting the complexity and ambiguity that one finds in this situation can reproduction theory move toward its conclusion. Bourdieu and Passeron, for instance, while admitting such complexity, base their theory on a model of communication between a "transmitter" (teacher) and "receiver" (student) which they admit turns out to be inadequate (RE 100–102; 107, 144).

On the other hand, the principle expounded by moderate hermeneutics is not one of *absolute* transformation. Transformation takes place within commonly shared frameworks that are slow to change—the constraints of tradition and social structures—and the undeniable historical objectivity of texts (for example, that a particular text was written by Shakespeare rather than Plato). Reproduction theory, in contrast, exaggerates these long-term constants. Indeed, even hermeneutical constraints are exaggerated by Bourdieu and Passeron. In their view, traditions and language, governed by social structure and power relations, overwhelmingly determine the outcome of education. Bourdieu and Passeron fail to acknowledge the enabling aspects of tradition, language, and social structure which allow for an indeterminate transformation rather than a determined reproduction. Thus they interpret pejoratively the fact that "the man who deliberates on his culture is already cultivated and the questions of the man who thinks he is questioning the principles of his upbringing still have their roots in his upbringing" (RE 37). But how could this be any different? There can be no significant questioning of or critical reflection on one's own tradition or culture or upbringing from the outside. If questioning or critical reflection is possible, it is only possible because one's tradition, culture, and upbringing enable it.

If traditions are transformed in educational experience, they are also, to some degree, reproduced. It would be politically naive and idealistic to deny what Plato had recognized in his cave allegory, that in every society cultural traditions and social structures are, through educational systems, renewed: never absolutely reproduced, but only somewhat transformed. Everything depends on to what degree one insists on the reproduction or the transformation.

In the larger and long-term framework, American education will continue to be characteristically American, distinct from European and other educational systems. But also over the long term, cultural systems change because, despite their conservative nature, they are always in a process of transformation even in the short term and in limited contexts. One generation does not interpret a work of art in the same way as the previous generation. One generation is more conservative or more liberal than another in its interpretation of political values. Understandings of gender, race, and class undergo significant reinterpretations from one time period to the next. The American educational system will pass on an American understanding, but that American understanding will not be the same from one time to another.

Education is not, as Bourdieu and Passeron would maintain, the inculcation or reproduction of "a system of (partially or totally identical) schemes of perception, thought, appreciation and action," an identical "habitus" (RE 35). Perception, thought, appreciation, and action at most are *partially* identical, which means *different* from one generation to the next; in the long term the word *identical* would be inappropriate. There is no doubt that tradition has a long-term "integrative function"; but the fact that practices and opinions are "phenomenally different or even contradictory" (RE 35) in the short term should not be dismissed as unessential. If, as the economist points out, we actually live our life in the short term, then we live the phenomenal differences and contradictions, whereas the concepts of "integrative function" and "generative habitus" are abstract images provided by sociologistic theorists. Relevant to the larger, long-term framework, such concepts cannot be denied; in hermeneutical theory they are expressed in terms of tradition and language. We are bound within political, economic, religious, scientific, educational, and other traditions which make our educational systems what they are. There is no absolute escape from these constraints. Yet they do not maintain an absolute hold on us. Constraining conditions are also enabling conditions which allow traditions to be questioned and transformed. There is never a pure reproduction or a pure transformation; the actuality is somewhere between these two abstract extremes.

From what methodological standpoint can sociologists declare that all education imposes dominant culture? From what external viewpoint can they declare the "objective truth" of education? (see RE 17, 31). At the very least, that place must be one from which they can see both education as an imposition (reproduction) and some other possibility which is not education as imposition. But what is that other possibility? Supposedly it is a viewpoint that does not suffer from a "misrecognition" of the objective truth— supposedly, then, the viewpoint of an ideologically free sociology. But how would that be possible, especially if in a strictly reproductive system there is no ideologically free education? If the attainment of such a neutral or disconnected standpoint is ruled out by hermeneutics, then the fact that reproduction theory is able to discover, in some way, "misrecognitions" and ideological determinants verifies the hermeneutical claim that traditions do not constitute absolute constraints but enable, in sciences like sociology, the discovery of something new, the reinterpretation of society, and the transformation of our understanding. Certainly the educational aim of Bourdieu and Passeron's text is not to reproduce in its readers the conservative ideology which it tries to unhinge. Yet their communication depends on and is enabled by a shared tradition which determines the nature of sociological inquiry.

In terms Bourdieu and Passeron might accept, education, if it produces false consciousness, or reproduces what they call the "happy unconsciousness," must also produce what Hegel calls the "unhappy consciousness": a consciousness aware of its falsehood.

Their own project and text—as attempts to educate the public—
affirm and give evidence of the productivity of educational experience. As critical theorists move beyond reproduction theory to
resistance theory—the project of critical reflection—they move
closer to a hermeneutical position which affirms transformation.

Hegemony, Critical Reflection, and Conversation

Gadamer's claim for the hermeneutical universality of language is
not a denial of so-called extralinguistic factors, but a way of ex-
plaining how they operate. Extralinguistic factors, such as power
relations and the political and economic relations of class, race,
and gender, have influence over educational experience only
through the medium of language. They are *power* relations only
insofar as they are *relations*, insofar as they influence. One could
say, then, that power itself is constituted in hermeneutical relations; power relations have their force only in social, that is, linguistic, relations. The intentional shove in the school hallway, the
slap on the hand by the schoolmaster—these examples of overt
force are also signs; they have meaning and require interpretation.
If they are not understood as signs, if they have no meaning, then
they are not really power relations. In the case of covert, hidden
power relations, or relations with hidden meanings, language, the
medium of ideology, law, and the organization of institutions, not
only mediates force, but hides it and thereby makes it more powerful. There is no such thing as "brute" force relevant to the issue of
hegemonic relations. Brute force can only be irrational force—the
accidental bump in the crowded hallway, or the kinds of phenomena which escape both planning and metaphysics (cf. RE 207). But
this kind of force does not systematically distort our interpretations and is not therefore relevant to these considerations. With
respect to considerations about hegemony, it is an abstraction to
speak of extralinguistic or extrahermeneutical forces. The only
forces that count are linguistic, hermeneutical ones.

That we are systematically caught up in hegemonic relations is
not denied by Gadamer. "Certainly I would grant that authority
exercises an essentially dogmatic power in innumerable forms of
domination: from the ordering of education and the mandatory
commands of the army and government all the way to the hierarchy of power created by political forces or fanatics."[61] It is not

only the conscious exercise of authority which explains power, however. Consideration of hidden, systemic power relations is precisely what led Gadamer to his concept of hermeneutical bias.

Admittedly, however, if Gadamer leaves room for an account of hegemonic relations in his hermeneutical theory, he does not develop such an account and seemingly underemphasizes such phenomena. Consider the following passage, which certainly seems, if not optimistic, then at least complacent with respect to power relations.

> In fact history does not belong to us; we belong to it. Long before we understand ourselves through the process of self-examination, we understand ourselves in a self-evident way in the family, society and state in which we live. The focus of subjectivity is a distorting mirror. The self-awareness of the individual is only a flickering in the closed circuits of historical life. *That is why the prejudices of the individual, far more than his judgments, constitute the historical reality of his being.* (TM 276–277)

Critical theorists would revise this thought to reflect the false consciousness involved in self-understanding. Long before we understand ourselves through a process of critical reflection, they would contend, we *misunderstand* ourselves in the power relations of family, society and state. Precritical experience is a distorting mirror. The precritical self-awareness of the individual is only a flickering of *misunderstanding* in the closed and hegemonic circuits of historical life. For Gadamer, however, even a misunderstanding is a way of understanding. Furthermore, he prefers to account for "distorted" understanding in terms of preconceptions and traditions into which we enter (are pulled) through the medium of language and a process that is larger than human subjectivity. Again, as the so-called extralinguistic factors affect us, they affect us through language, and we cannot understand or misunderstand them except within linguistic experience. If a child finds himself, for example, within a working-class family, and thus within a certain system of "attitudes towards the world and other people" (RE 134), this is the case because he has been acquired by working-class language and thus working-class perception and self-perception.

If a moderate theory of education is to make room for the

concept of hegemonic relations, it must deal with two preliminary problems. The first concerns distortion, and the second concerns authority. If I say that a particular communication or interpretation is distorted, must I not claim to know an undistorted truth which acts as a measure? Critical theorists claim access to such undistorted truth by way of critical reflection or an ideal speech situation. In relation to this last concept, Habermas holds a consensus theory of truth which states that truth is the consensus arrived at through communication which is accomplished in a distortion-free communication situation. Critical reflection enables us to move closer to such a situation. To the extent that Habermas admits the ideality of the ideal speech situation, however, he must agree that there is no such situation. More positively, all situations are hermeneutical situations and thus operate under hermeneutical constraints. The notion of "distorted interpretations" is a relative one. An interpretation is distorted only from the perspective of a different hermeneutical standpoint, which itself can be classed as distorted from the perspective of the first interpretation. Furthermore, relative distortions can never be absolutely adjudicated. Habermas holds for such absolute adjudication only by appealing to a transcendental, extrahistorical position, which on moderate hermeneutical principles is impossible to attain.

Critical hermeneutics must come to realize that distortion is simply part of the game. All interpretation, and all educational experience, is distorted, and one can only appeal to normative, ethical (and thus ideologically informed) judgments about which interpretation is better than another. Such would be a moderate relativism, one which does not deny a truth (as *alētheia*) in which one participates, but does question the possibility of certitude or correctness as *adequatio*. This has implications for the possibility of critical reflection, to which we will turn shortly.

The second problem, concerning the place of authority in educational experience, is the cause of a minor paradox for critical theorists. At least in the case of formal educational systems, education seems to involve hegemonic relations in its very nature, that is, authority relations between teacher and student or system and student. How is a critical (nonhegemonic) education possible? For critical theory, there is only one way out of this paradox; but this "way out" leads directly to principles of moderate hermeneutics. Specifically, one overcomes the problem of hegemony through conversation. But conversation, even conversation based on critical reflection, never comes close to the ideal speech situation. In this respect John O'Neill is right to prefer Freire to Habermas: "Habermas to the contrary, there is no ideal speech community. All there can be is that strenuous ethical commitment to the practice of communicative participation that Freire has improvised."[62]

Certainly there is room within a moderate theory of education to account for hegemonic relations. There is, in effect, room enough to learn from critical theory about how these relations function. Habermas is right to insist that systems can "distort" interpretation and educational experience. Gadamer fails to emphasize the effects of hegemonic relations on language. On the other hand, both theorists would agree that the way to deal with such distorted processes is by means of educational experience—enlightenment, critical or at least hermeneutical reflection. In this regard, however, everything depends on the power that is attributed to reflection within the educational process.

First, let us consider how by moving toward the solution of conversation critical theorists are forced to move beyond a theory of critical reflection. The fact that all reflection is itself linguistic suggests that reflection can be carried out in dialogue. This is clearly Freire's position. Only in such dialogue do teacher and student escape the authoritarian framework of precritical pedagogy. The fact that reflection can be carried out dialogically, however, implies not only the linguisticality of critical reflection, but its hegemonic nature as well. Reflection itself, as Gadamer contends, is "encumbered with dogmatism," and this is related to "the false objectification inherent in the idealist conception of reflection."[63] The claim to objectivity made for reflection implies a reflective process which has already come to a conclusion in a neutral, undistorted interpretation from which the critical reflector speaks with authority. Such reflection would be accomplished in the ideal speech situation. But all of this is impossible, an idealistic solution (and therefore no solution at all) to a real problem. Gadamer rightly objects to the ideal authority of the critical reflector: "the critique of ideology overestimates the competence of reflection and reason. Inasmuch as it seeks to penetrate the masked interests which infect public opinion, it implies its own freedom from any ideology; and that means in turn that it enthrones its own norms and ideals as self-evident and absolute."[64]

Reflection and critical conversation are not impossible. But reflection itself has the structure of conversation, and the structure of conversation is hermeneutical. One cannot escape hermeneutical constraints (which include hegemonic relations) in conversation. Michael Apple comes to this realization in regard to the conversation of critical theory itself. "The way we [critical theorists] talk to others in education and the language that we use to describe and criticize the workings of educational institutions embodies a politics in and of itself."[65] Even if this is a politics of enlightenment, the ideology of which can be traced from Kant through the Frankfurt School, it is not the neutral, objective politics which Enlightenment thinkers might claim. This same realization (which is critical but also hermeneutical) must also be applied to critical pedagogical conversation itself. If it is represented as a situation of dialogical conversation, it includes, in principle, hegemonic relations. Indeed, if, as Freire intends, educational conversation is meant to reflect on the real situation of the participants—their political and economic situations—such real situations do not magically disappear in conversation. The structure of critical conversation may even introduce other hegemonic relations into educational experience if, for example (as Freire proposes), teams of experts (teachers) are relying on previous research to guide the conversation. The way the conversation is *conducted* (for we are not speaking here of spontaneous gatherings), as well as the language used to describe and criticize the workings of relevant social institutions which determine the participants, "embodies a politics in and of itself."

The situation is never as clear as theorists of critical reflection lead us to believe. It is true *both* that "emancipation cannot be delivered from the outside" *and* that "schooling, regardless of its master, is always a form of imposition." Critical conversation is characterized by *both* autonomy and authority. This is not a paradox to be resolved, but a fundamental ambiguity to be recognized.

Incomplete Emancipation

The conversation of educational experience always falls short of the ideal educational situation. This is not because we do not yet have it right. Rather, it is a hermeneutical principle which applies to educational experience and which disputes Habermas's claim that "always, when we begin a discourse and carry it on long enough, a consensus would have to result which would be *per se* a true consensus."[66] There is a paradox here which Habermas and the critical theorists of education fail to recognize. If communication were totally "rational" (in Habermas's Enlightenment sense) and met the requirements of the ideal speech situation, then communication (interpretation, educational experience) would be a pure transference of unambiguous and undistorted knowledge. Educational experience, in an ideal educational situation, would amount to a pure reproduction! There would be no misinterpretation because the distorting power of hegemonic relations would be neutralized. Indeed, given such an ideal situation, no interpretation per se would be needed. But if there were not constraints could there be any productivity?

The paradox is purely theoretical; it has no bearing on reality. Educational situations are always less than ideal, in Habermas's sense, and are thereby always hermeneutical and never strictly reproductive. Precisely for this reason, emancipation is possible but is never accomplished in an absolute fashion. Moderate hermeneutics never denies the possibility of emancipation, but only the possibility of absolute emancipation. Emancipation is an ongoing process within educational experience, rather than the end result of critical reflection. The hermeneutical situation places constraints on any attempt at critical reflection. But this does not mean that critique is impossible or that if possible it lacks the power to avoid the reproduction of traditional ideological and social ills. "The fact that we move in a linguistic world and grow up into the world through an experience pre-formed by language does not at all remove the possibilities of critique. On the contrary, the possibility of going beyond our conventions and beyond all those experiences that are schematized in advance, opens up before us once we find ourselves, in our conversation with others, faced with opposed thinkers, with new critical tests, with new experiences" (TM 546).

Educational experience itself is productive of self-understanding and a relative, always incomplete autonomy. Pure heteronomy and pure autonomy are abstract extremes never reached in educational experience. Outside of theory, emancipation can never mean that an individual human subjectivity gains complete control over the human situation. It is appropriate to say that "the process of education and the process of liberation are the same,"[67] as long as we understand that neither education nor liberation are ever absolutely accomplished. It is equally appropriate for Habermas to say that "in the process of enlightenment there can only be participants," as long as the hermeneutical nature of participation is not denied. If it is the case, precisely, that emancipation must be worked on "from the inside," then it can never be accomplished outside of the hermeneutical constraints of the process of tradition and language.

Emancipation never means total escape from the process of tradition. Only through language is it possible to transcend a particular tradition, which means that one must work within a tradition to transform it or to produce a new one. Political and economic forces, as well as class relations, are mediated by language; but precisely for that reason they can be modified only through language. We reform them by reformulating them. Only through such reformulations (in conversations and educational experiences) is it possible to transform the power structures of domination and exploitation. Emancipation is a process that can only be effected through discourse, communication, and educational conversation.

To the extent that critical theorists move beyond strict reproduction theory to resistance theory, and to the extent that they move beyond an idealized notion of critical reflection toward the concept of critical conversation, and to the extent that they move beyond an Enlightenment theory of emancipation as absolute autonomy toward a theory of emancipation as participation, they must also move beyond the principles of critical hermeneutics to the more moderate principles which define educational experience.

The real difference between critical and moderate approaches should not be cast in terms of the contestation of the Habermas-Gadamer debate, but on a different level. Critical hermeneutics, rather than contesting the universality claimed by philosophical hermeneutics, should simply point out its inadequacy with regard to critical practice. From the critical perspective it is not enough to describe educational experience in universal terms. In the realm of educational experience, for example, particular pedagogies still need to be designed by employing a critical and thereby normative approach. More specifically, the critical approach to education shows that a moderate approach, based on universal hermeneutical principles, will never be sufficient for a complete analysis of educational experience. What the critical theory of education implies, and this is especially true of Paulo Freire's project, is that an educational theory which stays on the level of universal principles will never be of sufficient scope to assist in the development of a normative approach to education. This is not to deny the universality of hermeneutics, or even to say that it is irrelevant. A normative approach could still not get away with contradicting universal principles. That all educational experience is linguistic, for example, is not irrelevant or unimportant for normative theory. Rather, it is inadequate; it does not go far enough in its description to be of great use to a normative theory. Those who would develop a critical normative approach to education are primarily interested in changing educational experience and would require something less universal and more particular. This becomes especially clear when, following the critical approach, one recognizes, for example, that the educational situation is conditioned by hegemonic relations which are reflected in the contrast between school language and student language. In this case, if the aim is to design a set of critical and pedagogical canons that would address the particular situation, one would require something more than universal principles which state all educational experience is linguistic and hegemonic. Rather, one needs to know *specifically* how particular hegemonic relations condition a particular school language.

Freire's literacy teams are required to do preliminary research in order to ascertain the nature of the particular or local constraints that define the educational situation before they design their critical pedagogies. Certainly Habermas's use of the psychoanalytic model implies a similar approach. In effect, critical educational theory suggests that a universal theory which develops principles of educational experience in general must be supplemented with a local empirical description of educational experience in a particular school or system. A local description would not describe all interpretation but would describe the particular kind of interpretation which happens at a particular educational site. A normative theory could then be developed in light of local descriptions. Although a normative theory cannot contradict universal principles, it can prescribe against local circumstances. If, for example, the universal principle states that all educational experience is linguistic, it would not be legitimate for a normative theory to stipulate that this ought not to be the case. But if on a local level a particular school language discriminates against working-class students, then a local normative hermeneutics may in fact say that this ought not to be the case.

Especially on this local level, one can see that normative preferences will influence the description of local conditions. As a critical theorist, for example, one may be looking for precisely those kinds of phenomena which indicate "distorted" educational experience. This methodological fact not only reflects the universal hermeneutical principle that all interpretation is biased, but also shows how the normative constraints on description may be positive and productive, at least from the view of the critical theorist. We will return to the conception of a local hermeneutics in the final chapter.

CHAPTER 9

Radical Hermeneutics and Educational Theory

There is a growing body of educational theory that can be characterized as "poststructuralist." The concept of poststructuralism, however, encompasses a variety of approaches associated with names such as Foucault, Derrida, and Lyotard. Although Foucault's concept of genealogy, Derrida's deconstructive reading, and Lyotard's concept of postmodernism cannot be reduced to one common approach, it is not uncommon to regard all of these approaches as poststructuralist or postmodern. For our purposes we wish neither to eliminate any of these approaches from consideration nor to treat them as if they were all the same. For organizational reasons, however, we need to focus our discussion on one approach and yet retain the liberty to mention the others where relevant. For several reasons we will concentrate on the work by (and work inspired by) Derrida. First, in terms of clarifying a deconstructive or "radical" hermeneutics vis à vis our previous analysis, there exists a documented encounter between Derrida and Gadamer comparable to other debates we have already considered. Second, there exists a substantial body of material by Derrida and others on a deconstructive approach to education. Derrida himself understands deconstruction to have "in principle, a bearing on the apparatus and the function of teaching in general."[1] Finally, and in spite of the near encounter between Habermas and Foucault on the notion of enlightenment, and the exchanges between Habermas and Lyotard over the concept of consensus, the contrast between critical and radical hermeneutics can be made even clearer in a discussion which focuses on Derrida.[2]

PRINCIPLES OF RADICAL HERMENEUTICS

The task of Derrida's deconstructive interpretation is, as John Caputo contends in *Radical Hermeneutics*, "to keep the trembling and endless mirror-play of signs and texts in play," rather than to allow tradition to fix meaning (RH 117–118). Deconstruction is thus a hermeneutics "beyond 'hermeneutics', beyond the 'first essence' of hermeneutics, beyond the hermeneutics which looks for meaning and stability, a hermeneutics which takes the measure of deconstructive critique" (RH 119). We will try to see this for ourselves by turning to the question of radical principles. The principles of radical hermeneutics turn out to be grammatological principles, that is, principles that describe meaning as a product of grammatological form, the play of signs, or as Derrida puts it, the play of *différance*. These principles lead us not to the intention of the author, as in conservative hermeneutics, nor to a semantic system operating within the confines of a hermeneutical relation, as in Gadamer's philosophical hermeneutics, but to "textuality"— "an uncontrollable plurality of textual effects" (RH 150), a "bottomless abyss" of nontruth.[3]

Without doubt Derrida would claim that the only principle of deconstruction is that there are no principles, given the metaphysical nature of the very notion of principle (*archē*). Anything that looks like a deconstructive principle is really a nonprinciple. In a similar manner Derrida claims that there are no radical canons, no rules to follow in the game of deconstruction, no method to employ. Yet he qualifies this claim (as he must, in principle, every claim): deconstructive practices "allow for (no) method: no path leads around in a circle toward a first step, nor proceeds from the simple to the complex, nor leads from a beginning to an end. . . . We here note a point/lack of method [*point de méthode*]: this does not rule out a certain marching order" (D271). The marching order which constitutes the nonmethod of deconstruction prevents deconstruction from being an interpretive freeplay and allows for a coherent, yet at the same time uncontrollable, aesthetic play with language. Our procedure here will be to identify the "marching order" and to equate it with what we would term "radical hermeneutical canons" (noncanons). As in previous cases, we will then use these canons as clues to discerning hermeneutical principles. In all of this we run the risk of identifying something which Derrida would claim has no identity.

It is clear that even if deconstruction challenges the notions of identity and meaning, as well as the stodginess of hermeneutical practice, it does not champion arbitrary interpretation. With respect to reading, which Derrida characterizes as a game which requires risk, he states:

> That person would have understood nothing of the game who, at this [*de coup*], would feel himself authorized merely to add on; that is, to add any old thing. He would add nothing: the seam wouldn't hold. Reciprocally, he who through 'methodological prudence', 'norms of objectivity', or 'safe-guards of knowledge' would refrain from committing anything of himself, would not read at all. . . . The reading or writing supplement must be rigorously prescribed, but by the necessities of a *game*, by the logic of *play*, signs to which the system of all textual powers must be accorded and attuned. (D 64)

Deconstruction, then, is neither anarchy (without principles), where one reads anything at all into the text, nor conservative reproduction, where one reads nothing into the text. Deconstructive interpretation is located somewhere between arbitrariness and hermeneutical stodginess. These latter positions would contend that the logic of the play is totally under the control of the interpreter, whereas Derrida would look to the text itself for the prescribed sign that would enable a deconstructive reading. The question is whether there are any rules that would guide our looking to the text.

Textuality, Productivity, and Play

Despite any claim to the contrary, Derrida does not withhold a set of canons that would guide deconstructive reading. Indeed, precisely because they are concerned with reading, these canons resemble in form (although not in their prescriptive content) a traditional statement of hermeneutical canons. Derrida's textual hermeneutical (non)canons are clearly outlined in *Of Grammatology*. He expresses the ambition of a deconstructive reading to be to draw out of a text a signification (the "prescribed sign") that, once found, cannot be dismissed precisely because it operates within "the economy of a written text, circulating through other texts, leading back to it constantly, conforming to the element of a language and to its regulated functioning" (G 149). This search for a sign is not a search for the author's intention. Nor is it a search for a meaning that is "imposed by history and the language." Deconstructive reading ought not to go beyond the signifier, which is the text itself, toward a signified (intended or otherwise), but must try to uncover the play of language which constitutes the chain of significations which is also nothing other than the text itself. The sought-for signifier will be caught within a textual system that will allow a plurality of interpretations and will privilege none.

Derrida offers the following (non)canons which would allow the ambition of deconstructive reading to be fulfilled.

Canon (1): The reader must try to understand the linguistic constraints under which the author operates. If this sounds too much like Schleiermacher, we had better let Derrida say it. The "reading must always aim at a certain relationship, unperceived by the writer, between what he commands and what he does not command of the patterns of the language that he uses" (G 158). This (non)canon is enunciated in the shadow of a familiar principle: all interpretation, whether in the writing or the reading of a text, is linguistic. "The writer writes *in* a language and *in* a logic whose proper system, laws, and life his discourse by definition cannot dominate absolutely" (G 158). The reader ought to begin by "taking rigorous account of this *being held within* language. . . . the encompassing power of the language to which he [the author] is subject" (G 159–160). The reader herself is also held within a language and within traditions which in principle she cannot dominate (see, for example, G 160–161). This linguistic constraint is embodied as a "signifying structure," or "textuality." The deconstructive principle could be stated as follows: all interpretation is textualistic—that is, is caught up in a larger game, a play of signifiers.

Derrida would not dispute Gadamer's principle of the linguisticality of interpretation, or indeed, the hermeneutical universality of language (see WD 35). He would contend, however, that nonradical hermeneutics limits the linguisticality (textuality) of the text. The traditional practice of hermeneutics tends to decide on a meaning which excludes other meanings, and thus plays down the heterogeneity of the text. "Textuality being constituted by differences and by differences from differences, it is by nature absolutely heterogeneous and is constantly composing with the forces that tend to annihilate it" (D 98). In Derrida's view, nonradical hermeneutics, despite its attempt to limit textuality by excluding the plurality of meanings, is caught up within the play of signifiers anyway, yet in a way that is too trusting. Deconstruction is in the game more suspiciously. It wants to be aware that it is in the play of textuality. A deconstructive reading aims at allowing the full play of the heterogeneous textuality of the text. Nonetheless, even deconstructive interpretation limits textuality. The focus on a particular "prescribed signifier" (*supplément* in Rousseau; *pharmakon* in Plato, and so on) does frame an interpretation even if it has no privilege over other interpretations. Thus, a second principle emerges: all interpretation limits the heterogeneous textuality of the object of interpretation. Deconstruction claims to do this less than traditional approaches, or at least to do it knowingly.

If this textuality belongs to the text, still it must be activated, opened up, "produced" by the interpreter. Thus, *Canon (2):* The reader ought to open up the textuality of the text. This means, however, that the reader must open himself up to the text, since if something new is produced in reading, it is not totally the work of the interpreter. If deconstructionists do not unanimously agree with J. Hillis Miller's contention that "'deconstruction' is not something that the reader does to a text; it is something that the text does to itself," they at least agree that a deconstructive reading opens up both the text and the reader to an interpretive productivity.[4] We come close here to another familiar principle. Derrida tends to regard nonradical interpretation as simply an attempt at reproduction, a "doubling of commentary," which, he admits, has its own importance. It acts as a "guardrail" without which the productivity of deconstructive interpretation "would risk developing in any [arbitrary] direction at all and authorize itself to say almost anything. But this indispensable guardrail has always only *protected*, it has never *opened*, a reading" (G 158).

In the view of radical hermeneutics (and here Derrida fails to see his proximity to the moderate views of Gadamer) interpretation involves a productivity which goes beyond reproduction. Unlike conservative hermeneutics, which aims to accomplish a re-productive reading, radical hermeneutics, like its critical cousin, intends to escape the fascination with reproduction. In contrast to critical hermeneutics, however, radical hermeneutics construes reproduction in a larger framework. If for critical hermeneutics what gets reproduced are hegemonic traditions which limit the political and social possibilities of human existence, for radical hermeneutics it is this and more. Interpretation tends to reproduce the larger and more encompassing metaphysical framework which conditions all understanding. The characteristics of modernist metaphysics (for example, subjective and reflective control over the interpretation process, the objectivity of the text) are retained uncritically by both conservative and critical hermeneutics. In contrast, radical hermeneutics attempts to deconstruct the framework of metaphysics. Yet, as Derrida admits, there is no absolute or ultimate escape or emancipation; deconstruction always has to work "within the closure" of metaphysics (G 14).[5]

Canon (3): The interpreter ought not to look outside of the text for its explanation or meaning. Reading "cannot legitimately transgress the text toward something other than it, toward a referent (a reality that is metaphysical, historical, psychobiological, etc.) or toward a signified outside the text whose content could take place, could have taken place outside of language" (G 158). Reading ought to (must, if it is to be legitimate) remain within the signifier. Indeed, there is no going beyond the signifier.

The implied principle is that there is no transcendental signified to be interpreted. In Derrida's radical formulation, "*There is nothing outside of the text* [there is no outside-text; *il n'y a pas de hors-texte*]" (G 158). It is not simply the case that the text always goes beyond the author, as Gadamer says, but rather that the author does not exist outside of the text. The author is always "inscribed in a determined textual system," along with every referent or signified about which she writes (G 160). The play of signifiers embraces interpreter and the interpreted and constitutes a larger process beyond the control of writer or reader. We cannot gain an exterior control on this larger process (= textuality, play of signifiers); at most, we can operate within it, beginning wherever we find ourselves, and try to reveal it by subverting it in a deconstructive manner. Thus, *Canon (4):* "We must begin *wherever we are* . . . in a text where we already believe ourselves to be" (G

162). Derrida thus notes that there is no way to absolutely justify a point of departure.

Following the principle of textuality, a text is never closed in upon itself in self-identity, "complete with its inside and its outside" (D 130). Rather, it is an open system that produces a plurality of meanings. Thus, the interpreter ought not to set out to find or conclude with one identical self-enclosed meaning; "one must still take into consideration many other possibilities" (G 161). Since other paths are possible, no path is justifiable. Precisely on this point Derrida would argue against the notion of a deconstructionist method. Precisely this point demonstrates that deconstructionist canons are noncanons. Derrida cannot prescribe, from some exterior position, how interpretation ought to proceed, or where it ought to begin. The text itself must act as both the guardrail and the abyss. But deconstruction does not sit on the guardrail (depending upon a hermeneutics which prevents arbitrary interpretation) and simply acknowledge the abyss (the indeterminacy of interpretations). The "structural necessity of the abyss" always rules; we are already of necessity, rather than by "a happy or unhappy accident" (G 163), in the abyss, faced with the indeterminacy of interpretation. It is something that we as interpreters can neither avoid nor control. To the extent that we think we can, we live a fiction which itself is only one unjustifiable interpretation among others.

The principle operating here could be called the principle of play. Interpretation occurs only within the diacritical system of signifiers and without recourse to a metaphysical reality of the referent. "One could call *play* the absence of the transcendental signified as limitlessness of play, that is to say as the destruction of onto-theology and the metaphysics of presence" (G 50). Derrida's radical principle of play is an attempt (from the inside) to unravel the metaphysical belief in the reality and the identity of the referent—objectivity, subjectivity, presence, being, truth, or any other metaphysical concept operative in the Western tradition. The concepts that we have used to describe play—the transcending-appropriating structure, assimilation-accommodation, corrigibility-conservability, and so on—are, in the deconstructive view, metaphysical concepts that depend on an original subjectivity that gets transcended or reappropriated. The radical concept of play deconstructs the centered subjectivity seemingly implicit in the process. "This *play*, thought as absence of the transcendental signified, is not a play *in the world*, as it has always been defined, for the purposes of *containing* it, by the philosophical tradition. . . . to think play radically the ontological and transcendental problematics must first be seriously *exhausted*." (G 50). In the radical sense, play is not one form of experience among others; it is the principle of every experience, "the play of the world."[6] Interpretation itself is a way of situating ourselves within the abyss—the play of indeterminate meanings. The stability of every meaning is undermined by the shifting play of signifiers. Every "truth" that the interpreter closes in on becomes one of the plurality of fictions which constitute the play of differences within the system. Truth, as Socrates says of opinion, runs away; for deconstruction, it can never be tied down.

The Principle of Power

If, out of the incessant play of meanings, one meaning ends up as privileged, one must account for this in terms of a principle of power. The interpreter and the privileged meaning are products of the impersonal signifying practices and codes which reflect the metaphysical as well as the economic and political orders within which they operate, or which operate within them. An interpretation "corresponds to a condition of forces and translates an historical calculation," so that definite constraints which belong "to the discourse of our time" progressively determine a "chosen" interpretation (G 70). As in critical hermeneutics, the constraining principle of tradition is viewed in terms of reproduction and hegemony, but again in a larger framework. Traditions are always metaphysical impositions, and one must understand them in the widest possible sense in order to see them fully (see WD 41–42). Derrida could easily agree with Eugen Fink's characterization of metaphysical hegemony.

> The history of metaphysics conditions our every action, desire, and thought. Each attempt at thinking is, from the start, embedded in the large streams of thoughts that are [already] *realized* thoughts surrounding us as forms of social order which shape

our daily existence. Not in library books do old thoughts prove their power to prevail, but in the structures of the family, of the state, of law and community life, which actually penetrate us.[7]

The textuality of metaphysical hegemonic relations is not confined to libraries or texts; it overflows into the streets, houses, and workplaces of everyday human existence.

The nature of power, however, is not the same for critical and radical hermeneutics. For the latter it cannot be strictly reduced to hegemony. For critical theory hegemonic relations are external ones, imposed from the outside. For radical hermeneutics power relations are neither external nor internal, but constitute the very nature of interpretation. Critical theory adopts the model which Foucault terms "juridico-discursive power"—a one-way, unproductive, or counterproductive hegemonic power.[8] Traditional conceptions of law and monarchy constitute the explanatory models of the exercise of such power. Newer mechanisms of power, however, tied to modern technology, "are probably irreducible to the representation of law." These are "methods of power whose operation is not ensured by right but by technique, not by law but by normalization, not by punishment but by control, methods that are employed on all levels in forms that go beyond the state and its apparatus" (HS 89). From the viewpoint of radical hermeneutics, critical theory fails to adequately formulate this newer sense of power and thus fundamentally misconceives both hegemony and the possibility of emancipation.

Derrida shares Foucault's view (*contra* critical hermeneutics, but not in disagreement with Gadamer) that reflective acknowledgement of power relations does not amount to a liberation from them. For Foucault, discourses and power relations can undergo change, but not under the control of a subject's reflection.[9] For Derrida it is linguisticality which keeps us bound up within traditions, and linguisticality cannot be reduced in any sort of reflection, be it phenomenological, critical, genealogical, or even deconstructive: "to state the difficulty, to state the difficulty of stating, is not yet to surmount it" (WD 37). This skepticism about the power of reflection places into doubt the concept of emancipation developed in critical theory, as well as any hermeneutical trust in conversation.

Radical Suspicion

The Decentering of Subjectivity.   Emile Benveniste states clearly the structuralist and poststucturalist challenge to the concept of modern subjectivity. "It is in and through language that man constitutes himself as a subject, because language alone establishes the concept of 'ego' in reality, in *its* reality which is that of the being."[10] There is no lack of precedent in the history of philosophy for the poststructuralist suspicion of subjectivity. Even in the central development of modern philosophy, the very framework of which was set by Descartes' concept of *cogito* and Locke's notion of personal identity, Hume's famous skepticism concerning the status of the self represents a major contribution to a tradition of critical suspicion. But if Hume demonstrates the dispersion of the self in a stream of impressions, or the fictional nature of personal identity invented by the imagination, still he fails to go beyond the theater metaphor (disclaimers notwithstanding).[11] The theater remains as the mind, the stream of consciousness, the faculty of the imagination; if not the *cogito* then the *excogito* as locus for the event of subjectivity. Always behind the *cogitans* there lurks a transcendental subject, discovered by Kant and then again by Husserl. If the attempt is then made to disperse the transcendental ego, as Sartre tried to do, there still remains the empty stage: consciousness as the ultimate locus of subjectivity. Thus, Sartre's notion of the *pour soi* remains within the orbit of modern metaphysics, even if it is not a being, but a nothingness haunted by being. For this reason also, Sartre's theory of play, despite the possibility of transcendence, remains under the control of a subjective recovery.

Derrida wants to show that the locus of subjectivity is neither an identity that could be captured in the theater metaphor nor a definite nothingness recovering from and constituted by its possibilities, but a nonidentity, an u-topia (nonlocus) produced by an indefinite play of temporal difference. This is precisely the temporality that Husserl had analyzed as the absolute foundation of consciousness. But Husserl was unable to fully acknowledge that this temporal flow of retentional and protentional performances undercut the authority and control of the transcendental ego. Even if he had glimpsed this, he was not at all able to see that the performance of retentional-protentional relations was a play of

differences which undermined the identity and being of consciousness and which therefore displaced the transcendental flow itself
by an anonymous process which cannot even be measured in terms
of subjectivity, and is therefore not even a presubjective or passive
constitution.[12] Retentioning and protentioning are completely
caught up within an impersonal system of signifiers constituted by
the diacritical difference found in all sign systems. Subjectivity can
only be the sometimes result produced by this process, which lacks
any metaphysical characteristics of identity, being, or substance
and which can barely be captured in Derrida's deconstructive terminology of *différance*, trace, arche-writing, supplement, dissemination, and so forth.

We have already contrasted two conceptions of play (those of
Sartre and Gadamer) in terms of Husserl's analysis of temporality.
Here we can see the difference between them and Derrida's concept
of play. Whereas with both of the former concepts we could
characterize play in terms of an emphasis on one or other of the
temporal performances of retentioning (Sartre's emphasis on self-
recovery) or protentioning (Gadamer's emphasis on transcendence), deconstructive play cannot be so easily accommodated to
the phenomenological account of time and subjectivity. In Derrida's view, play is constituted by neither recovery nor transcendence, both of which imply a self or subject to be recovered or
transcended. Rather, the very possibilities of retentioning and protentioning depend upon the play of *différance*. Play is an in-
frastructural condition of possibility. Retentioning (or protentioning) can only be retentioning (or protentioning) on the basis of
something other than itself, something absent in the very presence
of what it represents. This anonymous game of presence-absence,
this play of differences which accounts for the traces of retentioning
and protentioning, is a play that cannot be described in terms of
self-recovery or self-transcendence (see WD 292). In the
deconstructive view, play according to the transcendence-
appropriation model is not really free play, and thus not true play
at all since it would be play already organized and under the
control of a metaphysics of subjectivity. Derrida's principle of play,
in contrast, is a principle which casts inescapable suspicion on the
very notion of subjectivity.

The poststructuralist displacement of subjectivity amounts to a deconstruction of humanistic philosophy insofar as humanism in the widest sense involves the metaphysics of subjectivity. Humanism places the human being at the center of things. It puts human subjectivity in charge of a technically ordered world. It makes the human subject the subject of a continuous history which represses difference and discontinuity and, according to Foucault, promises the possibility of reproduction: "that one day the subject—in the form of historical consciousness—will once again be able to appropriate, to bring back under his sway, all those things that are kept at a distance by difference, and find in them what might be called his abode" (AK 12). Derrida questions the very status and adequacy of historical science itself, as a human science. Denying the subject, deconstructing the concept of one's own (propre) self-identity, and in contexts of literary criticism dismissing the concept of authorhood, Derrida challenges the very nature of humanistic history. "We must also know that this history of metaphysics, to which the concept of history itself returns, belongs to an ensemble for which the name history is no longer suitable" (G 246; see WD 291). Derrida's grammatology (which is still not a nonhistorical account) displaces "man" with a play of différance. In agreement with Foucault, that Nietzsche's death of God really implies the death of man, Derrida's deconstruction of the subject is an attempt to move beyond the "metaphysical repetition of humanism."[13]

Postmodern Doubts about Conversation and Emancipation.   For both critical and moderate hermeneutics, conversation and emancipation are essentially linked. To contrast critical and moderate approaches, one can define a difference of degree between complete and incomplete emancipation, ideal and perfect consensus on the one hand, and ambiguous imperfect conversation on the other. Radical hermeneutics, however, casts doubt on any promise of conversation or emancipation. Since language is not just "the house of Being" (Heidegger) but also the house of metaphysics, radical hermeneutics holds that mere conversation will not, of itself, lead us beyond the walls of hegemonic traditions. Emancipation would mean moving "outdoors," but all of the doors seem to be locked shut. For this reason Derrida constantly casts doubt even on the pretentions of deconstruction to move beyond the language of metaphysics.[14] To the extent that it must always operate from within the metaphysical tradition, there seems no possibility of emancipation from that tradition which constrains all conversation.

Derrida distrusts the model of conversation and the "good will" required for it. The primacy which Gadamer gives to conversation as the essence of language is challenged by Derrida's deconstruction of the primacy of living speech. Derrida's analysis of the metaphysical tradition from Plato to Saussure, which makes speech primary and writing derivative, suggests that the alleged originality and self-presence involved in speech is subverted in a play of diacritical difference, an "arche-writing" which is other than self-present, identical, or original (see, for example, G 30ff.). For Derrida the "essence" of language consists in this play of signs (which is precisely a "nonessence") rather than in conversation. Whereas for Gadamer play and conversation share the same hermeneutical nature, for Derrida the more radical notion of play undercuts any appeal to the metaphysical conception of conversation.

This is the point of *aporia* which delineates moderate and radical hermeneutical approaches. We have termed it the *aporia* of conversation: interpretation must (according to the radical approach) escape the constraints of the ongoing hegemonic conversation of metaphysics, yet (according to Gadamer and Derrida) interpretation can only operate within the same conversation. For Gadamer, emancipation is attained in and through conversation; for Derrida, emancipation is the impossible liberation from the constraints of conversation. We will now see that this same *aporia* is played out in educational contexts.

RADICAL THEORIES OF EDUCATION

We have delineated a number of related principles of radical hermeneutics which, for purposes of our discussion of education, we will simplify to the following four.

The Principle of Play: All interpretation is caught up within a play of signifiers. This is both a constraining and an enabling principle. The play of difference is inescapable, but it is at the same time that which allows for deconstructive interpretation. *Corollary (I):* all interpretation is linguistic or textualistic. Both the interpreter and that which is interpreted are caught up within a system of language outside of which there is no transcendental signified. *Corollary (II):* all meaning is indeterminate—radically ambiguous. Textuality is heterogeneous.

The Principle of Limited Productivity: All interpretation limits the heterogeneous textuality of the object of interpretation. Nonradical interpretation attempts to exclude heterogeneity by the reproduction of metaphysical meaning. In contrast, radical interpretation seeks to be productive by allowing the play of heterogeneity to play itself out.

The Principle of Power: All interpretation is an exercise of power. The limitation on the heterogeneity of texts and the reproduction of the metaphysical framework reflect a power structure (sometimes hegemonic) which translates the metaphysical framework into a social and political ordering.

The Principle of Unjustifiability: All interpretations are ultimately unjustifiable in the sense that all strategies of justification depend on one or more categories that are themselves always products of another (metaphysical) interpretation. To oppose reproduction and hegemonic power structures, deconstructive interpretation is radically suspicious not only of traditional meaning and confident claims to truth, but also of any claim to a reflective method that guarantees emancipation. The notions of reflection, subjectivity, conversation, and emancipation are all placed in doubt. Ultimately, not even deconstruction is justifiable. Derrida presents deconstruction not as a position to be defended, but more as a strategy of radical nonpositionality, an undoing of the positions of others. Its goal is to be radically suspicious of any and all positions which make a claim to truth, value, being, justice, emancipation, and so forth. Indeed, the four principles just delineated are themselves open to deconstruction. They are principles that try to define a nonposition. In that sense, from the nonperspective of radical hermeneutics, they are nonprinciples.

To what extent are these (non)principles expressed in radical theories of education? Is the goal of radical education to turn us all into relativists and skeptics? Are the prevailing concepts and practices in education, or the concept of education itself, in need of deconstruction? We turn now to a number of radical theorists to seek answers to these and other related questions.

Derrida's Deconstruction of Education

For Derrida, educational systems (especially the university) are located on the side of metaphysics, reflecting the logocentrism that dominates philosophical thinking. Moreover, it is difficult for him to conceive of an educational or philosophical program or institution that would serve the interests of deconstruction.[15] It would first appear, then, that deconstruction must work in opposition to educational systems, outside of education, and against the very concept of education. But this would be a misunderstanding. Indeed, as Derrida's own practical association with GREPH (Le Groupe de Recherches sur l'Enseignement de Philosophie) shows, he understands deconstruction to be working within educational systems, not against them in the sense of trying to destroy them.[16] Deconstruction has two tasks within education: to develop a practical critique of education and "to engage in a positive rather affirmative, audacious, extensive and intensive transformation" of education.[17]

With respect to the first task, the deconstruction of metaphysical reason is at the same time a deconstructive critique of education. The educational institution—the university—is founded on the metaphysical principle of reason. "As far as I know, nobody has ever founded a university *against* reason. So we may reasonably suppose that the university's reason for being has always been reason itself, and some essential connection of reason to being" (PR 7). A deconstructive approach to the principle of reason (a principle which states, "nothing is without a reason") is simply to ask whether this principle has a reason. Derrida would thus use the paradox of reason—that reason has recourse only to itself, that one must use reason to account for the principle of reason—to lead us into the abyss: "The abyss, the hole, the *Abgrund*, the empty 'gorge' would be the impossibility for a principle of grounding to ground itself."[18] Ultimately, then, the university is situated over an abyss: it is open to a plurality of indeterminate interpretations. The university hides this situation from itself; it stops with reason and does not further ask the reason of reason. It masks its lack of grounding by justifying its existence in terms of utility with respect to "technology, economy, medicine, psychosociology or military power" (PR 11).

It is no longer a matter of saying, simply, that the university (or the educational system in general) is a tool of the state, an analysis that critical theorists easily pick up from Marx, and which Derrida also finds in Nietzsche.[19] Derrida is not questioning simply the notion of state-sponsored research in the university (which, of course, he does not ignore, and which he thinks is extremely obvious—one need only read the budgets which determine research agendas), but the general hegemonics which turn all research, even that which is referred to as "disinterested" research (mathematics, theoretical physics, philosophy), to account in terms of technical and economic "payoff." "One can no longer distinguish between technology on the one hand and theory, science, and rationality on the other. . . . [A]n essential affinity ties together objective knowledge, the principle of reason, and a certain metaphysical determination of the relation to truth. . . . [W]e can no longer dissociate the principle of reason from the very idea of technology in the realm of their modernity" (PR 12). The power relations which Derrida perceives in educational practice cannot be reduced to what Foucault identifies as juridico-discursive power; as Foucault himself would have it, they are much more comprehensive and basic, tied to the modern metaphysics of technology. They cannot be modeled on a legal-monarchical scheme. That might have been possible when "the entire topology of the university [was] organized around the exercise of royal censorship. Today, in the Western democracies, that form of censorship has almost entirely disappeared. The prohibiting limitations [which orient education to useful ends and the reproduction of society] function through multiple channels that are decentralized, difficult to bring together into a system" (PR 13). Derrida does not refrain from giving examples of these power relations.

> The unacceptability of a discourse, the non-certification of a research project, the illegitimacy of a course offering are declared by evaluative actions. . . . Within the university itself, forces that are apparently external to it (presses, foundations, the mass media) are intervening in an ever more decisive way. (PR 13)

The common denominator which allows philosophy and poetry, as well as physics and mathematics, to be manipulated and appropriated in these power relations is the concept of information. In the category of information metaphysics gets translated into technology. Everything can be reduced to information, encoded, and transmitted. Within the paradigm of information, language is seemingly brought under human control, and man is ensured of "his mastery on earth and beyond." The very notion of education found within this metaphysical-technological framework is that of transmitting information (PR 14).

If this amounts to a deconstructive critique of education, radical hermeneutics still must attempt its "audacious" transformation of education. For Derrida this transformation would involve a new questioning relation to language and tradition and a new way of taking responsibility. Although Derrida offers no formal curriculum, his own deconstructive approach to literary criticism is not irrelevant with respect to a transformed relation to language. Such a transformation would depend upon "the deconstruction of a pedagogical institution and all that it implies. What this institution cannot bear, is for anyone to tamper with [*toucher à*; also "touch," "change," "concern himself with"] language. . . . What this institution cannot bear is a transformation that leaves intact neither [linguistic nationalism nor universalism]."[20] If one studies the structure of "a poetic rather than an informative value of language" or "the effects of undecidability, and so on," one becomes "interested in possibilities that arise at the outer limits of the authority and the power of the principle of reason. On that basis, they may attempt to define new responsibilities in the face of the university's total subjection to the technologies of informatization" (PR 14). Some, at least from the side of conservative hermeneutics and cultural literacy, would certainly consider this an audacious suggestion.

In the most concrete of proposals, for reasons peculiar to the context of his lecture "The Principle of Reason" (thus following the canon that he must begin where he is), Derrida suggests a non-disciplinary faculty "at large," which in effect would be a practical implementation of what Habermas, in reference to Derrida, calls the leveling of genre distinctions, a dissolution of the disciplines which would not be the equivalent of an "interdisciplinary" approach but a "nondisciplinary" approach. The aim of non-disciplinary studies would not necessarily be the establishment of a position (philosophical, political, or moral), a community, or an institution. Indeed, such studies would question the very meaning of these concepts and their justification. The aim would be to maintain a radical suspicion of these concepts and to "also unmask . . . all the ruses of end-orienting reason, the paths by which apparently disinterested research can find itself indirectly reappropriated, reinvested by programs of all sorts" (PR 16). In a sense, the aim of a deconstructive program would be to maintain itself as a nonprogram, to maintain itself as deconstructive and to avoid deconstructivism.

For a critical hermeneutics, and specifically for Habermas, this would be going too far. He suggests that the leveling of genres—in effect, seeing all language in textualistic terms, having poetic or aesthetic value rather than informational value, or attributing primacy to rhetoric over logic—is Derrida's way of defeating the paradox of the self-referential critique of reason involved in asking about the reason of reason. In Habermas's view this "aestheticizing of language" is fatal, especially for an understanding of educational processes.[21] For Habermas, the disciplinary character of the educational context is essential because of "the independent logics" of problems defined within the structures of disciplines, and the specially tailored linguistic media to deal with them. Precisely such independently formed communicative practices make learning possible. "These learning processes unfold an independent logic that transcends all local constraints, because experiences and judgments are formed only in the light of criticizable validity claims." Derrida, by leveling disciplinary or genre distinctions, "permits the capacity to solve problems to disappear behind the world-creating capacity of language."[22]

Clearly, if in its first task the radical, deconstructive approach to education resembles a critical approach to education, here, in its audacious proposals, the differences begin to emerge. Critical approaches have a program; they champion emancipation, which they want to define in a definite Marxist or Freudian or critical way. They argue for a position that they would term "liberated." Derrida's response is that any program, any position, must be suspect and open to deconstruction. "Thus I shall go so far as to say that the discourse of Marxism and psychoanalysis, including those of Marx and Freud [clearly we could add Habermas and critical theory], *inasmuch* as they are standardized by a project [program] of scientific practice and by the principle of reason, are intra-institutional, in any event homogeneous with the discourse that dominates the university in the last analysis" (PR 16). This is the basis for a powerful critique of critical theories of education. Having formulated their discourse for years within the research structure of the university—indeed, a critical discourse which has usually been directed from the university toward educational systems at a lower level than the university—these theorists have only recently begun to ask themselves about their positions within the academy, about the language they use in their discourses, and about their relationship to the primary and secondary institutions which they study.[23] At the same time, Derrida realizes that this is a danger for his own deconstructive work and that the necessary involvement of deconstruction within the university framework, "with its memory and tradition, the imperative of professional rigor and competence," must also occasion self-critique and constant vigilance. Here we find the new responsibility "in the university or in the face of the university," proposed by Derrida (PR 14, 17).

This responsibility, however, is not a simple, straightforward, unambiguous one. It is an academic responsibility that suffers from the play of forces involved in deconstructive critique and transformation. "For the responsibility that I am trying to situate cannot be simple. It implies multiple sites, a stratified terrain, postulations that are undergoing continual displacement, a sort of strategic rhythm" (PR 17). Deconstruction runs a risk in this game. It risks "being reappropriated by socio-political forces that could find it in their own interest in certain situations." Again, deconstruction is operating within the heteronomous relations of the educational system, within "certain historical, techno-economic, politico-institutional and linguistic conditions" (PR 17). Thus radical suspicion is constantly needed.

Radical suspicion is required not only about disciplines and practices within the university but also about professions and the university's role in the "reproduction of professional competence" inside and outside of the university. The risk or danger of the deconstructive game is clear in this case. If deconstruction rejects the reproductive professionalization of the university, "which regulates university life according to the supply and demand of the marketplace and according to a purely technical ideal of competence," this rejection may "result in reproducing a highly traditional politics of knowledge" and, in effect, "a social hierarchy in the exercise of technopolitical power" (PR 17–18). Every move toward anarchy "risks producing or reproducing the hierarchy," and vice versa: as Derrida puts it in *Of Grammatology*, what we can call enslavement "can equally be called *liberation*."[24] Thus, one cannot settle into an easy position; the play of forces will not allow it. Any claim to eliminate this play and this risk is to fall into a trap. Deconstruction never comes to an end; it must be constantly vigilant: "Beware of the abysses and the gorges, but also of the bridges and the barriers" (PR 19).

This, then, is one outline of a radical approach to education: first, a critique which shows education to be the product of power relations and to be reproductive of those same relations; second, an audacious transformation of education which lets loose the play, promotes productivity, constantly risks reproduction, and maintains a radical suspicion of every end or final position. This is one deployment of radical hermeneutical principles within the educational context. Many of the radical approaches follow this deployment to some degree, in some partial or generalized way.

Radical Critique

Foucault's discussion of pedagogical power not only clarifies his own analysis of power relations and subjectivity but also represents a variation of the first, critical part of the radical scheme employed by Derrida. Foucault offers an intense critique of the design of educational institutions, from their physical architecture, which lends itself to hierarchy, continuity, and functional surveillance, to their power relations, which function in machinelike fashion. Educational practices are organized around a *"disciplinary power"* maintained in a pedagogical apparatus which reproduces its power "and distributes individuals in this permanent and continuous field" (DP 177). The power system implied in this disciplinary mechanism is summarized by Foucault in his reference to Bentham's panopticon, which allows for the complete visibility of subjects. This power is both visibly and invisibly installed within educational institutions. "This enables the disciplinary power to be both absolutely indiscreet, since it is everywhere and always alert, since by its very principle it leaves no zone of shade and constantly supervises the very individuals who are entrusted with the task of supervising" (DP 177). We only need consider the complaints of teachers in primary and secondary schools about how they themselves are treated as children with respect to access to materials and use of time. Within the educational system, the reproduction of social behaviors is guaranteed "by means of a whole ensemble of regulated communications (lessons, questions and answers, orders, exhortations, coded signs of obedience, differentiation marks of the 'value' of each person and of the levels of knowledge) and by the means of a whole series of power processes (enclosure, surveillance, reward and punishment, the pyramidal hierarchy)."[25] The "penal mechanism" of reward and punishment is articulated in terms of "time (lateness, absences, interruption of tasks), of activity (inattention, negligence, lack of zeal), of behavior (impoliteness, disobedience), of speech (idle chatter, insolence) of the body ('incorrect' attitudes, irregular gestures, lack of cleanliness), of sexuality (impurity, indecency)" (DP 178).

Foucault shows how subjects are constituted within the exercise of pedagogical power by identifying various operations manifested in reward-punishment practices. The pedagogical mechanism (we need only think of grading procedures for an example) "compares, differentiates, hierarchizes, homogenizes, excludes. In short, it *normalizes*" (DP 183). Pedagogical power is essentially different from the traditional notion of juridico-discursive power, which refers the individual to law rather than compares, which specifies acts "according to a number of general categories" rather than differentiates, which relies on an opposition between the permitted and the forbidden rather than hierarchizes, and which operates the "division of condemnation" rather than homogenizes.

> The Normal is established as a principle of coercion in teaching with the introduction of a standardized education and the establishment of the *écoles normales* (teacher's training colleges). . . .
> In a sense, the power of normalization imposes homogeneity; but it individualizes by making it possible to measure gaps, to deter-

mine levels, to fix specialties, and to render the differences useful by fitting them to one another. (DP 184)

By various educational procedures (Foucault analyzes the examination as an instance) the system subjects its subjects; it acts as a machine into which we put nonsubjects (children who live on the principle of play) and by which we produce *subjects*, in every sense of that word. These procedures constitute a special form of the exercise of power. (a) They objectify their subjects by making them *visible* in the light of certain measuring criteria; (b) they document their subjects bestowing upon them a personal history which captures and fixes them; and (c) they define each individual as a "case," which is the individual "as he may be described, judged, measured, compared with others, in his very individuality; and it is also the individual who has to be trained or corrected, classified, normalized, excluded, etc." (DP 191). Educational institutions thus create objectified, documented, fully described subjects who are open to methods of control and domination. For Foucault, the individual, the modern subject, is both a *fiction* of ideological representation (modern epistemology, modern political theory, economic utility theory) and a *reality*—"a reality fabricated by this specific technology of power that I have called 'discipline'" (DP 194).

Radical theories of education tend to follow rather closely the kinds of critique that we have seen in Derrida and Foucault. John Caputo, for instance, combines the discourses of Derrida and Foucault to provide a general critique of the university. He notes that within the university, power relations gather around the concept of reason to defend traditional positions and exclude new ones, with the result that the "university is put more and more to work by the society to which it belongs, and it has less and less time for the free play of ideas whose ground, reason, and practical purpose cannot be easily or directly shown" (RH 230–231). Other radical theorists focus their critiques on specific aspects of the educational scene. William Spanos, for instance, uses a Heideggerian deconstruction of metaphysics and Foucault's critique of the panopticon model of education to examine the notion of a core curriculum, its relation to existing power structures, and "its strategic tendency to *contain* and neutralize dissent." He concludes that the core curriculum reaffirms the "logocentric and elitist ideals of humanistic education," represses "the possibility of an authentic freeplay of ideals," and seeks after (attempts to reproduce) "a lost absolute origin and thus, ultimately, a disciplinary panoptic model of the college or university."[26]

Mas ud Zavarzadeh and Donald Morton focus on both curriculum and teaching method. They explore the implications of the postmodern decentering of subjectivity for the humanities curriculum. In this regard they offer a "postmodern critique" of current curricula which reinforce the concept of the individual subject as free agent within the existing social order. They argue that within existing curricula the pedagogical practice of the "interpretive essay" follows the principles of conservative hermeneutics and is based on an equation of truth with the author's intention. The author thus comes to stand as both a model of independent subject and a model of authority.[27]

Michael Ryan offers a deconstructive reading of the concept of academic freedom and its limitations. He also suggests that the academic division of disciplines reflects a "metaphysical" structuring of reality which serves the interests of established, hegemonic society. "The intellectual division of labor in the disciplines reflects and reproduces institutional divisions" which conceal real institutional relations. Furthermore, "the practice of knowing is itself already a form of bias, since it entails selecting and excluding, more often than not, according to historically determined institutional norms of what *should* be studied and known."[28] Since the university classroom cannot be isolated from the hegemonic relations found in society, and since all knowledge reflects a bias, Ryan concludes that the notion of academic freedom inappropriately describes the real situation.

The Postmodern Language of Possibility

For radical theorists of education there is no program or position that would escape the perpetual play of the mechanisms of power. One can only begin where one is, on a local level, within educational institutions, to resist the hegemonic practice of power, and remain wary (radically suspicious) that any chosen strategy for this resistance does not itself turn into a system of domination. Despite the caution that some radical theorists express about choosing an ultimate method, strategy, or position, one is not justified in claiming that their approaches do not offer what Aronowitz and Giroux call "a language of possibility." Nevertheless, a number of theorists from the points of view of critical theory and feminism have offered this criticism. Peter McLaren's suggestion, for example, that "little in the corpus of poststructuralist or postmodernist theories has been significantly appropriated for the purpose of educational reform, except by way of critique," is only partially justified.[29] McLaren, however, may be right in asking how far poststructuralist proposals have been implemented in reform programs. Radical theorists themselves admit that their pedagogical procedures have not been actualized.[30] Still, they do suggest numerous practical proposals for audacious transformation. The following incomplete inventory of the uncommon proposals made by poststructuralists should make clear the variety of the languages of possibility offered by the radical approach.

(1) Roland Barthes, following his own principle of textuality and emphasizing the principle of play in the teaching of literature, suggests that the "pedagogical problem would be to shake up the notion of literary text and to make adolescents understand that there is text everywhere, but that not everything is text; I mean that there is text everywhere, but repetition, stereotype, and *doxa* are also everywhere."[31] In order to disrupt, loosen, and baffle the power behind/in pedagogical discourse, Barthes recommends the use of digression or "excursion," adding "copious corrections and capricious revisions." Barthes' radical pedagogy consists of play and suspicion, which disrupt the "consistency of the self, of the subject," in order to approach the abandon of *jouissance*.

Beyond this disruptive and excessive style which emphasizes textuality and constantly corrects, adds, or wavers, Barthes also suggests pedagogy as "peaceable speech" which never judges, subjects, intimidates, or advocates a cause.[32] This pedagogical approach would amount to a radical suspicion ("floating") of pedagogical discourse. "For what can be oppressive in our teaching is not, finally, the knowledge or the culture it conveys, but the discursive forms through which we propose them."[33]

(2) Gregory Ulmer, citing the already developed critiques of education by Foucault, Derrida, and the critical theorists (he cites Bourdieu and Passeron specifically) and allowing for the possibility

of working within the existing structure of the university, offers his own audacious transformations of pedagogical practice, based not just on his reading of Derrida but also on his study of avant-garde movements in art, film, and television (see AG 168ff., 301ff.). With the humanities in mind he applies the notion of textuality to the lecture format, proposing to make the lecture a dramatic and play-ful discourse rather than a conceptual delivery of information.[34] "At issue in these lectures is the extent to which the *performance* aspect of the lectures (the scene of lecturing, rather than the refer-ential scene, the 'diegesis' of the lecture) is foregrounded, violating the student's expectation of information as message or content" (Textshop 43). In deconstructive lectures, the rhetorical system takes primacy over the content. The aim of such lectures would be to discourage reproduction and to elicit the student's productivity; students would activate "the natural capabilities of the mind to seek and achieve closure" (Textshop 45). Rather than the transmis-sion of information, then, the lecture would be a *text* which the student would have to actively interpret. The pedagogical presenta-tion is to be what Michel Serres calls an "invention" rather than a copy of an original signified (See AG 163–164).

Through radical pedagogy the student is to become "a partici-pant rather than a consumer."[35] This might be accomplished by providing visual and experimental tracks to supplement pedagogi-cal discourse, juxtaposing a traditional lecture and a parody of the same, or requiring students to rewrite texts (a technique of experi-mental "misreading . . . applied to plagiarized material," which constitutes a self-conscious move from reproduction to produc-tion) (Textshop 60). The aim of such techniques would be "to overcome the desire of the professors to *conclude*, to render a question inert through resolution, to reduce the tension of a prob-lem or an interpretation to the nirvana state of zero pressure by designing a decided meaning" (AG 145). Like the Socratic gadfly, the objective would be to keep questions open, to keep students thinking in a critical fashion, to keep the play of heterogeneous meaning alive.

(3) Jean-Francois Lyotard, in developing his conception of postmodernism, addresses the status of the university in this larger context. Lyotard might say, paraphrasing Freire, that "education is suffering from metanarrative sickness." Metanarratives or super-

discourses, which have served to legitimize the university, *seemingly* place us outside of hegemonic power relations, metaphysical frameworks, and relativistic language games while genuinely installing us deeper in precisely these economies. Furthermore, educational institutions serve to reproduce the metanarratives that legitimize them. For Lyotard the task is to "destroy" the authority of metanarratives, to give them the status of relativized narratives, and to break down genre-boundaries.[36] Such destructive experimentation, as Stanley Fogel expresses it, "dilutes the power of academic discourses which have been kept remote from one another and which have been hierarchized."[37]

A shift into a postmodern (postmetanarrative) society means the end of the university (see PMC xxiv–xxv). This, however, does not necessarily entail emancipation because the deconstruction of metanarratives simply means that we begin to see the reality of how we are living, without myths or superdiscourses concerning emancipation that hide or distort that reality. That which may replace the university, that is, educational institutes based on performativity or system efficiency, would be openly designed to serve the power interests of those institutions which already control the university and would simply "supply the system with players capable of acceptably fulfilling their roles at the pragmatic posts required by its institutions" (PMC 48). The honest criteria for judging the performance of such educational institutes would be power, practicality, efficiency, and marketability (PMC 51).

Lyotard calls for us to transform our modernist attitudes which tend to hang on to Enlightenment concepts like objectivity, truth, foundation, reason, and rational subject and which lead to the extremes of performativity. Lyotard favors a rule of paralogy: a playful pluralism in a plurality of local language games. Although Lyotard calls for "resistance against the academic genres of discourse," straightforward critique represents a risk: "the odds are that it will remain in the service of the apparatus it is out to get."[38] Given this risk, one possible approach to pedagogy might be to employ parody: "The destruction of theory can only take place through parody; in no way does it consist in *criticizing* theory, since criticism itself is a theoretical *Moment* from which the destruction of theory cannot be expected."[39]

For Lyotard the risk and the possibility of postmodernity are clear: the risk is that the electronic manipulation of information could lead to totalitarian control or "terrorist" exclusion (see PMC 63–64). The possibility is an ability to live with "paralogy," a plurality of language games, inventive experimentation, and efficient access to available information so that everyone has an equal chance in whatever language game they choose (see PMC 53, 66–67).

(4) In a proposal that equates critique with transformation itself, Zavarzadeh and Morton propose an alternative to the pedagogical practice of using the interpretive essay. They suggest an interrogative critique which would investigate "the enabling conditions of discursive practices." In contrast to the interpretive essay, the interrogative critique would displace the author (and thus displace authority and subjectivity) in order to discover the text as a system of "signifying practices and codes" which reflect the economic and political structure of society. In this case, the proposed transformation of the curriculum would coincide with the critique of the curriculum.

A postmodern critical practice would also substitute texts which "test the limits of intelligibility" for the classical texts of the humanistic curriculum, which "mystify" or camouflage or legitimize its hegemonic nature. The "heterogeneous reading list" of "innovative texts" would produce new options or alternatives ("new subject positions") for the student reader.

Radical pedagogy would not model itself on Socratic method, which Zavarzadeh and Morton view as totally noncritical, but on deconstructive approaches: "the teacher is a deconstructor and not a mere supporter in the traditional sense of the word. She helps to reveal the student to himself by showing him how his ideas and positions are the effects of larger discourses." This is characterized as an adversarial role, the aim of which is "to develop in [the student] a critical oppositional position in relation to the dominant order."[40]

One might wonder whether Zavarzadeh and Morton do not fall victim to one of the risks of deconstruction. In effect, their conception of radical education results in the *reproduction* of radicals in opposition to the dominant order. Ultimately this seems to be schooling for anarchy. The student, having been deconstructed as a subject, "having de-naturalized himself," would recognize "the arbitrariness of all the seemingly natural meanings and cultural organizations based on them." Culture and social arrangements are thereby opened up for an anarchy of interpretations and organizations. In contrast to critical approaches, they offer a conception of emancipation without consensus or even the possibility of consensus. But doesn't their postmodern critical theory, in its move toward anarchy, in Derrida's terms, "risk producing or reproducing the hierarchy," risk turning deconstruction itself into the new ideology (see PR 18)?

The Risks of Conversation

The risks of radical hermeneutics are sometimes explained in terms of its attempt to remain nonideological. To the extent that it does remain nonideological, it remains open to appropriation by any ideology—rightist or leftist.[41] Habermas makes this point in even stronger terms. He claims that poststructuralist approaches represent a "young conservatism" because they fail to identify theoretical reasons for moving in one direction rather than another. Thus, in Habermas's view, the hermeneutics of suspicion implied by Lyotard's "incredulity towards metanarratives" makes no sense without a theory of emancipation that would act as a standard of legitimation. According to Habermas, we need to "preserve at least one standard for [the] explanation of the corruption of all reasonable standards."[42] In opposition to Habermas's concern for reaching consensus in the social world, poststructuralists tend to suspect the idea of open discussion as serving ideological ends. They express a certain reluctance to be co-opted by hidden metaphysical systems, metanarratives, and power structures.

Not all theorists who would proclaim their theories to be radical, however, fall into the anticonversationalism criticized by Habermas. John Caputo, for example, attempting to follow out the implications of Derrida's deconstruction of conversation, introduces a certain problematic that illuminates the issue of emancipation and throws into relief the genuine *aporia* which delineates moderate and radical approaches.

For Caputo the liberation involved in radical hermeneutics (see RH 97) is not accomplished by a Gadamerian hermeneutics which allows for the continuity of traditions which are "extended, renewed, and perpetuated" in the incessant conversation which manifests the moral good will of *phronēsis* (see RH 108–109). Gadamerian conversation is too closely tied to the Platonic conception of dialogue and is based on a concept of recollection which, in Caputo's Kierkegaardian view, amounts to a metaphysical reproduction of "eternal truth" (see RH 13ff, 111). Gadamerian play "is a 'play' made safe by recollection" (RH 113). The traditional model of *phronēsis* is inadequate to the Derridian concept of play and to the deconstructive liberation from metaphysical rationality (see RH 210–211). For Caputo *phronēsis* is no match for the wisdom one needs to allow the play to play itself out—that is, the wisdom needed for hermeneutical emancipation. "*Phronēsis* functions only within an existing framework, an established paradigm. It is a fundamentally conservative notion" which is inadequate to the radical incommensurability of meanings implied by the principle of play.[43]

What is genuinely surprising is that, after dismissing Gadamer's hermeneutics as "the most liberal possible version of a fundamentally conservative idea" (RH 115), Caputo appeals to a metaphor originally offered by the conservative British philosopher Michael Oakeshott as the medium for translating Derrida's principle of play into the possibility of real political and moral liberation. It is doubly surprising when the metaphor refers us back to what had seemed to be dismissed by both Derrida and Caputo.

> I take it that, while Derrida provides no *criteria* for what makes for better or worse fictions, he does describe the conditions under which decisions should be reached. He thinks that things get worked out in a way which is very much like what Rorty (following Oakeshott) calls the conversation of mankind (but with no Rortian illusions about the charms of bourgeois liberalism)—by a kind of ongoing debate in which the forces of rhetoric clash and settle into a consensus of whose contingency it is the role of the Socratics and Derridians to remind us, to the point of distraction and infuriation. (RH 196)

This radical version of the "conversation of mankind" is not the historical discourse of metaphysical rationality, but a form of critical praxis. Everything hinges on whether the "conversation of mankind" (which, by the way, is not meant to exclude women[44]) is as different from the Gadamerian notion of conversation as Derridian play is from Gadamerian play. This, apparently, would be Caputo's contention. "This [liberation through conversation] is not merely a hermeneutic problem in the Gadamerian sense. . . . It is rather a deconstructive problem which requires vigilance about the subversion of discourse by a priori metaphysical schemes, by exclusionary practices, by a rhetoric systematically bent on sustaining the prevailing order" (RH 261). What seems to be a critical suspicion required to keep the conversation honest, however, is supplemented by a hermeneutical "trust in the dynamics of the *agora*" necessary to keep the conversation moving (RH 261).

Fair debate, perhaps, is part of the "double gesture" Derrida speaks of: deconstruction not in opposition to reason and the university, but "within the university, along with its memory and tradition, the imperative of professional rigor and competence" (PR 17). The ongoing conversation is, for Caputo, the "critique exercised from within" which keeps the play in play. In this regard Caputo does not shy away from the Enlightenment concept of emancipation (RH 254). He calls, not just for debate, but for the adjudication of views within that debate, that is, some form of consensus (RH 261). The consensus, however, is always tentative and open to a radical suspicion which Caputo, in contrast to Zavarzadeh and Morton, models on the Socratic art, and which consists of "local strategies for local action" (RH 263–264).

In educational theory also, we find that deconstruction is sometimes brought closer to the more moderate concept of productive conversation. John Trimbur, for instance, would combine the conservative propositions of Hirsch and William Bennett (aiming for cultural literacy using the classics of Western literature) with the radical approach of Lyotard and Derrida (attempting to thematize the hegemony that defines the classics as classics). The aim of such an approach would be to demonstrate a "network of intertextual relations" which constitute "the ongoing [but not necessarily harmonious or inclusive] conversation" of Western culture.[45]

In a similar fashion Kaufer and Waller propose a deconstructive practice which seems close to what Gadamer would call "hermeneutical reflection." They note that students carry around "sets of previously acquired and culturally sanctioned interpretive schemes of which they are unaware and through which they read the texts prescribed to them. What we can do [as teachers] is to encourage them to become more self-aware of the power of such schemes."[46] Part of this process consists of a "playful pedagogy" which combats the limitations of interpretations which "must make systematic omission of incompatible, though no less possible, interpretations" and asserts the undecidability of truth. Their positive proposals for the practice of this pedagogy incorporate the notion of textuality and of decentered subjectivity. Their pedagogical recommendations, however, inadvertently testify to the hegemonic situation which even radical education may not be able to escape: "As we have outlined the praxis above, the teaching of writing classes can be reinforced or redirected by the teacher's scheming and theorizing, and thus persuading or manipulating the students into becoming more critical and subversive about their residual assumptions."[47]

To what extent can radical theories of education avoid the paradox of authority and autonomy? To what extent can they do without the model of conversation? To what extent do they find themselves caught up within the ongoing, but not necessarily harmonious or inclusive, conversation of mankind? The *aporia* posed by the confrontation between radical and moderate approaches concerns precisely the risks of conversation.

A MODERATE RESPONSE: CONVERSATION, PLAY, AND EDUCATION

It may be possible for deconstructive approaches to define a position against conversation, but in principle they cannot maintain that position, not only because they must ultimately suspect any "position," but because by defining it, contending it, proposing it, arguing it, and debating it they are drawn into the very conversation they speak against. This is certainly Gadamer's point in response to Derrida's questions concerning good will, namely, that in posing questions Derrida shows the good will of which Gadamer speaks.[48] The issue here cannot be conversation versus nonconversation, but the possibility of two different types of conversation. Is conversation suspicious, agonistic debate which aims at paralogy rather than consensus? Or is conversation trusting communication which in principle aims for consensus? We find both views expressed in poststructuralist thought. On the one side, Lyotard argues against the consensus model of Habermas (see PMC 65). Consensus can only be one temporary state of conversation which must eventually issue in paralogy and the heterogeneity of language games. Consensus is merely local, tentative, and temporary (PMC 66). On the other side, Caputo's notion of radical conversation and Barthes' concept of "peaceable speech" retain a certain sense of trust in conversation. As Barthes expresses it, adding his own emphasis: "One of the things that can be expected from a regular meeting together of speakers is quite simply *good will*, that the meeting figures a space of discourse divested of all sense of aggressiveness."[49] But aren't both possibilities—paralogy and good will—motivations for continued conversation? Is it possible that the nature of conversation, and education, can accommodate both agonistics and consensus building?

We can discover one answer to this question by examining the notion of the "conversation of mankind" as it is proposed by Michael Oakeshott, appropriated by Richard Rorty, and employed by Kenneth Bruffee in developing the idea of collaborative learning. By such an examination we learn that a concept of conversation which embraces both suspicion and good will, both paralogy and imperfect consensus, is one which is adequately described by the principles of a moderate approach to education.

It is clear that for Oakeshott conversation is a metaphor of knowledge and human activity. As a metaphor it is quite easy to idealize it and to describe it as it ought to be. Ideally, for Oakeshott, the conversation is composed of a plurality of voices, each with its own idiom, and each being in relative emancipation from the others. In real terms, however, everything is not beyond suspicion with respect to conversation. If the conversation of mankind, ideally conceived, ought to be free of hegemony, ought to lack hierarchy, and ought not to require credentials for participation, still, it is not difficult to discover that some voices dominate and others are excluded.[50] Even Oakeshott acknowledges the *real* imperfection of the conversation—its political nature. This politics of conversation is an insidious politics because it not only hides itself under the guise of normalcy, but creates an "*impasse*." "An established monopoly will not only make it difficult for another voice to be heard, but it will also make it seem proper that it should not be heard: it is convicted in advance as irrelevant. And there is no easy escape from this *impasse*."[51] It is noteworthy that Oakeshott, the conservative thinker, and Derrida, the radical deconstructor, take the same side in their proposed strategies (which they both refuse to call "solutions") for dealing with this impasse. They both identify the dominating voice as belonging to the Enlightenment tradition, and in some fashion, although certainly not in an identical way, they both propose the voice of poetry as a rhetorical strategy.[52]

Certainly, in real conversation, one constantly meets with the kind of impasse Oakeshott describes. This is clearly Foucault's position with respect to the discourse of modern societies. Voices are excluded: the mad, the poor, the sick, the imprisoned, and the minorities have very little if any voice where it counts. Conversation in reality is hegemonic, and this is a constant. Political practice, in its essence and regardless of which particular ideology it follows, operates as exclusionary. Granted this hegemony, however, one could argue that there is always room in the conversation for the excluded voices, or at least, there is always room for a discourse like Foucault's, a discourse which speaks about the exclusion, or even further, an agonistic and paralogical discourse which champions the excluded. This is what attracts Caputo to the concept of conversation. Operating within the conversation of mankind, his "ethics of dissemination" would take its stand "with those for whom the system was *not* designed—women, children, the mad, the ill, the poor, blacks, the religious and moral minorities—those who are being excluded by the system" (RH 264). Rorty shows how it is possible to include agonistic, paralogical, or deconstructive discourses within the ongoing conversation.

Rorty distinguishes between normal and abnormal discourse within the conversation. Normal discourse is characterized by commensurability and is "conducted within an agreed-upon set of conventions about what counts as a relevant contribution, what counts as answering a question, what counts as having a good argument for that answer or a good criticism of it" (PMN 320). Within normal discourse one can locate trust (good will) and consensus. In general terms, normal discourse tends toward reproduction; it operates within already accepted paradigms and language games. Abnormal discourse, or what Rorty calls "edifying conversation," involves suspicion and incommensurability, and constitutes the basis for what Lyotard would call "paralogy." Abnormal discourse, like Lyotard's agonistics, challenges the metanarratives which guide normal discourse. It protests, Rorty says, "against attempts to close off conversation by proposals for universal commensuration through the hypostatization of some privileged set of descriptions" (PMN 377). Abnormal discourse occurs when someone joins the ongoing conversation "who is ignorant of conventions or who sets them aside. . . . The product of abnormal discourse can be anything from nonsense to intellectual revolution" (PMN 320). According to Rorty, these two types of discourse do not compete as two different conversations; they form two aspects of the conversation of mankind. Abnormal discourse is "edifying" to the extent that it is productive "of finding new, better, more interesting, more fruitful ways of speaking" (PMN 360). It is that aspect of conversation which allows us to transcend ourselves. It is possible, however, only on the basis of normal discourse; it is possible only if we start from someplace—for example, from where we already are, from where we find ourselves, as Derrida would insist. Agonistic, paralogical, abnormal discourse "is always parasitic upon normal discourse" (PMN 365), just as deconstruction is always parasitic upon the metaphysical discourse which it deconstructs, just as the productivity of interpretation rests upon the constraints of traditions and language, just as transcendence depends upon appropriation.

Participation in the conversation means pushing the *universitas* toward a *societas*. Rorty, borrowing this distinction from Oakeshott, associates normal discourse (funneled into acceptable disciplines) with the *universitas* ("a group united by mutual interests in achieving a common end") and abnormal discourse with the *societas* ("persons whose paths . . . [are] united by civility rather than by a common goal, much less by a common ground") (PMN 318). One can establish the *societas* of disparate, agonistic discourses only *within and against* the framework of a widely defined *universitas*. One participates in the larger conversation of knowledge—one enters into the process of educational experience—one enters into the play of discourse—through a sort of wisdom which adjudicates between normal and abnormal discourse, "the practical wisdom necessary to participate in a conversation" (PMN 372). *Phronēsis* is not, as Caputo would have it, inadequate to the conversation or relegated to normal discourse alone.[53] It is the only virtue available to deal with the ambiguity, the play involved in the incommensurability of discourses. It is the only virtue that will not deny the ambiguity.

Even if the poststructuralists present some cause to suspect and move away from the concept of the "conversation of mankind" (which indeed does operate as a metanarrative), they can never escape the hermeneutics of conversation. At best they cannot help but participate in a plurality of paralogical conversations, conversations which are nonetheless hermeneutically constrained. The concept of conversation, even if not the "conversation of mankind," is large enough to include all of the radical requirements of poststructuralist thought. It is a good metaphor to use in describing knowledge and educational experience, precisely because it is a good model of hermeneutical experience. Conversation reflects the same appropriation-transcendence structure of hermeneutical play, as Gadamer suggests. To be in conversation means to be in "the play of language itself, which addresses us, proposes and withdraws, asks and fulfills itself in the answer" (TM 490).[54] And, as Rorty claims, conversation takes on the shape of the hermeneutical circle (see PMN 319). As such, participation in the conversation calls for a *phronēsis* that recognizes and copes with the ambiguity and the agonistics, the imperfect consensus and the paralogy, the *universitas* and the *societas*, the good will and the suspicion involved in conversation. Deconstruction, whether it takes the form of paralogical discourse or "peaceable speech," is not something that falls outside of this hermeneutical model. Even agonistic discourse follows hermeneutical principles, insofar as it produces discursive meaning and requires a tradition to react against.

We can carry this argument into the educational context with the help of Kenneth Bruffee's concept of collaborative learning. Bruffee argues for the effectiveness of collaborative learning (peer tutoring, peer criticism, classroom group work, and so forth) in contrast to the traditional lecture.[55] Bruffee finds the conceptual rationale for the success of collaborative methods in the concept of conversation as developed by Oakeshott and Rorty. Education is misinterpreted if it is equated with the *acquisition* of information;

rather, knowledge is participation in a conversation, and, as Oakeshott contends, "education, properly speaking, is an initiation into the skill and partnership of this [knowledge] conversation."[56] For Bruffee, as for Gadamer (see TM 542–543), thinking itself, even reflective thought, is participation in the larger conversation.

Bruffee contends that in writing courses the act of writing ought to be thought of as participation in a conversation. Bruffee mixes the metaphorical and literal sense of conversation: not only does conversation stand as a metaphor for knowledge, as in Oakeshott and Rorty, but the act of conversation itself is proposed as the vehicle of collaborative learning. One can easily slide between the metaphorical and literal levels of this concept because the hermeneutical nature of conversation as it actually (literally) takes place makes it a perfect model (metaphor) for education.

With respect to writing as conversation, both normal and abnormal discourses are essential. Normal discourse serves a conservative function in education. "Teaching normal discourse in its written form is central to a college curriculum, therefore, because the one thing college teachers in most fields commonly want students to acquire . . . is the ability to carry on in speech and writing the normal discourse of the field in question" (Bruffee 643). One of the goals of collaborative learning is "to provide a context in which students can practice and master the normal discourse exercised in established communities" (644). This established knowledge, however, is not a permanent anchor in the conversation; it is always tentative and temporary, the product of a social process (the conversation) which changes. Only within certain contexts does established knowledge set the rules of the game, and ultimately the game of conversation itself produces and establishes knowledge. Abnormal discourse has an essential role to play in the generation of knowledge. "Abnormal discourse sniffs out stale, unproductive knowledge and challenges its authority. . . . Its purpose, Rorty says, is to undermine 'our reliance upon the knowledge we have gained' through normal discourse" (Bruffee 648).

At this point Bruffee rightly resists the temptation to say that writing courses must simply teach critique as a form of abnormal discourse. This would be the easy conclusion, which might attempt to equate something like deconstruction to abnormal discourse. Bruffee actually lists deconstructive criticism as a tool of normal discourse and apparently thinks of it as an established, professional approach to literary criticism. Bruffee argues against the deconstructionist concept of writing and in favor of the primacy of conversation (Bruffee 641). This argument, however, adds nothing to Bruffee's defense of collaborative learning, and perhaps even detracts from it. It is not necessary to show that writing is in some sense derived from spoken conversation in order to establish conversation as an educational model. One simply needs to show that writing has the same hermeneutical structure, that writing fits the hermeneutical model of conversation. Bruffee comes closer to this position in stating that "in every instance writing is an act, however much displaced, of conversational exchange" (642).

Following Rorty's contention that there is no discipline which describes abnormal discourse, Bruffee writes: "Abnormal discourse is therefore necessary to learning. But, ironically, abnormal discourse cannot be directly taught" (Bruffee 648). Would not Plato feel at home with a statement like this? Do we not discern the outline of *phronēsis* in abnormal discourse?

Any attempt to teach abnormal, agonistic discourse would be to normalize it and to turn it into an established discipline, just as any attempt to teach *phronēsis* would be to turn it into a set of rules or a particular *technē*. One acquires *phronēsis*, one picks up abnormal discourse, only by participating in a conversation that is beyond the explicit control of the participants. One cannot pedagogize the abnormal; one can only allow the abnormal to emerge within study, within conversation, which is always constrained by the process of tradition. The risk of normalcy is precisely the risk that deconstruction runs and precisely why a certain form of deconstructive criticism can be regarded as normal discourse.[57] Deconstruction can remain deconstruction only by running this risk, being constantly parasitic on the normalcy of traditions and constantly undermining that normalcy and transforming those traditions. Insofar as deconstruction follows this course, it is no different from education itself. In effect, radical hermeneutics and its pedagogy can only be effective by participating in conversations that are adequately described by moderate hermeneutical principles.

Bruffee suggests that the model of conversation challenges the traditional concept of pedagogical authority. "It challenges the authority of knowledge by revealing, as John Trimbur has observed, that authority itself is a social artifact" (Bruffee 649). Pedagogical authority, however, does not disappear in the conversation of education; teachers retain their authority, not on grounds of traditional justifications (value, truth, proximity to great minds or authors), but as "conservators *and* agents of change" (Bruffee 650). Even if we radicalize the concept of authority as social artifact, as Foucault would do, an authority framework still remains and embeds itself in the pedagogical process. The *aporia* of authority and emancipation, the paradox of authority and autonomy, is not resolved by either a moderate or a radical theory of conversation.

The literary critic Edward Said has argued that radical pedagogy, at least the deconstructive kind, shifts authority to the teacher by deconstructing everything except the deconstructor herself.[58] Since the student has no truth to hang on to, he hangs on to the text which is the teacher. Displacing the author and subjectivity does not necessarily involve displacing the teacher. The authority of the teacher may be apparent in traditional pedagogies, but the hidden, *implicit* control of the teacher over the radical pedagogical scene operates as an even more powerful authority structure precisely because it is disguised. That power operates more effectively when hidden is a principle that most poststructuralists recognize. Speaking against traditional systems of pedagogical authority (for example, the very architecture of the classroom, which gives the teacher a privileged place, the "[illusion of] the teacher's excentricity to the scene," and so on) does not change the fact that in each pedagogical scene the teacher is the stage director, manipulating the scene or the students to gain the sought-after effect. Following Barthes, Vincent Leitch contends that because speech, the teacher's medium, is inherently violent and authoritarian, "the depropriation demanded by deconstructive teaching is difficult, if not impossible, to attain in the classroom."[59] One might summarize by saying that pedagogy, like politics, of whatever type, inescapably involves a degree of force (sometimes conspicuous, sometimes hidden) which sets up an authoritative relation.

Whatever shape this authority relation takes, however, it is always under question in educational experience. In effect, one does not question unless there is something to be questioned. Ago-nistics is not possible without the existence of an authoritarian framework to be challenged. This is implied in Foucault's concep-tion of power. That agonistics is possible shows that educational experience involves both authority and emancipation, yet never in absolute forms.

If, as we argue, conversation is hermeneutical, if it reflects the same structure as play, and if it therefore captures the very sense of educational experience, then questions must be raised about any theory of education which prescribes for or against the reproduc-tion of normalized discourse. Indeed, the reproduction principle of either conservative or critical hermeneutics would be an impossible principle for radical approaches to education. Derrida holds for the radical play of textuality—that is, that language actually oper-ates as a chain of differential signifiers out of which there is no exit—and thereby implies the constant, albeit limited productivity of meaning in every interpretation. If language is as Derrida de-scribes, then reproduction could only be a completely arbitrary accident rather than the rule. Ulmer, in his *Applied Grammatol-ogy*, notes: "It is not surprising that a pedagogy committed to change rather than to reproduction would seize upon the irre-ducibility of the medium to the message . . . as the point of depart-ure for its program" (AG 162). The medium (the textuality of interpretation, the pedagogical presentation, the rhetoric) cannot be reduced to the message (that which is interpreted, the teacher's understanding, the meaning content). The medium always inter-feres with the message (and we have seen empirical studies by Olson that verify this claim). The pedagogical presentation is *al-ways* an "extra text," but this is a hermeneutical principle which applies to all pedagogy, whether it attempts to be conservative or radical. If this is so, then where is the possibility of strict reproduc-tion? As interpretation always involves understanding differently, so educational experience always involves a productive difference.

Perhaps it would be more appropriate to speak of ambiguity in this regard: educational experience is a play between reproduction and production which never involves pure reproduction or pure productivity but always remains between, a combination of appro-priation and transcendence. Rather than being a basis for a deconstruction of Derrida's educational theory, this ambiguity only verifies his claim that deconstruction never escapes the metaphysical framework, the process of tradition. Moreover, the fact that every discourse (conservative or deconstructive) is open to deconstruction may in fact prove the point that every discourse involves both a partial reproduction (appropriation of the traditional framework) and a partial production (a transcendence and transformation of that framework). Ulmer is right in this regard: "*Memoria*, in other words, as much as *inventio*, is an important aspect of the new pedagogy (which, like the new rhetoric, does not simply return to the old tradition but carries some of its principles into a new dimension)" (AG 179).

What happens in the conversation of education can be explained not by a principle of reproduction but by a principle of play. If hermeneutical experience, including the interpretation involved in reading, writing, and educational experience, has the nature of play, as both Plato and Derrida maintain (see D 156ff.), does this contradict any moderate principle? Everything, of course, depends on the nature of play. But in this regard, is Derrida's concept so radically different from Gadamer's? Within educational experience, which, Plato would suggest, aims at self-knowledge, Derrida maintains that interpretation rather than intuition is at play. "But this imperative of self-knowledge is not first felt or dictated by any transparent immediacy of self-presence. It is not perceived. Only interpreted, read, deciphered. A hermeneutics *assigns* intuition" (D 69). This assignment, the displacement of intuition by interpretation, corresponds to the decentering of the self (the subject) in play. More precisely, there is no original self-presence of self that is decentered; play itself is primary. Gadamer, no less than Derrida and the poststructuralists, holds to this decentering of the subject in play. "The actual subject of play is obviously not the subjectivity of an individual who, among other activities, also plays but is instead the play itself. But we are so accustomed to relating phenomena such as playing to the sphere of subjectivity and the ways it acts that we remain closed to these indications from the spirit of language" (TM 104).

Rather than being against conversation or education as a moderate hermeneutics would describe it, radical hermeneutics presupposes it and relies upon it. We are, after all, in a position to understand Derrida and the poststructuralists, and we are in a position

to accept innovation and *inventio*, only because we have undergone and are continuing to undergo a process of education which
deconstruction challenges. Derrida himself, having received a traditional education at the École Normale Supérieure and, even in
his deconstructive practice, having relied on classical texts from
Plato to Rousseau to Heidegger, still is able to think differently and
seemingly against that whole tradition. How is that possible? Why
is Derrida not another Husserl or Bergson, for instance? Precisely
because, as both moderate and radical hermeneutics claim, all is
not reproduction; traditions do not overwhelm the educational
process. Education, in its very nature, involves transformation,
whether it is tried for, as in deconstruction, or fought against, as in
conservative pedagogy. From the moderate point of view, education
is already and always a deconstructive process—one caught up
within an ambiguous play of reproduction-production, *memoria-
inventio*, authority-emancipation, appropriation-transcendence.

CHAPTER 10

Education and Hermeneutics

In previous chapters we explored the implications of hermeneutical theory for educational experience. We employed Gadamer's philosophical hermeneutics to work out a hermeneutical approach to education, and we pursued, for their relevance to education, various debates which have defined the major *aporiai* in hermeneutical theory. The main thrust of this inquiry has been to show how hermeneutics can make a contribution to educational theory. The connections between hermeneutics and education, however, are not one-way connections; they go both ways. If in the previous chapters we considered what hermeneutics had to say to educational theory, in this concluding chapter we want to consider what educational theory has to say to hermeneutics. What are the implications of the hermeneutics of education for hermeneutics itself?

Our considerations here will be guided by three questions. First, what model is most appropriate for the development of a universal philosophical hermeneutics? Here we will examine the traditional orientation of hermeneutics toward the textual paradigm and propose that the almost exclusive use of the text as a paradigm has introduced a distortion into hermeneutical theory which might be corrected by a consideration of educational experience. Second, how should the scope of hermeneutics be defined? Throughout our considerations we have been assuming the distinction between philosophical and prescriptive hermeneutics. We need to show that a universal philosophical hermeneutics, similar to what we have called a moderate hermeneutics, has well-defined limitations, and that prescriptive approaches are appropriate only in local contexts. Finally, to what extent and in what sense can the aporias which define the hermeneutical field be resolved? Here we shall offer some final considerations concerning hermeneutical principles.

THE INTERPRETATIONAL PROCESS

I suggested in Chapter 1 that there are essential connections between education and interpretation. If *hermeneutics* is a term which signifies both the art of and theory of interpretation, it should be clear from the analysis in the previous chapters that from the beginning to the end of the hermeneutical art, education is an issue. Yet hermeneutical theory has, for the most part, consistently ignored or repressed the educational dimension of interpretation. Considerations of educational experience have been excluded from the tradition of hermeneutics because interpretational theory has been oriented more toward the object of interpretation than toward the interpretational process. This is what I shall argue by returning to the issue of textualism which I raised in Chapter 1.

The primary model for the object of interpretation has been the text. There are, of course, good reasons for this orientation. Dilthey, citing "the immeasurable significance of literature for our understanding of spiritual life and history," remarked that speech fully expresses this spirit, and written text preserves speech. "That is why the art of understanding centers on the exegesis or *interpretation of those residues of human reality preserved in written form.*" He concluded that "*understanding* can attain general validity only in relation to written documents."[1]

Dilthey, of course, took his orientation from the textual hermeneutics of Schleiermacher. Historical accounts of the discipline of hermeneutics almost always begin with or focus on Schleiermacher. From Schleiermacher one can move forward to recount the development of Romantic hermeneutics and more recent twentieth-century developments. Also, from Schleiermacher one can move backwards in an attempt to measure the hermeneutical concepts of previous theorists of the Enlightenment or of medieval philology. Schleiermacher has been the measure of hermeneutics for a number of reasons. Within the realm of textual hermeneutics he clearly attempted to work out a general discipline to embrace the various specialized branches of hermeneutics. He also provided a systematic theory of interpretation which can easily be compared and contrasted with those of his predecessors. It was thus both easy and legitimate for almost everyone (Heidegger is one clear exception) since Schleiermacher to take Schleiermacher as a reference point, a bench mark of hermeneutical theory. We will see, however, that there is already operating, in Schleiermacher, a repression of the educational dimension of hermeneutics.

Schleiermacher's move from specific to general theory within textual hermeneutics is radically different from the move to a universal hermeneutics. This is what Heidegger understood, but Dilthey did not. Precisely here, in Dilthey's attempt to expand hermeneutics, we come upon the beginnings of the problem of textualism, that is, the use of the text as a model for universal hermeneutics. It is not only that Schleiermacher's textual hermeneutics becomes the measure of hermeneutical theory; the text itself becomes the paradigm of hermeneutics. All interpretation becomes modeled on textual interpretation. It follows that interpretation must be a kind of reading, since its object is always a kind of text. Hermeneutics and literacy go hand in hand.

To see what happens to hermeneutical practice as it is transformed into a scientific discipline by Enlightenment and Romantic thinkers one needs to contrast certain aspects of modern literacy to the ancient practice of oral performance. Indeed, the motivation for making hermeneutics its own discipline comes from modern literacy. Ancient and early medieval reading (*legere*) of poetry or prose was not the silent reading of a text. Interpretation was a pronunciation, a public performance, an explication, and was very much associated with rhetoric and education. In ancient Greece and Rome the priority of oral recitation was not limited to poetry but equally applied to the areas of law, medicine, agriculture, and religion. Rhapsodes were not only entertainers but teachers of history and social custom. In early Christian educational settings, prior to the rise of the universities, "reading" scripture meant an interpretation that was primarily an oral "exposition" and an "application" to one's own circumstances.[2] The medieval sermon and lecture developed not as an extra commentary on texts but as an oral reproduction and publication of scarce texts. The *lectio* of the scholastic teacher consisted "above all in exegesis, that is, in interpretation designed to set forth the objective contents of the text."[3] The interpretation of a text did not mean a silent reading, but an expository, pedagogical practice.[4] Interpretation was essentially an explication (pronunciation, articulation) of meaning which treated the text as a means or instrument of oral communication. A text was thought of, not as the object of interpretation, which in the view of Boethius, for example, was objective reality, but, like the spoken word, as the interpretation of the objective reality. A written text, according to the historian Paul Saenger, "was essentially a transcription which, like modern musical notation, became an intelligible message only when it was performed orally to others and to oneself."[5]

Only with the increasing use, from the twelfth century onward, of writing and written documentation in law, theology, philosophy, science, and education do we get a proliferation of texts and the necessity for a discipline of textual hermeneutics. The invention of movable type in the fifteenth century and educational reform a century later made the text the standard of legitimate knowledge.[6] With the text as standard of knowledge the status and practice of interpretation was transformed. Brian Stock has described how texts came to constitute a "reference system" which not only provided a structure for explanation but motivated a "systematic scrutiny" of the methods of interpretation. "Men began to think of facts not as recorded by texts but as embodied in texts, a transition of major importance in the rise of systems of information retrieval and classification."[7] David Olson observes that "the relation between a text and an interpretation becomes problematic only in literacy. In oral language the form and meaning form an indissoluble pairing." In conversation one can immediately question what something means, so that in preliterate societies, "there is little or no distinction between a text and its interpretation."[8] Interpretation is built into the oral performance. Moreover, as Stock notes, in an oral tradition, "one cannot check what is recalled against a presumably 'correct' version of things."[9] On the other hand, with written texts the words are preserved "while the meaning or intention is lost and must be reconstructed from the text." Olson concludes: "Literacy created hermeneutics," that is, the modern discipline of textual hermeneutics.[10]

Modern understanding, in contrast to ancient pronunciation and medieval *legere* and *lectio*, takes the text as an end. As Dilthey proposes, understanding has validity "only in relation to written texts." We know that modern reading (*inspixere, videre*) is a silent, internal operation. Indeed, modern notions of a private consciousness and internal reflection are tied to silent reading, the development of which begins in the twelfth to thirteenth centuries.[11] Modern interpretation, then, to the extent that it is considered on the model of silent reading, is something that happens internally, "in the mind." For Dilthey, the object of hermeneutics is "an inner reality" gained by the inner process of understanding. Dilthey inherited this view from Schleiermacher.

The rise of literacy, the corresponding transformation of hermeneutical practice, and the development of a modern discipline of hermeneutics which focuses on textual reading and construes understanding to be a process of interior reading all contribute to a repression of the educational dimension of interpretation. Schleiermacher and Dilthey represent two turning points in this development. Schleiermacher's specific contribution can be seen in contrast with Friedrich Ast's hermeneutics. Even in Ast, education was treated as something external, not *essentially* related to the inner works of mind, spirit, *Geist*—which is the thing which really counts for the interpreter's ability to understand others and alien cultures. Thus Ast, emphasizing the internal spiritual connections between interpreter and text, stated: "For it is only the temporal and external (upbringing, education [*Bildung*], circumstances) that postulate a difference of the spirit. If we disregard the temporal and external as accidental differences in relation to the pure Spirit, then all spirits are alike."[12] For Ast, the aim of hermeneutics was always to move beyond external accidents like education and background, and thereby to move into the spirit of the author, the meaning of the text. It is clear that Ast considered the external factors of education to be on the objective side of interpretation, an element of the author's experience to be understood.[13] If, on the object side, Ast did not completely disregard the temporal and external aspects of the author and text, he did subordinate them to a secondary position, important only insofar as we move through them to get to the real spiritual essence of the text. On the other hand, on the other side, the side of the hermeneutical process, Ast was willing to leave *explication* within the realm of hermeneutics, although subordinate to understanding.[14] Precisely here, in relation to the hermeneutical process, Schleiermacher made his advance.

Although Schleiermacher embarked on an attempt to move from specific to general hermeneutics, and is thereby perceived to have been broadening the description of textual hermeneutics, he simultaneously narrowed the field by excluding explication from the hermeneutical process. Under Schleiermacher, the central focus of textual hermeneutics became the *subtilitas intelligendi*. Moreover, Schleiermacher banished explication to the objective side of the hermeneutical relation; it became a text which itself is open to interpretation. "Only what Ernesti calls *subtilitas intelligendi* [exactness of understanding] belongs to hermeneutics; as soon as *subtilitas explicandi* [exactness of explication] becomes more than the articulation [*äussere Seite*, outer side] of understanding, it becomes itself an object for hermeneutics and belongs to the art of presentation [*Darstellens*]."[15] Hermeneutics, as he defined it, "deals only with the art of understanding, not with the presentation of what has been understood."[16] Hermeneutics takes as its task the exactness, correctness, *adequatio* of understanding, which is inner thought (silent reading) rather than the public performance of explication or pedagogical presentation.

Graham Nicholson, in his hermeneutical analysis of perception, rehearses this modern exclusion of explication from the hermeneutical process.

> The classical sense of the word [interpretation] assumed a context in which the *interpres* provided for his audience an oral or written *interpretatio*, a translation or exposition of some material. The aspect of a public performance of such an art is lacking to human perception. But was the outward, public performance an absolutely necessary part of the thing? Isn't it possible to say, rather, that in his oral or written performance he was communicating his interpretation to them? That would imply that the interpretation was his working out the translation or exposition in his own mind, the intellectual achievement.[17]

Nicholson lists two reasons for excluding explication and emphasizing "the 'interior' work" of understanding. First, understanding is more basic than explication in the sense of presentation. One finds this ordering already at work in Ast. Before one can explicate something, one first has to understand it. Second, someone can understand something without necessarily communicating it to an external audience. Explication, therefore, is only occasional.

The aspect of explication or presentation, which is degraded in Ast and excluded in Schleiermacher, is precisely what Chladenius had earlier equated with the pedagogical nature of interpretation.

Truer to the earlier sense of *hermēneía* and *interpres*—"to explain, expound, render clear and explicit"[18]—Chladenius defined interpretation as explication leading toward understanding, so that explication has a priority over understanding. Without explication there would be no understanding, since understanding is produced by explication. If we take our orientation from Chladenius rather than Schleiermacher, we might begin to see that Romantic hermeneutics represents an impoverishment of hermeneutical practice which excludes the pedagogical dimension in order to focus entirely on an interior realm.

The modern, Romantic emphasis on the interior subject, the mind as the theater of interpretation (in contrast to the public theater of the ancients), goes hand in hand with the focus on textual interpretation, where interpretation is reading and reading is an interior process. To the extent that modern hermeneutics takes its orientation from the text as its model object and makes interpretation a silent reading, and thus an interior understanding, it tends to exclude explication, pedagogical presentation, and educational experience from the interpretive process. This Schleiermachean exclusion would not be of such consequence if it simply remained a peculiar characteristic of textual hermeneutics. Dilthey, however, reinforced and broadened this exclusion by taking Schleiermacher's textual hermeneutics as the model for all hermeneutics. It is Dilthey who, while moving in the direction of universal hermeneutics, also moved in the direction of textualism by making *text* the paradigmatic object of all interpretation.

Dilthey was not concerned to develop simply a textual hermeneutics, as Schleiermacher was. Rather, Dilthey attempted to develop a general theory of understanding as a methodology for the social sciences. Nonetheless, he took as his model textual hermeneutics. In his appeal to Schleiermacher, who had explicitly excluded *subtilitas explicandi* from hermeneutics, Dilthey retained a narrowed conception of hermeneutics even while attempting to expand its scope and application. Dilthey meant to move hermeneutics beyond textual interpretation toward a more universal conception, and yet he retained the textual paradigm. Dilthey wanted to study life, but ended up reducing life to textual expression. "Life and history," he remarked, "have a meaning like the letters of a word."[19] Gadamer summarizes Dilthey's position:

> Like the coherence of a text, the structural coherence of life is defined as a relation between the whole and the parts. . . . It is the old hermeneutical principle of textual interpretation, and it applies to the coherence of life insofar as life presupposes a unity of meaning that is expressed in all its parts. (TM 223–224; see also TM 240–241)

Thus Dilthey not only carried over Schleiermacher's exclusion of explication in favor of understanding conceived of as an interior reading process, but he reduced the interpretation of historical and social life to the same notion of reading text. With Dilthey we have the advent of textualism, the use of the textual paradigm as a model for universal hermeneutics. Textualism involves the reduction of all forms of interpretation to one form: reading.

Textualism does not stop with Dilthey but characterizes most contemporary approaches to hermeneutics. Ricoeur represents a clear continuation of this tradition in his definition of hermeneutics as "the theory of the operations of understanding in their relation to the interpretation of texts" (HHS 43). In response to Heidegger's claim that textual interpretation is a derivative mode of interpretation, Ricoeur contends that "the example of textual exegesis is more than a particular case. . . . Heidegger may well call philological interpretation a 'derivative mode', but it remains the touchstone" (HHS 70). Ricoeur takes the text as paradigmatic when he employs it to explain distanciation (HHS 111): "In my view, the text is much more than a particular case of intersubjective communication; it is the paradigm of distanciation in communication."[20] For Ricoeur, the concept of the text is taken in both a literal and a metaphorical way; it is not, in all cases, to be identified with written expression (see HHS 132). Clearly Ricoeur's most pronounced textualism can be found in his attempt to use the text as a paradigm for the object of the human sciences. He proposes the hypothesis that "the human sciences may be said to be hermeneutical (1) inasmuch as their *object* displays some of the features constitutive of a text as text, and (2) inasmuch as their *methodology* develops the same kind of procedures as those of *Auslegung* or text interpretation" (HHS 197). Ricoeur thus attempts to find "readability-characters" in human action and further attempts to model the relevant methodology on reading (HHS 203, 209).

Despite his textualism, Ricoeur shows us precisely how taking the text as paradigm can lead to distortions. Thus, in attempting to use the text as a model for conversation, Ricoeur notes, "It does not suffice to say that reading is a dialogue with the author through his work, for the relation of the reader to the book is of a completely different nature. Dialogue is an exchange of questions and answers; there is no exchange of this sort between the writer and the reader. . . . The reader is absent from the act of writing; the writer is absent from the act of reading" (HHS 146–147). Wouldn't an analysis of conversation which tried to force it into the model of the text also introduce this type of distortion?[21]

The one clear exception to textualistic approaches in hermeneutics is, as already noted, Heidegger. One might think that Gadamer, who develops Heidegger's hermeneutics, would escape textualism. Gadamer, however, is not completely free of textualistic tendencies. First, it is clear that Gadamer is working out, not a textual hermeneutics, but a philosophical hermeneutics. He proposes models of interpretation other than the text, such as play and conversation. Indeed, in some cases conversation is used as a model to explain textual interpretation.[22] Yet it is also the case that Gadamer appeals to the textual model to explain several of his fundamental ideas: the logic of question and answer (TM 369ff.), application (TM 308ff.), the fore-structure of understanding (TM 267ff.), the hermeneutical circle and temporal distance (TM 293ff.), and language (TM 389ff.).

Gadamer's discussion of translation, which moves from the model of conversation to that of the text (see TM 384–388), motivates the argument that "in *TM* there is an ambiguity and vacillation between a conversation- and a text-oriented hermeneutic, and that the former possesses 'only a limited explanatory power.'"[23] Furthermore, it may be the case that Gadamer's emphasis on language and the process of tradition—specifically his conception that the object of interpretation is always, in some sense, tradition—led him, at times, into textualism.[24] Given the linguistic nature of tradition, the object of interpretation often appears to be a text. If, however, our relation to the process of tradition is, as we have stressed, always an anterior relation, a tradition is not something which poses itself in front of us in the form of an explicit textual object. The essential hermeneutical dimension of language is the one which operates "behind our backs"—the language which maintains and constrains the hermeneutical process rather than the language which confronts us as text.

In Gadamer's defense one might cite his insistence on the priority of speech over writing and argue that the primacy he gives to conversation should be enough to belie our suspicion of textualism. Yet even here his conception of speech is "textualized" by his frequent reference to the "inner ear." Interpretation is a *reading* which brings the text *to speech for the inner ear.* To the extent that the interpreter is construed as a reader who becomes "all [inner] ears," interpretation becomes a reading in the interior of the mind, and the object of interpretation is reduced again to text.[25] Furthermore, in the tradition of Romantic hermeneutics, Gadamer holds that "written texts present the real hermeneutical task. Writing is self-alienation. Overcoming it, reading the text, is thus the highest task of understanding. . . . Only in an extended sense do non-literary monuments present a hermeneutical task" (TM 390–391). That in some regards Gadamer derives his inspiration from the Romantics rather than from Heidegger, he admits. That this means that in some regards his hermeneutics is textualistic, he also admits. "Of course, in my attempt to describe the problems, I took as my guide the experience of meaning that takes shape in language in order to bring to light the limits that are posited for it. The Being-towards-the-text from which I took my orientation is certainly no match for the radicality of the limit experience found in [Heidegger's concept of] Being-towards-death" (DD 25–26). Gadamer, in this regard, asks for leniency: "One should be lenient with me, the old philologist, in my characterization of all this as 'being towards the text'. The hermeneutic experience truly is woven completely and utterly into the general being of human *praxis.* Although the understanding of that which is written is significant, it is included only in a secondary fashion."[26]

Given his textualism, it should not be surprising to see Gadamer, following Schleiermacher, exclude the educational dimension from the essence of interpretation. "We must not here abandon the insights of the romantics, who purified the problem of hermeneutics from all its occasional elements. Interpretation is not something pedagogical for us either; it is the act of understanding itself" (TM 397). Despite his claim that "the romantics recognized

the inner unity of *intelligere* and *explicare*" (TM 307), Gadamer
also recognizes that what Schleiermacher "has in mind is no longer
the pedagogical function of interpretation as an aid to the other's
(the student's) understanding; for him [in contrast to Chladenius,
who equates interpretation to pedagogical presentation and distinguishes it from understanding] interpretation [*Auslegung*] and understanding [*Verstehen*] are closely interwoven, like the outer and
the inner word, and every problem of interpretation is, in fact, a
problem of understanding. He is concerned solely with the *subtilitas intelligendi*, not with the *subtilitas explicandi*" (TM 184–
185).

Richard Rorty raises a concern about textualism primarily
against the thinkers of radical hermeneutics.[27] Derrida's famous
statement that "there is nothing outside of the text" (G 158) indicates a radical textualism. Derrida seemingly denies reference.
"From the moment that there is meaning there are nothing but
signs. We think only in signs" (G 50). Robert Sholes objects to this
liberation from reference, or what Foucault calls "the tyranny of
the text," and follows a distinction made by Edward Said between
"secular" and "hermetic" approaches to interpretation.[28] The secular approach would allow for a reference to something outside of
the text; the hermetic approach would be the equivalent of a radical textualism. With reference to radical textualism, Jameson takes
a different view. The textualist revolution, he writes,

> drives the wedge of the concept of a "text" into the traditional
> disciplines by extrapolating the notion of "discourse" or "writ-
> ing" onto objects previously thought to be "realities" or objects
> in the real world, such as the various levels or instances of a
> social formation: political power, social class, institutions, and
> events themselves. When properly used, the concept of the "text"
> does not . . . "reduce" these realities to small and manageable
> written documents of one kind or another, but rather liberates us
> from the empirical object—whether institution, event, or indi-
> vidual work—by displacing our attention to its *constitution* as
> an object and its *relationship* to other objects thus constituted.[29]

It may be that textualism has a "proper use," as Jameson indicates. In this respect, if, as Rorty claims, the most serious objections to textualism are moral rather than epistemological, it could
also be argued that one of the most productive uses of textualism

may be moral and critical. My objection to textualism, however, does not concern either the epistemological question of reference or the moral question concerning humanism. Rather, my objection involves the reduction and distortion involved in the employment of the paradigm of text to construct a universal philosophical hermeneutics. Such a construction reduces all interpretation to the form of reading. Insofar as textual interpretation becomes the model for all interpretation, hermeneutics introduces a distortion into the very nature of interpretation, namely, the interpretational process is construed as merely an internal operation of reading. Textualism, in its various forms and degrees, simply reinforces the exclusion of explication—a pedagogical dimension of interpretation.

But even this is not the whole story. It will not be enough to simply reinstate the pedagogical dimension so that hermeneutics will include both understanding and explication, if understanding continues to be thought in terms of an interior process of reading. If, however, the hermeneutical process is not to be modeled on reading, how should we characterize it? Here the import of our analysis in Part 1 should be clear. The hermeneutical process is better characterized as a process of learning rather than of reading. Reading itself is one important form of educational experience, but not the paradigmatic form. I want to suggest that the aims of a universal hermeneutics could be better accomplished, not by returning to Romantic or Enlightenment textual hermeneutics, but by retrieving the educational dimension of interpretation which has been obscured by textualism but which had been, albeit in an obscure way, involved in the possibility of hermeneutics even from the time of the ancient Greeks.

Learning, as a more adequate paradigm, cannot be reduced to an interior process but is genuinely interwoven with explication and application. The more complete picture of the hermeneutical process would include *subtilitas intelligendi*, as a learning process, *subtilitas explicandi*, as an educative practice of interpretation, and *subtilitas applicandi*, as a transformative self-understanding that comes through interpretation. Here we have Gadamer's universal hermeneutics, but on a basis other than textualism. These three moments of interpretation would accordingly not be three distinct parts but would constitute, as Gadamer would have it, an "inner fusion," an "interweave." There is no learning (understanding) without explication and application.

My intention is not to deny that the textual paradigm is a productive one which allows us to understand a great deal about interpretation. As often happens in the social sciences, however, the model itself can often mislead us. If we attempt to make secure the premise that all interpretation is analogous to textual interpretation, do we not close off the possibility of discovering more universal features of interpretation? For example, if, in our analysis of educational experience, we had simply followed the textualistic route, we would have come to the predictable conclusion that education is a kind of reading or rereading of traditions. But what if learning has a logical priority over reading? What if instead of education being a type of reading, reading is a type of education? Indeed, our analyses have suggested not only that educational experience is a kind of interpretation, but also that understanding itself is a kind of educational experience. In this case, educational experience offers a better paradigm—a more universal paradigm— than the text. It provides a model broad enough to include textual interpretation as well as conversation and play. The paradigm of learning is one that takes its bearing from the interpretational *process* rather than from the interpretational *object*. The process of interpretation is not one of reading, but one of learning, which at the same time is interwoven with explication and application. The object of learning can be anything, including a text. To the extent that learning is logically a broader category than reading, it offers a more appropriate paradigm for a universal hermeneutics.

THE CONCEPT OF LOCAL HERMENEUTICS

Throughout these discussions I have tried to stay almost exclusively on the level of a universal, philosophical hermeneutics. Indeed, I have made several attempts to exclude considerations of prescriptive hermeneutics. A universal, philosophical approach not only "treats interpretation as a universal feature of all human activity,"[30] but also attempts to identify those universal principles that apply (as conditions of possibility) to all interpretation. Having pursued these principles we now must discuss their limitations, for, although they have a universality, they are for that very reason limited. This limitation can be seen simply by noting that even if all interpretation is linguistic, there is no universal language; even if all interpretation is bound by traditions, there are no universal traditions; even if all interpretation is productive, all interpretations are not productive in the same way. Notwithstanding universal principles, one is immediately led to the fact that all hermeneutical practice, all "the action," takes place on a local level, within the realm of specific languages, traditions, and productivities. In effect, this fact itself may be formulated in a universal principle: all interpretation is local. A hermeneutical situation is always a localized one. It is not just that each culture has its own system of interpretation, as Foucault suggests, but that even within an interpretational system there exists a plurality and multiplicity of interpretational constraints and possibilities.[31]

In any empirical analysis of a particular interpretation or set of interpretations we need to see how the universal propositions of hermeneutics actually work in the specific location(s) of interpretation. But we need to be careful about how we do this. Specifically, we need to sort out the relations between the descriptive, the explanatory, and the prescriptive aspects of hermeneutics. Local hermeneutics attempts, in its descriptive and explanatory parts, to give an account of how and why a particular interpretation is actually taking place in specific circumstances and, in its prescriptive part, to prescribe how it ought to take place. In this context we can distinguish between (a) the meta-interpretation: the description and explanation generated by a local hermeneutical analysis; (b) the existing interpretation: the interpretation or interpretational process which is described/explained by the meta-interpretation; and (c) the prescribed interpretation: the interpretation which is prescribed as the result of the hermeneutical analysis.

It is clear that not only the prescribed interpretation, but also the existing interpretation and the meta-interpretation, on the local level run the risk of being biased by predetermined normative decisions. For example, if in a meta-interpretation of local hermeneutical conditions at work in a particular educational practice we say, in the fashion of critical hermeneutics, that in very real and specific ways this practice is distorted by a particular tradition, ideology, or power structure, we need to recognize that the concept 'distortion', which is used on the meta-interpretational level, is a normative concept. The concept of distortion can only be applied within the framework of a hermeneutical canon which would state, for example, that "all educational experience ought to be free from certain types of hegemonic traditions." Only within such a framework could we identify an existing interpretation or practice as "distorted" by a tradition. Such an approach, which depends upon the normative framework of already specified universal canons, can be associated with the *technical* application of general rules worked out independently of the situation. The prescriptive hermeneutical approaches of the conservative and critical type frequently operate in such a fashion.

I want to suggest that this is an approach which is not genuinely local, since it imports prescriptive canons predetermined in the abstract. I will propose that the proper model for a local hermeneutics is to be found in the concept of *phronēsis* rather than the concept of *technē*. In other words, prescriptives (canons, rules, and so forth), and even normative assumptions within the meta-interpretation, should be developed, as far as possible, at the local level on the basis of the local hermeneutical situation, not on the basis of a universal prescriptive hermeneutics. In effect, I propose that if there are legitimate universal canons (and I am not sure that there are), they must be dependent on or derived from local ones, and not *vice versa*.[32]

In a local hermeneutics the inquirer would set out to analyze existing interpretational practices at specific interpretational sites (communities, educational institutions, corporations, media sites, and so on). A local inquiry (the development of a meta-interpretation and prescribed interpretations) would be guided by the following kinds of questions: In any particular interpretational site, existing historically and in a specific place, what are the most immediate, the most local power relations at work? How do they produce and constrain the existing interpretations, and conversely, how are the existing interpretations used to support or transform such power relations? Only by answering such questions can the inquirer (who may be the interpreter herself involved in a self-reflection) determine what is to be done in terms of critical work. Of course, decisions on critical work in the local situation will always be informed by moral and political objectives that are already predetermined, but that involves prescriptive decisions of a kind different from strictly hermeneutical ones. Hermeneutical canons, developed on the local level, would specify how specific power relations should be reflected upon, continued, or transformed in continuing interpretation. A local hermeneutics, then, is not a theory of interpretation, but a practice of hermeneutics involving descriptive, explanatory, and prescriptive parts. Let us consider the descriptive and explanatory parts first.

The questions that can be raised in the local circumstances of interpretational sites are paraphrases of questions raised by Foucault with respect to discourses on sexuality. "In a specific type of discourse on sex, in a specific form of extortion of truth, appearing historically and in specific places . . . what were the most immediate, the most local power relations at work? How did they make possible those kinds of discourses, and conversely, how were these discourses used to support power relations?" (HS 97). These questions have a generic form which can be used with respect to any interpretational context, whether it involves education, sexuality, conversation, political institution, music, text, or something else. Moreover, they are questions that can be formulated on the basis of any universal principle. Foucault's questions are formulated to inquire about power relations. They can just as well be formulated to inquire about traditions, languages, preconceptions, productivities, self-understandings, and so on. Not only are power relations always local (HS 93), but traditions, linguistic practices, prejudices, and applications are always local. Thus, with respect to any specific local interpretation (discourse, communication, educational practice, institution, and so on), we can ask what are the most immediate traditions (linguistic practices, preconceptions, applications, and so on) at work. How do they make possible this kind of interpretation (etc.), and conversely, how are these interpretations used to support or transform these traditions (etc.)? How are these traditions (etc.) modified by their very exercise? Only in answering such questions would we be in a position to improve, support, or critique interpretation. Foucault's questions form the basis of a local hermeneutics which would seek out the constraints and possibilities which determine, in a particular time and place, the existing interpretational practices.

Another model for the descriptive and explanatory parts of a local hermeneutics can be found in the sociological-anthropological approach taken by Clifford Geertz. Geertz refers to his work as "interpretive anthropology," or a "cultural hermeneutics," to be taken not in the sense of a universal theory but in the sense of "actual interpretations of something" (LK 5). Geertz's procedure is not to "explain social phenomena by weaving them into grand textures of cause and effect," but to "explain them by placing them in local frames of awareness" (LK 6). His approach does not make the typical claim of value neutrality found in most social sciences. In a local hermeneutics the distinction between description or explanation and evaluation is never radical (see LK 6). Precisely for this reason we have to be careful to maintain a hermeneutical reflective attitude about the meta-interpretation, asking the same questions about our meta-interpretation as we ask of the existing interpretation. Such a reflection would never clear away all evaluative prejudices, but it would at least keep us attuned to the uncertain and tentative nature of the meta-interpretation.

Geertz acknowledges the problem of defining his method when the principle of approach is "not knowing, in so uncertain an undertaking, quite where to begin, or, having anyhow begun, which way to move" (LK 6). This is consistent, however, with the idea that in local hermeneutics one does not simply apply some predetermined rules or canons; rather, one develops those rules within the local context. Geertz uses the term *translation* to capture this procedure. The idea of translation is not to categorize cultural practices under abstract universal classifications ("experience-distant concepts") but to make diverse cultural practices ("experience-near concepts") define useful classifications (see LK 57ff.). "The reshaping of categories (ours and other people's— think of 'taboo') so that they can reach beyond the contexts in which they originally arose and took their meaning so as to locate affinities and mark differences is a great part of what 'translation' comes to in anthropology" (LK 12). One must steer a course set not by predetermined methodology, and therefore a course ("a continuous dialectical tacking") between the overdetermined universal and the underdetermined particular, or as Geertz puts it, "between overinterpretation and underinterpretation, reading more into things than reason permits and less into them than it demands" (LK 16). Geertz describes this procedure in terms of the hermeneutical circle. "Hopping back and forth between the whole

conceived through the parts that actualize it and the parts conceived through the whole that motivates them, we seek to turn
them, by a sort of intellectual perpetual motion, into explications
of one another" (LK 69). The meta-interpretation employed in a
local hermeneutics would, in this sense, be an art akin to the
Socratic art, an art because, for lack of any better method, the
practitioner is forced to ask questions and learn as she goes. It is
not a matter of applying predetermined procedural rules which
guarantee an objective interpretation; nor is it the case of adopting
a Romantic procedure of empathy. "The trick is not to get yourself
into some inner correspondence of spirit with your informant. . . .
The trick is to figure out what the devil they think they are up to"
(LK 58). Thus, in Geertz's ethnology, he proceeds "by searching
out and analyzing the symbolic forms—words, images, institutions, behaviors—in terms of which, in each place, people actually represented themselves to themselves and to one another"
(LK 58).

Foucault in discursive contexts, and Geertz in cultural contexts, provide models for the descriptive and explanatory parts of
local hermeneutics. It seems clear that in some cases we need to go
no further than description or explanation. Geertz's anthropological descriptions serve their scientific purpose, and, once having
understood how a culture understands itself, there is in anthropology no question of prescribing changes in behavior. As Geertz
acknowledges, this does not mean that his descriptions are value
neutral or that they do not have an effect on the society which may
become educated by them. Foucault, on the other hand, refrains
from pursuing prescriptives for philosophical reasons. Nonetheless, his meta-interpretations remain instructive, find application
for those who study them. We can, however, find a model for the
prescriptive part of local hermeneutics in the context of education.
It is clear, for example, that the critical approach to education
offers prescriptives that seek to change educational practice. The
same can be said of conservative and radical approaches. To what
extent, however, can these various prescriptive approaches function within a local hermeneutics?

That the proper level for prescriptive hermeneutics is the local
level is easily demonstrated. If on the universal level philosophical
hermeneutics tells us that we cannot help but be caught up within

traditions, linguistic practices, and power structures, and that in and through our interpretations we transform these constraints and ourselves, then prescriptives appear necessary simply on the basis that we tend to want to organize our lives and pursue objectives in and through our interpretive experiences. The specific constraints and possibilities of interpretive practice, however, can never themselves be universal because there are no universal traditions, languages, or power structures, and no universal applications or productivities involved in interpretation. Every interpretation is a local one insofar as it is affected by local constraints (etc.). So the prescriptives that we need to guide or regulate our interpretations must also be local ones.

A hermeneutical prescriptive must satisfy at least two conditions. First, it cannot contradict a universal principle. I cannot hold, for example, on the universal level, that all interpretation is bound by traditions, and then prescribe that this particular interpretation ought not to be bound by traditions. Second, it cannot itself be a universal prescriptive. As a prescriptive it must be tied to (and it must address) local hermeneutical conditions. So, for example, although an interpretation cannot escape all preconceptions, a prescription can legislate that it escape this or that specific preconception on the ground that the preconception in question is not productive. What constitutes a productive or nonproductive bias depends on specific objectives that are determined between local constraints and moral and political decisions already taken. Even with respect to the same set of facts, what constitutes a productive bias, for example, will differ for the politician and the political satirist, for the defense council and the prosecution, for the educator and the student. Similarly, within different contexts no interpreter will decide to operate in exactly the same fashion. More than that, if in the educational context language biases educational experience, and if the language of schooling fluctuates from one school to another, depending on type of school, location, social class of students, and so forth, then biases are always regional or local.[33] Any prescriptive designed to remedy such bias must begin with its local description. In a local hermeneutics the direction of movement is from the particular to the universal. One does not employ a universal prescriptive to determine interpretation in the specific situation.

A local *prescriptive* approach can be seen in the work of Paulo Freire. Freire is concerned about designing educational programs to liberate urban and rural workers. Educational programs which, of course, are prescriptive in nature are not decided centrally, however, and then taken to the local context. Such would be an oppressive education that would make the student (or worker) conform to a predetermined reality and truth. For Freire it is important to take into account the students *in their situation*; the educational program must be planned from the bottom up, rather than from the top down. Critical educators must first of all enter into a dialogue with those who would be students, in order to find out "their *objective* situation and their *awareness* of that situation" (PO 84). In a preliminary dialogue teacher and students become "co-investigators" of the themes to be explored in the educational program. In this meta-interpretive or "decoding" phase of program design, critical educators study the local situation, gathering "a series of necessary data about the life of the area."[34] Then, in carrying out the prescriptive phase, teachers "re-present" existing interpretation "to the people from whom [they] first received it— and 'represent' it not as a lecture, but as a problem" (PO 101). The aim of this explication is to have the students analyze "their own reality" and "become aware of their prior, distorted perceptions and thereby come to have a new perception of that reality" (PO 107).

We can see in Freire's educational proposals a model for local hermeneutics. A local hermeneutics would first study existing interpretations in order to describe, explain, and evaluate them. It would not, for example, be a *predetermined* principle that the interpretations of the peasant (or the urban worker, or the middle-class student) are always too trusting or reproductive of existing power structures, or that power structures are everywhere hegemonic. It would not be predetermined that an interpretation ought to be more reproductive or more suspicious. Within the meta-interpretation the local interpretations would not be evaluated in terms of any predetermined prescriptives or rules. The evaluative questions, while based on universal principles concerning the process of tradition, power, language, and so on, would develop prescriptives starting with the problems encountered within the existing interpretations themselves. In carefully avoiding the imposition of external, predetermined prescriptives, the process employed here would be one modeled on the concept of *phronēsis.*

In defining the proper model for local hermeneutics, whether in its descriptive or in its prescriptive part, we can appeal to two concepts: the concept of "paralogy" as it has been developed by Lyotard, and the concept of *phronēsis* as developed by Gadamer. The model for a local hermeneutics, and its relations to a universal philosophical hermeneutics, can be specified by examining how the concept of *phronēsis* can be properly employed in the paralogical situation.

Lyotard characterizes postmodernism as "an incredulity toward metanarratives" (PMC xxiv). A metanarrative should not be confused with what we have termed "meta-interpretation." A meta-interpretation, in contrast to a metanarrative, is always tied to and derived from local interpretations, or what Lyotard terms *"petit narratives."* In Lyotard's terms, the meta-interpretation would simply be the attempt to specify the rules of a particular local game or discourse. For Lyotard, there can be no universal knowledge because knowledge is always local knowledge, confined to local (nonuniversal) language games. Furthermore, knowledge is characterized by incommensurabilities, undecidables, conditions of incomplete information, fracta, discontinuities, and paradoxes (PMC 60). There is no one universal logic or metanarrative which covers all of these games; there are a plurality of logics, each specific to a local discourse. This is the situation which Lyotard calls "paralogy."

In dealing with issues of justice under conditions of paralogy, Lyotard condemns technocratic arrogance and "terrorist" exclusion—the elimination or threat to eliminate "a player from the language game one shares with him" (PMC 63). Since his conception of justice cannot be a traditional metanarrative of justice (Platonic or Marxist), Lyotard proposes the model of *petit narratives,* that is, temporary contracts rather than permanent institutions in areas concerned with professional, emotional, sexual, cultural, familial, political, and international relations (see PMC 66). Players in local contexts must reach a temporary consensus on the rules which define the game, a consensus which would be eventually cancelled. Justice also involves playing the game fairly.

Everyone should be granted access to the information they need to play (PMC 67).

Lyotard attempts to develop this concept of justice by turning explicitly to the Aristotelian theory of *phronēsis* (JG 26ff., 95). Justice is based on a judgment informed by *phronēsis*. The Aristotelian concept serves his purpose because, unlike the Platonic conception, it does not depend on a theoretical metanarrative for its legitimacy. *Phronēsis* is a purely prescriptive judging without appeal to theoretical criteria. "This is, after all, what Aristotle calls prudence. It consists in dispensing justice without models. It is not possible to produce a learned discourse [metanarrative] upon what justice is" (JG 26; see also p. 43). *Phronēsis* involves a dialectics which requires judging "case by case," "because each situation is singular" and there are no external criteria to guide judgment (JG 27). From case to case the mean is redefined; justice "cannot be determined in itself, that is, outside of the situation in which we find it" (JG 27). Thus the prescriptions one gets through *phronesis* are "dangling prescriptives" (JG 59); they are not grounded on theoretical descriptions or universal principles, but are developed "case by case."

Lyotard, however, denies an essential Aristotelian dimension of *phronēsis*, namely, that *phronēsis* depends upon education or on *héxis*, a habit of virtue, an *ēthos* (see JG 26). Clearly, without this *ēthos*, without a backdrop of educational experience, what Lyotard calls *phronēsis* is nothing more than what Aristotle would call "cleverness"—the ability to play the game with inventiveness, to play "master strokes" (JG 61). This is precisely what Lyotard defines as "justice": "Justice consists in working at the limit of what the rules permit, in order to invent new moves, perhaps new rules, and therefore new games" (JG 100).

Taking one's point of departure from the flux of paralogy rather than from the fixed *logos* of metaphysics, however, requires something more than cleverness. *Phronēsis*, which is more than Lyotard's concept of academic cleverness or speedy imagination, is a prerequisite for making our meta-interpretations knowledgeable and adequate to the local context. Lyotard is right, however, that *phronēsis* is not an external virtue introduced into the local situation from the level of a metanarrative. To see this we need to clarify the peculiar nature of the paralogical situation.

Lyotard describes the paralogical situation as one of shifting paradigms, where recourse to external standards is denied. In the situation outside of established paradigms there are no norms or fixed orders. But Lyotard fails to acknowledge that whatever situation we find ourselves in, no matter how paralogical, it is always a hermeneutical situation. We never find ourselves thrown into an *absolutely unfamiliar* situation. There is always some basis on which to interpret that which falls outside of established paradigms, simply because we are always situated, located at some already familiar locale. Our educational experience, our past, our traditions, our practical interests, always condition our situation, so that whatever temporary contract or consensus we agree to, whatever new paradigm we invent, it will never be absolutely without precedent.

Because the paralogical situation is always a hermeneutical situation, it will always be governed by universal hermeneutical principles. Indeed, to the extent that Lyotard refers to local discourses as "language games," he states a hermeneutical principle which applies to all cases: all interpretation is linguistic. To the extent that he admits that such games are played by different rules, he also implies that they operate under different regimes which can be described in terms of different traditions, biases, applications, and productivities. It is clear that if Lyotard were to allow for the necessary backdrop of educational experience in his conception of *phronēsis* (or, in other words, if he were to admit that prescriptives are never absolutely dangling), he would then be able to recognize that the paralogical situation is also a hermeneutical situation. Knowledge is always imperfect knowledge gained within the situation precisely because there is a backdrop of hermeneutical constraints, including the educational experience of the interpreter.

The model for such knowledge is *phronēsis*. In the paralogical situation, if we do not have recourse to external standards, pre-established rules, or already fixed frameworks as ready-made solutions, still we do have access to already existing information, we do have familiarity with old or other, perhaps unworkable or pre-empted standards, rules, and frameworks. Such familiarity is supplied by our educational experience. Our creation of new games is never ex nihilo, but always a creative transformation. If paralogy is a situation of uncertainty, if we do not operate out of a position of certainty (in the Cartesian or Husserlian sense), still, we do not operate outside of a hermeneutical situation within which we find some degree of familiarity.

Phronēsis, as either Aristotle or Gadamer explains it, is not the mechanical application of preestablished universal rules to particular circumstances (see TM 317–318). *Phronēsis* is not a skill or craft which founders when the situation is paralogical. It is neither a method nor a kind of *technē*. It is precisely the interpretational virtue that one can fall back on within a hermeneutical situation which is uncertain. For Aristotle, as well as for Gadamer, *phronēsis*, which depends on educational experience, is to be relied upon precisely on those occasions when no formula is available in advance, in those situations where, as Aristotle would put it, we must act *kata ton orthon logon*, that is, according to reason formed in educational experience.

Rather than being determined by rules, predetermined and external to the local situation, *phronēsis* enables us to work out the rules in and for the local interpretations. In effect, this is Gadamer's concept of "application" in which the universal gets determined by the particular, "case by case" as Lyotard says. According to Gadamer, application "does not mean first understanding a given universal in itself and then afterward applying it to a concrete case" (TM 341). Rather, the understanding of the particular case leads us to understand the universal. In local hermeneutics we move from an examination of existing interpretational cases to prescriptives that would transform our experience. Insofar as *phronēsis* cannot be specified outside the particular situation, which always remains hermeneutical, it does not lend itself to metanarratives. As such, it is the proper model for a local hermeneutics which begins at specific interpretational sites and takes its bearing from the local hermeneutical conditions rather than a set of universal prescriptives.

EDUCATION AND THE HERMENEUTICS OF AMBIGUITY

We began our study by noting three impasses which characterize the contemporary fields of both hermeneutics and education. First, the *aporia* concerning reproduction is signaled by both the conservative and critical hermeneutical principles of reproduction and the debates about cultural literacy and cultural reproduction in educational theory. There is disagreement about whether reproduction should be set as a goal, or treated as an ordinary result which must be avoided, or whether it is even possible. Second, the *aporia* concerning authority and emancipation is put in focus by the Habermas-Gadamer debate, but it is equally at issue between the critical and radical schools of thought. Here there is disagreement about the very nature of power, language, and the process of tradition, and about whether hegemonic relations can and should be avoided, or whether to some extent power itself can be productive. Third, the *aporia* concerning conversation is thematized in the encounter between Gadamer and Derrida, but is also operative in discussions of educational models and methods. The issues here concern whether a hermeneutics of trust or a hermeneutics of suspicion is the proper strategy, and whether conversation is something that exists under or beyond methodological control.

Although these aporias are respectively thematized in three debates within hermeneutical theory, we have seen that they genuinely cut across the entire field of hermeneutics. Since the same aporias appear within educational theory, our strategy has been to examine them in terms of educational experience. To what extent have we gained passage through these aporias, or to what extent do we remain on their threshold? Have we learned enough in our examination of educational experience to suggest their resolution in the field of hermeneutics?

In this concluding section I suggest that these three aporias are in fact three different expressions of one fundamental *aporia*, one, moreover, which is inescapable because it is part of the very nature of interpretation. This fundamental *aporia* concerns ambiguity and the finitude of understanding. Conservative theory wants to deny or fix ambiguity by the principle and canon of reproduction; critical theory seeks to rationalize and control it by neutralizing the effects of power, tradition, and authority; radical theory wants to radicalize it in the concept of play. Moderate theory, as we have called it, proposes to recognize that we cannot avoid ambiguity and therefore must not deny its operation but find a way to live with it without inflating its effect.

In the context of educational experience we have explained transformation by the principle of productivity and in terms of the concept of schema. We have shown that schemata (horizons, fore-structures) blur the distinction between original *meaning* and current *significance*. Any attempt to reconstruct (reproduce) an original meaning requires that the learner supplement or infer information that is lacking in the object of interpretation. In so doing, the learner shapes meaning within the framework of significance. All of this can be said of any interpretation. Because interpretation involves the operation of schemata, the reproduction of self-identical and unchanging meaning is not possible. But, at the same time, transformation is not absolute. With every interpretation we do not move into a completely new world; significance does not completely determine meaning. On the one hand, the process of interpretation, to the extent that it is constrained by traditions, language, biases, and power structures, is never absolute transformation. On the other hand, to the extent that it involves productivity, questioning, and self-understanding, it is never absolute reproduction. The truth lies somewhere between the absolutes of transformation and reproduction. The truth lies not in the resolution of the *aporia*, but in recognizing the fundamental ambiguity of interpretation.

There are clearly some cases in which reproduction seems to have the upper hand over transformation. This can be seen in local educational contexts in which traditional prejudices (taken here in a pejorative sense) are seemingly transmitted from one generation to the next. In some cases conscious attempts to transform the situation continually fail. Yet transformation is never completely absent. Transformations, which do not necessarily involve an improved or better understanding, but simply a different understanding, are constantly at work even within hardened traditions and immovable power structures.[35] Precisely because of what Habermas would call material factors (although not necessarily hegemonic ones), the possibility of strict reproductive interpretation is always undermined. It may be that the same traditions are carried over from one generation to the next, but they are always carried over differently.

It would be up to a prescriptive hermeneutics to work out the degree of reproduction and the degree of transformation each situation might require to meet some predetermined moral, political, or educational end. In some contexts a conservative approach may rightly emphasize a higher degree of reproduction, as long as it also recognizes the degree of transformation that unavoidably accompanies it. In other contexts, a critical approach may justly propose a critical transformation, as long as it would not deny that a degree of reproduction was inescapable. Even a radical theorist like Gregory Ulmer, who proposes "the central problem for poststructuralist education—*how to deconstruct the function of imitation* [reproduction] *in the pedagogic effect*" (AG 174), would have to admit that one never entirely deconstructs the reproductive effect. Whatever prescriptive approach one takes, one should not deny a certain degree of ambiguity that remains within any solution. Interpretations are both assimilative and accommodative, conservative and corrigible at the same time.

The same ambiguity is at work with respect to traditional and authoritative power structures. The truth always falls somewhere between absolute hegemony and absolute emancipation. Emancipation, we said, is always relative: we can always transform a specific power structure, but we can never escape power structures completely. Power, as Foucault put it, is everywhere, and yet always local. Critical transformation can only substitute one set of local power relations for another. Because of this, all interpretation is "distorted," and there is no possibility of undistorted interpretation. In this respect, to put it in Lyotard's vocabulary, not even critical theorists have recourse to a metanarrative which escapes the distortions of power. We are always within a paralogical situation precisely because of the plurality of traditions, biases, and power structures which constrain us. We can move from one local interpretational site to another, but never can we gain the language game of all language games. This, essentially, is Lyotard's critique of Habermas (see PMC 65–66, 72–73). It does not contradict the approach of a moderate hermeneutics as long as the paralogical situation is recognized as a hermeneutical situation.

The paralogical situation is fundamentally ambiguous. According to Lyotard, one cannot resolve the ambiguity by moving into a new language game, since, without appeal to metanarrative justification, one game is as good as another. This position is attacked by Habermas as "neoconservative," since there seems to be nothing that prevents the player from choosing, for example, a fascist game. Must we embrace a self-justifying metanarrative, dismiss paralogy, and repress ambiguity in order to avoid the risk of fascism? Clearly one is closer to fascism when one moves toward the metanarrative; the very definition of fascism must include an intolerance of difference, paralogy, and ambiguity. Affirming the ambiguity, rather than repressing it, is one way to reduce the risk of fascism.

Moderate hermeneutics, as a hermeneutics of ambiguity, proposes *phronēsis* (practical wisdom) as a way of coping with the ambiguity. In effect, some games *are* better than others, specifically those that allow us to encounter each other without violence, and those that promote educational experiences with great art and good ideas which challenge our established worldviews and allow us to transform our understanding of ourselves and the way things are. Because we learn these standards case by case, and we find ourselves only within hermeneutical situations, it is often difficult to discern which games are the better ones. *Phronēsis* does not involve denying the ambiguity or appealing to a metadiscourse that would justify one position over another. Nonetheless, by *phronēsis*, one position (or a number of positions) may be justified, although never absolutely or by appeal to transcendental reason. Faced with the ambiguity of the paralogical, hermeneutical situation, one must nonetheless interpret. Although there are no absolute criteria to determine which power structure, which tradition, which bias, or which authority to prescribe—indeed, because there are no such external criteria—we are forced to fall back on our own educational experience, our own critical reflection. And yet it is precisely here that we learn that these things are not precisely "our own," but that our educational experience and even our critical reflection are themselves linguistic, and constrained by the power structures, traditions, and biases that inform our situation. There is no neutral, undistorted interpretation from which a critical reflector speaks with authority. On the model of *phronēsis* we are caught between the absolutes of autonomy and heteronomy.

On this model, emancipation is possible, but never in an absolute fashion. In interpretation language, traditions, and preconceptions become enabling conditions of transformation. Emancipation is possible only within discourse, communication, and the conversation of educational experience. If paralogy rules out the absolute consensus of metanarrative, it does not rule out temporary, local, and imperfect consensus—partial consensus with persistent ambiguity.

Within a conversation the practice of *phronēsis* involves neither absolute trust nor absolute suspicion. Absolute suspicion would, of course, destroy the conversation and would push us not toward a transcendent metanarrative but to the opposite extreme of a radical nonposition. The idea of radical suspicion or nonposition itself fails to escape the ambiguity which radical hermeneutics tries to absolutize in the principle of play. One can remain positionless only by occupying, albeit temporarily and without justification, a position. Just as there is no metanarrative beyond all local conversations, so there is no nonposition outside of the plurality of language games. Conversation is ambiguously stationed between metanarrative and nonposition. If a position is always one within a local language game, as it must be, how do we choose to play that position, and why do we find ourselves within that particular language game rather than another? One can only acknowledge that our educational experience, which is more than we have chosen, has led us there.

Within a conversation, *phronēsis* is practiced somewhere between the extremes of absolute trust and absolute suspicion. One is able to be suspicious of X only by trusting in Y, where Y might be only our ability to ask the right questions. Trust, in order to be something more than naive or blind faith, is the informed outcome of previous suspicions. Dialogue is a dialectical relation worked out between trust and suspicion. Too much trust, as Derrida points out, would lead us unwittingly into traditions and power structures of domination; too much suspicion, as Gadamer points out, would cause the conversation to self-destruct.

Ambiguous play is not something that is opposed to conversation; it does not derail it, but is something that operates within conversation. Conversation involves the appropriation-transcendence structure of hermeneutical play, so that in conversation we never find absolute knowledge, but only imperfect interpretation which is constantly ongoing. Correlative to the distinction between language as an established system and ongoing conversation, we can distinguish between knowledge and interpretation. Although in the educational experience of conversation we may constantly seek knowledge as a complete and established system, we never get anything more than interpretation, that is, more of the educational experience of conversation, more of "the play of language." One never "has" knowledge; one participates in conversations at various interpretive sites.

A prescriptive hermeneutics cannot be designed to get the conversation completely under control, for in many respects the conversation transcends the interlocutors and carries them along. Neither can a prescriptive hermeneutics give up all control, as if we could not appropriate conversation for our own purposes. Both the possibility of a prescriptive hermeneutics and the possibility of reorganizing power relations attest to the control, indeed the responsibility, we have over the conversation. This responsibility comes in the ability we have to question and to thereby open the conversation in a new direction. Again, the model for a prescriptive hermeneutics is *phronēsis*, which proceeds by a logic of question and answer, a paralogic of many narratives, rather than by predetermined method or metanarrative imposition.

Within a conversational structure, constrained by language, traditions, preconceptions, power and authority structures, but also enabled by productivities, applications, questioning, and self-understanding, interpretation is ambiguously located between the extremes of reproduction and transformation, *memoria* and *inventio*, appropriation and transcendence, meaning and significance, hegemony and emancipation, consensus and paralogy, metanarrative and nonposition, trust and suspicion, accommodation and assimilation. Any attempt to reduce interpretation to one side, or to explode it toward the other, any attempt to prescribe our way out of the aporias, would be to deny interpretation's essential ambiguity. In every case interpretation involves something less than absolute; it is always something imperfect and incomplete.

We have tried to summarize this ambiguous structure of interpretation, play, conversation, and educational experience in our list of hermeneutical principles. (1) The principle of the hermeneutical circle holds that the projection of meaning in the fore-structure of understanding operates as a schema which is *both assimilative and accommodative* in a give-and-take adjustment process which undermines the objective-subjective distinction. (2) The principle of tradition states that all interpretation is *both con-*

strained and enabled by traditions, preconceptions, and structures of authority which operate "behind the back" of the interpreter, and yet in an anterior way to the extent that they are projected ahead of the interpreter through the fore-structure of understanding. Thus, the hermeneutical situation is never one of absolute paralogy because we can always fall back on already familiar and shared knowledge to make sense of the unfamiliar.

(3) The principle of the linguisticality of interpretation holds for a conception of language as something larger than subjectivity, yet never fully beyond our control. Language, as the vehicle of our traditions, *both limits and opens up the possibility* of interpretation, *appropriates and transcends* the interpreter, *memorializes and invents* the interpreted. (4) The principle of productivity (distanciation) states that all interpretation is transformative to some degree, but never in an absolute way. Productivity is never ex nihilo. Whatever interpretation starts with, however, is carried forward in a changed manner, and ends up somewhat different. There is some degree of transformation in any reproductive interpretation, just as there is some degree of reproduction in any innovative interpretation. (5) The principle of questioning states that through interpretation, the interpreter and the object of interpretation, as well as the traditions which define the hermeneutical situation, get opened up. This is not an absolute openness, but a play *between familiar and unfamiliar horizons.*

(6) All interpretation involves application in which meaning is construed within the framework of significance. In contrast to the conservative principle of application, significance cannot be disconnected from meaning. Interpretation involves a tension between remaining open to that which requires interpretation and tending to the claims made by the interpreter's own circumstance. The interpreter can never escape or disconnect from the local circumstances in which she is immersed; there is never the possibility of complete objectivity in this regard, so that every hermeneutical situation is ambiguous. In contrast to the critical principle of application, there is never a complete emancipation from this ambiguity, since even critical reflection is immersed in local circumstances. (7) All interpretation effects a self-understanding which is never fulfillable, since "the conversation that we are is one that never ends."[36] In self-understanding we find ourselves involved in a play

of interpretations which is *both an appropriation and transcendence* of ourselves.

(8) To these principles, which we have explored in some depth in Part 1, we need to add one which the moderate approach learns in its debates with critical and radical hermeneutics: the principle of power. It seems clear that this aspect of interpretation requires more emphasis than Gadamer had given it. But on this score, power should not be equated with purely hegemonic relations which are strictly reproductive. As Foucault holds, power is also productive. Interpretations never completely escape the power structures which define them, but they constantly transform those structures. Power itself is organized and reorganized through interpretation. Power, therefore, *both constrains and is constrained by interpretation.*

Precisely because these eight principles structure interpretation the way they do, we can say that interpretation is always local, tied to specific hermeneutical situations or interpretive sites. For this reason no interpretation constitutes a metanarrative which can legitimately be applied to all local discourses. Of course, this would motivate the following objection. Doesn't the universal hermeneutics expressed by these principles constitute a metanarrative which claims to range over *all* interpretations, in all locations? To answer this question we must clarify the concept of metanarrative.

For a discourse to be a metanarrative it must meet two conditions. (a) It must "cut across" or encompass all local narratives (conversations, interpretations, language games, and so on). If the discourse defines principles, they must apply to all cases in its domain. (b) It must be capable of adjudicating all differences; that is, it must be able to prescribe resolutions to conflicts (misunderstandings, misinterpretations). In other words, it must be able to insure the commensurability of all local discourses, and in that sense it must play a prescriptive role. Lyotard suggests that Plato's theory of justice claims the status of a metanarrative because it claims both universality and adjudicative power (see JG 19ff.). I would argue that the notion of the "conversation of mankind" makes similar claims. It signifies the largest and most all-embracing of conversations, and it prescribes that attainable solutions must be sought within the ongoing universal conversation. It prescribes against nonparticipation. Silence is always treated as a moment within the conversation rather than a sign of incommensurability. Clearly the universal conversation of mankind, taken as a metanarrative, fails to live up to its claims. The real case is rather that there are many conversations going on, a plurality of paralogical conversations at a multiplicity of interpretive sites. Many of the conversations cut across others, sometimes at cross-purposes and sometimes in a complementary way. There is, however, no ultimate adjudication possible among them all. There are no universal rational principles that would lead to a necessary consensus. This is where Habermas is wrong and Lyotard is right.

Philosophical hermeneutics, in contrast, does not claim the status of a metanarrative. It is simply one conversation among others. This follows from what hermeneutics itself discovers about language. As Gary Madison puts it, "Because of its essential linguisticality, that is, because there is no such thing as an ideal language which could ensure the commensurability of all partial discourses, human understanding is necessarily finite and pluralist."[37] The universality of philosophical hermeneutics is tied to the claim that it cuts across all other conversations because its object domain is interpretation itself. This is a claim similar to ones made by discourses like psychology, epistemology, anthropology, and history. The claim that any one of these discourses cuts across all others is a necessary but not sufficient condition for metanarrative status. For any one of these discourses to have the status of a metanarrative depends also on the condition that it could adjudicate all differences and constitute the ultimate theory of its object domain. Because it is not prescriptive, philosophical hermeneutics is not an adjudicative discourse at all. On the other hand, prescriptive hermeneutics, if it is rightly conceived as a local hermeneutics, is adjudicative but does not (or should not) claim to cut across all interpretation; it is always local, both in terms of its own discourse and in terms of its object domain. For these reasons neither philosophical hermeneutics nor a local prescriptive hermeneutics has the status of a metanarrative.

How, precisely, does philosophical hermeneutics "cut across" other discourses? It does not cut across all other discourses in the sense of having something to say about the specificity of local interpretive sites. Philosophical hermeneutics has nothing *particular* to say about the particular happenings which take place in a specific school or university, for example. It is rather the case that particular happenings at all interpretive sites have something to say to philosophical hermeneutics. Philosophical hermeneutics is a discourse which learns from other discourses. It cuts across all other discourses, not in the sense that it teaches, adjudicates, or prescribes, but in the sense that it learns from them. If philosophical hermeneutics professed to be a metanarrative, it would have to be one which could teach something that cannot be taught. From a plurality of interpretations philosophical hermeneutics learns not the already existing interpretational practices, but the essence of interpretation. It is not a theory or knowledge in the sense of *epistēmē*, superdiscourse, or metanarrative, but an interpretation which learns case by case to lay out the essence of interpretation.

NOTES

CHAPTER 1. THE NATURE OF HERMENEUTICS AND ITS RELEVANCE TO EDUCATIONAL THEORY

1. Wilhelm Dilthey, "The Rise of Hermeneutics," trans. Fredric Jameson, *New Literary History* 3 (1972), 234.

2. As early as the sixth century B.C. poetry was regarded as a source from which to take wisdom. As Xenophanes put it, by the interpretation of poetry the ancients attempted to learn what the gods were hiding from them (see frag. 18 and 9). See Werner Jaeger, *Paideia*, 3 vols., trans. Gilbert Highet (New York: Oxford University Press, 1939–1944), vol. 2, p. 360. The decline of poetic interpretation coincided not only with the rise of philosophy and prose but also with a crisis in the educational system and with the "struggle to determine the nature of true *paideía.*" (Jaeger, vol. 2, pp. 8, 10). Also see Rudolf Pfeiffer, *History of Classical Scholarship: From the Beginnings to the End of the Hellenistic Age* (Oxford: Clarendon Press, 1968), Part 1.

3. Johann Martin Chladenius, *Einleitung zur richtigen Auslegung vernünftiger Reden und Schriften* (1742), partial trans. in *The Hermeneutics Reader*, ed. and trans. Kurt Mueller-Vollmer (New York: Continuum, 1988), p. 58; also see pp. 61, 62, 69; hereafter this volume cited as HR. Johannes von Felde, *Tractatus de scientia interpretandi cum in genere omnis alias orationis, tum in specie leges romanas* (1689), p. 3; cited in HR, p. 3.

4. Friedrich Schleiermacher, *Hermeneutics: The Handwritten Manuscripts*, trans. J. Duke and J. Forstman (Missoula, MT: Scholars Press, 1977), p. 96; see also *Aphorisms of 1805*, in *The Hermeneutic Tradition: From Ast to Ricoeur*, ed. Gayle L. Ormiston and Alan D. Schrift (Albany: State University of New York Press, 1990), p. 57; hereafter this volume cited as HT.

5. Martin Heidegger, *Being and Time*, trans. John Macquarrie and Edward Robinson (New York: Harper and Row, 1962), p.188/148; hereafter cited as BT, English/German 8th ed. pagination.

6. Hans-Georg Gadamer, *Truth and Method* [*Wahrheit und Methode*, 1960], 2nd rev. ed., revised translation by Joel Weinsheimer and

353

Donald G. Marshall (New York: Crossroad Press, 1989), pp. 388, 397; hereafter cited as TM.

7.   There are many historical accounts of the development of hermeneutics. See, for example, Dilthey, "The Rise of Hermeneutics"; Richard Palmer, *Hermeneutics: Interpretation Theory in Schleiermacher, Dilthey, Heidegger, and Gadamer* (Evanston, IL: Northwestern University Press, 1969); and TM.

8.   Richard E. Palmer, commenting on a remark by Richard de George, in "Beyond Hermeneutics? Some Remarks on the Meaning and Scope of Hermeneutics," *University of Dayton Review* 17 (1984), 5.

9.   See Schleiermacher, *Hermeneutics*, pp. 95–97.

10.   Palmer, *Hermeneutics*, p.8.

11.   Paul Ricoeur, *Freud and Philosophy: An Essay on Interpretation*, trans. Denis Savage (New Haven: Yale University Press, 1970), p. 8.

12.   Wilhelm Dilthey, *Gesammelte Schriften* (Leipzig and Berlin: B. G. Teubner, 1958), vol. 5, p. 319; cited in Josef Bleicher, *Contemporary Hermeneutics: Hermeneutics as Method, Philosophy, and Critique* (London: Routledge and Kegan Paul, 1980), p. 10; see Palmer, *Hermeneutics*, p. 41.

13.   Gadamer, "Practical Philosophy as a Model of the Human Sciences," *Research in Phenomenology* 9 (1979), 83.

14.   Bleicher, *Contemporary Hermeneutics*, p. 1.

15.   Jürgen Habermas, "The Hermeneutic Claim to Universality," HT 245.

16.   Palmer, *Hermeneutics*, p. 9.

17.   Habermas, "The Hermeneutic Claim to Universality," HT 249.

18.   Gadamer, "Rhetoric, Hermeneutics, and the Critique of Ideology: Metacritical Comments on *Truth and Method*," HR 284.

19.   Paul Ricoeur, *Freud and Philosophy*, p. 25. Also see Ricoeur, *Hermeneutics and the Human Sciences*, trans. John B. Thompson (Cambridge: Cambridge University Press, 1981), p. 37; hereafter cited as HHS; and Jacques Derrida, *Of Grammatology*, trans. Gayatri Chakravorty Spivak (Baltimore: Johns Hopkins University Press, 1976), p. 9; hereafter cited as G.

20.   Richard Rorty, *Consequences of Pragmatism: Essays: 1972–1980* (Minneapolis: University of Minnesota Press, 1982), pp. 139ff.

21.   See, for example, Emilio Betti, "Hermeneutics as the General Methodology of the *Geisteswissenschaften*,"[1962], trans. Josef Bleicher, in Bleicher, *Contemporary Hermeneutics*, p. 53, hereafter cited as Betti; and E. D. Hirsch, Jr., *The Aims of Interpretation* (Chicago: University of Chicago Press, 1976), pp. 75ff.

22. This title has been used by John D. Caputo, *Radical Hermeneutics: Repetition, Deconstruction, and the Hermeneutic Project* (Bloomington: Indiana University Press, 1987); hereafter cited as RH.

23. James Duke, in Schleiermacher, *Hermeneutics*, p. 236, n.9.

24. See Hirsch, "Truth and Method in Interpretation," *Review of Metaphysics* 18 (1965), 492–494.

25. Habermas, "The Hermeneutic Claim to Universality," HT 250.

26. Gadamer, "Rhetoric," HR 289; also see Gadamer, "Hermeneutics and Social Science," *Cultural Hermeneutics* 2 (1975), 315ff; and "The Universality of the Hermeneutical Problem," in *Philosophical Hermeneutics*, trans. David Linge (Berkeley: University of California Press, 1976), p. 13; hereafter this volume cited as PH.

27. Anthony Giddens, "Hermeneutics and Social Theory," in *Hermeneutics: Questions and Prospects*, ed. Gary Shapiro and Alan Sica (Amherst: University of Massachusetts Press, 1984), p. 227.

28. Habermas, *Knowledge and Human Interests*, trans. Jeremy J. Shapiro (Boston: Beacon Press, 1971), p. 163; hereafter cited as KHI. See also p. 193.

29. Habermas, "The Hermeneutic Claim to Universality," HT 251.

30. Gadamer, "On the Scope and Function of Hermeneutical Reflection," trans. G. B. Hess and R. E. Palmer, *Continuum* 8 (1970), 90. Also see my essay "Language and Imperfect Consensus: Merleau-Ponty's Contribution to the Habermas-Gadamer Debate," in *Merleau-Ponty, Hermeneutics, and Postmodernism*, ed. Thomas Busch and Shaun Gallagher (Albany: State University of New York Press, 1992).

31. See Habermas, "A Review of Gadamer's *Truth and Method*" [1967], in *Understanding and Social Inquiry*, ed. Fred R. Dalmayr and Thomas A. McCarthy (Notre Dame, IN: University of Notre Dame Press, 1977), p. 360.

32. Ibid., p. 361.

33. Gadamer, "Hermeneutics and Social Science," p. 315. Also see "Reply to My Critics," trans. George H. Leiner, HT 277; and TM 495–496.

34. Derrida, cited in Alex Argyros, "The Warp of the World: Deconstruction and Hermeneutics," *Diacritics* 16 (1986), 47.

35. Heidegger, *What Is Philosophy?* [1955 lecture], trans. William Kluback and Jean T. Wilde (New York: Twayne, 1958), p. 73.

36. See John Caputo's excellent discussion of this, RH 153ff.

37. Derrida, *Spurs: Nietzsche's Styles*, trans. Barbara Harlow (Chicago: University of Chicago Press, 1979), pp. 107, 115.

38. Derrida, *Writing and Difference*, trans. Alan Bass (Chicago: University of Chicago Press, 1978), p. 292; hereafter cited as WD. Ac-

356 HERMENEUTICS AND EDUCATION

cording to John Caputo, Derrida's "anti-hermeneutic interpretation of interpretation," or "hermeneutics beyond hermeneutics," "denies all deep meanings, all hidden truth, indeed truth itself" (RH 118). Even if deconstruction provides a critique of hermeneutics and attempts to move beyond hermeneutics, Caputo (in RH) and Richard Palmer ("On the Transcendentality of Hermeneutics [A Response to Dreyfus]," in Shapiro and Sica, *Hermeneutics: Questions and Prospects*, pp. 84–95) argue that deconstruction is still a form of hermeneutics insofar as it involves a theory and practice of interpretation. I adopt this position and use Caputo's term *radical hermeneutics* to include deconstructive interpretation and its theory. See also Diane P. Michelfelder and Richard E. Palmer (eds.), *Dialogue and Deconstruction: The Gadamer-Derrida Encounter* (Albany: State University of New York Press, 1989), p. 9; hereafter cited as DD. Habermas also notes that Derrida, despite all disclaimers, falls within the tradition of hermeneutical thought insofar as he asserts the primacy of rhetoric over logic (see *The Philosophical Discourse of Modernity*, trans. Frederick Lawrence [Cambridge: MIT Press, 1987], pp. 187–188).

39. We might expect to see some common ground between Gadamer and Derrida in that they both find their philosophical inspiration in Heidegger. A number of commentators have delineated this common ground. See David Hoy, *The Critical Circle: Literature, History, and Philosophical Hermeneutics* (Berkeley: University of California Press, 1978), pp. 78ff., esp. 82–84; Manfred Frank, "Avant-Propos," *Revue internationale de philosophie* 151 (1984), 329–331; and DD 7–10.

40. This is a brief summary of a brief debate (or "nondebate"), the texts of which are collected in DD.

41. Ricoeur, *Freud and Philosophy*, p. 33.

42. Derrida, *Speech and Phenomena*, trans. David B. Allison (Evanston, IL: Northwestern University Press, 1972), p. 149; hereafter cited as SP. Also see *Spurs*, p. 53.

43. Gadamer, "*Destruktion* and Deconstruction," DD 109.

44. See Gadamer, "Text and Interpretation," DD 33; and Derrida, "Three Questions to Hans-Georg Gadamer," DD 52–53.

45. E. D. Hirsch, Jr., *Cultural Literacy: What Every American Needs to Know* (Boston: Houghton Mifflin, 1987); hereafter cited as CL.

46. It should be noted that Hirsch, in the context of working out his educational theory, assumes, but does not explicate, the relations between cultural literacy and his conservative hermeneutics. One can find the connection between his hermeneutics and educational theory mentioned in the educational literature (see, for example, Stanley Fogel, *The Post-*

modern University: Essays on the Deconstruction of the Humanities [Toronto: ECW, 1988], pp. 17–18) but rarely explicated.

47. See, for example, Michael Apple, *Ideology and Curriculum* (London: Routledge and Kegan Paul, 1979); Henry A. Giroux, *Ideology, Culture and the Process of Schooling* (Philadelphia: Temple University Press, 1981); Samuel Bowles and Herbert Gintis, *Schooling in Capitalist America* (New York: Basic Books, 1977); Pierre Bourdieu and Jean Claude Passeron, *Reproduction in Education, Society, and Culture*, trans. Richard Nice (London and Beverly Hills: Sage, 1977 [original French edition, 1970]), hereafter cited as RE; and R. E. Young, "Critical Teaching and Learning," *Educational Theory* 38 (1988), 47–59. These are only a few authors and works of an already large and developing school of thought.

48. See, for example, Jon Hellesnes, "Education and the Concept of Critique," *Continuum* 8 (1970), 40–51; Dieter Misgeld, "Education and Cultural Invasion: Critical Social Theory, Education as Instruction, and the 'Pedagogy of the Oppressed'," in *Critical Theory and Public Life*, ed. John Forester (Cambridge: MIT Press, 1985), pp. 77–118; John O'Neill, "Decolonization and the Ideal Speech Community: Some Issues in the Theory and Practice of Communicative Competence," in *Critical Theory and Public Life*, pp. 57–76; James Palermo, "Pedagogy as a Critical Hermeneutic," *Cultural Hermeneutics* 3 (1975), 137–146; and R. E. Young, "Critical Teaching and Learning."

49. See, for example, Henry A. Giroux, "Theories of Reproduction and Resistance in the New Sociology of Education: A Critical Analysis," *Harvard Educational Review* 53 (1983), 257–294. Even in this case, however, the concepts of reproduction and resistance are never discussed in hermeneutical terms.

50. Jacques Derrida, "The Principle of Reason: The University in the Eyes of Its Pupils," *Diacritics* 13 (1983), 3–20, here cited as PR; Michel Foucault, *Discipline and Punish: The Birth of the Prison*, trans. Alan Sheridan (New York: Pantheon Books, 1977), hereafter cited as DP; Also see, e.g., Gregory Ulmer, *Applied Grammatology: Post(e) Pedagogy from Jacques Derrida to Joseph Beuys* (Baltimore: Johns Hopkins University Press, 1985), hereafter cited as AG; William V. Spanos, "The End of Education: 'The Harvard Core Curriculum Report' and the Pedagogy of Reformation," *Boundary 2* 10 (1982), 1–33; and Vincent B. Leitch, "Deconstruction and Pedagogy," in *Theory in the Classroom*, ed. Cary Nelson (Urbana: University of Illinois Press, 1986), pp. 45–56. Again, this is an incomplete list of a growing body of literature.

51. Elaine Atkins, "Reframing Curriculum Theory in Terms of Interpretation and Practice: A Hermeneutical Approach," *Journal of Cur-*

riculum Studies 20 (1988), 444. Atkins nicely summarizes some work done by Richard Rorty (see "Hermeneutics, General Studies, and Teaching," *Selected Papers from the Synergos Seminars* 2 [1982], 1–15 [Fairfax, VA: George Mason University]) and Kenneth A. Bruffee (see, for example, "Collaborative Learning and the 'Conversation of Mankind'," *College English* 46 [1984], 635–652) in the area of curriculum studies. One exception to Atkins's observation is the German educational philosopher Günther Buck, who has been generally ignored (see *Hermeneutik und Bildung: Elemente einer verstehenden Bildungslehre* [Munchen: Wilhelm Fink, 1981]). Buck, noting the obscurity of the connection between hermeneutics and education, also suggests that the traditional identification of hermeneutics as exclusively concerned with the explication of texts conceals its relationship with education (*Hermeneutik und Bildung*, p. 24). Buck's *Hermeneutik und Bildung*, however, is not a systematic attempt to work out the details of a moderate hermeneutical approach to education. It is, as he explains, a collection of "occasional" essays that address various "elements" of such an approach; it is oriented toward pedagogical theory rather than educational theory in general, and it considers objections to moderate hermeneutics raised only by the critical theorists. See also Robert Hollinger, "Toward a Hermeneutical Approach to Education," *University of Dayton Review* 17 (1984), 13–20; and William R. Schroeder, "A Teachable Theory of Interpretation," in Nelson, *Theory in the Classroom*, pp. 9–44. Schroeder seems to be working somewhere between conservative and moderate approaches.

52.   R. Graham Oliver, "Through the Doors of Reason: Dissolving Four Paradoxes of Education," *Educational Theory* 35 (1985), 29.

CHAPTER 2. INTERPRETATION AND EDUCATIONAL EXPERIENCE

1.   Israel Scheffler, *Reason and Teaching* (Indianapolis: Bobbs-Merrill, 1973), p. 38.

2.   Chladenius, *Einleitung*, HR 61.

3.   See AG 161; and Jacques Derrida, *Dissemination*, trans. Barbara Johnson (Chicago: University of Chicago Press, 1981), p. 27, n.27; hereafter cited as D.

4.   Gadamer, "On the Scope and Function of Hermeneutical Reflection," p. 87.

5.   See Jean Piaget, *Science of Education and the Psychology of the Child*, trans. Derek Coltman (New York: Orion Press, 1970).

6. See, for example, Aquinas *Summa Theologica* I.76.1; I.51.1; and *De Spiritualibus Creaturis* 6 in *Quaestiones Disputatae*, vol. II (Romae: Marietti, 1965), p. 392.

7. Richard Rorty, in *Philosophy and the Mirror of Nature* (Princeton: Princeton University Press, 1979), hereafter cited as PMN, develops this distinction. David Olson ("Interpreting Texts and Interpreting Nature: The Effects of Literacy on Hermeneutics and Epistemology," *Visible Language* 20 [1986], 302–317) suggests that modern epistemology is itself not the opposite of hermeneutics, but an exaggerated form of hermeneutical practice.

8. See Edmund Husserl, *Logical Investigations*, trans. J. N. Findlay (London: Routledge and Kegan Paul, 1970), Investigation I; also see my paper, "Hyletic Experience and the Lived Body," *Husserl Studies* 3 (1986), 131–166.

9. Heidegger, *The Basic Problems of Phenomenology*, trans. Albert Hofstadter (Bloomington: Indiana University Press, 1982), p. 276.

10. Gadamer, "The Hermeneutics of Suspicion," in Shapiro and Sica, *Hermeneutics: Questions and Prospects*, p. 58.

11. See Graham Nicholson, *Seeing and Reading* (Atlantic Highlands, NJ: Humanities, 1984), pp. 3, 35ff.

12. John Dewey, *Democracy and Education* (New York: The Free Press, 1966 [1916]), p. 17.

13. Ibid., p. 102.

14. Cited by Gadamer, TM 246.

15. Jaeger, *Paideia*, vol. 2 (1943), p. 317.

16. Jean-Paul Sartre, *Being and Nothingness: An Essay on Phenomenological Ontology*, trans. H. E. Barnes (New York: Philosophical Library, 1956); see pp. 564 and 581; hereafter cited as BN.

17. TM 103; for a discussion very much akin to Gadamer's, see Heidegger, "What Are Poets For?" in *Poetry, Language, Thought*, trans. Albert Hofstadter (New York: Harper and Row, 1971), pp. 102ff.

18. Gadamer, "*Destruktion* and Deconstruction," DD 110; see also PH 57. For a Gadamerian account of play which places more emphasis on appropriation, see Jerald Wallulis, *The Hermeneutics of Life History* (Evanston, IL: Northwestern University Press, 1990), pp. 96ff.

19. See, for example, Susanna Millar, *The Psychology of Play* (Baltimore: Penguin, 1968), p. 13.

20. John Blackie, "How Children Learn," *NEA Journal* 47 (1968), 40–42; reprinted in *Readings in the Foundations of Education*, vol. 2, *Commitment to Teaching*, ed. James Stone and Frederick Schneider (New York: Thomas Crowell, 1971), p. 225.

21. Piaget, *Science of Education*, p. 155.

22. Also see James S. Hans, *The Play of the World* (Amherst: University of Massachusetts Press, 1981), pp. 51ff.

23. Their approximate agreement is not always apparent, because of their different employment of similar terminology. On the one hand, when Gadamer uses the terms *subject, subjective,* and *subjectivity,* he intends to signify the metaphysical-epistemological interpretation of subjectivity: the subject as substantial entity—soul, mind, ego, consciousness, personal identity, and so on. For Gadamer it is precisely this type of subjectivity that is displaced in play. On the other hand, when Sartre uses the term *subjectivity* he means, not the mind, ego, soul, or substantial consciousness, as in traditional substance ontology, but the egoless 'for-itself' which is the no-thingness, the freedom, the collection of possibilities that, as he puts it, "is what it is not and is not what it is." See BN lxv, 626; see also Jean-Paul Sartre, *The Transcendence of the Ego: An Existentialist Theory of Consciousness,* trans. F. Williams and R. Kirkpatrick (New York: Farrar, Straus and Giroux, 1957).

24. Jean Piaget, *Play, Dreams and Imitation in Childhood,* trans. C. Gattegno and F. M. Hodgson (New York: Norton, 1962), p. 147.

25. See Edmund Husserl, *Zur Phänomenologie des inneren Zeitbewusstseins (1893–1917),* ed. R. Boehm, Husserliana X (The Hague: Martinus Nijhoff, 1966). Also see Shaun Gallagher, "Suggestions towards a Revision of Husserl's Phenomenology of Time-Consciousness," *Man and World* 12 (1979), 445–464.

CHAPTER 3. INTERPRETATIONAL AND EDUCATIONAL CIRCLES

1. A similar distinction between "laws of understanding" (principles) and "practical rules" (canons) can be found in Philip August Boeckh, *On Interpretation and Criticism,* trans. J. Prichard (Norman, OK: University of Oklahoma Press, 1968), reprinted in HR, p. 133.

2. Hirsch, *The Aims of Interpretation,* pp. 75ff.

3. See Schleiermacher, *Hermeneutics,* p. 117.

4. Hirsch, *The Aims of Interpretation,* p. 81; also see pp. 31–32, 75.

5. Hirsch, "Three Dimensions of Hermeneutics," *New Literary History* 3 (1972), 245. Hirsch's own distinction between canon and principle does not correspond precisely to the one under discussion here. Making it clear that "interpretive canons are often relatively useless baggage," Hirsch does not recommend them as the basis for a reliable interpretive methodology. He contrasts canons to logical "principles of validation" (See *Validity in Interpretation* [New Haven: Yale University Press,

1967], pp. 203ff, 169ff, 207). Thus, what Hirsch calls "principles" are procedural rules meant to specify how interpretation ought to proceed, rather than the descriptive principles under discussion here.

6. See, for example, Palmer, *Hermeneutics*, p. 66; also, Hirsch, "Three Dimensions of Hermeneutics," pp. 246–247.

7. Jean-Francois Lyotard makes this point in broader terms. "There is nothing to prove that if a statement describing a real situation is true, it follows that a prescriptive statement based upon it (the effect of which will necessarily be a modification of that reality) will be just" (*The Postmodern Condition: A Report on Knowledge*, trans. Geoff Bennington and Brian Massumi [Minneapolis: University of Minnesota Press, 1984], p. 40; hereafter cited as PMC).

8. Schleiermacher, *Hermeneutics*, p. 198; also see pp. 59, 61–62, 68–69, 115–116, 195ff.

9. Dilthey, *Gesammelte Schriften*, vol. 7, p. 227; cited and trans. in KHI 170.

10. Husserl, *Experience and Judgment: Investigations in a Genealogy of Logic*, rev. and ed. Ludwig Landgrebe, trans. James S. Churchill and Karl Ameriks (Evanston, IL: Northwestern University Press, 1973), pp. 31–32.

11. Ibid., p. 37.

12. Despite Husserl's notion of *Vorwissen*, Gadamer criticizes Husserl for failing to accept the "primacy of interpretation." See "The Hermeneutics of Suspicion," pp. 59ff.

13. See Hirsch, *The Aims of Interpretation*, pp. 32ff; and CL 51ff.; for Piaget's notion of schema, see Piaget, *The Origin of Intelligence in Children*, trans. Margaret Cook (New York: International Universities Press, 1952), pp. 258ff.; and *Biology and Knowledge*, trans. Beatrix Walsh (Chicago: University of Chicago Press, 1971), pp. 176ff. Also see R. C. Anderson and P. D. Pearson, "A Schema-Theoretic View of Basic Processes in Reading Comprehension," in *Handbook of Reading Research*, ed. P. D. Pearson (New York: Longman, 1984), pp. 255–291.

14. See F. C. Bartlett, *Remembering* (Cambridge: Cambridge University Press, 1932). On the connection with Kant, see David E. Rumelhart and Andrew Ortony, "The Representation of Knowledge in Memory," in *Schooling and the Acquisition of Knowledge*, ed. R. C. Anderson, R. J. Spiro, and W. E. Montague (Hillsdale, NJ: Lawrence Erlbaum, 1977), pp. 100–101.

15. Richard C. Anderson, "The Notion of Schemata and the Educational Enterprise," in Anderson, Spiro, and Montague, *Schooling and the Acquisition of Knowledge*, p. 417.

16. Ibid., p. 423.

17. CL 53. Hirsch had previously confused the issue in his article, "Meaning and Significance Reinterpreted" *Critical Inquiry* 11 [1984], p. 204), where he equated the schema with Husserl's notion of intentional object and defined meaning as "a self-identical schema."

18. Hirsch, *The Aims of Interpretation*, p. 32.

19. See Gadamer, "The Problem of Historical Consciousness," in *Interpretive Social Science: A Reader*, ed. Paul Rabinow and William M. Sullivan (Berkeley: University of California Press, 1979), pp. 148–149; and Gadamer, "On the Circle of Understanding," in *Hermeneutics vs. Science?: Three German Views*, ed. John M. Connolly and Thomas Keutner (Notre Dame, IN: University of Notre Dame Press, 1988), pp. 71–72.

20. Buck, *Hermeneutik und Bildung*, pp. 51–52.

21. Hirsch, *The Aims of Interpretation*, p. 32.

22. Buck explains this in terms of widening the schema rather than shifting from one to another. See Buck, *Hermeneutik und Bildung*, pp. 55ff. Likewise, Piaget speaks of a "progressive complication of the schemata" (*The Origin of Intelligence in Children*, p. 153).

23. J. D. Bransford and M. K. Johnson, "Contextual Prerequisites for Understanding: Some Investigations of Comprehension and Recall," *Journal of Verbal Learning and Verbal Behavior* 11 (1972), 717–726; cited in CL, p. 40.

24. Chladenius, *Einleitung*, HR 55.

25. Schleiermacher, *Hermeneutics*, p. 149; see also p. 148.

26. Boeckh, *On Interpretation and Criticism*, HR 137–138.

27. Dilthey, *Gesammelte Schriften*, vol. 7, p. 214; see also pp. 137–138, 226, and vol. 5, p. 317; these texts are cited in KHI 180–183, 169, 177–178.

28. Schleiermacher, *Hermeneutics*, p. 112, 118; also Boeckh, *On Interpretation and Criticism*, HR 139.

29. The link between hermeneutics and induction can be traced back to the Romantics. See Wilhelm von Humboldt, "On the Task of the Historian," HR 112–113; Johann Gustav Droysen, "History and the Historical Method," HR 122; Boeckh, *On Interpretation and Criticism*, HR 146; Dilthey, "The Understanding of Other Persons and Their Life-Expressions," HR 163; see HR 156–158. Hirsch takes up this tradition and describes interpretation as an inductive process (see *Validity in Interpretation*, pp. 170ff., 203; "Truth and Method in Interpretation," p. 504).

30. Hirsch, *Validity in Interpretation*, pp. 206, 171–172.

31. Aristotle *Posterior Analytics* 71a1; also: "All teaching is based on what is already known," *Nicomachean Ethics* 1139b27, trans. Martin Ostwald (Indianapolis: Bobbs-Merrill, 1962). Comenius advances the

same axiom: "We learn the unknown only through the known. Or, whatever we learn, we learn through what we knew before, because no other course is possible" (*Analytical Didactic* [1657], 10, V).

32. For a critical discussion of Plato's theory of recollection, see Jacob Klein, *A Commentary on Plato's Meno* (Chapel Hill: University of North Carolina Press, 1965), pp. 108–172; see also John Sallis, *Being and Logos: The Way of Platonic Dialogue* (Pittsburgh: Duquesne University Press, 1974), pp. 65ff.; and James Risser, "Hermeneutic Experience and Memory: Rethinking Knowledge as Recollection," *Research in Phenomenology* 16 (1986), 41–55.

33. Dewey, *Democracy and Education*, pp. 180–181.

34. Ibid.

35. See Buck, *Hermeneutik und Bildung*, p. 52.

36. Frank Smith, *Comprehension and Learning: A Conceptual Framework for Teachers* (New York: Holt, Rinehart and Winston, 1975), p. 1; also see *Understanding Reading* (New York: Holt, Rinehart and Winston, 1971).

37. See, for example, Robert Glaser, "Education and Thinking: The Role of Knowledge," *American Psychologist* 39 (1984), 93–104; and Herbert A. Simon, "Problem Solving and Education," in *Problem Solving and Education: Issues in Teaching and Research*, ed. D. T. Tuma and F. Reif (Hillsdale, NJ: Lawrence Erlbaum, 1980), pp. 81–96.

38. Joseph J. Schwab and Paul F. Brandwein, *The Teaching of Science* (Cambridge: Harvard University Press, 1962), pp. 64–71; reprinted in *Teaching and Learning*, ed. Donald Vandenberg (Urbana: University of Illinois Press, 1969), p. 32.

39. Chladenius, *Einleitung*, HR 58.

40. Ibid., p. 61.

41. William M. Bryant, *Hegel's Educational Ideals* (Chicago: 1896, reprint ed: St. Clair Shores, MI), p. 94; cited in AG, p. 166.

42. Etienne Gilson, *A Gilson Reader*, ed. Anton Pegis (New York: Doubleday, 1957), p. 306.

43. Heidegger expresses the importance of this lack of completeness; see *An Introduction to Metaphysics*, trans. Ralph Manheim (Garden City, NY: Doubleday, 1961), p. 18.

44. James Hans has noted the hermeneutical circle involved in play, and his analysis is clearly relevant to our discussion. See *The Play of the World*, pp. 8, 10–11.

45. Augustine *De Trinitate* XII.14.23.

46. Gadamer, "Rhetoric, Hermeneutics, and the Critique of Ideology," HR 288; Habermas, "The Hermeneutic Claim to Universality," HT 247.

CHAPTER 4. HERMENEUTICAL CONSTRAINTS

1. Descartes, *Discours de la méthode* (1637); see translations by Laurence J. Lafleur (Indianapolis: Bobbs-Merrill, 1960), p. 11; and Donald A. Cress (Indianapolis: Hackett Publishing, 1980), p. 7.

2. See, Augustine *De Trinitate* XII.15.24.

3. Heidegger, *What Is Philosophy?* pp. 71–73; translation revised.

4. See Gadamer, "*Destruktion* and Deconstruction," DD 107ff.; "Hermeneutics and Logocentrism," DD 121; "Letter to Dallmayr," DD 99–100.

5. John Stuart Mill, *Utilitarianism* (Indianapolis: Bobbs-Merrill, 1957), p. 15.

6. Ibid., p. 30.

7. Gadamer, *Kleine Schriften*, vol. 1 (Tubingen: J.C.B. Mohr Verlag, 1967), p. 158.

8. Scheffler, *Reason and Teaching*, p. 2.

9. Ibid., p. 79.

10. *The Oxford English Dictionary*, "teach."

11. Gadamer, "On the Scope and Function of Hermeneutical Reflection," p. 92.

12. Ibid.

13. Karl Jaspers, *Philosophy of Existence*, trans. Richard F. Grabau (Philadelphia: University of Pennsylvania Press, 1971), pp. 48–51.

14. Mill, *On Liberty* (Indianapolis: Bobbs-Merrill, 1956), p. 7.

15. Ibid., p. 25.

16. Heidegger, *What Is Philosophy?* pp. 71–73.

17. Schleiermacher, *Hermeneutics*, p. 50.

18. Nietzsche, *The Will to Power*, trans. Walter Kaufmann and R. J. Hollingdale (London: Weidenfeld and Nicolson, 1968), # 484. See also *Beyond Good and Evil*, trans. Walter Kaufmann (New York: Vintage, 1966), sect. 17; and Bertrand Russell, *A History of Western Philosophy* (New York: Simon and Schuster, 1945), p. 567.

19. Augustine *De Trinitate* XV.12.22; 15.25.

20. Ibid., 10.19.

21. Descartes, *Meditations*, trans. Donald A. Cress (Indianapolis: Hackett, 1980), p. 65.

22. Heidegger, "Letter on Humanism," in *Basic Writings*, trans. David F. Krell (New York: Harper and Row, 1977), pp. 193, 213, 239.

23. Heidegger, "Building, Dwelling, Thinking," in *Basic Writings*, p. 324.

24. Heidegger, *Discourse on Thinking*, trans. John M. Anderson and E. Hans Freund (New York: Harper and Row, 1966), p. 70.

25. Habermas, "Review," p. 342, summarizing Gadamer.

26. Ibid., p. 336.

27. TM 398; see also TM 390. Gadamer's statement, "We are always situated within traditions and this is no objectifying process" (TM 282), expresses the general or primary relation. Joel Weinsheimer is one among many commentators who fail to clarify the difference between the anterior relation to a tradition and the case of reading a traditional text. Summarizing Gadamer, he states: "The object of interpretation is tradition in the form of language, and specifically silent, written language" (Joel C. Weinsheimer, *Gadamer's Hermeneutics: A Reading of* Truth and Method [New Haven: Yale, 1985], p. 221).

28. Jean Piaget and Barbel Inhelder, *The Psychology of the Child*, trans. Helen Weaver (New York: Basic Books, 1969), reprinted in *The Essential Piaget*, ed. Howard E. Gruber and J. Jacques Voneche (New York: Basic Books, 1977), p. 489.

29. Ibid., p. 490.

30. Ibid., p. 507.

31. Hans Furth, *Piaget and Knowledge: Theoretical Foundations* (Englewood Cliffs, NJ: Prentice-Hall, 1969), p. 108; see p. 111.

32. Piaget, *Essential Piaget*, p. 84.

33. E. Bates, B. O'Connell, and C. Shore, "Language and Communication in Infancy," in *Handbook for Infant Development*, 2nd ed., ed. J. D. Osofsky (New York: John Wiley and Sons, 1987), pp. 150, 151, 156, 157; see I. Uzgiris and J. McV. Hund, *Assessment in Infancy: Ordinal Scales of Psychological Development* (Urbana: University of Illinois Press, 1975).

34. See Merleau-Ponty, *The Primacy of Perception*, ed. James M. Edie (Evanston, IL: Northwestern University Press, 1964), p. 109; and *Themes from the Lectures at the College of France 1952–1960*, trans. John O'Neill (Evanston, IL: Northwestern University Press, 1970), pp. 21–22.

35. Furth, *Piaget and Knowledge*, pp. 112–113.

36. Merleau-Ponty, *The Primacy of Perception*, p. 99.

37. Merleau-Ponty, *Signs*, trans. R. C. McCleary (Evanston, IL: Northwestern University Press, 1964), p. 40.

38. Gadamer, "Summation," *Cultural Hermeneutics* 2 (1975), 330; see also "Reply to My Critics," HT 278.

39. Bryant, *Hegel's Educational Ideals* (1896), cited in AG, p. 166.

40. Piaget, *Essential Piaget*, p. 505; "Language and Intellectual Operations," in Furth, *Piaget and Knowledge*, pp. 122, 128; and Hans

Furth, *Piaget for Teachers* (Englewood Cliffs, NJ: Prentice-Hall, 1970), pp. 67–68.

41. Noam Chomsky, *Language and Mind* (New York: Harcourt Brace, 1968); see also David McNeill, *The Acquisition of Language: The Study of Developmental Psycholinguistics* (New York: Harper and Row, 1970).

42. Piaget, "Le langage et la pensée du point de vue génétique," *Acta Psychologica* 10 (1954), 51–60.

43. D. W. Hamlyn, *Experience and the Growth of Understanding* (London: Routledge and Kegan Paul, 1978), pp. 103ff. Further page references given in text.

44. Merleau-Ponty, *Signs*, p. 40.

45. Merleau-Ponty, *The Visible and the Invisible*, trans. Alphonso Lingis, (Evanston, IL: Northwestern University Press, 1968), p. 201, trans. revised.

46. See Hans Furth and Harry Wachs, *Thinking Goes to School: Piaget's Theory in Practice* (New York: Oxford University Press, 1974), pp. 12–13.

47. Michael Polanyi, *Personal Knowledge: Towards a Post-Critical Philosophy* (New York: Harper Torch Books, 1964), pp. 56–57.

48. See Augustine, *De Magistro*, trans. John H. S. Burleigh, in *Augustine's Earlier Writings* (Philadelphia: Westminster Press, 1953), pp. 69–101.

49. Scheffler, *Reason and Teaching*, p. 74.

50. Ibid., p. 62, emphasis added.

51. Ibid., p. 75.

52. Ibid., p. 78.

53. Ludwig Wittgenstein, *Philosophical Investigations* (New York: Macmillan, 1968), p. 23; See, for example, pp. 29, 30, 43, 49.

54. See, for example, Ferdinand de Saussure, *Course in General Linguistics*, trans. Wade Baskin (New York: McGraw-Hill, 1966); and G 50.

55. Heidegger, "What Calls for Thinking," in *Basic Writings*, p. 365; see also, Heidegger, *On the Way to Language*, trans. Peter Hertz and Joan Stambaugh (New York: Harper and Row, 1971).

56. PH 56; see also Gadamer, "The Problem of Language in Schleiermacher's Hermeneutic," *Journal for Theology and the Church* 7 (1970), 76.

57. Hans, *The Play of the World*, pp 85ff.

58. See, for example, Phyllis Levenstein, "Cognitive Development through Verbalized Play," in *Play—Its Role in Development and Evolution*, ed. Jerome S. Bruner, Alison Jolly, and Kathy Sylva (New York: Basic Books, 1976), pp. 286–297.

59.   P. M. Greenfield, "Playing peekaboo with a four-month old: a study of the role of speech and nonspeech sounds in the formation of a visual schema" (1970), unpublished manuscript, cited in Jerome S. Bruner and V. Sherwood, "Peekaboo and the Learning of Rule Structures," in *Play—Its Role in Development and Evolution*, p. 277.

60.   Piaget, "The Language and Thought of the Child" (1923), trans. Marjorie Gabain, in *Essential Piaget*, p. 84.

61.   Dewey, *Experience and Nature* (New York: Dover, 1958), p. 191.

62.   Dewey, "Meaning and Existence," in *Dewey and his Critics: Essays from the Journal of Philosophy*, ed. Sidney Morgenbesser (New York: Journal of Philosophy Inc., 1977), p. 477. This is also Merleau-Ponty's contention. See *Phenomenology of Perception*, trans. Colin Smith (London: Routledge and Kegan Paul, 1962), pp. 193–194, 183–189.

63.   Gadamer, "The Problem of Language in Schleiermacher's Hermeneutic," p. 76; see also p. 83.

64.   PH 56; see p. 66, and TM 490.

65.   Gadamer, "Text and Interpretation," DD 21; see the French translation: "Le Défi Herméneutique," *Revue Internationale de Philosophie* 151 (1984), 333.

CHAPTER 5. HERMENEUTICAL POSSIBILITIES

1.   "On the Problem of Language in Schleiermacher's Hermeneutic," p. 75; also TM 447.

2.   Michel Foucault, *The Archaeology of Knowledge*, trans. A. M. Sheridan Smith (New York: Pantheon Books, 1972), p. 120; hereafter cited as AK.

3.   *Oxford English Dictionary*, "trade." As noted, the gains-from-trade doctrine is not uncontroversial. There is a broad-based debate about its validity, part of which is contained in an exchange between Paul Samuelson and Arghiri Emmanuel. See, for example, Paul Samuelson, "Illogic of Neo-Marxist Doctrine of Unequal Exchange," in *Inflation, Trade, and Taxes: Essays in Honor of Alice Bourneuf* ed. Belsley et al. (Columbus: Ohio State University Press, 1976); and Arghiri Emmanuel, *Unequal Exchange: A Study of the Imperialism of Trade* (New York: Monthly Review Press, 1972).

4.   Rousseau, *Essay on the Origin of Language*, in *On the Origin of Language*, ed. and trans. John H. Moran (New York: F. Ungar, 1967), p. 33.

5.   Dilthey, *Gesammelte Schriften*, vol. 1, p. 225; cited in KHI, p. 164.

6.   See Ricoeur, HHS 61, 103; see also "Ethics and Culture: Habermas and Gadamer in Dialogue," *Philosophy Today* 17 (1973), 153–165.

7.   Graham Nicholson, "Transforming What We Know," *Research in Phenomenology* 16 (1986), 57–71.

8.   See Otto Kurz, *Fakes* (New York: Dover, 1967), pp. 329–334, for a detailed account of the forgeries.

9.   Ibid., p. 331.

10. Ibid., p. 332.

11. HHS 131–132; Ricoeur refers to "productive distanciation" in "Ethics and Culture," pp. 160ff.

12. Dewey, *Democracy and Education*, p. 157.

13. Ibid., p. 159.

14. Ibid., p. 160.

15. Scheffler, *Reason and Teaching*, p. 59.

16. See, for example, Gabriel Marcel, "On the Ontological Mystery," in *The Philosophy of Existentialism*, trans. Manya Harari (New York: Citadel Press, 1971), pp. 9–46; See Gadamer's related discussion of the concepts of "problem" (TM 376ff.) and hermeneutical situation (TM 301–302).

17. Gadamer, *The Idea of the Good in Platonic-Aristotelian Philosophy*, trans. P. Christopher Smith (New Haven: Yale University Press, 1986), p. 170.

18. Ricoeur, *The Conflict of Interpretations: Essays in Hermeneutics*, trans. Don Ihde (Evanston, IL: Northwestern University Press, 1974), p. 17. This principle can also be found in Dilthey. Palmer clarifies its normative significance in his summary of Dilthey's position. See *Hermeneutics*, p. 115; see Dilthey, *Gesammelte Schriften*, vol. 7, pp. 145, 191, 215–216.

19. Gadamer, "The Hermeneutics of Suspicion," p. 59.

20. Ricoeur writes: "By the expression '*self*-understanding', I should like to contrast the *self* which emerges from the understanding of the text to the *ego* which claims to precede this understanding" (HHS 193).

21. See, for example, John Dewey, "Interest in Relation to Training of the Will," [1896], in *The Philosophy of John Dewey*, vol. 2, *The Lived Experience*, ed. John J. McDermott (New York: G. P. Putnam, 1973), pp. 421–442.

22. See Dewey, *Democracy and Education*, pp. 124ff. See Alfred

North Whitehead, *The Aims of Education* [1929] (New York: Free Press, 1967), p. 37; and Piaget, *Science of Education*, pp. 158–159.
23. Dewey, "Interest in Relation to Training of the Will," p. 424.
24. Ibid., pp. 425–426.
25. Ibid., p. 426.
26. Ibid., p. 431.
27. Like Gadamer, Dewey relates play to aesthetic experience and suggests that it involves a self-transcendence; see ibid., p. 432.
28. Heidegger, *Der Satz vom Grund* (Pfullingen: Neske, 1958), p. 188.
29. See Carol Gould, "From the Dialectic of Questions to Social Critique: Proposals for a Concrete Phenomenology of Education," *Philosophical Forum* 6 (1974), 16–17; J. T. Dillon, *The Practice of Questioning* (London: Routledge, 1990), pp. 7–15; and Dillon, "Questioning in Education," in *Questions and Questioning*, ed. Michael Meyer (New York: Walter deGruyter, 1988), pp. 98–117.
30. Dewey, *Democracy and Education*, p. 161.
31. See TM 359ff. and, for example, the discussion of Buber's I-thou model for the educational situation in John Scudder and Algis Mickunas, *Meaning, Dialogue, and Education: Phenomenological Philosophy of Education* (Lanham, MD: University Press of America, 1985), pp. 24ff.
32. Aristotle *Nicomachean Ethics* 1177a27–35; see also 1177b22; 1178b35ff.

CHAPTER 6. THE NATURE OF EDUCATION

1. See, respectively, John Dewey, *Democracy and Education*, pp. 152ff.; Joseph J. Schwab and Paul F. Brandwein, *The Teaching of Science* (Cambridge: Harvard University Press, 1962), pp. 64ff.; reprinted in Vandenberg, *Teaching and Learning*, pp. 32–38; and Foster McMurray, "The Problem of Verification in Formal School Learning," in *Essays for John Dewey's 90th Birthday* (Urbana, IL: Bureau of Educational Research, 1950), pp. 47ff, reprinted in Vandenberg, *Teaching and Learning*, pp. 39–45.
2. Dewey, *Democracy and Education*, p. 165.
3. Dewey, "My Pedagogic Creed," [1897], in Dewey, *The Philosophy of John Dewey*, vol. 2, *The Lived Experience*, p. 450; and *Democracy and Education*, pp. 76, 77, 182ff. Also see *The Child and the Curriculum, The School and Society* (Chicago: University of Chicago Press, 1956), p. 11.

4. Dewey writes: "Education is not infrequently defined as consisting in the acquisition of those habits that effect an adjustment of an individual and his environment. The definition expresses an essential phase of growth. But it is essential that adjustment be understood in its active sense of *control* of means for achieving ends" (*Democracy and Education*, p. 46).

5. See, for example, Frank C. Wegener, "The Logic of Subject Matter," *School and Society* 77 (1953), 306–308; reprinted in Vandenberg, *Teaching and Learning*, pp. 46–51.

6. Whitehead, *The Aims of Education*, pp. 4, 6–7. With respect to the definition of education in terms of 'life', see Dewey, *The Philosophy of John Dewey*, vol. 2, *The Lived Experience*, pp. 445–446, 450. In the 1940s this progressivist idea was translated into "life adjustment training." See U.S. Office of Education, *Life Adjustment Education for Every Youth* (Washington, DC: U.S. Government Printing Office, n.d.), p. 15; cited in CL, p. 124.

7. R. S. Peters, *Education and the Education of Teachers* (London: Routledge and Kegan Paul, 1977), p. 17.

8. McMurray, "The Problem of Verification in Formal School Learning," pp. 40–41. This is not far from Hirsch's argument in *Cultural Literacy*.

9. Scheffler, *Reason and Teaching*, p. 59.

10. B. F. Skinner, *The Technology of Teaching* (New York: Appleton-Century-Crofts, 1968), p. 19.

11. Harlan Lane, cited in Scheffler, *Reason and Teaching*, pp. 165–166.

12. Bruce Romanish, "Critical Thinking and the Curriculum: A Critique," *Educational Forum* 51 (1986), 52; and former U.S. Secretary of Education William J. Bennett, "What Works in Education? The Scientific Approach," *Education* 108 (1987), 138.

13. John Wilson, *Preface to a Philosophy of Education* (London: Routledge and Kegan Paul, 1979), p. 17; emphasis added.

14. Ibid., p. 21; also Harold Loukes, John Wilson, and Barbara Cowell, *Education: An Introduction* (Oxford: Martin Robertson, 1983), for example, p. 20.

15. William K. Frankena, *Three Historical Philosophies of Education: Aristotle, Kant, Dewey* (Chicago: Scott, Foresman, 1965), p. 6.

16. J. Gordon Chamberlin, *Toward a Phenomenology of Education* (Philadelphia: Westminster Press, 1969), pp. 159–160; emphasis added.

17. Romanish, "Critical Thinking and the Curriculum: A Critique," pp. 46–47; emphasis added.

18. Scheffler, *The Language of Education* (Springfield, IL: Thomas, 1960), pp. 13–22.

19. Peters, *Education and the Education of Teachers*, p. 10.

20. Ibid., pp. 13, 19, 7.

21. The last phrase is from Robert V. Bullough, Jr., "School Knowledge, Power and Human Experience," *Educational Forum* 51 (1987), 260.

22. Nietzsche, *The Will to Power*, #466.

23. Heidegger, *On the Way to Language*, p. 74.

24. Heidegger, "The Question Concerning Technology," in *Basic Writings*, p. 288.

25. Ibid., p. 300. Also see "What Are Poets For?" pp. 110ff.

26. Allan Bloom, *The Closing of the American Mind* (New York: Simon and Schuster, 1987), pp. 170–171.

27. See Heidegger, "The Question Concerning Technology," p. 309; and "What Are Poets For?" pp. 115ff.

28. Heidegger, "Letter on Humanism," p. 210.

29. Werner Jaeger noted these same connections (*Paideia*, vol. 1, pp. 229, 301.

30. Heidegger, "Letter on Humanism," p. 203; see p. 191.

31. George Grant, *Technology and Justice* (Notre Dame, IN: University of Notre Dame Press, 1986), p. 22.

32. Ibid., p. 33.

33. Peters, *Education and the Education of Teachers*, p. 3.

34. Gadamer, "On the Scope and Function of Hermeneutical Reflection," p. 83.

35. Gadamer, "The Hermeneutics of Suspicion," p. 65.

36. Gadamer, *The Idea of the Good in Platonic-Aristotelian Philosophy*, p. 80; also see Heidegger, "What Are Poets For?" pp. 110–111.

37. Alternatively, we could focus on those educational theorists who emphasize content or literacy and show that such emphasis can never really reduce subject matter to a storehouse or standing reserve of knowledge, or reduce the power of tradition to purely instrumental power. I discuss such theories in the next chapter, however.

38. Kant, *Critique of Pure Reason*, B xiii, trans. F. M. Müller.

39. See Dewey, *Reconstruction in Philosophy* (Boston: Beacon Press, 1957), Chapter 3.

40. Although *art* is often used to translate *technē*, there is no etymological link between the English *art* (Latin *ars*) and the Greek *technē*. It can be noted, however, that the English *art* once meant "learning" in general. Today it is used in this sense only for the liberal arts.

41. See Gilson, *A Gilson Reader*, p. 66.

42.   Aristotle *Nicomachean Ethics* 1143a15. Gadamer notes that the Greek word for the act of understanding, *synesis*, "tends as a rule to be encountered in the neutral context of the phenomenon of learning and in exchangeable proximity to the Greek word for learning (*mathesis*)" (*Reason in the Age of Science*, trans. Frederick G. Lawrence (Cambridge, MA: MIT Press, 1981), p. 132).

43.   See *Republic* 346a; *Protagoras* 331c; *Gorgias* 495a; *Euthyd* 275d.

44.   See Sallis, *Being and Logos*, pp. 65ff.

45.   This peculiar preconception of knowledge, and the contrasting one held by Socrates (see below), explains the significance of the words *to parapan* in Meno's version of the paradox, and their disappearance in Socrates' version. This significance is missed by both John E. Thomas (*Musings on the Meno* [The Hague: Nijhoff 1980], pp. 123, 128–129) and Alexander Nehamas ("Meno's Paradox and Socrates as a Teacher," *Oxford Studies in Ancient Philosophy* 3 [1985], pp. 9–10).

46.   See Sallis, *Being and Logos*, pp. 73–74, 78–79.

47.   Ibid., p. 65.

48.   All citations of the *Meno* are taken from the G. M. A. Grube translation.

49.   See, for example, William S. Cobb, Jr., "Anamnesis: Platonic Doctrine or Sophistic Absurdity?" *Dialogue* (Canada) 12 (1973), 604–628.

50.   See Samuel Scolnicov, "Three Aspects of Plato's Philosophy of Learning and Instruction," *Paideia* 5 (1976), 50.

51.   See I. M. Crombie, "Socratic Definition," *Paideia* 5 (1976), 94–101.

52.   See Sallis, *Being and Logos*, pp. 101–102.

53.   Skinner, *The Technology of Teaching*, p. 61.

54.   See Gadamer, *The Idea of the Good*, pp. 23, 25–27, 33, 35–42, 46–50, 80–81, 111, 121, 166, 168, 170.

55.   See Heidegger, "Plato's Doctrine of Truth," [1942], trans. John Barlow, in *Philosophy in the Twentieth Century*, vol. 3, ed. William Barrett and Henry D. Aiken (New York: Harper and Row, 1971), pp. 173–192.

56.   Heidegger, "Letter on Humanism," pp. 194–201; "Plato's Doctrine of Truth," p. 191.

57.   Heidegger, "Letter on Humanism," p. 225.

58.   Heidegger, "On the Essence of Truth," [1943], trans. John Sallis, in *Basic Writings*, p. 134.

59.   See Heidegger, "The End of Philosophy and the Task of Thinking," [1966], trans. Joan Stambaugh, in *Basic Writings*, p. 390. Heideg-

ger's change on this issue and the reading of the *Meno* that I present here are clearly opposed to the interpretation offered by Angelo A. Giugliano, "Toward a Heideggerian Paideia," *Philosophy of Education* 42 (1986), 87–98.
    60. Scolnicov affirms this interpretation: "*Adequatio*, or correspondence of state of mind (or proposition, judgment, etc.) to state of affairs ceases then to be the distinguishing mark of knowledge, or at least ceases to be its sufficient criterion" (Scolnicov, "Three Aspects," p. 52).
    61. Gadamer, *The Idea of the Good*, p. 11.
    62. Heidegger, *What is Philosophy?* p. 71.

CHAPTER 7. CONSERVATIVE HERMENEUTICS AND EDUCATIONAL THEORY

    1. Betti 59; Hirsch provides a similar description ("Truth and Method in Interpretation," p. 502).
    2. See, Husserl, *Logical Investigations*, Investigation I.
    3. Hirsch, "Truth and Method in Interpretation," p. 498.
    4. Hirsch, *Validity in Interpretation*, p. 8. We note that the meaning (or at least the significance) of the distinction between meaning and significance seems to have changed for Hirsch. See his "Meaning and Significance Reinterpreted," *Critical Inquiry* 11 (1984), 202–225. In this article he qualifies the relation between meaning and author's intention, and gives more importance to application. Hirsch even admits to moving closer to Gadamer's position, but still disagrees with Gadamer over the nature of meaning.
    5. This principle can also be traced back to Romantic hermeneutics. See Ast, *Grundlinien der Grammatik, Hermeneutik und Kritik*, HT 46; Schleiermacher, *Hermeneutics*, p. 111; Dilthey, "The Understanding of Other Persons and Their Life-Expressions," HR 159; and *Gesammelte Schriften*, vol. 5, p. 317.
    6. Hirsch, "Truth and Method in Interpretation," p. 498.
    7. Hirsch, *Validity in Interpretation*, p. 46.
    8. See Betti, *Die Hermeneutik als allgemeine Methodik der Geisteswissenschaften* (Tubingen: J. C. B. Mohr, 1962), pp. 45–49; cited in Palmer, *Hermeneutics*, p. 58.
    9. Schleiermacher, *Hermeneutics*, p. 111.
    10. Droysen, "History and the Historical Method," HR 129.
    11. Hirsch, *Validity in Interpretation*, p. 134.
    12. Ibid., p. 47.
    13. Schleiermacher, *Hermeneutics*, p. 110;

14. Hirsch, *Validity in Interpretation*, p. 219; see Husserl, *Logical Investigations*, Investigation I.

15. Hirsch, ibid., p. 222.

16. Ibid., p. 236.

17. Ibid., p. 180.

18. Hirsch, *Cultural Literacy* (CL).

19. Schleiermacher, *Sämmtliche Werke*, Part 3, vol. 9, *Zur Pädagogik*, p. 40; cited in Jeffrey Hoover, "The Origin of the Conflict between Hegel and Schleiermacher at Berlin," *The Owl of Minerva* 20 (1988), 74.

20. Hirsch, *Validity in Interpretation*, p. 140.

21. This is Hirsch's claim, which he bases on research by Rummelhart, Goding, and Norman (see CL 224, n.47). But this is neither a simple nor a settled issue. See, for example, Glaser, "Education and Thinking," pp. 93–104; Jonathan Baron, *Rationality and Intelligence* (Cambridge: Cambridge University Press, 1985), pp. 245ff.; Raymond S. Nickerson, David N. Perkins, and Edward E. Smith, *The Teaching of Thinking* (Hillsdale, NJ: Lawrence Erlbaum, 1985), pp. 57–59; Simon, "Problem Solving and Education," pp. 81–96; and Joanne G. Kurfiss, *Critical Thinking: Theory, Research, Practice, and Possibilities* (Washington, DC: ASHE-ERIC Higher Education Report No. 2, 1988), pp. 19ff.

22. Richard W. Paul, Announcement for the 9th Annual Conference on Critical Thinking and Educational Reform, August 6–9, 1989; the statement is in direct opposition to Hirsch's contention, "Only by piling up specific, communally shared information can children learn to participate in complex co-operative activities with other members of their community" (CL xv).

23. See, for example, Nelson Quimby and Robert J. Sternberg, "On Testing and Teaching Intelligence: A Conversation with Robert Sternberg," *Educational Leadership* 43 (1985), 53; Chet Meyers, *Teaching Students to Think Critically* (San Francisco: Jossey-Bass, 1986), p. 1; Barry K. Beyer, *Practical Strategies for the Teaching of Thinking* (Boston: Allyn and Bacon, 1987), p. 4.

24. I argue that both cultural literacy and critical thinking are based on conservative principles, in spite of the fact that certain critical theorists of education adopt a critical thinking approach which seems consistent with critical hermeneutical principles. For example, Stanley Aronowitz and Henry Giroux oppose critical thinking to conservative cultural literacy movements and interpret critical thinking to be an approach consistent with a "liberal," critical theory of education (see *Education under Siege: The Conservative, Liberal, and Radical Debate over Schooling*

[South Hadley, MA: Bergin and Garvey, 1985], for example, pp. 49–50, 61). I return to this issue in the next chapter.

25. Theorists of progressivism sometimes claim, without contradiction, that cultural literacy is an essential part of progressive education. See, for example, McMurray, "The Problem of Verification in Formal School Learning," p. 40.

26. Hirsch considers the objection that students will merely memorize but not really possess information (CL 142). Also see Donald Walhout, "Philosophy in the Cultural Literacy Project," *Teaching Philosophy* 12 (1989), 8; and Thomas J. Donahue, "Promoting 'Philosophical Literacy'," *APA Newsletter on Teaching Philosophy* 88 (1989), 106.

27. See Hirsch, *Validity in Interpretation*, p. 197.

28. Ibid., pp. 204–206.

29. Robert H. Ennis, "A Concept of Critical Thinking: A Proposed Basis for Research in the Teaching and Evaluation of Critical Thinking Ability," *Harvard Educational Review* 32 (1962), 81–111.

30. Kurfiss, *Critical Thinking*, p. 2.

31. Nickerson, Perkins, and Smith, *The Teaching of Thinking*, p. 48. This is precisely the position that Dewey outlines in *Democracy and Education*.

32. See J. Q. Bransford et al., "Teaching Thinking and Problem Solving: Research Foundations," *American Psychologist* 41 (1986), 1078–1089; J. G. Greeno, "Trends in the Theory of Knowledge for Problem Solving," in Tuma and Reif, *Problem Solving and Education*, pp. 9–23; Simon, "Problem Solving and Education," pp. 81–96; and Frederic Charles Bartlett, *Thinking: An Experimental and Social Study* (New York: Basic Books, 1958), pp. 11–12, 31–32; see also Kurfiss, *Critical Thinking*, pp. 33ff; and Beyer, *Practical Strategies for the Teaching of Thinking*, pp. 68–71.

33. Baron, *Rationality and Intelligence*, pp. 193, 251; Baron is not alone in his appeal to the schema in the theory of critical thinking. See, for example, Nickerson, Perkins, and Smith, *The Teaching of Thinking*, p. 255; Robert Glaser, "Education and Thinking," pp. 93–104.

34. Baron, ibid., p. 193.

35. Ibid., p. 251; also see p. 195.

36. See, for example, Nickerson, Perkins, and Smith, *The Teaching of Thinking*, p. 98.

37. See Baron, *Rationality and Intelligence*, pp. 222–223, 253; and Meyers, *Teaching Students to Think Critically*, p. 6.

38. See, for example, Nickerson, Perkins, and Smith, *The Teaching of Thinking*, pp. 119ff.; and Baron, *Rationality and Intelligence*, pp. 108ff.

39. See, for example, ibid., pp. 131ff.

40. Harvey Siegel, "Rationality and Ideology," *Educational Theory* 37 (1987), 153–167.

41. Ibid., p. 161.

42. It is interesting to note that while proponents of critical thinking often admit that a great deal of what is said in critical thinking theory is never put into educational practice, proponents of cultural literacy contend that schooling has become nothing other than the teaching of skills without content. At the same time, while the proponents of cultural literacy complain that schools have not been teaching cultural literacy, proponents of critical thinking claim empirical evidence to the effect that current practice amounts to nothing more. See, for example, Anthony Petrosky, "Critical Thinking: Qu'est-ce que c'est?" *The English Record* 37 (1986), 3.

43. Glaser, "Education and Thinking"; related discussions can be found in Meyers, *Teaching Students to Think Critically*, pp. 12ff; and R. J. Yinger, "Can We Really Teach Them to Think?" in *Fostering Critical Thinking*, ed. R. E. Young (San Francisco: Jossey-Bass, 1980). Dewey also makes the case for the essential connection between literacy and thinking; see *Democracy and Education*.

44. Discussions of the concept of schema or related concepts which also suggest a relation to the moderate hermeneutical approach include H. S. Broudy, "Types of Knowledge and Purposes of Education," and Richard C. Anderson, "The Notion of Schemata and the Educational Enterprise," both in Anderson, Spiro, and Montague, *Schooling and the Acquisition of Knowledge*, pp. 12–15, 415–431.

45. Glaser, "Education and Thinking," p. 100.

46. Ibid.

47. See Anderson, "The Notion of Schemata and the Educational Enterprise," pp. 419ff.

48. Glaser, "Education and Thinking," p. 101.

49. Ibid.; see also Anderson, "The Notion of Schemata and the Educational Enterprise," pp. 427ff.

50. Baron, *Rationality and Intelligence*, p. 193.

51. Richard Rorty, "That Old-Time Philosophy," *The New Republic* 3820 (April 4, 1988), 28–33.

52. David R. Olson, "The Languages of Instruction: The Literate Bias of Schooling," in Anderson, Spiro, and Montague, *Schooling and the Acquisition of Knowledge*, pp. 65–89; in the same volume Richard C. Anderson ("The Notion of Schemata and the Educational Enterprise," pp. 421–422) shows how Olson's thesis challenges the notion of reproduction.

53. Olson, "The Languages of Instruction," pp. 68–69.

54. On this same point, see Stephen Toulmin, *The Uses of Argument* (Cambridge: Cambridge University Press 1958), p. 181; and RE 114ff. This argument could also be put in terms of "common sense," which might be mistaken for a culturally neutral kind of knowledge. On this point see Clifford Geertz, *Local Knowledge: Further Essays in Interpretive Anthropology* (New York: Basic Books, 1983), pp. 73–93; hereafter cited as LK.

55. Olson, "The Languages of Instruction," p. 75.

56. The work of Basil Bernstein shows the complexity of these relations. For example, "Aspects of Language and Learning in the Genesis of the Social Process," *Journal of Child Psychology and Psychiatry* 1 (1961), 313–324; and *Class, Codes, and Control: Towards a Theory of Educational Transmission* (London: Routledge and Kegan Paul, 1977). See also Paul Atkinson, *Language, Structure and Reproduction: An Introduction to the Sociology of Basil Bernstein* (London: Methuen, 1985), pp. 156ff.

57. See Olson, "The Languages of Instruction," pp. 80 and 88ff.

58. Harvey Siegel, *Educating Reason: Rationality, Critical Thinking, and Education* (New York: Routledge and Kegan Paul, 1988), pp. 59–60.

59. Scheffler, *Reason and Teaching*, p. 79; see Siegel, *Educating Reason*, p. 59.

60. Siegel, *Educating Reason*, pp. 74–75.

61. See, for example, Kurfiss, *Critical Thinking*, pp. 42ff.; Nickerson, Perkins, and Smith, *The Teaching of Thinking*, pp. 100ff.; and Beyer, *Practical Strategies for the Teaching of Thinking*, pp. 192ff.

62. Aristotle *Nicomachean Ethics* 1139a.

63. P. Christopher Smith outlines many of these points with reference to Plato and Gadamer; see "Towards a Discursive Logic: Gadamer and Toulmin on Inquiry and Argument," *Proceedings of the 23rd Annual Heidegger Conference* (Notre Dame, IN: University of Notre Dame, 1989).

CHAPTER 8. CRITICAL HERMENEUTICS AND EDUCATIONAL THEORY

1. In some cases sociological approaches are employed. See, for example, RE. Others take more philosophical approaches, for example, Henry A. Giroux, "Theories of Reproduction and Resistance in the New Sociology of Education: A Critical Analysis," *Harvard Educational Review* 53 (1983), 257–294. For an accessible summary of various critical

approaches to education, see Rex Gibson, *Critical Theory and Education* (London: Hodder and Staughton, 1986).

2. See Gadamer, "The Hermeneutics of Suspicion," pp. 54–55; TM 20ff.

3. See his discussion of Dilthey in KHI 180–181; and "A Review of Gadamer's *Truth and Method*," pp. 344–345.

4. Habermas, "Review," p. 360.

5. Ibid., p. 361.

6. Habermas, "Summation and Response," *Continuum* 8 (1970), p. 127.

7. Habermas, "Review," p. 356.

8. Ibid., p. 357.

9. Ibid.

10. Habermas, "The Hermeneutic Claim to Universality," HT 270.

11. Habermas, "Review," p. 358.

12. Ibid., p. 305.

13. Habermas, "Summation and Response," p. 129.

14. Habermas, *Theory and Practice*, trans. John Viertel (Boston: Beacon Press, 1974), p. 40.

15. Habermas, "Summation and Response," p. 126; see pp. 130–131.

16. Other often cited sources include Bowles and Gintis, *Schooling in Capitalist America*; and Bernstein, *Class, Codes, and Control*.

17. George H. Wood, "Schooling in a Democracy: Transformation or Reproduction?" *Educational Theory* 34 (1984), 224.

18. Giroux, "Theories of Reproduction and Resistance," p. 259; Aronowitz and Giroux, *Education under Siege*, pp. 70–71; and Wood, "Schooling in a Democracy," p. 230.

19. Wood, "Schooling in a Democracy," pp. 230–231; Wood cites Paul Willis, *Learning to Labour: How Working-Class Kids Get Working-Class Jobs* (London: Saxon House, 1977); also, Women's Study Group, Centre for Contemporary Cultural Studies (eds.), *Women Take Issue* (London: Hutchinson, 1978); Giroux, "Theories of Reproduction and Resistance," p. 259ff.; and Michael Apple, *Education and Power* (Boston: ARK, 1982), pp. 14ff., 18ff., 67ff..

20. Giroux, "Theories of Reproduction and Resistance," p. 260.

21. Antonio Gramsci, *Selections from Prison Notebooks*, ed. and trans. Quinten Hoare and Geoffrey Smith (New York: International Publishers, 1971), p. 33; cited in Aronowitz and Giroux, *Education under Siege*, p. 10.

22. See, for example, Jean Anyon, "Social Class and the Hidden Curriculum at Work," *Journal of Education* 162 (1980), 67–92; for the notion of "implicit pedagogy" see RE 47–48.

23. See RE 11, 13, 39–40, 167, and 206; also Apple, *Education and Power*, pp. 5 ff., 13 ff.

24. Apple, *Education and Power*, p. 12; see RE 53; see also Giroux, *Schooling and the Struggle for Public Life: Critical Pedagogy in the Modern Age* (Minneapolis: University of Minnesota Press, 1988), pp. 117–123, on Hirsch and conservative theories.

25. See Aronowitz and Giroux, *Education under Siege*, p. 25; for the theoretical background of this argument in Frankfurt School critical theory, see Theodor Adorno and Max Horkheimer, *The Dialectic of Enlightenment* (New York: Herder and Herder, 1972); also see Michael Ryan, "Deconstruction and Radical Teaching," *Yale French Studies* 63 (1982), 54.

26. Michael Apple, *Teachers and Texts: A Political Economy of Class and Gender Relations in Education* (New York: Routledge and Kegan Paul, 1986), p. 5.

27. Apple, *Education and Power*, p. 29.

28. See, ibid., pp. 181–182, n.53; and Todd Gitlin, "Primetime Ideology: The Hegemonic Process in Television Entertainment," *Social Problems* 26 (1979), 252, cited by Apple; see also Aronowitz and Giroux (*Education under Siege*, pp. 154 ff.), who object to an oversimplified and negative definition of power.

29. Aronowitz and Giroux, *Education under Siege*, pp. 28–29.

30. Aronowitz and Giroux cite Wittgenstein on this point. "But as Wittgenstein has remarked, language is—'a form of life', not *the* form of life. It is bound up with social relations" (ibid., p. 65).

31. See RE 120–121; Olson, "The Languages of Instruction," pp. 65–66; and studies by Basil Bernstein in *Class, Codes, and Control*. For an alternative view, see Catherine E. Snow, "Literacy and Language: Relationships during the Preschool Years," *Harvard Educational Review* 53 (1983), 165–189.

32. Ryan, "Deconstruction and Radical Teaching," p. 54.

33. See, for example, Giroux, *Ideology, Culture and the Process of Schooling* (Philadelphia: Temple University Press, 1981), p. 57.

34. Aronowitz and Giroux, *Education under Siege*, p. 7.

35. Ibid., p. 8. We note that the aim of education is the same for Dewey, for Hirsch, and for Aronowitz and Giroux, that is, for progressive, conservative, and critical theorists: to prepare students "for the broad requirements of citizenship in a democratic state" (ibid).

380 HERMENEUTICS AND EDUCATION

36. Thus Aronowitz and Giroux fault Dewey "for not bringing his theory of education into the context of problems of state and institutional life. Although he has a clear idea of what schools *ought to be*, he carefully avoids making a social and political analysis of what schools actually *are*" (ibid., p. 9).

37. Ibid., pp. 9, 49–50.

38. Ibid., pp. 51–54; also Wood, "Schooling in a Democracy," p. 234; and Misgeld, "Education and Cultural Invasion," p. 108.

39. Aronowitz and Giroux, *Education under Siege*, pp. 49, 65.

40. Ibid. p. 65.

41. Ibid., pp. 38–39.

42. Ibid., p. 38.

43. Michael Katz, "Critical Literacy: A Conception of Education as Moral Right and Social Ideal," in *The Public School Monopoly*, ed. Robert Everhart (Cambridge: Ballinger Press, 1982), p. 209. Also see Wood, "Schooling in a Democracy," p. 234.

44. Giroux, "Marxism and Schooling," *Educational Theory* 34 (1984), p. 132; also, Aronowitz and Giroux, *Education under Siege*, p. 133.

45. Wood, "Schooling in a Democracy," p. 225; also, on the non-neutrality of literacy, see RE 23–24, 53; Apple, *Education and Power*, p. 12; and David R. Olson, "From Utterance to Text: The Bias of Language in Speech and Writing," *Harvard Educational Review* 47 (1977), 257–281.

46. See Freire, *Pedagogy of the Oppressed*, trans. Myra Bergman Ramos (New York: Herder and Herder, 1970), hereafter cited as PO. On the relation between Freire and Habermas, see Misgeld, "Education and Cultural Invasion," pp. 97ff.

47. Paulo Freire, *Cultural Action for Freedom* (Cambridge: Harvard Educational Review, 1970), p. 12.

48. John O'Neill puts this in terms of overturning the hegemonic structure of language. See "Decolonization and the Ideal Speech Community: Some Issues in the Theory and Practice of Communicative Competence," in Forester, *Critical Theory and Public Life*, p. 68. Also see Misgeld, "Education and Cultural Invasion," pp. 106–108.

49. Kevin Harris, "The Politics of Literacy," *Educational Theory* 39 (1989), 170; see Apple, *Teachers and Texts*, p. 178.

50. "Education has fundamental connections with the idea of human emancipation. . . . the process of education and the process of liberation are the same." (R. W. Connell et al., *Making the Difference* [Sidney: George Allen and Unwin, 1982], cited in Wood, "Schooling in a Democracy," p. 230).

51. Carnegie Commission Report on Higher Education, *Priorities for Action* (New York: McGraw-Hill, 1973), p. 61. This is cited and discussed in Ryan, "Deconstruction and Radical Teaching," p. 50.

52. Jacques Derrida, "Otobiographies: The Teaching of Nietzsche and the Politics of the Proper Name," in *The Ear of the Other: Otobiography, Transference, and Translation,* ed. Christie McDonald, trans. Peggy Kamuf (Lincoln: University of Nebraska Press, 1985), p. 33.

53. Aronowitz and Giroux, *Education under Siege,* p. 65.

54. Wood, "Schooling in a Democracy," p. 231.

55. See R. E. Young, "Moral Development, Ego Autonomy, and the Questions of Practicality in the Critical Theory of Schooling," *Educational Research* 38 (1988), 394.

56. Habermas, *Theory and Practice,* p. 40.

57. Aronowitz and Giroux, *Education under Siege,* p. 39.

58. Peters, cited in Young, "Moral Development," p. 400.

59. Habermas, "Review," p. 338.

60. Olson, "From Utterance to Text," p. 82.

61. Gadamer, "On the Scope and Function of Hermeneutical Reflection," pp. 88–89.

62. O'Neill, "Decolonization," p. 73. But even Habermas himself comes to this position; see "The New Obscurity," in *The New Conservatism,* trans. S. W. Nicholsen (Cambridge, MA: MIT Press, 1989), p. 69.

63. Gadamer, "On the Scope and Function of Hermeneutical Reflection," p. 90. Even Bourdieu and Passeron admit that false consciousness spreads to critical reflection (see RE 37).

64. Gadamer, "Hermeneutics and Social Science," p. 315.

65. Apple, *Teachers and Text,* p. 199.

66. Habermas, "Summation and Response," p. 132.

67. Connell et al., *Making the Difference,* cited in Wood, "Schooling in a Democracy," p. 230.

CHAPTER 9. RADICAL HERMENEUTICS AND EDUCATIONAL THEORY

1. Jacques Derrida, "Où commence et comment finit un corps enseignant," in *Politiques de la Philosophie,* ed. Dominique Grisoni (Paris: Bernard Grasset, 1976), p. 65.

2. For the issues between Foucault and Habermas, see Habermas, "Modernity versus Postmodernity," *New German Critique* 22 (1981), 3–14; and *The Philosophical Discourse of Modernity,* pp. 238–293; Michel Foucault, "What Is Enlightenment?" in *The Foucault Reader,* ed. Paul Rabinow (New York: Pantheon, 1984); see also Nancy Frazer,

"Michel Foucault: A 'Young Conservative'?" *Ethnics* 96 (1985), 165–184. For the Habermas-Lyotard exchanges, see Habermas, *The Philosophical Discourse of Modernity*; PMC, *passim*; and Jean-Francois Lyotard and Jean Loup Thebaud, *Just Gaming*, trans. Wlad Godzich (Minneapolis: University of Minnesota Press, 1985), *passim*, hereafter cited as JG. See also Richard Rorty, "Habermas and Lyotard on Postmodernity," in *Habermas and Modernity*, ed. Richard J. Bernstein (Cambridge: MIT, 1985), pp. 161–225.

3.   Derrida, *Spurs*, p. 119.

4.   J. Hillis Miller, "The Two Rhetorics: George Eliot's Bestiary," in *Writing and Reading Differently: Deconstruction and the Teaching of Composition and Literature*, ed. G. Douglas Atkins and Michael L. Johnson (Lawrence: University Press of Kansas, 1985), p. 101.

5.   The reproduction of a metaphysical framework occurs within critical theory to the extent that it depends on psychoanalysis, the critique of ideology, or depth hermeneutics (see G 161). Critical depth hermeneutics is caught up within the larger framework of the modern metaphysics of the Enlightenment—the metaphysics of subjective control. Derrida attempted to show that something similar is the case for Gadamer's philosophical hermeneutics. By focusing on the concept of 'good will' in his Paris encounter with Gadamer in 1981, Derrida claims to reveal a hidden metaphysical presupposition. He construes Gadamer's concept of the trust involved in conversation as belonging "to a particular epoch, namely that of a [modern] metaphysics of the will," a modernist determination which seems to place the interpreter's subjectivity in control of the process of interpretation (see Derrida, "Three Questions to Hans-Georg Gadamer," DD 53).

6.   This is a phrase Derrida uses quite often. See G 259; WD 292; and *The Ear of the Other*, pp. 68–69.

7.   Eugen Fink, "Ontological Problems of Community," trans. Michael R. Heim, *Contemporary German Philosophy* 2 (1983), 3.

8.   See Foucault, *The History of Sexuality*, vol. 1, trans. Robert Hurley (New York: Vintage, 1980), pp. 82ff.; hereafter cited as HS. See also "The Subject and Power," Foucault's afterword to Hubert L. Dreyfus and Paul Rabinow, *Michel Foucault: Beyond Structuralism and Hermeneutics* (Chicago: University of Chicago Press, 1982), p. 226.

9.   "I have not denied—far from it—the possibility of changing discourse: I have deprived the sovereignty of the subject of the exclusive and instantaneous right to it" (AK 209).

10.   Emile Benveniste, "Subjectivity in Language," in *Problems in General Linguistics*, trans. Elizabeth Meek (Coral Gables, FL: University of Miami Press, 1971), p. 224.

11. See David Hume, *A Treatise of Human Nature* (Oxford: Clarenden Press, 1868, 1975), p. 253: "The mind is a kind of theatre where several perceptions successively make their appearance; pass, re-pass, glide away, and mingle in an infinite variety of postures and situations. . . . The comparison of the theatre must not mislead us. They are the successive perceptions only, that constitute the mind."

12. Derrida's reading of Husserl is contained in SP, especially Chapter 5. For further discussion of these points, see my essay "The Theater of Personal Identity," *The Personalist Forum* 8 (1992).

13. Derrida, *Margins of Philosophy*, trans. Alan Bass (Chicago: University of Chicago Press, 1982), p. 136.

14. See Derrida, *Positions* (Chicago: University of Chicago Press, 1981), p. 27; SP 51–52; WD 280.

15. See Derrida, "Où commence et comment finit un corps enseignant," p. 66.

16. See GREPH, *Qui a peur de la philosophie?* (Paris: Flammarion, 1977). See also Vincent B. Leitch, "Deconstruction and Pedagogy," in Atkins and Johnson, *Writing and Reading Differently*, pp. 16–19.

17. Derrida, "Où commence et comment finit un corps enseignant," p. 67. See also "Mochlos ou le conflit des facultés," *Philosophie* 2 (1984), 21–53.

18. PR 9; Derrida's lecture was delivered at Cornell University, which is geographically situated over a gorge. The gorge, which has a guardrail around it, comes to symbolize the image of the abyss.

19. See Derrida, *The Ear of the Other*, pp. 33–37.

20. Derrida, "Border Lines," in Harold Bloom et al., *Deconstruction and Criticism* (New York: Seabury Press, 1979), pp. 94–95.

21. See Habermas, *The Philosophical Discourse of Modernity*, pp. 185–210.

22. Ibid., p. 205.

23. See, for example, Apple, *Teachers and Texts*, p. 199; also Hank Bromley, "Identity Politics and Critical Pedagogy," *Educational Theory* 39 (1989), 207–223.

24. G 131. In the educational context he quotes Levi-Strauss: "The fight against illiteracy is therefore connected with an increase in governmental authority over the citizens. Everyone must be able to read, so that the government can say: ignorance of the law is no excuse" (Levi-Strauss, *Tristes Tropiques*, trans. John and Doreen Weightman [New York: Antheneum, 1984], p. 300). Derrida refuses to go along with Levi-Strauss's implied conclusion: that we can associate nonexploitation and liberty with illiteracy.

25. Foucault, "The Subject and Power," pp. 218–219.

26.   William V. Spanos, "The End of Education: 'The Harvard Core Curriculum Report' and the Pedagogy of Reformation," *Boundary 2* 10 (1982), 8–11.

27.   Mas ud Zavarzadeh and Donald Morton, "Theory Pedagogy Politics: The Crisis of 'The Subject' in the Humanities," *Boundary 2* 15 (1986–1987), 1–22.

28.   Ryan, "Deconstruction and Radical Teaching," pp. 53, 55.

29.   Peter McLaren, "Postmodernism and the Death of Politics: A Brazilian Reprieve," *Educational Theory* 36 (1986), 393; McLaren contrasts postmodernism with the success of Paulo Freire's critical approach. This line of criticism is also followed up in respect to feminism in Sandra Harding, *The Science Question in Feminism* (Ithaca, NY: Cornell University Press, 1986); and Carol Nicholson, "Postmodernism, Feminism, and Education: The Need for Solidarity," *Educational Theory* 39 (1989), 197–205.

30.   Stanley Fogel, for example, states that "humanities teachers have in some cases presented a content-oriented postmodernism while leaving its implications for pedagogy and the humanities untouched" (*The Postmodern University* p. 33).

31.   Roland Barthes, *The Grain of the Voice: Interviews 1962–1980*, trans. Linda Coverdale (New York: Hill and Wang, 1985), p. 149. See Leitch, "Deconstruction and Pedagogy," pp. 19–22, for a good outline of Barthes' pedagogical theory. See also Steven Ungar, "The Professor of Desire," *Yale French Studies* 63 (1982), 81–97.

32.   See "Writers, Intellectuals, Teachers," trans. Stephen Heath, in *A Barthes Reader*, ed. Susan Sontag (New York: Hill and Wang, 1982), pp. 380, 402.

33.   Barthes, "Lecture," trans. Richard Howard, *October* 8 (1979), 15; cited in Leitch, "Deconstruction and Pedagogy," p. 21.

34.   He cites examples of lectures by Derrida, Joseph Beuys, Antonin Artaud, and John Cage. See "Textshop for Post(e) Pedagogy," in Atkins and Johnson, *Writing and Reading Differently*, pp. 39–43; hereafter cited as Textshop; see also AG 174ff.

35.   Textshop 46; Ulmer here quotes Gerald Holton; see AG 184.

36.   See Lyotard, *Instructions paiennes* (Paris: Galilee, 1977), pp. 86–87; Grisoni, *Politiques de la philosophie*, p. 125.

37.   Fogel, *The Postmodern University*, p. 26.

38.   Lyotard, *Rudiments paiens: genre dissertatif* (Paris: UGE, collection 10/18, 1977), p. 34; trans. Georges Van Den Abbeele, cited in Fogel, *The Postmodern University*, p. 22; see Lyotard, "Interview," *Diacritics* 14 (1984), 17.

39.   Lyotard, *Rudiments*, p. 29; Fogel, *The Postmodern University*, p. 23.

40.   Zavarzadeh and Morton, "Theory Pedagogy Politics," pp. 6–10.

41.   See, for example, Leitch, "Deconstruction and Pedagogy," p. 24.

42.   Habermas, "The Entwinement of Myth and Enlightenment: Re-reading *Dialectic of Enlightenment*," *New German Critique* 26 (1982), 28.

43.   RH 217; on Caputo's critique of *phronēsis*, see my "The Place of *Phronēsis* in Postmodern Hermeneutics," in *Essays in Radical Hermeneutics*, ed. Roy Martinez (Bloomington: Indiana University Press, forthcoming).

44.   See RH 196; but see also Nicholson, "Postmodernism, Feminism, and Education," pp. 197–205.

45.   John Trimbur, "To Reclaim a Legacy, Cultural Literacy, and the Discourse of Crisis," *Liberal Education* 72 (1986), 118.

46.   Kaufer and Waller, "To Write Is to Read Is to Write, Right?" in Atkins and Johnson, *Writing and Reading Differently*, p. 68; they cite Fredric Jameson in this regard.

47.   Ibid., pp. 82–83.

48.   See Gadamer, "Reply to Jacques Derrida," DD 55–56.

49.   Barthes, "Writers, Intellectuals, Teachers," p. 401.

50.   See Michael Oakeshott, "The Voice of Poetry in the Conversation of Mankind," in *Rationalism and Politics* (New York: Methuen, 1975), pp. 198, 202.

51.   Ibid., p. 202.

52.   See ibid. Their approaches are not identical; we cannot translate Oakeshott's "images" into Derrida's "signs." From a defensive, Enlightenment position, Habermas criticizes Derrida for precisely translating what Oakeshott calls "the voice of practical activity and the voice of 'science'" into literary genres. Indeed, for Habermas, this is why Derrida misunderstands the nature of education. He criticizes Rorty for a similar "aestheticizing of language" (Habermas, *The Philosophical Discourse of Modernity*, pp. 204–206). Habermas, however, would not be able to criticize Oakeshott on this point, since he, like Habermas, defines the voices of practical activity, science, and poetry as three irreducible idioms.

53.   See RH 261; Caputo eventually gives in to Rorty's notion of *phronēsis* or "civility," but insists on calling it "meta-*phronēsis*," "the skill to cope with competing paradigms. Civility is the virtue of knowing how to like and live with the dissemination of *ēthos*" (RH 262); see also Gallagher, "The Place of *Phronēsis* in Postmodern Hermeneutics."

54.   See DD 110 and TM 542–543. Jeff Mitscherling clarifies the essential differences between the concepts of conversation found in Gadamer and Rorty. See "Philosophical Hermeneutics and 'the Tradition,'" *Man and World* 22 (1989), 247–250.

55.   See Kenneth Bruffee, "Collaborative Learning and the 'Conversation of Mankind,'" *College English* 46 (1984), 635–652; hereafter cited as Bruffee.

56.   Oakeshott, "The Voice of Poetry in the Conversation of Mankind," p. 199; cited in Bruffee 638.

57.   Carol Nicholson, in an article which defends the view of education as conversation, focuses on this risk by citing Hannah Arendt. See "Postmodernism, Feminism, and Education," pp. 203–204.

58.   Edward Said, "Textuality," summarized in AG 158.

59.   Leitch, "Deconstruction and Pedagogy," p. 49; see AG 174; also Zavarzadeh and Morton, "Theory Pedagogy Politics," p. 10.

CHAPTER 10. EDUCATION AND HERMENEUTICS

1.   Dilthey, "The Rise of Hermeneutics," p. 233.

2.   See A. H. Armstrong, *Hellenic and Christian Studies* (Hampshire, GB: Variorum, 1990), Chap. 10, pp. 8, 12–14; Eugene Bahn and Margaret L. Bahn, *A History of Oral Interpretation* (Minneapolis: Burgess, 1970).

3.   M.-D. Chenu, "Les *magistri.* La 'science théologique'," *La théologie au douzième siècle* (Paris: 1957), p. 344; cited and trans. in Brian Stock, *The Implications of Literacy: Written Language and Models of Interpretation in the 11th and 12th Centuries* (Princeton: Princeton University Press, 1983), p. 328. See also George E. Ganss, *St. Ignatius' Idea of a Jesuit University* (Milwaukee: Marquette University Press, 1954), pp. 250ff.; and Friedrich Paulsen, *The German Universities and University Study*, trans. James F. Thilly and William W. Elwang (New York: Scribners, 1906); and in relation to the study of law in this regard, see Hastings Rashdall, *The Universities of Europe in the Middle Ages* (Oxford: Clarenden Press, 1936), vol. 1, p. 218.

4.   See Brian Stock, *The Implications of Literacy*, pp. 90, 105. On the monastic practice of *legere*, see p. 408.

5.   Paul Saenger, "Silent Reading: Its Impact on Late Medieval Script and Society," *Viator* 13 (1982), 371.

6.   See David R. Olson, "Introduction," *Media and Symbols: The Forms of Expression, Communication, and Education*, 73rd Yearbook of

the National Society for the Study of Education, Part 1, ed. David R. Olson (Chicago: University of Chicago Press, 1974).

7. Stock, *The Implications of Literacy*, p. 62; also see pp. 3, 71–85.

8. Olson, "Interpreting Texts and Interpreting Nature: The Effects of Literacy on Hermeneutics and Epistemology," *Visible Language* 20 (1986), 302–317; see pp. 305–306; see also Stock, *The Implications of Literacy*, p. 14.

9. Stock, *The Implications of Literacy*, p. 15.

10. Olson, "Interpreting Texts and Interpreting Nature," p. 305. One could argue, in a related fashion, that the development of the modern (Protestant, Romantic) conception of the hermeneutical circle, expressed in terms of parts and whole, was dependent upon transformations of writing and printing technology. See Saenger, "Silent Reading," p. 385.

11. Olson, "Interpreting Texts and Interpreting Nature," p. 385; Saenger, "Silent Reading," p. 384; and Stock, *The Implications of Literacy*, pp. 4, 18.

12. Ast, *Grundlinien der Grammatik, Hermeneutik und Kritik*, HT 40.

13. Ibid., pp. 44–45.

14. Ibid., pp. 41–45.

15. Schleiermacher, *Aphorisms on Hermeneutics from 1805 and 1809/10*, HT 57.

16. Schleiermacher, *Hermeneutics*, p. 96.

17. Nicholson, *Seeing and Reading*, pp. 4–5.

18. Nicholson summarizes the lexical material on *interpres* in *Seeing and Reading*, p. 3. On *hermēneía* see Palmer, *Hermeneutics*, pp. 14ff.

19. Dilthey, *Gesammelte Schriften* vol. 7, p. 291; cited and trans. in TM 241 and 231, n.113.

20. HHS 131; also see Ricoeur, "Ethics and Culture," p. 160; and "Philosophical Hermeneutics and Theological Hermeneutics: Ideology, Utopia, and Faith," in *Protocol of the Colloquy of the Center for Hermeneutical Studies in Hellenistic and Modern Cultures* 17 (Berkeley: 1976), pp. 2–3.

21. See Jonas Soltis, "Logics and Languages of Pedagogical Research," *Philosophy of Education* 40 (1984), 273–282.

22. See TM 368, 378; Frank M. Kirkland ("Gadamer and Ricoeur: The Paradigm of the Text," *Graduate Faculty Philosophy Journal* 6 [1977], 131–144), focuses on this aspect of Gadamer's hermeneutics and contrasts it to Ricoeur's textualism. Kirkland, however, sides with Ricoeur's concept of text as the proper paradigm of hermeneutics.

23.   Joel Weinsheimer, *Gadamer's Hermeneutics*, p. 220, n.9, citing an argument made by Horst Turk, "Warheit oder Methode? H. G. Gadamers 'Grundzüge einer philosophischen Hermeneutik,'" in *Hermeneutische Positionen*, ed. Hendrik Birus (Gottingen: Vandenhoeck and Ruprecht, 1982), p. 128.

24.   See, for example, David Hoy's textualistic reading of this in David Hoy, *The Critical Circle* (Berkeley: University of California Press, 1978).

25.   Gadamer, "Text and Interpretation," DD 42–43, 49. The argument I am developing here is opposed to Werner Hamacher's interpretation ("Hermeneutic Ellipses: Writing the Hermeneutical Circle in Schleiermacher," in *Transforming the Hermeneutical Context: From Nietzsche to Nancy*, ed. Gayle L. Ormiston and Alan D. Schrift [Albany: State University of New York Press, 1990], 177–210). In contrast to Hamacher, Robert Dostal reaches a conclusion similar to the one represented here; that is, Gadamer makes the literary text "paradigmatic for the problem of interpretation." See Robert Dostal, "The World Never Lost: The Hermeneutics of Trust," *Philosophy and Phenomenological Research* 47 (1987), 433–434.

26.   Gadamer, "Reply to My Critics," HT 292.

27.   Rorty, *Consequences of Pragmatism*, pp. 139ff.

28.   Robert Sholes, *Textual Power: Literary Theory and the Teaching of English* (New Haven: Yale, 1985), pp. 74ff.; see AK 47; and Said, *The World, the Text, and the Critic* (Cambridge, MA: Harvard University Press, 1983).

29.   Fredrick Jameson, *The Political Unconscious*, pp. 296–297; cited in Sholes, *Textual Power*, p. 84.

30.   Caputo, "Horizontal Hermeneutics and Its Delimination," *Man and World* 19 (1986), 242.

31.   See Michel Foucault, "Nietzsche Freud Marx," in Ormiston and Schrift, *Transforming the Hermeneutical Context*, p. 60.

32.   I would distinguish local hermeneutics from what William Schroeder terms "local theory," which seems to be a "special" hermeneutics in Schleiermacher's sense, that is, a theory which "seeks principles and evaluative criteria relevant to the interpretation of a restricted set of objects (narrative literature and film and drama)" ("A Teachable Theory of Interpretation," p.10).

33.   See p. 234; Giroux and Aronowitz (*Education under Siege*, p. 72) suggest that conditions vary from "school to school and from neighborhood to neighborhood." Michael Apple also proposes the analysis of conditions on the level of neighborhoods and with respect to actual practices of education, such as textbook design and marketing practices. In

terms of discerning the aims of education, John Dewey also indicates a local perspective (see *Democracy and Education*, p. 108).

34. PO 102. Freire, like Geertz, admits that such a study will not be value free.

35. The seemingly intractable situation in Northern Ireland may serve as one example out of many. If in the local educational and interpretational contexts of Belfast or Derry transformation seems to be absent, it is never completely absent. Interpretation and reinterpretation by the press and mass media constantly affect the way people understand themselves and their neighbors. Changes in production relations (the introduction and administration of civil rights legislation with respect to employment and housing) transform not only the "real" situation but also the hermeneutical situation. Changes in political structure and practice (the constant formation of new governmental administrations, the peace movement, and so on) transform the reproductive effort of various groups. For more detailed discussion, see Shaun Gallagher, "Violence and Intelligence: Answers to the Irish Question," *Political Communication and Persuasion* 2 (1983), 195–221.

36. Gadamer, "Letter to Dallmayr," DD 95; see p. 97.

37. Gary Madison, *The Hermeneutics of Postmodernity* (Bloomington: Indiana University Press, 1988), p. 51.

SUBJECT INDEX

NAME INDEX

399